THE JOURNAL

OF

NEGRO HISTORY

CARTER G. WOODSON

Editor

VOLUME XXX

1945

THE ASSOCIATION FOR THE STUDY OF NEGRO LIFE AND HISTORY, INC.,

WASHINGTON, D. C.

CONTENTS OF VOLUME XXX

Vol. XXX—January, 1945—No. 1

Vol. XXX—April, 1945—No. 2

Vol. XXX—July, 1945—No. 3

THE JOURNAL
OF
NEGRO HISTORY

Vol. XXX—January, 1945—No. 1

PROCEEDINGS OF THE ANNUAL MEETING OF THE ASSOCIATION FOR THE STUDY OF NEGRO LIFE AND HISTORY HELD IN BOSTON, MASSACHU-SETTS, OCTOBER 27-29, 1944

For the first time the Association for the Study of Negro Life and History assembled in annual meeting in Boston, Massachusetts. When the proposal first came to the national offiffice the reaction was that during the days of restrictions on travel the attendance might be too small to justify the effort. On the contrary, most of the historians interested believed that it would be advantageous to all concerned to carry to that area a demonstration of the objectives and achievements of the Association and at the same time to profit by meeting in an atmosphere where so much of our history has been made. The conference proved to be about as well attended as the average attendance at our annual meetings, and the people of the city had reason to rejoice with the delegates that they assembled in that city.

The first session opened with introductory remarks by Mrs. Alberta C. Valentine, the wide-awake chairman of the local committee which so successfully sponsored the conference under the inspiration of Miss Wilhelmina M. Crosson. Mrs. Valentine introduced for a welcome address Mr. Charles C. Dasey, a member of the Governor's Committee for Religious and Racial Understanding. The speaker was

1

alert to the gravity of the social upheaval attendant upon
the present international conflict and expressed the desire
that this conference may give more light from the past to
illuminate the present and clarify the future for a new program of toleration which will guarantee equality and justice
to all men without regard to race, religion or national origin.
Attorney Louis R. Mehlinger, secretary-treasurer of the
Association, responded. He assured the preceding speaker
and the Boston audience of the arduous labors of the Association to hasten the coming of the new order by presenting
in scientific form the achievements of the Negro to justify
his recognition as a positive force in the progress of mankind. In the record of the Association during the last thirty
years he found much which, when properly utilized, will
advance the thinking public far in the direction of real democracy.

Next spoke Dr. James G. Leyburn, of the Department
of Sociology of Yale University, on ''The Disabilities from
which the Natives of South Africa Suffer.'' He had just
recently returned from a lend-lease mission to the Union of
South Africa and spoke of what he actually observed in
that country. His address, which was carefully outlined
and effectively delivered, appears in this number of this
magazine. His discussion articulated with the address by
the Director who, from the international point of view,
spoke on the participation of the American Negro in the
wars of America. He contended that because the Negroes
of the United States are unable to register their will in the
policy-making of the Federal Government they have fought
just as often to their own detriment as they have to their
advantage. In support of his position he recited the issues
of all the wars in which the country has been engaged from
the colonial period down to the present time. He concluded
with the thought that Negroes, instead of looking for ordinary political jobs to reward a few sharp politicians should
clamor for the carrying out of lofty principles in the in-

terest of actual democracy. The effect of these addresses was deepened by the beautiful music rendered by a local minister at the suggestion of Mrs. Gladys M. Purdue, chairman of the committee on music.

On Saturday morning at the Teachers College of the City of Boston, Mrs. Lucy Harth Smith, of Lexington, Kentucky, a member of the Executive Council of the Association, presided with grace and dignity. She briefly discussed the topic of the morning—"The Negro in the Curricula of the Schools." Mr. W. M. Brewer, head of the Department of History of the Colored High Schools of Washington, D. C., then read a paper entitled "Acquainting the Negro with History." His emphasis upon introducing the Negro to history in general and to his own history in particular tended to set forth anew the important objectives of the Association for the Study of Negro Life and History. This paper appears in the December issue of *The Negro History Bulletin*. Next appeared Mr. Harvey C. Jackson, of the Public Schools of Highland Park, Michigan, a member of the Executive Council of the Association. He discussed from experience in race relations in his own work exactly how the youth of both races may be taught at an early age to appreciate the achievements of all elements of our population and learn thereby to have a more favorable attitude toward others than their parents who are so set in their ways that little change is possible. Mr. W. F. Savoy, of the Ohio Branch of the Association, spoke next along the same line emphasizing what seemed to him to be certain desirable approaches to this question and methods of dealing with it effectively, as shown by his paper, which appears in same issue of *The Negro History Bulletin*. The discussion was further extended by Mr. Collins Reynolds, intercultural fellow at the Harvard University Graduate School. A most profitable general discussion followed and aroused so much interest that the session was reluctant to adjourn.

At the close of this session the Association went into its

annual business session. In the absence of Mrs. Mary Mc-
Leod Bethune, the national chairman, Attorney Louis R.
Mehlinger, secretary-treasurer of the Association, presided.
There were no reports from special or standing committees,
and the reports of the national officers were read, discussed
and finally adopted with the thanks of the body. These reports for the year ending June 30, 1944, were published in
the July issue of THE JOURNAL OF NEGRO HISTORY. The present officers, with one exception—President Joseph J. Rhoads,
who resigned—were reelected. Mr. Harvey C. Jackson, of
Detroit, Michigan, was chosen to fill the vacancy. Various
suggestions for the promotion of the work were then welcomed. Mr. A. G. Lindsay urged that those paying $10.00
annually be considered as Sustaining Members and that
those paying only $1.00 annually be designated as Associate
Members. By motion it was so ordered. More simplifica-
tion of *The Negro History Bulletin* in order to reach a
larger number of smaller children was also urged. Dr.
L. P. Jackson emphasized the need for more information
in each issue of the magazine as to who the contributors
are and what they represent. The body decided to meet in
Columbus, Ohio, next year.

In the afternoon on the same day the topic for discussion
was "The Negro among the Pioneers." Professor A. M.
Schlesinger, of Harvard University, presided. The first
speaker, Dr. W. Sherman Savage, of Lincoln University in
Missouri, read a paper on "The Negro on the Mining Frontier," which appears in this issue. The paper aroused much
interest because of the considerable number of Negroes
reported as penetrating the Far West, and also because of
the race prejudice encountered in spite of the fact that the
frontier is supposedly a democratizing force in American
life as pointed out in the general discussion by Dr. L. D.
Reddick, curator of the Schomburg Collection of the New
York Public Library. In the absence of Dr. Kenneth W.
Porter, of Vassar College, his paper entitled "Negroes and

the East Florida Annexation Plot, 1811-1813,'' was read very satisfactorily by Dr. Merze Tate, of Howard University. The discussion of this paper did not follow in view of the fact stated above, but the time was devoted profitably to the discussion of the first address. Among those participating was Mr. Dred Scott Neusom of Detroit, Michigan. Dr. Porter's paper appears in this issue of THE JOURNAL OF NEGRO HISTORY and speaks for itself as a scholarly production.

At the evening session the same day Mr. Matthew W. Bullock, chairman of the Massachusetts Parole Board, presided. The topic of the hour was "The Free Negro of the Ante Bellum Period.'' On taking the chair, he expressed his sustained interest in the work of the Association and his delight to have the body assemble in Boston. He next introduced Dr. Lorenzo J. Greene, of Lincoln University in Missouri, who in spite of suffering from a cold read effectively his paper on "The Anti-Slavery Movement in New England, 1637-1761.'' This paper is a by-product of his prolonged research into the Negroes of New England, which resulted in the recent publication of his monumental production, *The Negro in Colonial New England*. Boston was surprised to know that its most aristocratic families owe the beginning of their wealth and position to slavery and the slave trade.

The next speaker Mr. Robert D. Reid, of Tuskegee Institute, read a paper on "The Free Negro of Alabama before the Civil War.'' He followed the usual pattern of dealing with this element from the point of view of social condition, economic status, political disabilities, and objects of the personality of law. Then followed a general discussion in which participated Dr. John Hope Franklin, of North Carolina State College, and Dr. L. P. Jackson, of Virginia State College, both of whom have made scientific studies of the Free Negro in their respective states. Some remarks were made also by Professor Henry J. Cadbury, of the Harvard Divinity School, and by Mr. James J. Green, of Boston.

Several others made observations and suggestions with respect to the ante bellum studies. The session then adjourned to attend an informal reception at the Women's Service Club at 464 Massachusetts Avenue, where, under the direction of Miss Susie Jones and her coworkers the visitors and their entertainers enjoyed themselves immensely.

The next session followed a breakfast at the Home of the League of Women for Community Service at 558 Massachusetts Avenue. Miss Odile Sweeney, of the Cambridge Community Center, presided. The repast was promptly and nicely served without a hitch and the chairman proceeded to take up the topic of the morning, "Untouched Fields." Dr. John Hope Franklin of North Carolina State College delivered an address from "The Papers of James Boon, a Free Negro." He gave abundant evidence of having done a thorough piece of research and showed how the papers of this one progressive Free Negro reflected the failures and successes of the element to which he belonged in North Carolina. This successful study revealed a large untouched field of the past of the Negro in this country. Dr. L. P. Jackson followed to present his observations on "The Unexplored Fields in the History of the Negro in the United States." He reviewed the efforts made in various fields but did not consider the works thus produced as sufficiently comprehensive and definitive. Among the fields requiring further effort are the compilation of directories of Negroes, slave and free, before the Civil War, the Negro family, the Negro barber, the Negro local business man, and the Negro in local politics. This paper was published in the December issue of *The Negro History Bulletin*. Helpful comment was made thereupon by Mr. Harvey C. Jackson, of Michigan, Atty. Raymond Pace Alexander, of the Philadelphia Bar, and several others who spoke briefly on the two papers delivered.

Those unacquainted with Boston went on a sight-seeing

tour of the city and vicinity, conducted by Mrs. Mollie L. Bell. Miss Wilhelmina M. Crosson, with her car, assisted an overflow group on this tour which ended at Faneuil Hall at 3:30 P. M., where the final session was held. There the Director of the Association presided. The session opened with appropriate selections arranged by the Committee on Music. Before introducing the speakers to discuss "The Negro as a Citizen of the United States," he reversed the order and had Prof. A. M. Schlesinger, of Harvard University, present the History Prizes. The First Prize of One Hundred Dollars for the best article submitted to THE JOURNAL OF NERGO HISTORY for the year ending September 30, went to Mr. W. M. Brewer, head of the Department of History of the Colored High Schools of Washington, D. C., for his article entitled "The Poll Tax and the Poll Taxers." The Second Prize of Fifty Dollars for the next best article thus submitted went to Mr. Reuben Sheeler, of Alabama State College, for his "Development of Unionism in East Tennessee." The Prize of Fifty Dollars for the best review submitted to this magazine during the same period went to Professor Kenneth W. Porter, of Vassar College, for his estimate of James Truslow Adams's *The American.* The Prize of Twenty-five Dollars for the next best review thus submitted went to Dr. Benjamin Quarles, of Dillard University, for his evaluation of Madeline Hook Rice's *American Catholic Opinion in the Slavery Controversy.*

The first speaker of the afternoon was Governor Leverett Saltonstall of Massachusetts. He came, accompanied by the Secretary of State of Massachusetts, to bring greetings on behalf of the Commonwealth. Mayor Maurice J. Tobin, who could not be present, sent greetings through Mr. Joshua A. Jones. Professor Louise Overacker, of Wellesley College, was then introduced to discuss "The Negro's Struggle for Participation in Primary Elections." She restricted her discussion to the recent decisions culminating in the one in which the United States Supreme Court

reversed itself and gave the opinion that the Negro should
be permitted to participate in the Democratic Primary of
Texas. This well delivered paper appears in this issue of
this magazine. The next speaker was Attorney Raymond
Pace Alexander, of the Philadelphia Bar, who spoke enter-
tainingly and instructively on "The Upgrading of the Negro as a Citizen as Shown by the Recent Decisions of the
United States Supreme Court." He covered briefly some
of the ground of the preceding speaker, but traced the development of the idea of the Negro as a citizen from the
very beginning of our history to the present day and in a
most satisfactory manner. The last speaker, President
Charles H. Wesley, of Wilberforce University, was at his
best as a scholar and an orator in speaking on "The Negro's
Struggle for Freedom in its Birthplace." All three speakers
were heartily applauded by an appreciative audience because, taken together they abundantly enlightened them on
the working of the laws and constitution of this country
and the devices which Negroes have had to employ in order
to enjoy the rights and privileges therein guaranteed. The
meeting then adjourned to meet in Columbus, Ohio, the last
week-end of next October.

NEGROES AND THE EAST FLORIDA ANNEXATION PLOT, 1811-1813*

South of the United States borders, in the territory still precariously held by the Most Catholic King of Spain, the Negroes and Indians of East Florida were, in 1812 and '13, being entangled in a net of international intrigue.[1] "The persistent desire of the United States to possess the Floridas," which K. C. Babcock declares "between 1801 and 1819, amounted almost to a disease, corrupting the moral sense of each succeeding administration," had resulted, after a local insurrection, in a proclamation of Oct. 27, 1810, annexing to the United States the "territory from the Mississippi to Perdido."[2] Congressional confirmation of this presidential action was followed, Jan. 15, 1811, by a secret act of Congress authorizing the President to take possession of all or any part of Florida in case of agreement with the *local* authorities or in the event of any attempt by a foreign government to occupy any part of that territory. Gen. George Mathews, formerly governor of Georgia, was accordingly dispatched to East Florida to obtain the transfer of that region to the United States.

"Local authorities" was a term capable of being liberally construed, and Gen. Mathews therefore devoted himself to nurturing the ambitions of American settlers in the Spanish territory of East Florida, who might be encouraged to set themselves up as a "local government" favor-

---

*In the absence of Dr. Porter on account of illness, this paper was read by Dr. Merze Tate of Howard University at the annual meeting of the Association for the Study of Negro Life and History in Boston, Massachusetts, on October 28, 1944.

[1] Unless some other source is specified, statements concerning the Patriot and annexationist movement in Florida are based on Julius W. Pratt, *Expansionists of 1812*, N. Y., 1925, pp. 61-127, 189-237, esp. 104, 117, 193, 194, 201-202, 207-209.

[2] Babcock, Kendric Charles, *Rise of American Nationality* (American Nation, xiii), N. Y., 1906, pp. 22-25; Adams, Henry, *History of the United States During the First Administration of James Madison*, i, N. Y., 1891, pp. 306-312; Channing, Edward, *History of the United States*, iv, N. Y., 1917, p. 417.

able to annexation by the United States. United States troops on the border were expected to assist in any such movement. On Mar. 14, 1812, the so-called "Patriots"—consisting mostly of citizens of Georgia—hoisted their flag at Rose's Bluff and, with the threatened assistance of American gun-boats, forced the surrender, Mar. 18, of Amelia Island, which was thereupon turned over to the United States, represented by Gen. Mathews. St. Augustine, the capital of East Florida, was the next objective, and was invested by the Patriot forces; Picolata, their headquarters, was in due course turned over to Lieut. Col. Smith, USA, on April 12.

The fall of St. Augustine, and with it the whole province of East Florida, seemed at this point inevitable. The entire garrison of the province consisted of only about 400 men, mostly untrained city militia. In this emergency, however, the Spanish authority still possessed two potential sources of military strength: the Indians and the Negroes. Gov. Estrada had gotten into communication with the Seminole Indians of the Alachua towns immediately upon the insurrection of the Patriots and the invasion by American troops, but in his despair felt that the Indians might even side with the Americans. There was actually little danger of this, for the Patriots were contemptuously obvious in their attitude toward the Indians, coolly apportioning their land as bounties to volunteers, regardless of Aesop's fable concerning the man who sold the lion's skin while it was still on the beast's back. The Spanish authorities indeed asserted that the Patriots had not even been content to allow their actions to speak for them, but had put their intentions into unmistakable words. Gen. Mathews, it was said, had told King Payne, the principal Seminole chief, that "he intended to drive him from his land," while John H. McIntosh, a leading Patriot, had notified another prominent chief, Boleck or Bowlegs, Payne's brother, that "he intended to make him as a waiting man." But, cut off from St. Augustine and munitions by the blockading force at Picolata, the Indian for a time took no overt action.

The Indians of Florida were threatened with the loss of their homes to the land-grabbing Patriots and the flood of colonists to whom Florida would be opened by annexation to the United States, but the Negroes were confronted with a more serious menace. Even the slaves dreaded the stricter slave-code of the southern United States, but the numerous free Negroes, many of them runaways from the United States, or their descendants, saw themselves and their families deprived of hard-won freedom should Florida come under United States rule. It had long been a policy of the Spanish government, dating back at least as far as 1688, to encourage Negroes from the British settlements to take refuge in Florida. The Spaniards, of course, had slaves of their own, but they were far-seeing enough to realize that the flight of Negroes from the British colonies weakened the traditional enemy and strengthened the Spanish colony, and that this unofficial migration would continue only so long as the fugitives were assured that they would not be merely exchanging one slavery for another. A colony of runaway Negroes was consequently established in 1739 near St. Augustine, and a fort constructed for their protection and garrisoning; the settlement was known as Gracia Real de Santa Teresa de Mosé, the fort, in brief, as Fort Mosé or Moussa.

Negro sergeants, with secret *rendezvous* in Carolina, were sent into that colony to instigate desertions from the plantations and, if possible, insurrection. The slaves were informed that the governor of Florida had formed a regiment of runaway slaves, "appointing officers from among them, and placing both officers and enlisted men upon the pay and rations allowed to the regular Spanish soldiers." This propaganda contributed to a constant leakage of runaways from the Carolina plantations to strengthen the manpower and military strength of the Spanish settlements, and it was a factor in at least one large-scale, though unsuccessful, uprising. The participants in this affair revealed their inspiration, after a preliminary slaughter of twenty whites, by marching toward Florida, banners displayed and drums beating, crying out "Freedom!", but were eventually cut to pieces and dispersed. Among the troops at St. Augustine reported at one point in the early 1740's were: "One regiment of Negroes, regularly officered by Negroes, One ditto of Mulattos, Ninety Indians, and 15 Negroes who ran away from South Carolina"—these last, presumably, recent arrivals. When, by the Treaty of Paris in 1763, Florida was ceded by Spain to Great Britain, the colony at Fort Mosé was transferred to Cuba.[3]

With Florida under British rule it was, of course, no longer such a tempting haven of refuge to discontented slaves on Georgia and South Carolina plantations; certainly it no longer offered any official welcome, overt or covert. But about the middle of the eighteenth century a body of discontented Lower Creeks from Georgia, under the leadership of a chief named Secoffee, perhaps the same as the one known to the English as The Cowkeeper, began to move into northern Florida and establish settlements,[4] where runaway slaves could find refuge. In welcoming and giving protection to such fugitives, the Seminole, no more than the Spanish authorities, were inspired by philanthropic motives, nor were they moved by a similarity of their own condition—"Seminole" means separatist—to that of the Negro "seceders" from plantation-society.

The Seminole had observed that prestige was attached by the Florida settlers to the presence of Negroes, and some

[3] "Dispatches of Spanish officials bearing on the free Negro settlement of Gracia Real de Santa Teresa de Mose, Florida," *Journal of Negro History*, ix (1924), 144-195; Southall, Eugene P., "Negroes in Florida Prior to the Civil War," JNH, xix (1934), 76-86; Jones, Charles C., Jr., *The History of Georgia*, 2 vols., Boston, 1883, i, 298-300, 344.

[4] Swanton, John R., *Early History of the Creek Indians and Their Neighbors*, Washington, D. C., 1922, pp. 398-400.

of the chiefs were sufficiently impressed to purchase a few black people in exchange for the half-wild cattle which, along with horses and hogs, they had acquired in their earlier home and had driven with them on their migration. Forty cattle are said to have been the standard price for a Negro slave. Once in possession of Negroes, however, the Seminole were rather at a loss to know what benefit they were supposed to derive from them, since they had no intention of devoting their lives to the management of slaves. They soon solved the problem, however, in much the same manner as the barbarians invading the Roman Empire had dealt with a similar situation when they found themselves in possession of Roman slaves whom it was beneath a warrior's dignity personally to supervise. The Seminole simply supplied their Negroes with axes and hoes, and told them to cut down trees, build houses for themselves, and raise corn. When the crop was harvested, the master was satisfied with a reasonable proportion of it—one observer said that it was never more than ten bushels annually—and the remainder served as sustenance and compensation for the so-called slaves, who soon also acquired cattle, horses, and swine, with which the master never presumed to meddle so long as he was supplied with a fat hog or side of beef at slaughtering time.

It was a mutually advantageous arrangement, in which the master furnished protection and the slave paid a moderate rent in kind, rather than anything even approaching the familiar system of plantation slavery.

The grapevine telegraph soon informed slaves in Georgia and South Carolina of the advantageous position enjoyed by the "slaves" of the Seminole, and fugitives from plantations of the Deep South began to find their way through woods and swamps to the Seminole villages. These fugitives put themselves under the protection of prominent Seminole chiefs and in turn supplied an annual tribute in corn and other such products. The implication was that each Negro's patron would assert ownership over his *protegé* should the latter be claimed by his former master or any other white man. White men in general, however, not well acquainted with this arrangement, understood this relationship to be the only one familiar to him as existing between Negro on the one hand and Indian or white on the other—that of slave and master; actually, it seems, the Indians did not so regard it. The Negroes lived apart from the Indians, in their own villages—an evidence of independence which they greatly prized, were under no supervision by their masters or patrons, dipped their spoons into the sofky pot along with their lord and his family whenever they happened to be at his home, habitually carried arms, frequently possessed large herds of livestock, and, save for their annual tribute, were under no greater subordination to the chiefs than were the Seminole tribesmen themselves. The relationship might be described as one of primitive democratic feudalism, involving no essential personal inequality between lord and vassal. Gen. Gaines, a generation later, spoke with approximate accuracy of "the Seminole Indians with their black vassals and allies."[5]

The Indians eventually found the Negroes useful in ways other than that of relieving their patrons of a part of their agricultural responsibilities, and allowing them greater opportunity for the more congenial activity of the chase. The Negroes all spoke some European language—English, or, in case of fugitives from Florida and Louisiana plantations, Spanish or French; they soon learned the Muskhogean tongue of the Seminole. They were thus almost the only interpreters available for intercourse between the Indians and the whites—and the only interpreters in whom the Indians could put any confidence, since their opinion of the Creek half-breeds who sometimes fulfilled that function was usually not high. The Negroes who had fled to the Seminole as adults were also acquainted with the white man's ways—

[5] *American State Papers, Military Affairs*, vii, 427.

at the least much better acquainted than the Indians—and were capable of giving advice as to his probable intentions in any particular situation. In a time of actual or threatened hostility a runaway Negro could wander into a white man's town or camp and gather information unobserved, when an Indian would immediately be apprehended. From interpreters and spies it was an easy transition for the Negroes to become unofficial advisers, and then to be recognized, in some cases, as tribal counsellors. A relationship which had originally been merely one of mutual material advantage eventually became cemented by reciprocal respect and affection. Intermarriage inevitably took place, though probaby not to such an extent as would have been the case had the Negroes lived less independently and separately.

The contrast of the Seminole Negro's existence with that of their kinsmen on the plantations was so striking as to call forth comment from all observers. His everyday life was universally described as positively idyllic. He lived in a Negro village, separate from that of the Indians with whom he was associated, in a house built after the Indian style of palmetto planks lashed to upright posts and thatched with palmetto leaves, but usually of better construction, in the midst of well-cultivated fields of corn, rice, sweet potatoes, melons, beans, peppers, and cotton. Horses, cattle, and swine belonging to him grazed in the woods and on the savannas. He dressed after the Indian fashion, on occasions of particuar festivity wearing moccasins, leggins, a long full smock, or hunting shirt, of gaudy hue, belted at the waist, and a turban composed of bright-colored bandannas, or a similarly brilliant shawl, ingeniously twisted about his head and topped with plumes; a series of brightly-polished metal crescents hung about his neck and descended upon his chest. A more sober and less elaborate variation of this costume sufficed for everyday wear. The younger boys, of course, ran about nude or, as they approached adolescence, were invested with a long homespun shirt. The Seminole Negro was not a slave of the hoe, but spent a part of his time hunting and fishing. In time of war the men and grown boys of the Negro villages assembled, equipped with rifle or musket, axe, and knife, under their own captains, who were in turn responsive to the orders of the Seminole chief to whom they owed allegiance. Under this regime they throve amazingly. An observer a decade later, when the Seminole Indians and Negroes were in a considerably less prosperous condition, nevertheless declared: "The Negroes . . . both men and women [are] stout and even gigantic in their proportions . . . the finest looking people I have ever seen. . . . They are much more intelligent [sic] than their masters, most of them speaking the Spanish, English, and Indian languages. Though stouter than the aborigines . . . they resemble the Indians in figure, being longer limbed, and more symmetrically formed than the Negroes of the plantations. . . ."[6]

There was consequently no group of people in Florida with a greater stake in resistance to invasion and annexation by the United States than the Seminole Negroes; the Spaniards would lose thereby their independence, the Indians their land, but the Negroes would lose at once their independence, their homes, and the very freedom of themselves and their families. By no means all the free Negroes in Florida in 1812 were among the Indians. There were many who owed their freedom to the lenient Spanish emancipation laws; there were others who had escaped to the British during the turmoil of the Revolution, or to the Spanish, again, after the retrocession of Florida; but the Seminole Negroes were the boldest, the best trained to arms, and

[6] The best of the numerous accounts describing the idyllic relations between the Seminole Indians and their Negroes, and the enviable situation of the latter, are: (Simmons, William Hayne), *Notices of East Florida*, Charleston, 1822, pp. 41, 50, 76; ASP, MA, vi, 533-534; Williams, John Lee, *The Territory of Florida*, N. Y., 1837, p. 240; Kennedy, William, *Texas, the Rise, Progress, and Prospects*, London, 1841, i, 350.

the most strategically located for bringing into the struggle not only themselves but their Indian masters or patrons as well.

Such were the only allies to whom in this dark hour the Spanish authorities at St. Augustine could turn with any hope for relief. But at the darkest hour, a thin ray of light penetrated. The United States Government, under Federalist and Northern pressure, belatedly decided that its agent, Gen. Mathews, had proceeded too openly in his relations with the Patriots and early in April, 1812, he was dismissed. This by no means meant, however, an immediate withdrawal of United States troops and was, indeed, in large measure a subterfuge, for a few days later the Secretary of State requested Gov. D. B. Mitchell of Georgia to assume control of affairs in East Florida and to arrange with the governor of the province for the restoration of the original situation—but only on condition that the governor would agree to extend amnesty to the Patriots who, under the encouragement of the United States, had hoisted the banner of rebellion. This left the agent with an excuse to retain United States troops in Florida—and, since the United States agent was also the governor of Georgia, he could even draw on the militia of that state for additional military support. A part of the latter, indeed, was immediately mobilized, its commander expressing the hope that the Florida Indians would "take up the cudgels" in behalf of the Spanish government, since this would "afford a desireable pretext for the Georgians to penetrate their country, and Break up a Negroe Town: an important Evil growing under their patronage."

Still, the withdrawal of Mathews sufficiently discouraged the Patriots that the Spanish authorities enjoyed a brief breathing-spell. This they utilized in recruiting and obtaining reinforcements. The forces in St. Augustine were presently said to consist of 400 white and 500 black troops.[7]

[7] *Niles Register*, iii (Jan. 23, 1813), 330.

"They have armed," Mitchell indignantly announced, "every able-bodied negro within their power, and they have also received from the Havana a reinforcement of nearly two companies of black troops. . . ."—some of them, perhaps, descendants of the colonists evacuated from Fort Mosé half a century before. "It is my settled opinion," Mitchell continued, "that if they are suffered to remain in the province, our southern country will soon be in a state of insurrection." Mitchell consequently protested to Gov. Kindelan: "Your certain knowledge of the peculiar situation of the southern section of the Union in regard to that description of people [Negroes] one might have supposed, would have induced you to abstain from introducing them into the province, or from organizing such as were already in it."

The wrath which the Spanish governor must have experienced on being read this self-righteous lecture, by the agent of a government which had instigated a rebellion in his province, and was even then in occupation of a part of it, on the impropriety of his use of the only troops available for resisting this uprising and invasion, may be more easily imagined than described; it is best expressed in his own words in a letter of Dec. 12, 1812, in which he points out that the colored population served in the militia of all Spanish provinces on an equality with the whites, and sarcastically compares Mitchell's protest to that of a burglar who complains that a householder is provided with a blunderbuss whereas the burglar possesses only pistols![8]

Matters must soon come to a head. The Spanish garrison at St. Augustine, although reinforced from Havana, were closely besieged from the land-side and cut off from provisions. Some diversion was necessary or St. Augustine must fall from starvation if not by military force. This diversion must be supported by the Indians to be effective, but, to bring it about, Negro agency was required. Before

[8] *N. E.*, iii (Jan. 16, 1813), 311-312.

leaving Florida, Gen. Mathews had summoned the Indian chiefs to a talk, and warned them against intervention; they had since sat peacefully if sullenly in their villages. But in July a Negro from St. Augustine, speaking the Indian language, arrived at Payne's town of Alachua to warn its inhabitants and those of the town of Alligator Hole, and of the Negro villages in the region, against the designs of the Americans. "The Americans are playing with you," he said. "They are going to take your country beyond the St. John's; your young men, then, will be forced to work for them, the young females will be put to spin and weave for them, while the old people will sweep the yards of the white men." This incitement, which coincided so well with what Payne's people had so long feared and observed, tipped the balance in favor of war and against the Americans, so far as the 200 Indian "gun men" of Alachua and Alligator Hole, and the 40 "negro gun men" of the neighborhood were concerned.[9]

On July 25, accordingly, the Seminole Indians and Negroes fell upon the plantations along the St. John's belonging to Americans who were cooperating with the Patriots, killed eight or nine settlers, and "carried off" a large number of probably not altogether unwilling slaves. Patriots began to desert their camp to look to the safety of their families and property. Negroes of the St. Augustine region seem to have joined with the Seminole Indians and Negroes on these raids. Lt. Col. Smith reported, Aug. 21, 1812: "The blacks assisted by the Indians have become very daring & from the want of a proper knowledge of the country the parties which I have sent out have always been unsuccessful."[10] Despite the arrival on Aug. 15 of Maj. Daniel

[9] *State Papers and Publick Documents of the United States*, ser. 1, vol. ix, pp. 181-187, "Talk of Tuskegee Tustumugee (sic), Creek Agency, Sept. 18, 1812, to Col. Benj. Hawkins."

[10] Davis, T. Frederick, ed., "United States Troops in Spanish East Florida, 1812-13 (letters of Lieut. Col. T. A. Smith)," *Florida Historical Quarterly*, ix (July, Oct., 1930, Jan., Apr., 1931), 3-23, 96-116, 135-155, 259-278, x (July, 1931), 24-34: ix, 111.

Newnan of the Georgia militia with 250 volunteers, the position of the United States troops and Patriots before St. Augustine was rapidly becoming untenable, not only because of the strengthening of the Spanish garrison and the Negro-Indian raids upon the besiegers' rear, but also because the invasion, which, from the beginning, had been supported by Georgia volunteers, was now being resisted by other volunteers from Georgia—Negro slaves who, taking advantage of the confusion, were deserting the plantations and making their way to the allied Spanish, Indian, and Negro forces. Gov. Mitchell, Sept. 9, declared that the Spanish "governor has proclaimed freedom to every negro who will join his standard, and has sent a party of them to unite with, and who are actually at this time united with the Indians in their murderous excursions. Indeed the principal strength of the garrison of St. Augustine consists of negroes . . . the most of our male negroes on the seaboard are restless and make many attempts to get off to Augustine, and many have succeeded."[11]

The siege of St. Augustine ended suddenly and disastrously. On Sept. 12, a train of wagons, escorted by 20 United States Marines and Georgia volunteers, under the command of Capt. Williams, USMC, and Capt. Fort of the militia, was proceeding from Davis Creek to the besieging camp. At Twelve Mile Swamp—so-called from its distance from the St. John's—lay ambushed a company of about 50 Negroes, or Negroes and a few Indians, warned by scouts of the wagon-train's approach, and under the command of "a free Black named Prince"—a free man who intended to remain so. His orders to his troop were to immobilize the wagons and pick off the officers. Out of the darkness crackled a volley, mortally wounding the Marine captain in eight places, wounding the militia officer, killing the sergeant, wounding six privates, laying several of the horses dead in their harness. Out of the shadows Negroes and

[11] *S. P. & P. D.*, ix, 168-172.

Indians leaped in for the kill, axe and knife in hand, but the dozen Marines and militiamen still on their feet, responding to the commands of their wounded officers, returned the fire and followed it up with a charge so unexpectedly fierce that the enemy melted away into the darkness, enabling the survivors to make their escape, carrying their wounded and abandoning the horseless wagons and their contents.

But though the little company had escaped absolute annihilation, this action of only twenty-five minutes had nevertheless been decisive. Lt. Col. Smith frantically summoned the Georgia militia to his aid with men and horses, and with their assistance retreated from before St. Augustine to the supply depot on Davis Creek, where he could be protected by United States gunboats. "Thus ingloriously ended the siege of St. Augustine," is Julius W. Pratt's comment—raised, be it noted, by a Negro-instigated diversion in the rear by Seminole Indians and Negroes, followed up by a cutting of the supply lines by a force of Negroes and Indians under Negro leadership.[12]

Although the siege of St. Augustine was at least temporarily lifted, it might be resumed were the enemy in the rear crushed. Maj. Daniel Newnan, adjutant-general of Georgia and commander of the Georgia volunteers in Florida, had on Aug. 21, a few days after his arrival, been ordered to proceed against the hostile Indians and destroy their towns and supplies. Difficulty in obtaining horses and provisions, and the ravages of malaria, had delayed his departure until after the catastrophe of Twelve Mile Swamp, at which time his volunteers had less than a week to serve. He was resolved, however, to carry out his orders if at all possible, so asked for volunteers to serve as long as the expedition required. Only 84—about a third—of his own force vounteered, but enough Patriots and militiamen from other

---

[12] *S. P. & P. D.*, ix, 175-177; Williams, John Lee, *The Territory of Florida*, N. Y., 1837, p. 197; McClellan, Maj. Edwin N., *Indian Fights* (Hist. U.S.M.C., 1st ed., 1st rev., i, ch. 19: mimeographed).

detachments were added to bring the total to 116. With this force, twelve horses, and four days' provisions, on Sept. 24 he marched jauntily but determinedly off to destroy the Alachua towns.

The morning of the fourth day when, it was thought, they were only six or seven miles from the Alachua settlements, they suddenly encountered a force of 75 to 100 Indians on the march, some mounted, most on foot, either moving on the St. John's for a final blow at the American forces or warned by scouts of the approach of an invading army. They were led by the aged head-chief Payne, mounted on a white horse, and by his brother, the war-leader, Bowlegs. At sight of the enemy the Seminole promptly threw down their packs, "trimmed their guns," formed a line of battle, and opened fire. The octogenarian King Payne rode to and fro, encouraging his men, but as the Seminole closed in the border rifles crackled and the white horse ran riderless.

The Seminole, infuriated by the death of their chief, fought desperately and, although somewhat outnumbered by the Georgians and though the muskets with which most were armed were outranged by the frontier rifles, they kept up the action for two and a half hours, constantly endeavoring to outflank the enemy. The Georgians, however, eventually drove them back, taking with them the body of their chief, into a swamp where the whites dared not follow. After scalping the bodies left on the field, Newnan's forces took advantage of the enemy's withdrawal to erect log-barricades and dig fox-holes. The Georgians were left undisturbed—save for the sight of Indians in the distance, on the edge of the swamp, painting themselves and consulting —until half an hour before sunset.

The next attack was heralded by a furious yelling, in which for the first time the deep-chested shouts of Negroes mingled with the shrill outcries of the Indians. Word of King Payne's death had reached the Negro villages, and their warriors, resolved to avenge their protector, were arriving on the battlefield. Crouching low, led by their chiefs, the Indians and Negroes, now perhaps 200 in number, closed in rapidly and, at about 200 yards, opened fire on the entrenched borderers who replied with their usual accuracy. The attack continued until eight o'clock, the Negroes in particular displaying conspicuous bravery, which led Maj. Newnan to comment, "Negroes . . . are their best soldiers," but finally the Seminole again retired.

Then began the severest test of the expedition. For two days no attack ensued, but the Georgians knew themselves constantly under observation. A messenger had been sent back for reinforcements, but it was four days to the St. John's and another four to return, and their provisions had been exhausted on their march. They had been depending on the beef and corn of the Alachua towns, still six or seven miles distant, but now horse-meat was their only resource. It must have been almost a relief when after two days the attack re-commenced, but in a form harder to endure than the previous frontal actions. The enemy had learned respect for the deadly accuracy of the Georgia rifles and henceforth were determined to play by their own rules. Riflemen, carefully concealed, began a desultory and nerve-wracking sniping which continued for five or six days, while more and more of the invaders succumbed to wounds, disease, and starvation until over half were *hors de combat.*

After a week of siege, Newnan, in desperation, determined on a night-retreat and, carrying the sick and wounded on stretchers, set out for the St. John's. The enemy, who could hardly have been ignorant of this move, let them go; the Indian and Negroes had suffered perhaps as many as 50 casualties, and were unwilling to incur further loss in the extermination of an enemy now desirous only of escape. Perhaps they were far-seeing enough to consider the moral effect of this battered half-starved band upon other would-be invaders. Newnan's party struggled on through the wilderness for several days. They lived on "gophers, alligators, and palmetto stocks," missed one relief party, were briefly attacked by about 50 Indians, finally encountered another relief expedition, were escorted to the St. John's, and conveyed by gunboat to Col. Smith's camp. "The punitive expedition," says Pratt, "had degenerated into a desperate retreat. Newnan ... had not come within sight of an Indian town or supply depot."[13]

The Georgians and Patriots for the time being could only rend the air with dire prophecies of slave insurrection; the danger was really too great for them to do more than remain passive and hope for relief. Their only forces were inadequate, in the face of the growing enemy strength, for any aggressive action. A letter of Jan. 3, 1813, declared: "A number of slaves have lately deserted their masters & gone to Augustine from the St. John's."[14] The Patriot leader, McIntosh, on Jan. 24, complained to James Monroe: "Our slaves are excited to rebel, and we have an army of negroes raked up in this country, and brought from Cuba to contend with. . . . St. Augustine, the whole province will be the refuge of fugitive slaves; and from thence emissaries . . . will be detached to bring about a revolt of the black population in the United States." These appeals were not without effect upon a government in which the slavery interests were so powerfully represented, and the general government prepared to reinforce its troops in Florida for the suppression of the Indians and Negroes and the ultimate seizure of the province.

The citizens of East Tennessee, however, were so situated as to be more immediately concerned and capable of taking action. Observing their brothers in the western part of the state preparing for a march against Mobile and Pensacola under Gen. Jackson, they had been organizing a regiment of volunteer cavalry. East Tennessee was not a

---

[13] *N. R.*, iii (Nov. 14, 1812), 171; *ibid.*, iii (Dec. 12, 1812), 235-237; Williams, *Territory of Fla.*, 198.

[14] *Davis, loc. cit.*, ix, 269.

plantation area, and its citizens were probably chiefly concerned with the Indian menace, but other Tennesseans were conscious of the danger to slavery in the Florida situation and one of them, Willie Blount, wrote from Nashville, Dec. 12, 1812, to William Eustis, complaining of "disaffection among the blacks" and incitement "to commit murder and depredations."[15]

Upon learning of Newnan's defeat the Tennesseans acted immediately. Under John Williams of Knoxville over 200 mounted volunteers set out for the south early in December, 1812, and arrived at Colerain on the St. Mary's River, Jan. 7, 1813, when they put themselves under the command of Brig. Gen. Flournoy. The Indians, alarmed at these preparations, had sued through the Creek agent, Benjamin Hawkins, for peace; Maj. Gen. Pinckney, nevertheless, decided to order the expedition to proceed and to unite with it 200 regulars under Col. Smith. The Georgians were determined to proceed independently to oust the Indians from the coveted Alachua lands if the Federal Government refused to take action and the East Tennesseans would probably have put themselves under the command of Georgia state authorities had United States officers refused to coperate. It seemed wise, therefore, to take advantage of the presence of so large and determined a body of volunteers and to give them all the assistance available; otherwise they might proceed on their own responsibility, and should they be defeated, this, added to the Newnan debacle, would greatly reduce the prestige of the United States.

The East Tennesseans, accordingly, joined by a few Georgians, started out early in February for the "Aulotcheewaus." They intended to drive the Indians from their fertile lands and, in many cases no doubt, themselves ultimately assume occupancy. For those who had no such intentions the lure of adventure and plunder sufficed. They were informed of the rich stores of deerskins and beeswax

[15] *S. P. & P. D.*, ix, 155-160.

accumulated in the villages, the horses grazing on the savannas which could be used for the transport of the loot and which, together with the large herds of cattle, could be driven north to a market; probably most important of all was the possibility of capturing some of the women and children of the Negro villages who, roped together, could be driven off with the other livestock and restored at a good price to the slavery from which they or their parents had escaped. Col. Smith was to unite with this company of adventurers near the first Seminole town.

The plan proceeded according to schedule. The two forces united on Feb. 7 and moved upon the Alachua towns. The Indians and Negroes, who had mustered at the most 200 warriors against the early Georgian invasion, knew themselves incapable of resisting a force nearly four times as large as Newnan's and over twice their own. They had hurried their women and children deep into the swamps, and the warriors, lurking on the borders of their fastnesses, watched for an opportunity to harry the foe. The expeditionary force reached Payne's town on the 9th and found it deserted. The next objective was Bowlegs' town, ten or twelve miles southwest, and a body of volunteers under Williams set out for it on the 10th. This division of the enemy gave the Indians and Negroes an opportunity, and on the first day of the march 200 warriors attacked the Tennessee column but were repelled with heavy casualties. The resistance, however, held up the invaders long enough so that they did not reach Bowlegs' town until the 12th. The expeditionary force, the enemy driven from the field, turned with enthusiasm to the work of plunder and destruction, burning 386 houses, together with several thousand bushels of corn, in the two large towns and in the smaller villages, including a Negro town, appropriating 2,000 deerskins, and rounding up 400 horses and as many cattle. Driven to desperation by the sight of smoke from their homes and storehouses, the Indians and Negroes again and again took advantage of the invaders' preoccupation with plunder, to emerge from their fastnesses and strike at the ravagers. They were always beaten off, but the resistance was sufficient to convince the invaders that it would be unwise to proceed against a third more distant Indian town. They decided to be satisfied with the destruction of the two principal towns, and with the fact that "the balance of the Seminole Nation is completely in waste." Perhaps a desire to convey their plunder to safety was also a factor. Fifty or sixty Indians, it was declared, had been killed at the cost of only one white man dead and seven wounded. The Alachua region was open to white settlers. Almost the entire Seminole food supply was destroyed and by spring the survivors were "literally starving." It had indeed been "a famous victory."[16]

One victory, however, does not necessarily win a campaign. The Indian and Negro resistance to American occupation had held it up until Northern and Federalist opposition in Congress had forced a suspension of the attempt. By May 15, 1813, United States troops had been withdrawn from Florida, leaving the Patriots, scornful of an offer of amnesty, to cope with the Spanish government for themselves. Some of them removed to the United States and those who remained justified the reference to them by the leading authority on the movement, as "a band of unscrupulous adventurers," by confiscating the property of their recreant erstwhile comrades and selling such free Negroes as were unlucky enough to fall into their hands.[17] They had the impudence to suggest to the Spanish governor an armistice on condition of the removal of Negro troops, a grant of the Alachua lands, and complete amnesty—a proposal which was ignored. The Patriots then moved into the

[16] *N. R.*, iv (Mar. 13, 1813), 29; (Mar. 20, 1813), 48; (Mar. 27, 1813), 67; (Apr. 17, 1813), 116; Davis, *loc. cit.*, ix, 271-274; McClellan, 15-16.

[17] For plundering activities of the Patriots, see "United States vs. Ferreira," 36th cong., 1st sess., sen. misc. doc. no. 55.

Alachua lands, cleared of Indians a year earlier, built a fort, and requested annexation to the United States, which on Apr. 19, 1814, was finally and conclusively refused.[18] Thus ended, for that time, the attempt to annex East Florida to the United States.

That it ended in failure rather than in success was in large part due to Negro resistance. That the majority of the Spanish garrison in St. Augustine were black troops is a matter of no great significance in this connection; they were merely acting under orders, as were their white comrades. It is important, however, to note that the initial action in raising the siege of St. Augustine was a diversion in the rear by Seminole Indians and Negroes acting at Negro instigation, that local Negroes, joined by runaway slaves from Georgia and Florida plantations, harried the besieging force in co-operation with the Indians, and that the besiegers' supply-lines were cut and the siege finally raised by a force consisting almost entirely of Negroes under Negro leadership. Maj. Newnan's final desperate attempt to strike at the center of Indian and Negro resistance was thwarted by a force in which, as the major himself testified, the gun-men of the Negro towns were the best soldiers.

To be sure, had not Congressional action resulted in the recall of United States troops from East Florida, the Negro-Indian resistance would have proved ultimately ineffective, but, on the other hand, a Congress confronted by a *fait accompli*, which was prevented only by the Negro-Indian opposition, would probably not have withdrawn its army of occupation.

It might, indeed, be said with truth that, from the long-range viewpoint, the Negro and Indian resistance to the East Florida annexation plot was of little effect. Five years

---

[18] The Patriots accepted peace terms from the Florida government in 1816. Wyllys, Rufus Kay, ''The East Florida Revolution of 1812-1814,'' *The Hispanic American Historical Review*, ix (Nov., 1929), pp. 415-445, esp. 445, quoting from Brevard, Caroline, *A History of Florida*, 2 vols., Deland, Fla., 1924, i, 31.

after the Tennesseans' vengeful destruction of the Alachua towns, Andrew Jackson marched at the head of another Tennessee force through East Florida, defeated the hopelessly outnumbered Negroes on the Suwanee, broke up the Indian and Negro settlements, and sent their inhabitants flying southward, thus making inevitable that annexation of East Florida which was agreed upon the following year, in 1819, and which went into effect two years later. Negro-Indian resistance thus delayed annexation less than a decade.

What is, then, the ultimate significance of Negro resistance to the East Florida annexation plot? Simply that it demonstrates a fact which would hardly seem to require demonstration had it not been so generally disregarded, perhaps even concealed, by many writers in the field of American history: namely, that Negroes, as well as Indians or whites, have, in an international situation, displayed a capacity for recognizing their own interests and taking action to safeguard them. In the face of the East Florida annexation plot the Negroes potentially affected—free Negroes, Seminole Negroes, Florida and Georgia plantation-slaves—readily discerned that the maintenance of Spanish rule in East Florida was essential to their well-being; the action they took in its defense was courageous, skilful, and effective.

KENNETH WIGGINS PORTER

Vassar College, Poughkeepsie, N. Y.

THE NEGRO ON THE MINING FRONTIER*

The frontier in American history is one of the most significant contributions to the development of the American nation, a subject which has been exploited by many of the leading writers in the literary and historical fields. This phenomenon has been a motivating influence in the growth of the West, perhaps more than any other section of this country. Much has been made of this frontier hypothesis and there have been pros and cons on the amount of influence it has exerted on the development of the history of the United States, but all will agree that it has exerted some influence on the growth and development of the West. The West itself probably needs to be defined for the scope of this paper. It has meant different sections at different times, but for this discussion the West will mean west of the Mississippi River. The very nature of the subject will define it even more.

There were many motives and several factors which made for the rapid development of the Western frontier. Some persons moved West because they were restless in spirit, for one reason or another; others migrated because they sought cheap land; others moved West because they had failed in life; some went West because they were fugitives from justice, among these being several who became the notorious bad men and women of the American frontier; and for still others who migrated the motives were overlapping. Those who were influenced by the aforementioned motives made for the slow and gradual development of the Western frontier. The factor which made for the rapid settlement of the West was the development of the mining frontier. All types of people went West in the "gold rushes" and they changed the West from a region of unsettled communities, laying the basis for the agricultural and urban development which came at a later time. In spite

* An address delivered at the annual meeting of the Association for the Study of Negro Life and History in Boston, Massachusetts, October 28, 1944.

of the participation in these "rushes" by all types of persons, one writer has said, "While every race and nationality was represented in the mining population very few Negroes migrated to the camps."[1]   Since this movement began at the time slavery was at its zenith, it would seem at least plausible.

Upon closer examination it will be observed that there were Negroes on the mining frontier and they seemed to have been in the mineral empire, furnishing labor which aided the development of these mines in almost every section of the mineral empire.   Many of those who came from slave states brought their slaves with them as laborers. Such a person was Major Edwin Sherman, who arrived in California in June, 1849, and located at Rose Bar on the Sacramento River, an active mining center.   There came from Texas to that same mining center a month later Thomas Jefferson Green, with others interested in the same project along with their slaves.   They at once staked out claims for themselves and their slaves without consulting anyone.[2]   There was an unwritten law in the mining country that when a miner staked out a claim it was sacred, but in doing so he must take into consideration others who were already in the country.   Thomas Jefferson Green did not consider this, but staked his claim and began to work with his slaves.   This action was not pleasing to the miners already at Rose Bar and they protested vigorously, since it was against the rules set up under the preëmption claims. A meeting was held on July 29 at which it was decided that no Negro would own a claim or would be permitted to work in the mines.[3]   At this same meeting a committee was appointed to inform Green and the Texans of the action of the meeting.   The miners achieved the objective, for Green and

[1] Briggs, H. E., *Frontiers of the Northwest*, p. 74.

[2] Sherman, Major Edwin, Biographical Material.   Document in Bancroft Library.   Godwin, Cardinal, *The Establishment of State Government in California*, p. 110.

[3] *Ibid.*

the others decided to abide by the decision of the miners and took their slaves and moved away.[4] Whether they went to other mining fields or went back to Texas is not clear.

Daniel Woods in his narrative of a mining company in California said there were two servants with the group, belonging to various members. They worked in every way with the others in the operation of the project. One of these Negroes was an athletic type of man and, according to his own statement, as strong and vigorous a specimen of humanity as it had ever been Woods' pleasure to observe. This strong vigorous man did all of the work that required great strength about the mines and with it he was jovial and merry, always singing some catchy tune. The other was an old man, who belonged to the president of the company, called by the name of Allen. This old man was to get his freedom when he left that country, it was said.[5] The wonder is that it was not given him while he was in the mining country where he might have had an opportunity to stabilize himself and where he could secure independence quickly. Whether he was able to reap this reward or not is not known.

In 1850 there occurred another case of some significance that involved a slave in the mineral empire. In this year Thomas Gilman, a planter of Mount Pleasant, Tennessee, agreed to permit one of his slaves to go to the gold fields of California on the condition that the slave would pay for the privilege with the very first gold he was able to secure in the mining country.[6] Tom, the slave, who had been given the name of his master, moved to California and settled in Dragoon Gulch, where he struck a pocket of considerable size in his claim. This friendly obliging young Negro, true to his agreement, forwarded to his master the amount of

---

[4] Sherman, Major Edwin, Biographical Material. Members of the committe were a Mr. Rose, Governor Shannon and Edwin A. Shannon.

[5] Woods, Daniel B., Sixteen Months at Gold Digging, p. 155.

[6] Buckbee, Edna B., The Saga of Old Tuolumne, p. 308.

gold they had agreed upon for his liberty.[7] This gold was paid in good faith and Tom Gilman had every right to think he was free, but the planter by some way, which is not clear according to the records at hand, forced the Dragoon miner to pay for his freedom a second time. This case shows to what lengths some slaves had to go to secure their freedom; it also shows this slave owner had no respect for any agreement he made with a slave. Thomas Gilman was not yet through with his slave in the California gold field, for on June 29, 1855, the former, in a letter to this Negro, urged Tom to return to him in Tennessee. He reminded Tom of a promise he was supposed to have made to take care of the planter in his old age. The slave could not remember making any such an agreement, but had so much respect for his duty, as he saw it under the supposed promise, that he began to pack up and make ready to return to Tennessee. He would have accomplished his aim but was prevented from it by other miners in the vicinity who persuaded him not to leave his claim, and this saved him from going back into slavery.[8] Gilman lived in this section long after the "gold rush" was over; he could be found in his cabin on Shaw's Flat Road which leads to Sonora. He took pride in after years in providing water at his cabin for the weary traveler. In 1935 when the Saga of Old Tuolumne was written the cabin had rotted away, and all that remained was the chimney. Tom Gilman not only worked on the mining frontier but became a part of it and remained long after the gold fever had subsided, until the end of his earthly career.

As early as 1848, the very year of the discovery of gold

[7] *Ibid.*, p. 309.

[8] *Ibid.* Excerpts from a letter on file in Mississippi House in Shaw's Flat: "Uncle Joseph and your colored friends are generally well and wish to be remembered to you and hope to see you again. If you have lost your gold by the banks come just as soon as you get enough to bring you, if you cannot make as much in this country perhaps you can save what you make.

Signed: THOMAS GILMAN,
Mount Pleasant, Tennessee"

at Sutter's Fort, a group of gold seekers started out on May 1 from Buchanan County, Missouri. They journeyed westward by slow stages, as was the custom in those days. Along the route they came in contact with the Hays train, also from Missouri. They traveled westward together, sharing the hardships of the journey and offering mutual protection for each company. At Fort Hall they found a Negro slave who had escaped from Colonel Hays in Jackson County, Missouri.[9] Hays did not attempt to force the slave to return to Missouri, as he might have done under the laws then in operation in the territories; rather he made an agreement with the Negro so that he might secure his freedom if he would go along and drive one of the teams of oxen. In addition he had to work a year in the gold fields. This arrangement was satisfactory to the Negro slave, for it offered him a way to secure his freedom and put him in a section where he could find employment as a free man.

The social aspect of the mining frontier in California is interesting. One of the best known sections of the Northern California gold field was Negro Bar, situated on the American River. This village was settled in 1849 but was destroyed in 1850 when the Virginia Mining Company was formed to drain the river bed at this point.[10] In this settlement, while it was in existence, there were both slaves and free men. There was also a great deal more tolerance of Negro blood in the mining area than was usual in the states. Negroes were not expected to sit at tables with whites but were allowed to lose their money in the gambling rooms like others.[11] These Negro dollars helped the whites overcome their prejudice. The Negroes both free and slave on the frontier liked to gamble and were frequent patrons of the gambling houses. In spite of the accommodations which were offered to Negroes by the regular hotels, in any town

[9] Gibson, J. W., *Recollection of a Pioneer*, p. 30.
[10] *California Historical Quarterly*, vol. x, p. 293.
[11] Brotherwick, J. D., *The Gold Hunters*, p. 163.

or camp of any size there was always a hotel kept by a Negro proprietor for the special benefit of Negro people. Where there was no hotel operated especially for Negroes, the Negro was accommodated with the whites, always last.[12]

A little distance from Rose Bar, William Carpenter, a California pioneer, says in the fifties men were there from every section of the country, of all colors and all ages. Gambling and vice of all kinds existed without interference from the constituted authority, which was then the Vigilance Committee. Carpenter felt that California would never become a farming section but in this he proved himself a poor prophet.[13]

There were some parts of the mining section in which Negroes were quite numerous but not as numerous as they were in the South Atlantic States, as might be expected. The fact that this region was so far from the center of Negro population in the United States, together with the facts that the section was unorganized and the only labor required was in the mines, made for a small Negro population. There were frequent examples of Negroes receiving their freedom as a result of their working in the mines of California.[14] There were instances of slaves being left in the mines by their masters and working diligently to secure their freedom.[15] They were free according to the laws of California, but most of the Negroes in the mines made no effort to use their freedom. The reason probably is that only those were brought whom the owners could expect to remain faithful to the masters and respect the bonds of slavery.

Early in 1850 an attempt to use Negro miners failed because of the opposition of the white miners. Dr. Earl and Colonel Thorn brought to Los Angeles from the Southern

[12] *Ibid.*, p. 164.
[13] Carpenter, William, *A California Pioneer*, p. 6.
[14] Brotherwick, J. D., *Three Years in California*, p. 164.
[15] *Ibid.*

states a large number of Negro slaves whom they proposed to work in the mines and who were to furnish the principal source of labor for this project. This idea did not work out as was anticipated because the white miners stampeded the mines and drove the Negroes away.[16] The owners did not get even the cost of bringing the slaves to the gold fields and the slaves got their freedom without much effort on their own part.

There is a case on record of a mine worked entirely by slaves and owned by Colonel William English and other Georgia slave owners. They invested in Nevada in a mine known as the Old Kentucky Ridge. The slaves were promised their freedom as a compensation for working in the mines.[17] This work was very difficult; the slaves had to carry the ore on their heads in large baskets back a half mile to the mill. The mine failed and Colonel English died destitute of funds. The slaves took what they had been able to save by working at odd jobs about the mines in their spare time and purchased land and paid for his funeral. After the death of Colonel English his nephew took over control and forced the slaves to purchase their freedom again.[18] When they did get their freedom they settled at Grass Valley, where they became an important part of the community. These cases show that Negro slaves furnished a portion of the labor on the mining frontier and formed a larger part of the population on this frontier than has been thought by some persons.

There were some slaves who made rich finds while working with their masters. Such a person was Elijah Baker, a Negro slave who was working in Downings Ravine in the fifties. He had been brought there by his master, James Baker, who was unreliable and was soon out of money. He then hired Elijah out and decided to go back to Georgia,

---

[16] *History of San Diego County, California*, p. 70.
[17] *San Francisco Chronicle*, October 11, 1903.
[18] *Ibid.*

leaving Elijah to work. Elijah soon discovered a mine and was shortly thereafter in possession of considerable gold.[19] When his master asked him to return to the plantation he started back to Georgia, but fortunately for him, perhaps, he died on the way and his master took over his property. The slave showed his loyalty to his master and was willing to return if in all probability it would have cost him his freedom.

There was in Hangtown in the year 1851 a young Southerner who brought one of his slaves to California with him to work in the mines. They worked and lived together, master and man, sharing equally the labors and hardships of the mines.[20] One night the slave dreamed that he and his master had been working inside of a certain cabin and had taken out a great pile of gold. He told this to his master. Neither he nor his master paid much attention to the dream and passed it off as only a normal dream meaning little or nothing. A few nights later the slave had the same dream again and this time his master took it seriously. He bought the house and began dismantling and digging under the floor. This proved a wise step, for before they were half through they had taken out $20,000. Negroes in some cases found rich veins even while they were working for their masters. They were said by one writer to be proverbially lucky in the mines of California.[21]

Some of the large companies formed for the purpose of mining had Negroes with them as a part of their labor supply. Such was the case of a company that set out from Arkansas in 1849. It took the name of the Washington County Mining Company because a large percentage of the members came from Washington County, Arkansas. The company consisted of 126 persons: 86 were from Washington County, 15 from the Cherokee Nation, 8 from Madison

[19] Quaife, M. M. *Echoes of the Past*, p. 260.
[20] Brotherwick, J. D., *Three Years in California*, p. 163.
[21] *Ibid.*, p. 164.

County, Arkansas, 10 from Benton County, Arkansas, 2 from Tennessee, and 3 were women. There is no way of telling where the women made their homes before starting West, since they were included in the groups already named. There were five Negroes in the company, but whether they were free Negroes or slaves is not clear.[22] Just a year later another company set out from the Cherokee Nation on April 20 and was captained by Clement Van McNair. It was composed of 105 whites and 15 Negro servants, and comprised the group that made the Ralston Creek gold discovery.[23] The Negroes, as servants or as partners in the companies, were a part of the mining population and gave labor to those companies which were formed solely for the purpose of unearthing ore in the mining section.

The Negro slave was in California, all will agree; the question comes, was he happy in his bondage? William Kelly, who made a trip in the mining country when it was at its height, thought the Negro slaves in the mining country were happy because they made no attempt to escape or to exercise their freedom. The slaves in the South were always on the lookout for a chance to escape, or by sheer thrift they would strive to secure enough money to purchase their freedom. This very question was the most important political question in the Eastern states in 1851. In spite of all these favorable circumstances, not a single instance came before this observer's notice of a slave's deserting the mines.[24] They were there in great numbers, he says, without any law to restrain them and no punishment could be meted out to them. This would seem strange on the part of the Negro under ordinary circumstances; but in most cases the slaves brought to the frontier were the docile, kind and obedient type who were fond of their masters and reluc-

[22] Bieber, Ralph, *Southern Trails of California in 1849*, p. 334.

[23] Hafen, Leroy, *Pikes Peak Gold Rush*, p. 35.

[24] Kelley, William, *An Excursion to California Over the Prairie, Rocky Mountains and Great Sierra Nevada*, p. 190.

tant to leave them. Perhaps the Negroes did not attempt to run away because they were in free territory and could soon secure enough money to purchase their freedom either by working in the mines or by doing domestic service in their spare time.

The evidence at hand shows that the slave was an important factor on the mining frontier. What was the contribution of the free Negro to the mining country? On October 5, 1849, Major William Downie formed a company and started for the mines of California. This company consisted of two white men, one white boy (Michael Durvarney) and seven free Negroes.[25] The names of two of these Negroes are Charles Wilkins and Albert Callis, both of whom acted as cooks for the company. The company decided to go up in the high mountains because it was believed that there was better gold higher up.[26] They went up to the fork of the Yerba River, where the north and south branches come into the main stream. When they had reached the section they selected to work, the land was assigned to the men. The piece allotted to Albert was particularly rich, and gold could be seen in considerable quantities by removing the dirt with the foot. They arrived on Sunday but Albert and the other Negroes would not work on Sunday, even though they saw the gold in his plot. Albert came from Mathew County in Virginia and was believed to be a runaway slave, but if true he was free in California so long as it was not proven that he was a slave.[27] This was a successful undertaking and proved that gold was in the high reaches of the mountains. The town of Downieville grew up from this settlement, which is 2,000 feet above sea level in one of the highest regions in California.[28] Some of the Negroes who settled in

[25] Downie, Major William, *Hunting for Gold*, p. 34; Hittel, Theodore, *History of California*, vol. iii, p. 92, says that Downie came to California by sea and had 10 Negroes.

[26] Hittel, Theodore, *History of California*, vol. iii, p. 92.

[27] Downie, Major William, *Hunting Gold in California*, p. 51.

[28] Hittel, Theodore, *op. cit.*

Downieville when the mining had ceased remained to work
at various jobs. Albert worked at his trade as a barber in
the town.[29] As late as 1851 one of the original Negroes was
working a tunnel on the south fork of the Yerba opposite
Ranaka Bar.[30]

Another Negro who struck a rich find was Moses Drinks,
a miner who started in 1852 from his cabin, which was between Jackass Hill and Tuttle Town. On his way at the
base of the mountain within sight of Shaw's Flat he noticed
a gleaming object which proved to be a piece of gold weighing five pounds.[31] He did not want to turn back to his cabin
so decided to bury his gold on the spot until he returned. At
the end of three weeks when he returned a company of
Italians were working the ground where his gold was
buried, but fortunately they had not reached his gold and
it was saved.

An Englishman who was influenced by the gold rush was
Joseph Batty, who came to America to visit his brother in
Wisconsin. They decided to start out to seek gold, but the
expedition failed because proper provision had not been
made at the start. The brothers separated, the older brother going back home to Wisconsin, while Joseph remained on
the frontier taking whatever odd jobs he could find.[32] After
doing this for a while he decided to continue his search for
gold by going into the mountains. After equipping himself
he set out alone for the fields. While walking by the Feather
River he met a Negro, who saluted, as was the custom at
that time in the mines, and entered into a conversation with
him. It was soon ascertained that he had been in this section but was planning to go farther up into the mountains.
Batty says that he was surprised that the Negro was such
an intellectual person and was ready to agree with the good

---

[29] Downie, Major William, *op. cit.*

[30] *San Francisco Daily Alta California*, May 11, 1860.

[31] Buckbee, Edna B., *op. cit.*, p. 329.

[32] Batty, Joseph, *Over the Wilds of California*, p. 41.

Dr. Watts in saying that it was the mind which made the man. The Negro was well versed in the Bible and had been a clerk in Baltimore, but like others in this period had come West seeking his fortune.[33] This Negro was very generous and offered Batty a partnership and with it the privilege of sharing his cabin. In spite of this hospitality on the part of the Negro, Batty says something just revolted within him against living with a Negro.[34] Batty stayed a while because he could not do better, but soon left in spite of the Negro's kindness. There were many other Negroes in this settlement and it was supposed that they were there because they desired to be alone. It was probably because the prejudice which existed in the Southern states had been carried to the mines. Time and experince were needed, one writer thought, before community spirit could spring from such diverse elements as were found on the mining frontier.[35] There was such a domineering attitude on the part of the whites that in some cases Negroes did not go to the mines at all, but took jobs in the city.[36] The fact that in some sections Negroes did not go to the mines probably accounts for some writers believing that there were few Negroes in the mining country.

There were some Negroes as operators of companies and prospectors of mines on the mining frontier. One Mr. Edgar, a Negro prospector in the Black Mountains country, brought in to the office of the *Rocky Mountain News* the finest specimen of quartz bearing gold which the editor had seen that year.[37] This showed the effort made by the individual prospector. In the Southern California gold fields a vein of gold was discovered by a Negro known as Dick.[38] The vein was so rich that it made for the ruin of the fortu-

---

[33] *Ibid.*, p. 42.
[34] *Ibid.*, p. 44.
[35] *History Nuggets*, iii, p. 92.
[36] Soule, Frank, *Annals of San Francisco*, p. 42.
[37] July 31, 1865.
[38] Hittel, Theodore, *op. cit.*, p. 118.

nate Negro. Dick first sold several portions to various persons and worked what was left. This proved so rich that in a comparatively short time he left and went to Sacramento taking with him one hundred thousand dollars with the intention of having a good time.[39] He soon lost it in a wild frontier town, such as Sacramento was at that time. He was looked upon as a loafer after he lost his money and he ended it all by cutting his throat.

James Williams was another free Negro who went to the mining camps in the early fifties. He went up to the mines on the little boat, *Jennie Lind,* from San Francisco. He first worked at Negro Hill but did little good there.[40] He then went into the restaurant business in Sacramento and apparently did well, but left that section when he got into a controversy with a slave owner over his slave. From there he went to Mexico; in later years he went back to San Francisco, then back to the mines around Sacramento at a hundred dollars per month, but before he could collect he was driven out of the mines by the element that was determined that Negroes should not work in there.[41] Williams finally settled in Sacramento as a junk dealer.

There were also mines operated by Negro companies, such as the one mentioned by a correspondent giving his reminiscences in *The Green Wood Valley,* El Dorado County, June 24, 1874, in which he speaks of a mining colony made up of Georgia Negroes.[42] They could not carry on their own correspondence and this correspondent acted as their legal adviser. These Negro miners had difficulty with the Chinese also. Some Negroes were forced to go into business for themselves, in some form, in order to remain on the frontier. In Idaho Lewis Walker, an old resident of that Territory, was engaged in the mining business.[43] He

[39] *Ibid.*
[40] Williams, James, *Life and Adventures,* p. 28.
[41] *Ibid.*
[42] *The Sacramento Daily Union,* June 27, 1878.
[43] *The San Francisco Elevator,* December 20, 1873.

was evidently doing well, for it was announced that he had purchased property in Portland which he felt would be of great value.

The Rare Ripe Gold and Silver Mining Company was located in Brown's Valley, Yerba County. This was an incorporated company for quartz mining with all the equipment necessary for the work and it was first class.[44] This company was ready to expand its business by offering 300 shares for sale to the public. Negroes were at work in the Utah mines. T. H. Grice of Salt Lake in a private letter to the editor said that he had been at the mines nearly all of the past season and would write soon on the mines and prospects of Negroes in that inland region. The writer goes on to say that the Elevator Mine was sold by the company last summer for the sum of $15,000.[45] Most of the money was invested in a capital prospect in Big Cotton Wood Mining District. He thought the company would make money unless something happened out of the ordinary during the next year, and that furthermore the prospects were bright in Utah for Negroes in mining.

When the gold rush in California had subsided, the Negroes who had gone to that frontier left and went to other sections, as did other miners, wherever they heard of gold. It would seem that several came to Colorado and joined with others in that mining frontier. During the early history of Summit County, a small party of Negroes came in with the first prospectors. They found what was true generally, that there was hostility toward them, so they drifted together in order to better protect themselves. They took up considerable placer ground in French Gulch, which proved very profitable. Later they were the victims of racial hatred, so they had to move farther, on land which was apparently barren, but which after a brief interval

44 *Ibid.*, April 10, 1868.
45 *Ibid.*, December 14, 1872.

turned out to be very rich.[46] The place was called Nigger Hill, a designation which began as a term of contempt but turned out to be a badge of honor. This hill extended between French and Indiana Gulches on Bald Mountain about eight miles from the timber line. There were several mines on this ridge and many prospects just waiting for men and money to develop them.

There was also the Morning Star Mine in Hillsdale County, Colorado.[47] The editor of the *Rocky Mountain News* said nothing more had been received about this mine, but the Negroes were working right along and taking some nice ore. There were Negroes operating their own mines. Aunt Clara Brown, who came to Colorado with the gold seekers at the age of sixty after serving as a slave until emancipation, became one of the well known Negro citizens of Colorado.[48] One correspondent in speaking of her said that she was a Negro woman with a state if not a national reputation as a successful miner and philanthropist. Her property was in Crisman's Camp. She was elected to membership in the Colorado Pioneer Association back in the seventies.[49] She was one of the first Negroes elected to that association and when she died at the age of 85 she was buried with honors. She was so well known that she was considered an institution in Central City.[50]

There were individual miners in Colorado who made important finds, just as in California. In 1880 a half dozen capitalists spent the Sabbath entertaining Negro Jim. Jim came to George Town, Colorado, from North Carolina and was getting this consideration because he owned a thick vein of mineral out toward Decatur which ran $1,000 to the ton. The reason for all the attention was to persuade Jim to take

[46] *Rocky Mountain News*, May 2, 1880.

[47] *Ibid.*, September 8, 1885.

[48] Baker, James H. and Hafen, Leroy, *History of Colorado*, vol. iii, p. 1095.

[49] Harvey, James, *Negroes in Colorado*, p. 20 (unpublished thesis now in the University of Denver Library).

[50] Young, Frank, *Echoes from Arcadia*, p. 3.

$100,000 for his property.[51] Jim refused the offer and kept his property for the time being. Another such miner was John Frazier, who also lived in George Town and struck a find on Brown's Mountain.[52] He called the name of his lode the Black Prince and he had struck three hundred ounce ore. These unusual claims show that Negroes were lucky here as they had been in the California mines.

The labor supply for the Colorado mines, like those elsewhere, was furnished partly by Negro miners in spite of opposition to them. This item appears in the *Rocky Mountain News,* that the imported Negro miners at Walsenburg had departed and the company would have to get along with common plain miners.[53] John W. Dobbs, who was known as the Uncle Tom of the Rockies, also furnished labor in the Colorado gold fields. He came to the Rockies from Georgia in 1884 and when the work in the mines was not so profitable he worked in a saw mill owned by one John Newman.[54]

John Sanderlin was in 1890 a retired business man devoting his time to the supervision of his mining and farming interests. He was one of the first to come to Colorado in the Pikes Peak excitement.[55] Sanderlin was probably the best known Negro in Denver for businesslike ability and success as a business man.

Some of these Negroes became experts in the technical phases of mining. Moses Rodgers was born a slave in Missouri and suffered all the hardships that slavery imposed, but finally learned by great effort to read. He moved later to California, where he owned several mines and became an expert on mining.[56] He was one of the most distinguished workers in California. He was respected as any other mining capitalist and his advice was constantly sought.

[51] *Rocky Mountain News,* September 28, 1880.
[52] *Ibid.,* July 3, 1884.
[53] *Ibid.,* May 22, 1885.
[54] Harvey, James, *op. cit.,* p. 129.
[55] *Ibid.,* p. 20.
[56] Beasley, Delilah, *Trail Blazers of California,* p. 107.

The evidence given shows that the Negro was a factor on the mining frontier. He was not only a laborer but an operator and prospector. The condition in the mines at times was a difficult one for the Negro, and especially for the slaves, but in many cases it pointed to their freedom. It is reasonable to conclude that the Negroes were on the frontier in considerable numbers and that they were found on every mining frontier from California in 1849 to the end of the gold rush in the Black Hills of the Dakotas.

W. Sherman Savage

Lincoln University in Missouri

DISABILITIES OF THE SOUTH AFRICAN NATIVE*

In South Africa the word "Negro" is not used at all. The terms employed to describe the chief divisions of the population are, rather, European and non-European.

"European" means 2,000,000 whites, of whom about 60% are descendants of Dutch and Huguenot settlers of the seventeenth century. They used to be called Boers, but since that word means "farmers," they are now called Afrikaners. Their language, Afrikaans, a modification of Dutch, is one of the two official languages of the Union of South Africa. The other 40% of the European group is the English, who are either descendants of the 1820 settlers (South Africa's equivalent of the Mayflower group) or of the relative newcomers drawn to South Africa since the discovery of diamonds and gold in the 1870's and 1880's.

"Non-European" means 8,000,000 other people, divided into three main groups: the Natives, or Bantus, about 7,000,000 of them, who will be discussed in this paper; the Coloureds, some 750,000, descendants of the mixed unions between the early Boers and Hottentots or between whites and Malay coolies; and the Indians, 220,000 in number, descendants of coolies brought in some fifty years ago to work on the sugar plantations of Natal. As is evident, the Natives are the largest element of the population, yet they suffer under disabilities which for the moment seem tragic, and for the future grim, in their portent for strife.

In any discussion of South African affairs, two facts should be constantly borne in mind: half the white population of the continent of Africa is in the Union; and racial prejudice and fear are general among the whites. They see themselves as a small island of whites in a dark continent, in constant danger of engulfment by the 7,000,000 blacks

* An address delivered at the opening session of the annual meeting of the Association for the Study of Negro Life and History in Boston, Massachusetts, on October 27, 1944.

within their own borders and the 160,000,000 others to the north. Hence the primary essence of their statecraft is to keep the Native in his "place." What is his place, as the whites see it? The answer is shown by the disabilities under which the Native must live, disabilities not only actual but also legal.

First, the Native is not a citizen of South Africa, but a subject. Except in rare instances and limited fashion, he cannot vote, and in no case can he sit in Parliament. Legislation is passed for him, not by him. He may not even bear arms in defense of his country, although he may join the army as a manual laborer. It is considered dangerous to allow weapons to be placed in the hands of Natives.

Next, the Native may not own land where he pleases. He endures the ultimate in segregation, in that the only land he may own is in Native Reserves, which constitute only 13% of the area of the country. This means that the whites, who are only one-fifth of the population, own more than four-fifths of the land. Some of the land in the Reserves is good, some bad; everywhere there is overcrowding, soil erosion, and the ill effects resulting from these in undernourishment and disease. Of the four provinces of the Union, in Transvaal the Natives constitute 70% of the population but are permitted to occupy only 3.5% of the land; in the Orange Free State they are 67% of the population and hold 0.2% of the land.

The Native suffers tax discrimination. There is a poll tax *on Natives only* of one pound ($4) a year, and another tax, the hut tax, of ten shillings ($2), upon each family. White legislators are perfectly candid about their reasons for these taxes: the Native cannot possibly secure cash for the payment so long as he lives in his Reserve; therefore he will be forced to come out and work on the farms of the white men or in the gold, diamond, and coal mines. Since a monthly wage to Natives of £4 is considered high, one may imagine the financial burden imposed by the taxes. This bur-

den is quite aside from the effects of the enforced absence
from one's family for several months a year. The white
farm bloc has seen to it that there is no tax on land, so that
it often happens that Natives pay more taxes, actually, and
not merely proportionately, than whites.

The Native is segregated in all cities. Except where
servants' quarters are provided, he must live in a district
set aside for him on the outskirts of the city, pay rent for
a shanty in a township which generally has no sewage, no
electricity, no paved streets, and only one water pump for
every four blocks. In two of the four provinces he is shut
in his district at night and a guard is kept at the gates. If
his township is far away from the centre of the city, where
he must perform his daily work (and these Native townships are almost always at a distance), he has to pay his
own bus, tram, or train fare twice each day, and must travel
third-class in Jim Crow conveyances.

In two provinces the Native must always carry a pass
when he is outside his Reserve. The pass must be shown
on demand, and failure to present it is an offense punishable by fine and imprisonment. Some hundred thousand are
so convicted each year and are mulcted of thousands of
pounds of their meagre wages. If a Native is out of his
district in a city after ten o'clock at night he must have a
special pass. If he leaves a farmer to seek work elsewhere,
he must secure still another pass. Even to come to the city
at all, to look for work, requires a special pass. Natives of
exceptional education are exempt from carrying passes, but
since, if challenged, these men have to produce proof of
their special status, they gain little from this exemption.
Of all the Native disabilities, this particular one of carrying
passes is probably the most deeply resented.

The Native is by law prohibited from becoming a skilled
worker. The Labour Party, which in other countries often
takes a liberal position, in South Africa has seen to it that
Natives should in no wise compete with whites for good

jobs and wages. Because of this Colour Bar legislation, therefore, the actual manual labor is generally done by the Native under direction from a white man, and the employer has to pay wages to two or three men instead of to one. Wages to Natives range generally from the £5 with food and housing paid monthly to exceptional house servants, through the £3-£4 with food and housing to mine workers, down to 10s. or less paid to some farm workers.

The Native does not receive an equal education with the whites. Most of the education provided is paid for from the tax money collected from the Natives; in addition the children have to pay for their books, transportation, and any special fees. The result is that few Natives attend school, and these rarely go beyond the fourth grade. There is one Native college in the Union, and two universities permit Natives to attend their classes. One might ask what the point of education would be for the ambitious Native, since the Colour Bar prevents his entry into a skilled job.

The Native does not receive equal justice with the whites. The highest courts are scrupulously fair; but the majority of cases come before the magistrates of the lower courts, who are harried, impatient because the Native cannot understand English or Afrikaans or the complications of legal terminology, and probably contemptuous of the Native. Within the past two years a white farmer received a sentence of 18 months for flogging a Native to death, while a Native was executed for having attacked a white man with a knife. A white man was fined for his third conviction of rape of Native girls, while a Native was executed for attempted assault on a white woman.

The Native is prohibited from striking. Even his right to join trade unions is limited, but for a Native to participate in a strike is a legal offense punishable by fine or imprisonment or both. There is thus no way in which the laborer can effectively express his economic grievances. Just as his wage is less than the white man's, so is his compensation for industrial accident and disease; and social security laws apply hardly at all to him.

The Native is subject to special legislation in many fields. It is illegal to sell liquor to a Native but not to a white. It is not only illegal for a Native to marry a white but also to have sexual intercourse with a white. A Native finds it almost impossible to comply with all the requirements for opening a store, so that trade is generally in the hands of non-Natives. Not only may Natives not share conveyances with whites, but also they may not attend theatres or other gatherings of whites. If a white householder employs both male and female servants, only one sex may live in the servants' quarters on the premises, even though the servants be husband and wife. Of the Four Freedoms, therefore, only one, freedom of religion, seems to be allowed the Native in South Africa.

In this generally dark picture one may note certain influences at work to improve conditions. Although the Native has no political power, he may, in the Cape Province, choose three whites to represent him in Parliament—three out of 153, three whites to represent seven million people, with 150 to represent the other three million. In the Senate eight political appointments are made of white men to "represent the Native interests." The three M.P.'s and an occasional Senator do a splendid work in attempting to secure fairer dealing for the Natives. Some of the churches, especially the Anglican and the Methodist, strive hard to be Christian. There are, for example, forty-two Native clergymen in the Anglican diocese of Johannesburg who have no more supervision than do their white colleagues. It is, nevertheless, a rare Christian who would insist upon the validity of the doctrine that "God hath made of one blood all nations." Finally, there are the anthropologists at the universities, devoted groups of social workers, American missionaries, and numbers of humble citizens with a perception of the meaning of justice and decency. All of these work hard for Native rights—but their numbers are small.

One hopeful sign is the increasing number of business men who want South Africa to become an industrial country. If industries are to flourish, there must be greater purchasing power than that of the two million whites. If the seven million Natives had higher wages they could buy more. This is often as far as the thinking of these business men has gone; but if their counsel prevails, and the economic condition of the Natives is improved, other changes might be expected to follow.

The question naturally arises as to why, if the Native has so few rights and so many disabilities, he does not combine with his fellows and take forcible steps to relieve his people. There are at least three major reasons. First, most of the Natives are but one generation removed, and many not that, from tribal life. A person thinks of himself primarily, therefore, as a Zulu, a Xosa, or a Suto, not as an African; and the ancient tribal hostilities persist to the exclusion of any feeling of oneness and coöperation. Second, each tribe has its own language, and there is as yet no common tongue nor any common culture to provide a sound basis for coöperation. Third, it is illegal for Natives to own arms, to strike, to vote, to hold public office; and so all the agencies for forceful action are in the hands of the whites.

Such conditions of discrimination, such disabilities, cannot forever continue to exist without an explosion, no matter how long postponed. The thoughtful whites are aware of this. An American is always eagerly questioned by white South Africans about the Negro problem in this country. In the discussion someone invariably betrays the lurking fear of the whites by remarking, "Yes, but in America you have ten whites to every Negro, while in South Africa we have four Natives to every white." Because of this fear, there is no slight intention on the part of the South Africans to give effect to Article 3 of the Atlantic Charter, in which was promised "the right of all peoples to choose the form of government under which they will live."

It is ironical to discover that the best educated of Natives look upon America as a paradise for people of their race. The Zulu messenger in our office, wearing a uniform on which appeared the name of the office, told me with glowing pride that he had been asked by several Natives if he were an American. The effect of that episode upon me was to make me feel renewed sympathy for the South African Native, but even more a deep humility as an American.

James G. Leyburn

Department of Sociology,
Yale University

THE NEGRO'S STRUGGLE FOR PARTICIPATION IN PRIMARY ELECTIONS*

Last summer *Life* published a picture entitled "Lonnie Smith votes by order of the Supreme Court." It showed a Negro casting his ballot in the Democratic primaries in Texas. It was indeed an historic occasion for it marked the end of Texas' fight to bar Negroes from effective participation in political affairs by excluding them from the primaries of the Democratic party. It was the end of an important chapter in the larger struggle for equal franchise rights. It is a chapter which might well be entitled Texas *v.* The Supreme Court, for Lonnie Smith's right to vote was established only after the constitutionality of Texas' so-called "white" primary had come before that tribunal in four separate cases. It might even be called the Supreme Court *v.* the Supreme Court for it involved cleavages within that august body and an important reversal of position.

The first of the "white" primary cases came before the Court in 1926, but in order to appreciate the importance of the court's position in the Lonnie Smith case one must go back a little further—to the Newberry decision of 1922.

The Newberry case arose out of the 1918 Michigan primary campaign in which Truman H. Newberry opposed Henry Ford, and in which members of the Newberry family spent $195,000. It raised the question whether limitations upon expenditures of *congressional candidates,* imposed by Congress in 1910, applied to Newberry, a candidate for a senatorial nomination. All members of the court agreed that because of errors in the charge of the trial judge to the jury, his conviction should be set aside. Upon the constitutional question, however, the court was badly split. *Four* judges held that the primary was an essential part of the

* An address delivered at the final session of the annual meeting of the Association for the Study of Negro Life and History in Faneuil Hall in Boston, Massachusetts, on October 29, 1944.

electoral process, which Congress could regulate under Article I, conferring upon it power to regulate "the manner of holding elections." *Four* judges held that the act of nomination was *not* part of the electoral process and that consequently Congress had no power to regulate expenditures in *primaries*. The ninth judge (McKenna) refused to commit himself on this point. Although since this decision it has been frequently stated, in Congress and out, that the court held that Congress had no power to regulate *primaries,* because primaries were not elections within the understanding of the Court, that important point was left undecided. As the record will show, it was a point which the Court carefully dodged until 1941, when the Classic case was decided.

Keeping the Newberry case in mind, let us turn our attention to the Texas "white" primary cases. Since Reconstruction days, in all southern states, an attempt has been made to bar the Negro from membership and participation in the Democratic primary by party rule or custom. At first these rules were private *party* rules with which the State had no concern. However, with the introduction of statutes regulating the nominating process, and particularly after the passage of direct primary laws which made the primary election a trial heat in the election process—a trial heat protected by the machinery and safeguards of the general election,—the situation was very different. In the Southern states, most of the statutes after extending to primaries the requirements for participation in general elections, specifically recognized the right of the party to enact additional rules of eligibility. But it was not until the State of Texas incorporated a white primary provision into its statutes that the issue came to the Supreme Court.

In Nixon *v.* Herndon, the first of the so-called white primary cases, the Supreme Court held invalid a 1923 Texas statute which expressly stated that "in no event shall a negro be eligible to participate in a Democratic party pri-

mary held in the State of Texas, and should a negro vote in
a Democratic primary election, such ballot shall be void and
election officials are hereby directed to throw out such
ballot. . . .'' The Court held that this was clearly *state* action depriving Negroes of the ''equal protection of the law''
assured them by the 14th amendment. By not taking up the
question of the *15th* amendment the Court avoided commit-
ting itself on the important question left in doubt since the
Newberry decision, namely, is the primary part of the election, and does the 15th amendment protect voting in *primaries* as well as general elections?

Following this decision Texas promptly repealed the invalidated provision of its primary election law, substituting
one which gave the party state committee power to pre-
scribe qualifications for membership. The Democratic
Party State Executive Committee promptly did the expected and passed a resolution barring Negroes from participating in primaries. In 1932 the same Nixon who had
figured in the earlier case brought the question of the constitutionality of this provision to the Supreme Court in the
case of Nixon *v.* Condon. The majority of the Court argued
that since the State Executive Committee operated under
authority clearly granted by the legislature, Negroes were
barred by *state* action and that this, too, violated the 14th
amendment. Although the majority of the Court so held,
four of the nine judges dissented, arguing that the general
powers of the party were inherent in the *party* and were
not derived from the legislature of Texas. According to
their view, in Texas at least, parties were private rather
than governmental organizations; the legislature had not
granted power but simply recognized power which was inherent in the party.

With this encouragement, Texas tried once again, and
eventually succeeded in framing legislation mutually satisfactory to herself and the Supreme Court, although just as
discriminatory. The legislature repealed *all* provisions of

the primary election law which had related to the power of the party state committee to fix qualifications. With no legislation on this point, it was within the power of the state convention, as the governing authority of the party, to determine qualifications for participation. It is not surprising that the next Democratic state convention resolved: "That all *white* citizens of the State of Texas, who are qualified to vote under the constitution and laws of the state, shall be eligible to membership in the Democratic party and as such entitled to participate in its deliberations."

The action was at once challenged by R. R. Grovey, admittedly qualified on all grounds but color. In 1935, in the case of Grovey *v.* Townsend, Texas emerged triumphant in its struggle with the Supreme Court—temporarily at least. A unanimous Court, speaking through Justice Roberts, held that the Democratic party in Texas was now a "voluntary association," *not* an organ of the state; that hence no *state* action was involved. Justice Roberts laid much emphasis upon the status of the primary in this particular state, pointing out that it was financed by the party, not the state, and that the party furnished the ballots and counted them. This suggests that in Justice Roberts' opinion, whether the party is a "voluntary association" or a governmental agency, depends upon the degree to which it is regulated by the state. A state may discriminate against Negroes but it must pay the price of leaving the entire conduct of the primary, as well as the determination of the qualifications for participation, to the *party.*

So matters stood until April, 1944, when the same question, coming before the Supreme Court in the Lonnie Smith case, was viewed in a very different light. Between 1935 and 1944 the inexorable hand of Fate had made many changes in personnel of the Court; seven of the nine justices participating in the Grovey case had died or retired in those nine years. Only Roberts and Stone remained.

In the meantime, the "New" Supreme Court had rendered a decision in a case which although not involving voting rights of Negroes paved the way for the Lonnie Smith decision. I refer to the important opinion in U. S. v. Classic.

In the Classic case the Court at last faced squarely the question it had dodged since the Newberry decision in 1922 —Is the primary an integral part of the electoral process protected by the Constitution? In holding that the right of a qualified voter to participate in a Louisiana primary at which congressmen were nominated, and to have his vote counted, was protected under Art. I of the Constitution giving Congress the power to regulate ''the manner of holding elections,'' the Court pointed the way to a reversal of its earlier stand in the Grovey case.

The opinion in the Classic case, written by Justice Stone, stressed the following points: that in Louisiana the primary is subject to comprehensive state regulations; that it is conducted by the State at public expense; and that it is ''as a matter of law and in fact'' the only stage at which the choice of the voter has any significance. Justice Stone concluded that ''since the primary is the only stage when such interference could have any practical effect on the ultimate result—i.e., the choice of the Congressman to represent the district—the primary in Louisiana is an integral part of the procedure for the popular choice of Congressman.''

Justice Douglas, who dissented on the narrow ground that the clauses of the Criminal Code applied in this instance were not *specifically* intended to include primaries, went even further in defending the power of Congress to regulate the nominating process. ''The manner of holding elections,'' he said, ''becomes *an arsenal of power* ample to protect congressional elections from any and all forms of pollution. The fact that a particular form of pollution has only an indirect effect on the final election is immaterial. The fact that it occurs in a primary election or nominating convention is likewise irrelevant. *The important considera-*

tion is that the Constitution should be interpreted broadly so as to give to the representatives of a free people abundant power to deal with the electoral process. It means that the Constitution should be read so as to give Congress an expansive implied power to place beyond the pale acts which in their direct or indirect effect, impair the integrity of Congressional elections. For when corruption enters, the election is no longer free. To hold that Congress is powerless to control these primaries would indeed be a narrow construction of the Constitution, inconsistent with the view that that instrument of government was designed not only for contemporary needs but for the vicissitudes of time.'' From these words it is clear that Justice Douglas is ready not only to strike down action within the states, but to uphold Congress' power to protect the nominating process, whatever its form and at whatever stage, from ''pollution.''

The Lonnie Smith case applied to participation in the Democratic primaries of Texas the principles formulated in the Classic case. Smith, a Texas Negro who had been denied a ballot at the Democratic primary of July, 1940, brought suit for damages. The issue was exactly the same as that raised in Grovey v. Townsend, nine years earlier. The lower Federal courts, relying upon the Grovey decision, denied him the relief sought. April 3, 1944 the Supreme Court handed down the historic decision upholding Lonnie Smith's right to vote. Justice Reed, speaking for all but one member of the Court [Roberts], emphasized the effect of the Classic case, which he said removed all doubt that primaries were part of the ''elections'' subject to Federal control and fused ''the primary and general elections into a single instrumentality for choice of officers.'' He went on to say:

''Classic bears upon Grovey v. Townsend not because exclusion of Negroes from primaries is any more or less *state* action by reason of the unitary character of the electoral process, but because the recognition of the place of the primary in the electoral scheme makes clear that state delegation of power to fix the qualification of primary elections is delegation of a *state* function that may make the party's action the action of the state.''

Applying these principles to a re-examination of the Texas law the Justice held that, although the qualifications for voting were fixed by the party convention, the primary elections were conducted under state statutory authority of such a character that the action of the party became the action of the state.

The Lonnie Smith case went far toward establishing the Negro's right to participate in the nominating process—the only point at which participation can be effective in the "one party" states of the South. It leaves in doubt one point, however. Suppose a state repeals *all* laws pertaining to the nomination process? Suppose it leaves the party free to nominate its candidates in any way it sees fit? Following the Lonnie Smith decision, South Carolina took exactly that step, repealing all of its primary laws. If Negroes are barred from participating in nominations in that state by party authority and the issue comes up to the Supreme Court, what will that body decide? Certainly some of the language in the opinions in both the Classic and Smith cases suggests that some members of the Court may be ready to stand squarely on the following broad principles:

1. That the franchise is an essential attribute of democracy.
2. That in American democracy nominations are an integral part of the electoral process, whether regulated by state law or not.
3. That discrimination on the basis of race at any stage, by party officials as well as state officers, is unconstitutional.

It seems to me highly probable that a majority of the present Court could be brought to such a position.

These opinions suggest another possible development. Suppose Congress decides that the solution for the problem of discrimination against Negroes must be found in the enforcement of *federal* legislation regulating primary elections as well as general elections? Some parts of the opinions in the Classic and Lonnie Smith cases suggest that the Court would view with favor the exercise of such wide federal power over *primary* elections, as well as general elections.

I do not need to tell you that Lonnie Smith's victory is not the last mile-stone on the road to equal participation by Negroes in the primaries of southern states. Poll tax requirements, literacy tests unfairly administered, unreasonable residence requirements, even intimidation, which keep many from participating in the general elections, also exclude them from the primaries. But at last their right to participate in primaries rests upon the same basis as their right to participate in general elections. I do not hesitate to say that the Lonnie Smith case is an important mile-stone on the road up; perhaps it is no exaggeration to say that it is as important a mile-stone on the way up as the Dred Scott case was on the road down. It has been a long, uphill road, but the obstacles which remain are not obstacles imposed by judicial interpretation, and the top of the hill may well be in sight.

LOUISE OVERACKER

Wellesley College

THE NEGRO'S STRUGGLE FOR FREEDOM IN ITS BIRTHPLACE*

The State of Massachusetts and the City of Boston have been referred to often as the birthplace of freedom. It was here that the voyagers of the Mayflower and their descendants found a haven and established homes free from the chains which bound them in their homeland. It was here that the struggles for the freedom of Americans from that which they regarded as tyranny had its origins. This story is well known to every school child—the scene of the Stamp Act Congress, the Boston Massacre, the Boston Tea Party, Lexington, Concord, Bunker Hill, Faneuil Hall and the work of Adams, Hancock, Gerry, Ames, King, Otis and a host of immortals. Most Americans are proud of these origins of freedom and the struggle through which they have come. Another story, that of the Negro American's struggle for freedom is not so well known. George H. Moore, in *Notes on the History of Slavery in Massachusetts,* (New York, 1866) has described the rise and fall of slave labor in the colony and state and revealed the record of the suppression of freedom for a minority in the midst of those who were themselves struggling to be free. John Daniels, in *In Freedom's Birthplace: A Study of Boston Negroes,* (New York, 1914) has presented a kind of exploratory study of the same subject in slavery and in freedom. Dr. Lorenzo Greene, in his *The Negro in Colonial New England, 1620-1776,* (New York, 1942) has written a painstaking and revealing study of slavery and the free Negro in New England, which included the Colony of Massachusetts.

The study of the Negro in his struggle for full citizenship rights and the opportunity to accept the duties of citizenship, particularly in the nineteenth century, has not received the attention which either the subject or the birthplace of freedom deserve.

*An address delivered in Faneuil Hall in Boston, Massachusetts, on the occasion of the final session of the annual meeting of the Association for the Study of Negro Life and History, October 29, 1944.

Citizenship in the State of Massachusetts rises out of the Massachusetts Bill of Rights of 1780. It was through court interpretations of this constitution that slavery was abolished in this state, for equality for all men was decreed by it although slavery was not formally prohibited by its legislation. The emphasis given to freedom by anti-slavery agitation led to the view that it was "considered as abolished." This process has been called by one writer "emancipation by judicial process" and is regarded as the "distinctive honor of Massachusetts."[1] The Constitution of 1780 stated that "all men are born free and equal, and have certain natural, essential, and unalienable rights; among which may be reckoned the right of enjoying and defending their lives and liberties; that of acquiring, possessing and protecting property; in fine, that of seeking and obtaining their safety and happiness."[2] Such rights were guaranteed as freedom of worship, speech, free press, elections, the impartial administration of justice, trial by jury and the protection of life, liberty and property. In spite of this background and these assertions, there were distinctions based upon law and custom which affected the status of the Negro citizen and limited his advancement. The Negro had to struggle, therefore, both against the usual limitations which faced the average citizen and the special ones placed upon him by reason of his distinctive color. If one could expect the Negro to be considered a citizen, it would have been in the place in which the echoes of freedom were sounded the loudest by tongue, pen and arms.

Until the first constitution of 1780 and its judicial interpretation, the colony kept the Negro in chains which deprived him of the same freedom, as was granted to other Americans. There were about 7,000 Negroes in a white population of 516,419 in Massachusetts in 1780. There were

[1] George H. Moore, *Notes on the History of Slavery in Massachusetts.* New York, 1866, p. 241; Mary S. Locke, *Anti-Slavery in America*, 1619-1808. Boston, 1901, p. 80.

[2] Poore, *The Federal and State Constitutions*, Part I, p. 956.

766 Negroes in Boston in 1790, which was about 4 per cent of the population. There were 1,174 in 1800, 1,468 in 1810 and 1,690 in 1820. Their friends wrote, made speeches, enacted legislation and contested cases at court. The Negro conspired and revolted in the very spirit of independence and freedom which his oppressors had employed for themselves. Petitions were presented by them. One of these declared that the Negroes were in sympathy with the struggle for freedom in which the peoples of Massachusetts were engaged and that they expected "great things" of those "who had made such a noble stand against the designs of their fellowmen to enslave them."[3] Another petition stated that "they have in common with other men a natural right to be free and without molestation to enjoy such property as they may acquire by their industry."[4]

Such endeavors were supplemented by champions of freedom in other spheres of citizenship activity. In the debates of the Constitutional Convention of 1777-1778, the opponents of free suffrage won their battle, for they succeeded in this first debate on Negro suffrage in American history in having the ballot excluded from use by Negroes, Indians and Mulattoes. This was not accomplished without opposition, for Dr. Gordon wrote, "Would it not be rediculous, inconsistent and unjust, to exclude free men from voting for representatives and senators, though otherwise qualified, because their skins are black, tawny or reddish?" and a writer in the *Independent Chronicle*, September 23, 1779, stated, "The principle on which we engaged in this opposition, Sir, I take to be this, that representation and taxation are reciprocal—that we, not being represented in the Parliament of Great Britain, Parliament had no right to tax us without our consent. . . . On this principle, Sir, we engaged in the present war, . . . on this principle we suppose ourselves justified in resisting, even in blood, that power

---

[3] *Journal of the House of Representatives*, 1772-1773, p. 195.
[4] *Massachusetts Historical Society Collections*, vol. iii, pp. 395-396.

which would thus arbitrarily exact upon us; and on the same principle, I conceive the persons excepted in the clause now before the Convention would be justified in making the same opposition against us which we are making against Great Britain."[5] The incongruity of this situation was as apparent to some eighteenth century patriots as it is today to some twentieth century patriots, when we again fight a war of freedom and other men in our midst remain unfree.

While this constitution was disapproved by vote of the people and a provision for the abolition of slavery also failed of adoption, court decisions and the initiative of Negroes in pressing their claims, notably in the town of Dartmouth, gradually led to the establishment of the right to suffrage on the part of Negroes.[6] Paul and John Cuffee, free Negroes, decided at first not to pay the personal taxes required by the Selectmen of Dartmouth, but finally decided to do so under protest. They paid the taxes and appealed to the legislature on the well-known principle of no taxation without representation. Their petition was received by the General Court on February 10, 1780 and was subsequently dismissed. There is no historical basis for the view that this petition led to the grant of suffrage to Negroes. However, by 1783, under interpretation of the Constitution of 1780, this right was established.[7] It is evident that some Negroes were permitted to vote in some localities and that in others they were denied this privilege.

The path to a recognized citizenship was still a tortuous one for the Negro inhabitants of the state. By the dawn of the nineteenth century, they were regarded as free, but the spirit of slavery was still active and they continued to be re-

[5] Moore, *op. cit.*, pp. 186, 188.

[6] Moore, *op. cit.*, p. 198; W. C. Nell, *Colored Patriots of the Revolution*, pp. 87-90.

[7] Moore, *op. cit.*, p. 199; H. M. Sherwood, "Paul Cuffee," *The Journal of Negro History*, vol. viii, January, 1923, pp. 162-166.

garded as inferiors.[8] Their rights in the courts were under question. Their right of election to office in the Commonwealth and the townships remained to be established. The opportunity to live in the localities in which they desired to live, to work at the jobs for which they were capable and to attend the schools of their choice, were all in the lap of the gods of their future. The inevitable result was a struggle which continued throughout the nineteenth century, although Massachusetts reported no slaves by the census of 1800 and by this token manifested its loyalty to the physical freedom of all Americans. Nevertheless, there were disadvantages facing Negro-Americans in this city and state. The relative unimportance of their numbers in relation to the majority population element, their poverty and relative lack of property holdings, their social ostracism and their deficiencies in education and cultural life were also obstacles against which they were compelled to struggle. There were in-group and out-of-group barriers which faced the Negroes of Massachusetts seeking recognition as citizens. In spite of these difficulties, they continued their onward march with the help of sympathetic friends to a fuller citizenship.

During the first decades of the nineteenth century, there was little change in the status of the Negro population. They were regarded as free but actually they were unfree. In the Boston City Directory of 1829, there were listed only 224 Negroes by name and occupation, although the census of 1830 gave the city Negro population as 1,875.[9] On the one hand, this may lead to the conclusion that the unlisted population was sub-standard and sub-marginal or that the records were incomplete, and this is regarded as the fact for the entire city population. Of the 224 listed in the record, 54 were designated as laborers, 30 were in domestic work, 36 were sailors and among other trades were cordwainers,

---

[8] J. P. deWarville Brissot, *New Travels in the United States of America*, London, 1794, vol. i, pp. 261-263; John Daniels, *In Freedom's Birthplace*, p. 23.

[9] Daniels, *op. cit.*, pp. 18, 19; U. S. Census of 1830, p. 12.

housewrights, grain-measurers, soap-makers, bootmakers, and one individual strangely known as a "hair-renovator." There were fourteen clothing shops, a provision shop, a junk shop, four tailor shops, a general shop, and two ministers. Twenty-six were listed with independent residences but no occupations were given for them.

The state census for 1830 listed 7,048 Negroes in Massachusetts, a total of 319,599 free Negroes in the United States and a total slave population of 2,009,043. It seems probable from varying evidences that a similar proportion of the Negroes of the state, as of the City of Boston, accepted the opportunities which came to them and, making use of them, created worthy economic enterprises for themselves. There were those who had generations of freedom back of them and, not accepting willingly the position of inferiority, acquired positions requiring ability and intelligence.

In spite of these evidences of progress, there were others who were shiftless, lazy and improvident. Fleeing from slavery in which they were compelled to work, and arriving in places of legal freedom, they easily drifted into idleness. Some writers of history who saw these members of the Negro population concluded that this was a cross-section of the free Negro population. The fact that these persons were to be seen, especially in the cities, was not so much an indictment of all the Negroes themselves as of the system which by custom and attitude debased them and forced them down to the lower rungs of the economic ladder. On the contrary, the fact that there were Negroes with some achievement to their credit demonstrated that the causes of failure were not entirely inherent in the Negro population of itself.

These causes were to be found also in the environment in which the Negro population lived. They were denied freedom of worship, and in struggling against it, they found their own solution in similar manner to those who struggled for the same principle in Europe. The early relationship between church membership and voting in Massachusetts had subsequent influence on the attitude of the church toward the baptism and church membership of Negroes. While George Bancroft asserts that, "The servant, the bondsman might be a member of the church, and therefore a freeman of the company," it has been regarded as doubtful that there was any extensive application of this principle.[10] As the number of Negroes increased, they were denied the choice of pews in the churches, although they were assigned certain sections. A Negro of Boston described these sections as "places similar to pigeon-holes," and stated that a sexton was known to be placed at a church door to see that Negroes sat in these places.[11] Other Negroes were served communion after the white members had been served.

These experiences induced the Negroes to plan for the establishment of places of worship free from such treatment. There is no evidence that Negroes wanted to be to themselves or that they sought in this way to segregate themselves. The first Negro church was established in 1809. It was known as the African Meeting House, and was located in the West End in Smith Court off Belknap Street, now Joy Street. The presence of abolition assemblies in this church soon obtained for it the title of "Cradle of Liberty for Negroes." Separate churches were established during the same period in New Bedford and other places.[12]

A similar experience was had by Negroes who sent their children to the public schools. These schools had received Negro children but gradually they were being excluded or were made to feel that they were not wanted. A private school was opened in 1798 in Boston in the home of Primus Hall, a Negro. The teacher was Elisha Sylvester, a white

[10] Greene, *op. cit.*, p. 261-262; George Bancroft, *History of the United States*, vol. i, p. 360; C. G. Woodson, *History of the Negro Church*, p. 15.

[11] *Proceedings of the Third Annual New England Anti-Slavery Convention*, Boston, May 24-26, 1836.

[12] Frederick Douglass, *My Bondage and My Freedom*, p. 371.

man, and the parents paid for the instruction. The Rev. Mr. Morse, the father of Samuel F. B. Morse, Messrs. Kirkland of Harvard College, Channing, Lowell and Emerson of Boston, took an interest in the school and supported it for two years.[13] Two students from Harvard University taught in the school until 1806. The school was then moved to the Belknap Street Church and was continued there until 1835, when a building was erected. This African School was under the supervision of the School Committee. John B. Russwurm, the first known Negro college graduate in the United States, was a teacher in this school from 1821 to 1824. A separate primary school was established in 1820.

Other Negroes were opposed to these efforts to develop separate schools for Negroes, because they knew that these would lead to inequalities in education. These persons sent petitions against the schools and succeeded finally in having Negroes admitted in all towns except Boston. The latter did not abolish these schools until 1855. The admission of Negro students to colleges in Massachusetts as in many other states was denied, for it was not until 1826 that John B. Russwurm received from Bowdoin College the first college degree awarded to a Negro.[14]

Limitations upon freedom were faced by Negroes in most public services and places in Massachusetts. Separate cars were provided for Negro travelers on several roads. Frederick Douglass has preserved in his autobiography his bitter experiences on the railroads and in inns.[15] Those Americans who were willing to accept Negroes as equals were in the minority and their voices were weak and the general public seemed indifferent.

[13] *Special Report of the U. S. Bureau of Education*, Washington, D. C., 1871, p. 357; *Historical Records Survey*, W.P.A., Boston, Massachusetts. The African Baptist Church, p. 97.

[14] George W. Williams, *History of the Negro Race in American from 1619 to 1880*, vol. ii, p. 163; C. G. Woodson, *Education of the Negro Prior to 1861*, p. 265.

[15] Frederick Douglass, *My Bondage and My Freedom*, p. 329 ff.

The freedom of the right to work was restricted. As one observer stated, "They (Negroes) cannot obtain employment on equal terms with whites and wherever they go, a sneer is passed upon them. They have been and mostly are servants or doomed to eccept such menial employment as the whites decline. They are poor with small means and opportunities for enjoying the social advantages and comforts at the command of the whites. Thus, though their legal rights are the same as the whites, their condition is one of degradation and dependence." The enrollment of Negroes in the militia and the bearing of arms were prohibited by legislative act, in spite of the services rendered by Negroes in the war with Great Britain, and their expressed willingness to continue this part of their duty as citizens.

Facing limitations upon their freedom to worship, to work, to learn, to mingle socially with their fellows, driven to fear by the enforcement of the fugitive slave acts, generally discounted by their fellow citizens as inferiors, Negroes did not willingly accept such chains in the state where freedom was born. They began to organize themselves just as some of them had petitioned in the earlier years. They organized among themselves and also in conjunction with whites. In Boston in 1826, they organized the Massachusetts General Colored Association. Among its members were William C. Nell, John T. Hilton, Thomas Dalton, James G. Barbadoes, Coffin Pitts, John E. Scarlett, Hosea Easton, Joshua Easton, Thomas Cole, Frederick Brimley, Walker Lewis. Their objectives were the improvement of the conditions in which they found themselves and the abolition of slavery. It should be remembered that this organization began its work prior to the organization of Garrisonian Abolition.

One of the courageous members of this Association was David Walker of Boston, who delivered a stirring address at its meeting in 1828 and urged Negroes to form societies to end slavery. He had come to Boston from Wilmington,

North Carolina, where he was born in 1785. He began to conduct a clothing business in Boston and by 1827 he was regarded as a prosperous merchant. In 1829 he published his well known *Walker's Appeal in Four Articles, together with a Preamble to the Colored Citizens of the World, but in particular, and very Expressly to those of the United States of America, written in Boston, in the State of Massachusetts, September 28th, 1829.* This *Appeal* of some eighty pages ran through three editions in less than twelve months and was widely distributed. His *Appeal* began with the Preamble addressed to his "beloved Brethren and Fellow Citizens." He stated that his travels over a considerable part of the United States had led him to the conclusion that the colored people of the United States were "the most degraded, wretched and abject set of beings that ever lived since the world began." In a defiant and severe manner, Walker made his attacks upon slavery. He called upon Negroes to make "tyrants quake and tremble on their sandy foundations." He urged them not to fear and to contend for their lawful rights. "The man," he wrote, "who would not fight under our Lord and Master, Jesus Christ, in the glorious and heavenly cause of freedom and of God—to be delivered from the most wretched, abject and servile slavery, that ever a people was afflicted with since the foundation of the world, to the present day—ought to be kept with all of his children or family, in slavery, or in chains, to be butchered by his cruel enemies." He declared that there was "no greater mockery of religion than the way in which it is conducted by Americans." This was a new voice of freedom. This was a New Negro. But what else could one expect in this place of freedom where its echoes rang in the ears of the mighty as well as of the lowly.

Some anti-slavery leaders looked upon the pamphlet as too radical. Benjamin Lundy said that "a more bold, inflammatory publication, perhaps, never issued from the press of any country." Garrison declared that "While the

American people might denounce it as bloody or monstrous but that Walker was paying them in their own coin.'' And he added, ''as for me, I do not preach rebellion.'' The distribution of Walker's pamphlet from the birthplace of freedom led to considerable alarm in the South. Its circulation was prohibited in five states. A reward of one thousand dollars was offered for Walker's head and ten times this amount for ''the live Walker.'' The Mayor of Savannah, Georgia, wrote to the Mayor of Boston and asked that the publication of this work be stopped. The Mayor of Boston replied that ''notwithstanding the extremely bad and inflammatory tendency of the publication he does not seem to have violated any of these laws.'' Threats against Walker's life became so frequent and numerous that his friends advised him to go to Canada. But he declined to do so and remained in Boston, where he died in 1830. His sudden death led to the persistent rumor that he had been poisoned through the plans of Southern slaveholders. This rumor has not been proved.[16]

While this effort was the work of an individual, the organization of individuals who were conscious of the need of unity was also begun in the third decade of the nineteenth century. It was not strange that a call should be made for a convention which assembled in Philadelphia in June 6-11, 1831.[17] While Massachusetts did not send delegates to this convention, a provisional committee of Boston Negroes was appointed, in a list of committees in fifteen cities, to spread the purpose and work of the Convention, to advance the welfare of the Negro population and to cooperate with the anti-slavery cause. These men were Rev. Hosea Easton, Robert Roberts, James G. Barbadoes and Rev. Samuel Snowden.

[16] Clement Eaton, ''A Dangerous Pamphlet in the Old South.'' *Journal of Negro History*, vol. ii; George W. Williams, *op. cit.*, vol. ii, p. 553-554; *Niles Weekly Register*, Vol. 38, p. 157 ff; William Lloyd Garrison, *The Story of His Life by His Children*, vol. i, pp. 435, 436.

[17] *Minutes of the First Annual Convention of the People of Color.* June 6-11, 1831. Philadelphia, 1831.

At the second Convention of the People of Color, June 4, 1832, two delegates from Massachusetts were present, Rev. Hosea Easton from Boston and Nathan Johnson from New Bedford.[18]

The student of history who studies the evidence can see clearly that abolition endeavors were undertaken by Negroes prior to the rise of Garrison. The voice of David Walker, the work of the Massachusetts General Colored Association and participation in the conventions of the People of Color contribute to this conclusion. They organized not only by themselves but also in cooperation with other Americans who undertook the fight for freedom.

When the New England Anti-Slavery Society was organized in 1832, it was not only held in the Sunday School room of the African Meeting House with a Negro minister leading in prayer, but an invitation was also extended to Negroes to form auxiliaries to this organization.[19] The Massachusetts General Colored Association accepted this invitation and selected Joshua Easton of North Bridgetown as its delegate to the annual meeting in 1833.[20] The work of this Association was gradually taken over by the New England Anti-Slavery Society. Negro citizens seemed to be more interested in the integration of themselves into the main stream of freedom than to continue to be small segregated eddies near the shore. However, separate societies of Negroes with anti-slavery opinions continued to exist and numerous meetings of free Negroes were held in Boston, Nantucket, New Bedford, Salem, Lynn.[21] Negroes were

[18] *Minutes and Proceedings of the Second Annual Convention for the Improvement of the Free People of Color in the United States; Held by Adjournments in the City of Philadelphia from the 4th to the 19th of June, inclusive, 1832.* Philadelphia, 1832.

[19] *The Constitution of the New England Anti-Slavery Society, with An Address to the Public.* Boston, 1832, p. 6.

[20] *First Annual Report of the Board of Managers of the New England Anti-Slavery Society,* presented January 9, 1833, p. 7; *The Abolitionist,* vol. i, No. II, p. 20.

[21] *The Emancipator,* vol. i, No. 6, p. 21.

chosen as officers of the anti-slavery societies and were placed on the Board of Managers of the American Anti-Slavery Societies. Among the sixty-two signers of the Declaration of Sentiments of the American Anti-Slavery Society in 1833 was James G. Barbadoes of Massachusetts. Barbadoes also served on the Board of Managers of this society. A Negro woman, Susan Paul, of Boston, was a counsellor for the Boston Female Anti-Slavery Society.[22] Charles Lenox Remond, who had served as an anti-slavery lecturer, was elected president of the Essex County Anti-Slavery Society and vice-president of the New England Anti-Slavery Society.[23]

The association of Negroes with whites in the work of the anti-slavery societies brought about criticisms of them. William Ellery Channing was criticized by Garrison for expressing the belief that "we ought never to have permitted our colored brethren to unite with us in our associations."[24] A resolution, sponsored by Professor Charles Follen of Harvard College, was adopted by the Massachusetts Anti-Slavery Society on January 20, 1836 stating that the anti-slavery cause was considered "the cause of Philanthropy, with regard to which all human beings, white men and colored men, citizens and foreigners, men and women, have the same duties and the same rights."[25]

Nevertheless, Negroes continued to organize themselves and to push forward their own advancement. This is a story which needs still to be told. They had supported the anti-slavery societies. They had helped with their efforts and their small means to keep the *Liberator* alive. In 1834,

[22] *Third Annual Report of the Board of Managers of the New England Anti-Slavery Society presented January 21, 1835.* Boston, 1835, p. 22; W. C. Nell, *Colored Patriots of the American Revolution, with Sketches of Distinguished Colored People.* Boston, 1855, pp.346-347.

[23] *The Liberator,* vol. viii, No. 29, 1938, p. 114.

[24] *Garrison to Lewis Tappan,* December 17, 1835. (mss.) Se also Elizabeth Buffum Chase, *Anti-Slavery Reminiscences.* Central Fall, R. I. 1891, pp. 16-17.

[25] *Fourth Annual Report of the Board of Managers of the Massachusetts Anti-Slavery Society,* January 20, 1836. Boston, 1936. p. 49.

a circular issued by Garrison and Knapp, publishers of the *Liberator,* stated that only one-fourth of the total number of subscribers to the paper were white. It was further stated, "the paper then belongs especially to the people of color —it is their organ—and to them its appeal will come with peculiar force."[26] They continued to hold meetings to aid the paper, and in 1840 appointed a committee of Negro citizens for this purpose, consisting of John T. Hilton, James G. Barbadoes, J. W. Lewis, J. B. Smith, Thomas Cole, S. S. Cook, W. C. Nell, Reverend S. Saunders, B. Weeden, S. R. Alexander, W. Wright, Joseph H. Gover and B. Bassett.[27]

While meetings were being held for abolition purposes, others were held to organize for the extension of political and civil privileges. A convention of 1839 in New Bedford appointed a committee of five to nominate a list of candidates as representatives to the Massachusetts General Court. It was also resolved that the cause of liberty and equal rights was paramount to all considerations. Representatives of Boston, New Bedford and Salem formed, in 1840, an organization known as the Colored Citizens of New England to cooperate in the fight against slavery and for the extension of political rights.[28] Meetings were held also in the interest of the Liberty and Free-Soil parties, in which Negro leaders played active parts.[29] These meetings prepared petitions asking for full citizenship privileges to be sent to the Legislature and for Congress.

Negro citizens served as anti-slavery lecturers. Notable among these were Charles L. Remond, Frederick Douglass, William Wells Brown. They interested themselves actively as agents in the Underground Railroad. They aided fugitives to escape from prison and made history for themselves in fugitive slave cases. They marched with the leadership

[26] *Shall the Liberator Die?*—A Circular. Boston, 1834.

[27] *The Liberator.* vol. ix, No. 24; vol. x, No. 25, 1840. p. 98.

[28] *The Liberator.* vol. ix, No. 24; No. 44, 1938. p. 175.

[29] Charles H. Wesley, "The Participation of Negroes in Anti-Slavery Political Parties." *Journal of Negro History.* January, 1944. Pp. 32-74.

and in the ranks of the armies of American freedom. They were advancing their economic status and by industry and increasing intelligence were taking more prominent places in their communities. The census of 1860 showed that for Massachusetts 78.44 per cent of the Negroes were returned as following some gainful occupation and in Ward 6 of Boston 90.91 per cent were found to be following some distinct occupation. The percentage for the total population following some gainful occupation was 90.60 per cent, which showed a favorable comparison.[30] Manifestly these Negro citizens were engaging in a magnificent struggle for freedom. There were several lawyers, physicians, dentists, teachers and authors among them. The first Negro admitted to the bar in the United States seems to have been Macon B. Allen, who was admitted at Worcester, Massachusetts, on May 3, 1845.[31] There were skilled mechanics and other workers in common labor among them and there were proprietors of small businesses and owners of property.

These Negro citizens were now prepared to wage two significant battles against prejudice and for a larger citizenship in this state. The first of these important struggles was against separate public schools. The Negroes had earlier agreed upon the plan and sought to establish separate schools so as to relieve their children of ridicule and abuse. As they witnessed the development of segregation, they saw that it meant inequality. They began to petition the municipal authorities to abolish these schools, and in this endeavor they were aided by abolitionists and liberal whites. The admission of Negro children without separation to the schools of Salem, Nantucket, New Bedford, Lowell and other places gave evidence of the possibilities of unrestricted admission in a city like Boston. The most effective petitions requesting that the separate schools

[30] *Abstract of the Census of Massachusetts*, 1860. Pp. 356-358.
[31] John Daniels, *op. cit.*, Appendix, p. 450.

should be abolished were adopted and signed by white and colored persons in 1840 and in 1844. The first was not given full consideration but in the latter year a discussion arose. The majority of the Boston school committee declined to approve the request and based their action upon the natural differences between the races which "no legislature, no social customs can efface." The City Solicitor rendered a decision that the committee had the legal right to exclude white as well as colored from certain schools. The minority expressed the view that the schools were for all pupils and that the restriction of any advantage was illegal and arbitrary.[32] The attack was renewed in 1846 through the presentation of another petition. The Primary School Committee stated that the separate schools for Negroes had been started not to degrade Negro children but to bring them into the schools in larger numbers. A Negro teacher was then appointed as school master of the Negro school. It seems to have been thought that this would bring satisfaction to the Negro leaders. Such a bargain, however, did not satisfy them.[33]

An organized effort was then made under Jonas Clark and two hundred twenty-seven other persons of both population groups. They called themselves the Negro-School Abolition Party. They decided first to surround the school and prevent the chidren from entering; second, they started a school which was opened to both groups of pupils and selected a Negro teacher; and third, they encouraged the bringing of a suit by Benjamin F. Roberts, whose daughter had been refused admission to the public schools. With Senator Charles Sumner as counsel and a Negro lawyer, Robert Morris, in association, the case was argued on December 4,

[32] *Report of the Minority of the Committee on the Primary School Board on the Caste Schools of Boston.* 1844; Daniels, *op. cit.*, pp. 446-447; C. G. Woodson, *Education of the Negro Prior to 1861*, pp. 320-323.

[33] *Report of the Primary School Committee, June 15, 1846.*

1849.[34] The decision was an adverse one, the court claiming that the General School Committee had power under the Constitution to make this provision for separate schools. The struggle, however, was not abandoned, and a report, made in 1854 by George F. Williams, a white lawyer, and a petition signed by 1,500 white and colored persons were so influential that an act was passed on April 28, 1855 by the Legislature abolishing separate schools for Negroes.[35] This action removed a barrier to education and climaxed a struggle of sixty-seven years for the Negro people and their friends. The struggle could now be changed by the leadership to one of preparing to meet the competition of teaching positions in a mixed school system.

A second important citizenship struggle was the establishment of the right to bear arms. Throughout the abolition period, Negroes had protested against their exclusion from the militia. At a national convention in Rochester, New York, in 1853, at which Negro delegates from Massachusetts were present, a resolution was passed emphasizing the citizenship of Negro-Americans. They said, "By birth, we are American citizens; by the principles of the Declaration of Independence, we are American citizens; within the meaning of the United States Constitution, we are American citizens; by the facts of history and the admission of American statesmen, we are American citizens; by the hardships and trials endured—by the courage and fidelity displayed by our ancestors in defending the liberties and in achieving of our land, we are American citizens."[36] It was also resolved that the denial of the enlistment of Negroes

---

[34] Sarah C. Roberts vs. The City of Boston, December 4, 1849. *Massachusetts Reports*, 1849. vol. vi, pp. 198-210; *The Works of Charles Sumner.* vol. ii, p. 334.

[35] *Laws of Massachusetts, 1855;* Daniels, *op. cit.*, p. 448; Woodson, *op cit.*, pp. 320-325.

[36] *Proceedings of the Colored National Convention held in Rochester, July 6th, 7th and 8th, 1853.* Rochester, 1853. Pp. 8 ff; *The Liberator*, vol. xxiii, No. 29, July 22, 1853; No. 31, August 5, 1853.

was unconstitutional and undemocratic, and that action declaring them unworthy to bear arms in defense of their country consigned them to general contempt.

These opinions were very widespread among Negro citizens. They began an active campaign in 1853, with petition after petition pouring into the legislature. Motions were made to strike out the word "white" from the military act and legislative debates continued for several years.[37]

The need for soldiers in the war which was undertaken by the South to secure its independence and to defend its institution of slavery was of far greater value than words. The opposition to the use of Negro soldiers was decreased by the draft of white civilians as soldiers.[38] The decision of the United States Government to employ Negro soldiers led to state enlistments. When Governor John A. Andrew of Massachusetts was notified on January 26, 1863 that the state could raise two regiments, recruiting was begun on February 16. Negro leaders, among whom were Frederick Douglass, William Wells Brown, Charles L. Remond, Lewis Hayden, John S. Rock and others became interested recruiting officers. The enrollment was completed within three months. This has been called the first Negro regiment raised in a Northern state, but there was already in service the First Kansas Colored Regiment. However, this was the first enlistment on a large scale under the new government policy.[39]

There were three regiments of Massachusetts Negro soldiers, The Fifty-fourth Massachusetts Regiment, the Fifty-fifth Massachusetts Regiment and the Fifth Cavalry. Other Negroes enlisted in the Navy at Boston.

When the United States Government desired to pay

[37] William Schouler, *History of Massachusetts in the Civil War.* Boston, 1868. P. 175 ff; Edith Ellen War, *Political Opinion in Massachusetts during the Civil War and Reconstruction.* New York, 1916.

[38] *The Springfield Republican.* January 20, 1863.

[39] M. A. DeWolfe Howe, Boston, *The Place and the People.* New York, 1903. Pp. 291-292.

these soldiers the wages of military laborers, ten dollars a month, instead of the pay of soldiers, thirteen dollars a month, they refused to accept the payments, in spite of hardships experienced by their families. They also declined to have the state of Massachusetts assume the difference in payment. Their determination to resist this injustice was a high point in the history of the struggle of the Negro citizen to bear arms and to demand equal treatment. Not only does their courage in war stand out in the pages of history, but also their bravery in insisting upon equality in the ranks of the soldiers of the nation.

While the struggle of the Negro people for freedom in the Birthplace of Freedom was not ended with the Civil War, the basis had been laid for the continuation of the struggle for larger freedom. This basis was in group organization, for here the beginning must be made, cooperation with white Americans who believed in freedom for all and who had the courage of their convictions, group petition and individual argument, political pressure and advancing economic status. These formed the basis of the struggle. This struggle for status as a citizen continued throughout the nineteenth century and to the present day.

Negro citizens, their friends and allies who are believers in democracy still carry on the fight for freedom now as then. When John S. Rock, first Negro admitted to practice in the United States Supreme Court, attended the National Convention of Colored Men in 1864, he made an inspiring address. As we engage in another war, the sons of Massachusetts may repeat his sentiments. These sons come also from Freedom's Birthplace and are its fighting ambassadors to an unfree world. Said Rock, "I come from Massachusetts, where we are jealous of every right. All we ask is equal opportunities and equal rights. This is what our brave men are fighting for. They have gone to the battlefield for the sake of killing and being killed, but they are

fighting for liberty and equality.''[40]   Thus spoke a leading
Negro citizen of the United States in 1864.   Need we say
more in 1944?   Again we are in a war for freedom.   This
nation seems also to be the birthplace of the modern concepts of freedom, as we now know them—the Four Freedoms—and yet in this national birthplace of freedom, from
which we carry on the struggle to bring freedom to the rest
of the world, there are those among us who are unfree.   This
phase of history in Massachusetts shows clearly that freedom has to be striven for, struggled for, fought for, paid for,
and that we must work together for it, both in the birthplace
of freedom and elsewhere in the world.   As paradoxical as
this may appear, it is the pathway which is open for us to
follow, and courageously let us, with manly and womanly
courage, follow it.

CHARLES H. WESLEY

Wilberforce University

[40] *Proceedings of the National Convention of Colored Men* held in Syra-
cuse, New York. October 4-7, 1864.

DOCUMENT

A SIDELIGHT ON EDMONIA LEWIS

Edmonia Lewis was the Negro's "first woman artist of note."[1] Born in 1845, by the time she was thirty she had won an international reputation for her sculptures.[2] The following letter, written while Miss Lewis was on the threshold of her career, is a candid appraisal by a woman who was in the habit of speaking her mind. The writer, Lydia Maria Child, had been a staunch abolitionist, owing her conversion to anti-slavery principles to William Lloyd Garrison. Mrs. Child's pamphlet, "An Appeal in favor of that class of Americans called Africans," was one of the most moving pieces in the catalogue of abolitionist literature. Mrs. Child had also served as editor of the *Anti-Slavery Standard,* the official organ of the American Anti-Slavery Society. Mrs. Child's letter is written to Sarah Shaw of Boston, and is found in the Shaw Family Correspondence at the New York Public Library.

Wayland [Mass.], Apr. 8th, 1866.

DEAR SARAH,

With regard to Edmonia Lewis, I partly agree with you, and partly I do not. I do not think she has any genius, but I think she has a good deal of imitative talent, which, combined with her indomitable perseverance, I have hoped might make her something above mediocrity, if she took *time* enough. But she does *not* take time; she is in too much of a hurry to get up to a conspicuous place, without taking the necessary intermediate steps. I do not think this is so much "self-conceit," as it is an uneasy feeling of the necessity of making things to sell, in order to pay for her daily bread. Then you must remember that *youth,* in its fresh strength and inexperience, naturally thinks itself capable of doing anything. How contemptuously I smile now to read things which seemed to

[1] Alain Locke, *Negro Art: Past and Present* (Washington, 1936), p. 17.

[2] Miss Lewis' career is outlined and her approach, technique and subject matter is described in James A. Porter, *Modern Negro Art* (New York, 1943), pp. 57-63. See also Freeman Henry Morris Murray, *Emancipation and the Freed in American Sculpture* (Washington, 1916), pp. 21, 225.

me very beautiful when I wrote them, years ago! And it should
not be forgotten that Edmonia is younger than young—brought
up, as she was among the Chippewas and negroes without any education. I think it is a pity that she has undertaken to be a sculptor;
and when she first told me of her design, I tried hard to dissuade
her from it. The sight of her bust of Voltaire modified considerably
my disapprobation of her undertaking. It seemed to me rather
remarkable, considering her antecedents. But that was copied
from a *bust*. Her medallion of John Brown, also copied from a
bust, is better than any of her other medallions. Those of Garrison and Phillips, taken from *life,* are horridly vulgarized. Mrs.
Chapman's[3] bust, taken from *life,* is a tolerable likeness, with her
refined beauty left out.

When she told me she was going to make a bust of Col. Shaw,[4]
I remonstrated against it. I had a feeling about him that made me
reluctant to have any practice-hands tried upon his likeness. I
did not send her any suggestions, or any assistance of any kind,
hoping she would give it up. After she had done it, it seemed to
me to have many obvious defects, and yet, on the whole, it was
better than I had expected. It does give the idea of a *gentleman,*
I think, likeness or no likeness. I certainly should not be *ashamed*
of a son that looked like it. Edmonia came to see me, to say good-
bye, a few days before she went to Europe; and when she saw the
book of photographs which you gave me, containing four likenesses
of Robert, taken at different times, I think she was a little piqued
that I had not loaned them to her, while she was making the bust.
I bought one of the busts of Robert; and, wishing to make it look
more military, I sawed off a large portion of the long, awkward-
looking chest, and set the head on the pedestal again, in a way that
made it look much more erect and alert. When she saw it, she did
not seem displeased, but said, "why didn't you tell me of that,
before I finished it? How much you have improved it!" I was
very reluctant to send her request to Mrs. Minturn,[5] but I did not
see how I could back out of it. I don't think it is so much "self-
conceit," as it is utter inexperience. Brought up among the Chippewas, how *can* she know anything of the delicate properties of re-

[3] Maria Weston Chapman had been the key figure in the Boston Female
Anti-Slavery Society, editing its annual reports and conducting its annual
anti-slavery bazaars.

[4] Robert Gould Shaw was colonel of the Fifty-fourth Massachusetts Volunteers, a regiment of Negro soldiers. Shaw was killed leading his troops at
Fort Wagner, S. C., in July, 1863.

[5] Mrs. Minturn was the wife of Robert Bowne Minturn, a merchant-philan-
thropist who had made large contributions in aid of the Freedmen's Relief
Association.

fined life. The *new* bust, to which she alludes, she says she did in Florence. Whether it is the one Mr. Garrison exhibited I know not. I can readily conceive how such things must annoy you.

The group of the Freedwoman and her Child strikes me disagreeably. The face is pretty good, but the figure is shockingly disproportioned. The feet are monstrous. I understand Mr. Waterston[6] is trying to get it cut in marble, but I think he had far better not. I agree with you that, looked at in the light of *Art*, nothing she has produced is worthy a second glance; but I am more disposed than *you* seem to be to give her time for a fair trial. If she will only *take* time! I doubt whether we *can* treat our colored brethren *exactly* as we could if they were white, though it is desirable to do so. But we have kept their minds in a state of infancy, and children *must* be treated with more patience and forbearance than grown people. How can they learn to swim, if they don't dive into the water? They will sprawl about, at first, doubtless, but they will find the use of their limbs by dint of trying. . . .

Your affectionate old Mariechen
[Lydia Maria Child]

BENJAMIN QUARLES

Dillard University

---

[6] Very likely Robert Cassie Waterston, author of *American Art and Art Unions* (Cambridge, 1850).

BOOK REVIEWS

An Anthology of American Negro Literature. Edited by Sylvestre
C. Watkins. (New York: The Modern Library, Random House,
Inc., 1944.)

At best the compiling of an anthology is a laborious and exacting
task, requiring enormous technical knowledge, superior taste, and
wholly mature judgment. Much more than he desires, the anthol-
ogist is forced to make his collection appear "all things to all people." Even so, there is certain to be quibbling over the omission of
well known "favorite" selections, some grumbling over the inclu-
sion of strange, little known ones, and the unlucky compiler is
eventually set down as a fellow of low taste and little learning
largely because of what he does and what he does not include in his
collection. *An Anthology of American Negro Literature,* edited
by Sylvestre C. Watkins, does not escape the general limitations
of the anthology form, and in addition, shows serious faults within
the special province that the editor has chosen.

In the preface the editor says, "This collection represents the
vigorous thinking and writing that characterizes today's Negro
author," and further states that this anthology "has been compiled
as an introduction to the vast store of information and general
writings that have been written by Negroes." If these statements
represents the editor's purpose, then the title is certainly misleading.
To achieve adequately the purpose indicated in the first statement,
the trite term, "Contemporary," or some happier equivalent of the
editor's imagining, is essential in order to convey specifically and
definitely to the reader the true nature of the contents. Besides,
the editor handles rather loosely his phrase, "today's Negro author." Difficult as it is to determine what "today" really means
when viewed with any historical perspective, is the editor justified
in including Chestnutt's "The Goophered Grapevine," published
in 1887, with the work of writers born since the turn of the century?

The second statement quoted from the preface reveals another
weakness of this collection. While the editor presents his work as
"an introduction to the vast store of information and general writings that have been written by Negroes," he limits his selections
to four types of writing: the short story, the essay, biography, and

autobiography. Even though the editor frankly admits his collection is incomplete, selections from these four fields alone can by no means serve as an introduction to Negro literature. Any such arbitrary delimiting to so few fields, while purporting to represent the entire range of Negro Literature is a grave injustice. Again, how can any collection, which in the main includes work done in the past forty years only, be representative of a body of writing which extends over at least two centuries and a half? The editor should ponder such collections as *The Negro Caravan, Early Negro American Writers,* and *Readings from Negro Authors* and then note the adequacy of *An Anthology of American Negro Literature* as an introduction to the entire field.

In spite of these limitations, this work does have definite value and usefulness. Within the narrow limits he has set for himself, the editor has chosen representative selections from the most distinguished present-day Negro writers in the four fields which make up the anthology. And what is perhaps the most encouraging feature is the number of pieces by writers born since the beginning of the twentieth century. More than a third of the writers in Mr. Watkins' collection fall into this grouping. Taken as a whole, the selections by these younger Negro writers suffer in no way through comparison with the work of the older writers. To judge from their work in this anthology, the younger writers are producing work that is artistically mature, vigorous, and entirely free from self-pity. This indicates a healthy condition of present and distinct promise for future writings by Negro American writers.

The theme of all the material in this collection is the "Negro Problem." For a long time yet this will continue to be the dominant theme for Negro American writers. While some Negro writers in the past have broken away from this all-absorbing theme, and even more are doing so now, the peculiar situation of the black American in this still partly contemptuous, partly hostile America consumes the energies of most Negro writers. However, the charge, frequently made, that such complete absorption with the "Negro Problem" seriously limits and circumscribes the black writer and has a deleterious effect upon his thought and art, can be challenged successfully by even a superficial examination of the variety of viewpoint, the deft handling of material, the incisive thinking displayed in the contents of this work. So long as Negro writers continue to look at the ''Problem'' with similar honesty, objectiveness, and artistic vigor, the body of writings by black Americans will continue to justify collections such as the present one and will merit thoughtful critical appraisals containing no vestige of contempt or disparagement.

J. WELFRED HOLMES

Winston-Salem Teachers College

Tuskegee Institute and the Black Belt: A Portrait of a Race. By Annie Kendrick Walker. (Richmond, Virginia: Dietz Press, 1944. Price $3.00.)

This is another effort of the better class of the South to take notice of the Negro. Almost all white Southerners, making desire father to the thought, have refused to concede anything of worth in the Negro. To them he has been merely the embodiment of man power to be used in drudgery and debased to the ghetto. The Negroes achieving and struggling for recognition and interesting such a large number of sympathziers beyond the frontier of social repression, however, have compelled the unwilling public in the land of segregation to speak out on the so-called race problem.

All of the writers of the former secession area are not speaking in the same tone. Their words are of varying tenor. Some would grant the Negro everything the race wants and others would make no concessions at all. The author of this volume herein evaluated occupies middle ground. The Negro is entitled to more than he receives, but he must not expect to be recognized as a citizen. He must continue contented with his lot as a subject under the control of the white man. Some of these days he may become a citizen, but he must not expect that transformation to take place overnight. The time is not ripe for sudden and radical changes.

Tuskegee Institute is played up because of the supposedly sound basis of its conservative educational program, but while this and other schools have done little openly to direct the Negro toward agitative methods these schools in spite of their fears and restrictions have prepared the way somewhat for the Negroes' demands of the hour. The schools have taught the fundamentals which have so developed the Negroes' minds as to lead them to think. These Negroes have been stirred up by the dissemination of information and the advancement of ideas from centers outside of the South. While all Southern Negroes have not spent long periods outside of their section, they have been visited by those who have and they read extensively Negro newspapers and magazines which are fearlessly waging the battles of the Negroes on all fronts.

During the ante bellum times the ruling class defended themselves from such onslaughts on the strongholds of slavery by preventing the education of the Negro and forbidding the circulation of literature prejudicial to the interests of the slavocracy. Following the Civil War the South, until recently, prevented the thorough education of the Negro at public expense, but could not prevent the missionary educators from doing for the race what the aggrieved slavocracy refused to do. The Negro reformers have risen in the South, therefore, like the ghost that will not down. The present state of affairs is alarming. It is the self-imposed duty of authors like the writer of this volume to present the situation as it is and to restrain the reformers and the unreformed from demanding so much that the effort for change may end in merely self-exterminating conflict.

It is a mistake for writers to play up the Tuskegee plan of education as a reason for conservatism. Booker T. Washington never advocated the abandonment of the struggle for the rights of his race. No man living at that time raised or spent more than he did to contest laws in the courts and to defend Negroes who were imposed upon unjustly. His five-fingers philosophy in his Atlanta speech in 1895 was misinterpreted and applied by the segregationists. Booker Washington later denounced segregation as unjust as slavery itself. And even if it could be proved that he believed in such a downward course, he spoke in the light of things half a century ago. Things change in the course of time and measures once advocated have become outmoded. Men make progress and to stimulate the universe toward the best it can make of itself, one generation, as Thomas Jefferson advocated should not bind the other, for the living would thereby be subject to government by the dead. The living past must live, but the dead past must be buried.

C. G. WOODSON

The Negro in American Life. By John Becker. With an introduction by Lillian Smith. (New York: Julian Messner, Inc., 1944. Pp. 58. Price $1.00.)

Meet the Negro: A Positive Picture of "America's Tenth Man." By Karl E. Downs. With an introduction by E. Stanley Jones (Pasadena, California: The Login Press, 1944. Pp. 179. Price $1.50.)

These two publications, like scores of others which may be grouped herewith, hardly merit an historical criticism except to warn the public against meretricious works. For the propaganda required to place before the American public facts concerning the despised and rejected Negro who is now scheduled for a new hearing they have a purpose and may do some good. Likewise they will do the Negro considerable harm in presenting a conglomeration of half-baked ideas labeled as a portraiture of Negro achievement and present day activities. The noted and the notorious are thrown together into the same sack. The meritorious and the questionable are likewise jumbled without exhibiting any judgment as to proportionate values or knowledge of causes and their effects.

For example, Becker in his *Negro in American Life* devotes half of his space to what may be picked on the sidewalks of Harlem and the remaining portion to the Negro in the war. He hardly touches the life of the Negro laborer, the business man and the professional class. These few Harlem snapshots can not picture the life of fourteen millions of Negroes in the various walks of life in which they are engaged. The prize fighter, the sprinter, the agitator, and the entertainer are given as much space as Frederick Douglass and Booker T. Washington. Carver, who was a lover of nature rather than a scientist, is given more mention than all; and it seems that the author never heard of Charles H. Turner, Ernest E. Just, and W. A. Hinton who distinguished themselves in science. Charles S. Johnson and E. Franklin Frazier, sociologists, come into the picture as competitors with the Sage of Anacostia and the Wizard of Tuskegee.

Meet the Negro shows most of the shortcomings of *The Negro in American Life* and, besides, the bias in playing up unduly acquaintances and leaders of Methodism to which the author belongs. Hugh Mulzac is worthy of honorable mention because of being the first Negro captain to serve in the marines. The Negro leaders who made the opportunity for Mulzac deserve the credit in this case. He is merely an incident. Willa B. Brown had to be included because she is a vivacious aviatrix. Ernest Wilkins deserved space with the great because he obtained the degree of Doctor of Philosophy at nineteen. Jimmy Mundy had to be headlined because he arranges music for Paul Whiteman. Alexander P. Shaw attained greatness by being elected a bishop of the Methodist Church. Lillie M. Jackson reached the roll of honor by becoming a successful agitator in Baltimore. Now thousands of other Negroes have achieved more than the persons of this type, and they would be surprised to see themselves publicized to the exclusion of persons who are unselfishly serving humanity.

The authors of works of this sort do not rise higher than the level of chronicling current news. They have no standard by which they arrive at the truth by careful investigation. Some of what they say is true, but things currently reported must be checked. In many cases, moreover, in sketching the careers of those of some merit the authors do not show sufficient judgment to emphasize the important achievements of these persons rather than the unimportant. For example, instead of merely mentioning the fact that William L. Dawson has been elected to Congress the author should have informed the reader as to what Dawson has accomplished in Congress. Instead of merely reporting on the promotion of Benjamin O. Davis to the rank of brigadier general the author should have informed the reader as to what this soldier has achieved in the military campaigns in which he has participated. Citations in the bibliography show inaccuracies in keeping with the general trend of the volume. The book does not show proper use of the works mentioned.

C. G. Woodson

What the Negro Wants. Edited by Rayford W. Logan. Fourteen Negro Contributors. (Chapel Hill: University of North Carolina Press, 1944. Pp. XXIII, 352.)

These fourteen essays, ably edited by Rayford Logan, are in essential agreement as to "what the Negro wants." All of the writers say that nothing less than complete equality is what the Negro wants and intends to achieve. Indeed, representing the organizations and broad segments of the Negro population, they could say nothing less. Logan selected the contributors, "four of whom might be called conservatives, five liberals and five radicals." Frankly, this reviewer does not know from the content and tenor of these essays where to place each respective writer and perhaps the unanimity of these Negro writers prompted the representative of the publishers, W. T. Couch, to write the preface which he uses to attack the essential thesis of this book.

Couch advances many theses as methodological procedures in order to set up straw men and then knock them down. He advances what he calls "three theories which are widely held concerning the condition of the Negro in America": one, that the Negroes' condition is produced by inferiority, but that this inferiority can be overcome, and last, that the Negro is not inferior, that he only appears to be so and that American white supremacy is the chief cause of this inferiority. Now, the publisher uses these views in order to inveigh against the contentions of Myrdal's *An American Dilemma*, against the anthropological views of our leading scientists, and primarily against the "equality" argument advanced by the authors. Couch asks, "Is it possible that *An American Dilemma* is the final, authoritative word on this subject—that this third view is dominant because it is thoroughly buttressed with facts and sound reasoning?" Then Couch proceeds to advance a typical white supremacist argument about "equality," "inferiority," "superiority" and in favor of segregation and discrimination. Obviously, he does not mean "equality" before the law. He does mean that white supremacy must remain if the Negro is to be kept "inferior," for he says, "The white Southerner, reading this book, must remember that the task of the *superior* man is not to prate of being *superior* but to be really so." (Italics the reviewer's.) Couch has allowed us to witness one of the strangest spectacles in American publishing history, of soliciting a book and then using his position and prestige to attack the book.

All of the essays are well-written and up to the standards of a first-rate anthology. Most of these writers are professional writers and have been busy for half of their lives writing in defense of the Negroes' rights. Logan leads off with a well documented account of the historical denial of the rights of citizenship and properly sets the tone for the book by bringing his account up to date. The "Dean of American Negro Thought," W. E. B. Du Bois, who is now director of special research of the National Association for the Advancement of Colored People, reviews his fifty-year long struggle for the equality of the Negro in America, thus providing a summary model for any who are of stature enough to follow in his steps. Leslie Pinckney Hill, Charles H. Wesley, Roy Wilkins, all tell slightly different stories, but they too are in complete agreement as to the full equality the Negro wants.

Willard S. Townsend, the trade union leader of the United Transport Service Employees of America (Congress of Industrial Organizations), supplies valuable economic and labor history, with a very fair appraisal of the defects of the American Federation of Labor and the achievements of the Congress of Industrial Organizations. Doxey Wilkerson, former Howard University professor and now executive editor of *People's Voice,* contributes a Marxist historical essay to the discussion, in which he does not omit the part which ought to be played by global thinking and by a necessity to see the picture as a whole if the war is to be won. The "Gloomy Dean," Gordon B. Hancock and Frederick D. Patterson, as Southerners, are at one in their demands for a fuller participation in American democracy. Mrs. Bethune, the founder and president of the National Council of Negro Women, contributes a very realistic review of the position of the Negro in a changing situation.

Langston Hughes and Sterling Brown write, not only as the experienced poets and literary craftmen they are, but as onlookers of the American scene. They write as travelers, as sensitive, penetrating critics of an undemocratic Southern plantocracy. Brown's essay, one of those literary gems, is worth the attention of any discerning critic of regional literature. The odd and disturbing notes in the book are the essays of A. Philip Randolph and George S. Schuyler. Randolph presents us with a program, the all-black March on Washington Movement with its non-violent good will action. His essay contains the only anti-Soviet and red-baiting remarks in the book. Schuyler shows himself as a racialist with a pseudo scienitfic account of race, though there are cogent details in his historical review of "race." These are the only two essays in which no mention is made of the war.

In addition to the editor's preface, the publisher's preface, there is an excellent *Who's Who* of the contributors.

EUGENE HOLMES

Howard University

Capitalism and Slavery. By Eric Williams. (Chapel Hill: The University of North Carolina Press, 1944. Pp. 285. Price $3.00.)

This book marks the beginning of the scientific study of slavery from the international point of view and shows the necessity for a definitive study of slavery in all parts of the new world. Only a few scholars like Pares, Burn, Beer, Klingberg and Mathieson have penetrated that mist sufficiently to show its international implications, and the studies produced in the United States as treatments of slavery in the various commonwealths are all but travesties of American historical literature. In most cases the authors have not had the mental grasp of the meaning of the social, commercial and industrial factors involved; and they have been too near to the age discussed or too closely connected by ties of blood with the participants in the slave trade and slavery. Dr. Eric Williams, a product of Oxford, is an able scholar equal to the task undertaken, and he has done it scientifically.

Dr. Williams's book does not consist of spun-out theories and opinions. He marshals facts, many of which others have mentioned but did not understand; and he gives many other valuable data taken from sources which so many investigators do not generally touch. All the important archives of the British Empire yielded materials for this essay. The author understands Europe, Africa, and America; and through the papers of the statesmen and the promoters of slavery with whom they were connected and closely cooperated he became acquainted with these human factors. The book is therefore a convincing study of that master and servant order in its commercial and industrial ramifications.

Dr. Williams supports the contention that capitalism and slavery had the same trend in one European country as in the other. While his book deals with the situation in British Empire, the study of that of other European nations thus involved would not be a different story. The industrial revolution likewise affected all slaveholding nations. He says, "Commercial capitalism of the eighteenth century developed the wealth of Europe by means of slavery and monopoly. But in so doing it helped to create the industrial capitalism of the nineteenth century which turned round and destroyed the power of commercial capitalism, slavery and all its works." Hoping to recoup the losses suffered in the failure to subdue the American colonies, the British after 1783 turned to India and other possessions for creative wealth. This sort of development of the Empire, however, was long a debatable policy. Statesmen and reformers have conflicted with their proposals because of their inability to understand these relationships and interrelationships; and thus at times they have opposed what they believed they were advocating. For this reason, "Politics and moral ideas of the age are to be examined in relation to economic development." "Politics and morals in the abstract make no sense" (211). Everything had its value in dollars and cents and based its defence on that ground. Yet slavery an outworn interest which had ceased to serve the purpose for which it was established was defended by West Indian statesmen among whom it was strongly intrenched. The tendency of these worn-out systems thus to endure prevents progress long after men of vision have seen the evil of the old ways. This the author finds as stemming from the same source as the uprooted theory that a white man is unfit for labor in the tropics and that the Negro is inferior and justly consigned to slavery.

The examination of this period of long ago, which was followed by universal revolution, just as the crisis now upon us seems to indicate, may help us considerably in evaluating the confusing men and measures of today which all but baffle human understanding. Industrial capitalism followed commercial capitalism which it destroyed. Today we have economic imperialism which holds the natives of the dependencies of the British Empire beneath the heel of the oppressor. What hope is there for India, or Native Africa under the present system? What system under the impact of democratizing forces at work will be devised to supplant the policy of government mainly concerned with the production of wealth? Dr. Williams does not answer these questions, and it was not his purpose to do so; but he has written a scholarly account of how these matters worked out in the case of one revolution and would have us learn from the past how to understand the present and to deal wisely with the problems at hand.

This work should make a strong appeal to those who now array themselves against the British Empire because of its present policy of grabbing all of the universe which it can find any excuse for taking over. The evils of the British system are enormous, and should be attacked whenever the opportunity presents itself, but the opposition must proceed consistently and intelligently. This book will help those thus concerned to understand what they desire to do and may suggest some methods of procedure by its exposition of developments in the British Empire when the present system had its beginning. The British Empire is not the United States, and it is not conducted as our Government is administered by its present incumbents. Churchill is often denounced because of what he says and does, but any other premier of Britain would say and do just what he says and does. The British Empire must grab the lands of weaker peoples, control their raw materials, and maintain there a monopoly of trade. It is thus that the British Empire is constituted. Britain is a democracy of privileged interests not one of individuals. Evil ends are reached in Britain in a more subtle way than in the United States. Changes are made in the light of the interests involved. Whatever the demand for reform may be, one highly favored interest in the final analysis must overcome the other before there can be any change as was the case of the destruction of commercial capitalism by industrial capitalism. In our excoriation of the British Empire we must learn to attack the substance rather than the shadow.

C. G. WOODSON

La Fondation de la République d'Haiti par Alexandre Pétion. By Dr. François Dalencour. (The Author, 3 Rue Saint-Cyr, Port-au-Prince, Haiti, 1944. Pp. 344. Price $2.00.)

This is not a biography of a great Haitian leader. It is the narrative of the efforts to establish a permanent government in Haiti after the overthrow of the French there and the final emergence of the republic under Alexandre Pétion. For some time it was difficult for the majority of the people concerned with political affairs to decide which way the country would develop—whether it would reestablish under the rule of certain freedmen a government like the one which had been overthrown or a democracy like those developing in other parts of the Western Hemisphere. For almost half a century the island seemed to swing first one way and then the other in accordance with the will of the leader who might contrive to make himself master of his enemies.

It was just as natural for certain leaders to undertake the rule of the despot as it was to initiate a regime of equality for all. The

Haitians doubtless desired liberty, but they had to become acquainted with democratic rule before they could appreciate it. Often so-called democracy of that day did not differ much from monarchy, for in the United States, which has often been referred to as the greatest democracy on earth, only one white man out of every fifteen could vote as late as 1800. Real democracy does not yet exist in the United States, and we need not be surprised to learn that the supposedly democratic rule in Haiti has not meant much in the elevation of the majority of the people.

Pétion deserves credit for establishing the Republique in 1806, although it did not grant democracy to every inhabitant of the island. Yet, even if the government remained in the hands of the upper crust of the Haitian society, democracy had a better chance for development down to the lower orders than it would have had under imperial rule like that of Dessalines, Christophe and Soulouque with absolute power invested in one man and his lieutenants. When one class began to register its will in the government all other classes might reasonably expect to do likewise some day.

The author traces the tendency toward democracy in showing the rise of the liberal party under the Constitution of 1806 which effected a generous apportionment of landed property and the grant of civic and social rights never before enjoyed by the inhabitants of the island. The author makes Pétion a hero. After establishing the republic he craved not for power and was elected president against his will. He proved the justice of his cause in establishing principles of government which in spite of many upheavals endured even in the revised Constitution of 1816, and the efforts to maintain an empire finally ceased to afflict the people of Haiti.

It is fortunate that Dr. Dalencour has produced this work. Foreigners have written about Haiti from the point of view of the man on the outside. They are unable to see and understand the country as it really is. The history of Haiti, however, must be produced in definitive form by the Haitians themselves. The work under review is based mainly upon secondary authorities, although here and there the author quotes some interesting documents like the fine tribute paid Pétion by Simon Bolivar who gave the former high rank among the advance guard of the freedom of mankind. The achievements of Pétion, like those of other leaders, however, must be recorded exactly as they were and with adequate documentation to inspire confidence in the account. The historians must do more than merely correct certain erroneous impressions received from the misinforming treatments on Haiti published by Americans and Europeans. They must tell their own story in full and to the satisfaction of the best critics of modern historiography.

This brings up another question. To what extent have the documentary materials of Haiti been preserved? To what extent have they been used? Most of the works bearing on Haiti are based on the documentary materials of countries which have had relations with that island. Haiti has not yet told enough of its own story out of the mouths of its own witnesses. Until these speak and give their version of the past of that island we shall always have to question not only what foreigners say about Haiti but some things which the Haitians may say about themselves. We need less of the eulogistic personal accounts and more of the beginning and development of things through men and measures. Dr. Dalencour was trained in medicine not in history, and he has done well to write so fully under the handicaps which are but natural. It is earnestly desired that from the Haitian youth may come historians who with scientific objectivity will tell the story anew to an uninformed world.

C. G. WOODSON

The Haitian-American Anthology: Haitian Readings from American Authors. By Mercer Cook and Dantes Bellegarde. (Port-au-Prince, Haiti: Imprimerie de l'Etat, 1944. Pp. 160.)

Dr. Mercer Cook, head of the department of Romance Languages of Atlanta University, is now on leave in Haiti, serving as the Supervisor of the English-Teaching Project. To facilitate his task he has compiled and edited these readings in collaboration with Dantes Bellegarde, former director of the Lycée Pétion and sometime minister of Haiti to the United States. The book is of importance to the historian for the reason that the authors planned it with the thought that the duties of a teacher of foreign languages transcend the limits of grammar, pronunciation, and vocabulary, for "he must also introduce his pupils to the civilization of the country whose language they are studying." These selections, with three exceptions, are comments of North Americans on Haiti. Along with the thought of these foreigners are those of Maurice

Dartigue, Dantes Bellegarde, and Judge J. B. Cineas for the reason that no other writers have expressed such sentiments so accurately as these three commentators of Haiti.

These selections are presented under five headings: History, life and customs, nature, art and folklore, and the occupation and its aftermath. For brief accounts of the beginnings of Haiti the editors made selections from the works of Frederick Douglass, Blair Niles, Percy Waxman, Lokke and Adams, W. E. B. Du Bois, H. P. Davis, Rayford Logan, John W. Vandercook, and Richard Pattee. In this part are included Leslie Pinckney Hill's "Capture of Toussaint" and Wendell Phillips' eulogy of that hero. The life and customs of the Hatian people appear in the selections from the works of Raymond Leslie Buell, Robert Parsons, W. B. Seabrook, Maurice Dartigue, John H. Craige, William Beebe, Melville J. Herskovits, John W. Vandercook, and George E. Simpson. Nature in Haiti is portrayed in extracts from Blair Niles, who enlarged upon the beauty of Haiti; the birds pictured by Wetmore and Swales; and snapping shrimps, described by William Beebe.

For folklore the selections are from the works of George E. Simpson and J. B. Cineas, Melville J. Herskovits, Zora Neale Hurston, Harold Courlander, Joseph H. Craige, and Edward Larocque Tinker. Next follow five Haitian poems: Massillon Coiucu's "Oblivion," translated by Edna W. Underwood and Jessie Redmond Fauset; Roussan Camille's "Nedjé," translated by Mercer Cook; Carl Brouard's "The Negro Women Pray," translated by Edna W. Underwood; Oswald Durand's "If," translated by the same author; and Jean Brierre's "To Paul Robeson," translated by Frances Waldman.

The occupation of Haiti and its aftermath, as others saw it from the foreign point of view appear in "An American Negro Visits Haiti," by James Weldon Johnson; "Accomplishments and Problems of Occupation," by A. C. Millspaugh; "The Haitian Press in 1926," by Grace Watson and Emily Balch; "Poetic Protest," by John F. Matheus; "William Allen White Throws a Kiss," by Augusta Hinshaw; "An American Liberal Describes the Situation in 1931," by Ernest Gruening; "Haiti's Economic Ills," by James Leyburn; "A Review of Leyburn's *The Haitian People*," by L. L. Montague; "Tony Bloncourt," by Mercer Cook; "The Good Neighbor Policy," by Latante and Wainhouse; "The President of Haiti

Visits Washington;'' and ''President Roosevelt Proposes a Toast to President Lescot.''

It is clear from the contents herein given in detail that this volume of readings, although intended to meet a special need in Haiti, may be used profitably in schools elsewhere engaged in the study of the history and language of Haiti. The work was not published for sale, but those especially in need of the helpful manual may address themselves to the authors for whatever copies they may be able to make available where some good may thereby be accomplished.

C. G. WOODSON

Panorama de la Musica Afroamericana. By Nestor R. Ortiz Oderigo. (Buenos Aires: Editorial Claridad, 1944. Pp. 301. Price $5.00.)

The lovers of American Negro music will be delighted to see in Spanish the reproduction of the record of the Negro in this art in the United States. A few more works like this will serve the commendable purpose of convincing Latin Americans that the so-called Negroes of the United States have made a distinct contribution to culture. While various centers are disseminating information to the contrary this book will help considerably to expose the present propaganda worked out from an agglomeration of traditional falsehoods with respect to the Negro in the United States.

The critics may not agree with the author on what he says as to the authenticity of Negro music, but his listing of these achievements and appraisal of the artists who have popularized them will prove to be interesting. He is concerned with the work songs, the spirituals, the blues, minstrelsy, ragtime, and jazz. He emphasizes such as the hammer song, the water carrier, the mule song, and the John Henry legend. He invites attention especially to such spirituals as ''I Have a Shoe,'' ''Sometimes I Feel Like a Motherless Child,'' ''You May Bury Me in the East,'' etc., paralleling for the most part treatments of the same in English, with many of which he shows acquaintance. The book gives biographical sketches of the Negro performers who have done most to interpret this and other music in America and Europe. The work is illustrated well with cuts of these artists, many of which are duplications of those

in Maud-Cuney-Hare's *Negro Musicians and Their Music,* on which
the author leaned very heavily without giving due credit.

On reading the title of this book the reader may be disappointed
in finding that it is restricted almost altogether to what the Negro
has achieved in music in the United States and what the white
critics are now saying to prove that this music was originated
among the whites rather than among Negroes. The scientist would
expect in a work of this sort adequate treatment of the Afro-American music developed in the West Indies and Latin America, especially in Brazil where there are more persons of African blood than
in the United States of America. Probably the author neglected
these achievements because they are nearer to the primitive stage
than in the case of those of Negroes farther North. It would have
added greatly to the value of the work, however, to see the Afro-
American music of all parts adequately treated and evaluated by
comparison with respect to forces and influences. For example, the
scientist would like to hear more about the music emerging from
the *Macumbas* and the *Candomblés* of Brazil, more about the *Tango
Brasileiro,* the *Samba,* the *Modinhas,* and the *Lundús.* Did these
musical manifestations retain more or less of the African element
than the Negro music of the United States of America. Is the music
in Haiti African, French or Haitian? Fernando Ortiz believes that
the culture of Cuba must become Cuban. Has that culture reached
that stage with respect to its music and what are the forces at work
to determine what it is or shall be? Until all these conflicts and
fusions of culture are examined for this broader and commanding
point of view we shall still be subject to the opinions of contro-
versialists like John Powell and George Pullen Jackson, who have
assumed as their indispensable duty the proving that the Negro in
America has not created anything.

C. G. WOODSON

Without Bitterness: Western Nations in Post-War Africa. By A.
A. Nwafor Orizu. (New York: Creative Age Press, Inc., 1944.
Pp. 395. Price $3.00.)

About a hundred years ago European nations were in doubt as
to what they would do with Africa. They finally decided in the
Berlin Congress of 1885 to conquer the Continent and exploit the
Natives as peons and serfs by a new method of creating wealth

known as economic imperialism. There was no thought of the elevation of the Natives except to aid stintingly the efforts of missionaries, most of whom in turn became tools in the hands of the conquerors. Considerable enlightenment of some Natives, however, resulted inevitably from the use of Africans as laborers trained to do things according to modern ways, and certain other Natives educated themselves in foreign parts. Because of less restrictions on the West Coast the Natives have made more intellectual progress than in South Africa where they are practically enslaved or in East and Northeast Africa where Native culture was once at a higher level than in the other parts of that land. These more modernized Natives of the West Coast, therefore, are the first of the so-called "Dark Continent" to combine as workers toward a common goal and to say to the European conquerors that they must change their way of administering affairs in Africa and eventually they must get out.

The voice of Africa crying through this volume is that of a Native of Onitsha in Southern Nigeria. He was educated in the United States after having come under the influence of Mnandi Azikiwe, who is also a product of schools on this side of the Atlantic. Orizu makes it clear in the beginning of his story that he stands for the aggressive policy of Azikiwe in contradistinction to the conservative course of cooperation advocated by the late missionary-teacher J. E. K. Aggrey. The old philosophy of complacency has lost its grip on the African mind and the medieval church has lost its force there. Africa, he contends, has awakened and in spite of the chains of imperialism it must attain freedom and take its place among the nations of the world. The author would have spoken more accurately if he had restricted these claims of self-assertion to the few enlightened Natives like himself and Azikiwe who are bringing about the awakening of Africa. If Native Africa were alive to its actual situation the European conquerors could not remain on the continent a year longer. These assertions, therefore, must be accepted more as preachments of changes devoutly to be desired than as recording what has been actually achieved.

In the first chapters of the book the author makes helpful comment on the present European claims and control of Africa which one must bear in mind in order to understand the message of the volume. He classifies Liberia, Egypt and Ethiopia as independent states but with considerable qualification shown in the brief histories of those nations in their relation to the European imperialists. The author probably may be pardoned for saying more about Nigeria than about other parts, because he is a native of that area. Relying upon well-known authorities, he gives a fair glimpse of the history of West Africa and the Sudan, but neglects the history of the other parts of the Continent. In that part of the history set forth, however, appear sufficient facts to condemn the European imperialists and these missionaries who have given their evil deeds the white-wash of the sanctuaries of the Church of God.

The author brings out that, while there are in Africa those Natives who consider the religion of the missionaries essential to the progress of the continent, there are others who are indifferent and still others who are militantly arrayed against the so-called Christian workers. He says, "When the proper light operates among the Africans to regenerate their society, to emancipate their mentality, to nationalize their activities, and to secure their existence, Christianity will have accomplished its mission in Africa. But if Christianity fails to solve these problems in Africa it will have no basis for a preferred position over other organized religions in Africa (174). The African must be given the opportunity to chose his own religion and his own government. Imperialism means decay to the African and likewise to the European agent of the system. Christianity has too long played into the hands of the imperialists instead of promoting the brotherhood democracy which Africa needs.

Finally the author would suggest that West Africa be made an independent state. He is doubtless on sound ground in contending that West African Natives have sufficiently advanced along modern lines to manage their own affairs. Likewise he is right in contending that, if the European conquerors are sincere in their past and present proclamations the disabilities and burdens must be removed from the shoulders of Natives in other parts that they may develop toward freedom and equality. In the final analysis the author advocates revolution with respect to Africa. If the conqueror will permit it to work out peaceably the blood of both Natives and Europeans will be spared; but, if the new order must come by force, let it be at the expense of those who block the wheels of progress.

C. G. WOODSON

NOTES

Books of United States History

Books in which the Negro in particular is treated include the following: *Tuskegee and the Black Belt: A Portrait of a Race,* By Anne Kendrick Walker (Richmond, Virginia: Dietz Press, 1944); *Jim Crow Joins Up,* a study of the Negro in the armed forces, by Ruth Dannenhower Wilson (New York: Press of William J. Clark, 1944; *The Negro in American Life,* an unbalanced effort to portray mainly in pictures the past and present of the American Negro, by John Becker, for the Council against Intolerance (New York: Julian Messner, Inc., 1944); *Seeking a Way,* a reprint from the Biennial Report of the American Missionary Association showing what this organization has done for the education of the Negro. The reprint is dedicated to Dr. W. E. B. Du Bois, who retires this year from teaching service most of which he rendered in connection with schools assisted by the American Missionary Association.

Books which bear indirectly upon the Negro include these: *John C. Calhoun, Nationalist, 1782-1828,* by C. M. Wiltse (Indianapolis: Bobbs-Merrill Company, 1944); *The First Lincoln Campaign,* by Reinhard H. Luthin (Cambridge: Harvard University Press, 1944); *Jefferson Davis and His Cabinet,* by R. W. Patrick (Baton Rouge: Louisiana University Press, 1944); *Pitchfork Ben Tillman: South Carolinian,* by Frances Butler Simkins (Baton Rouge: University of Louisiana Press). Here may be added *By Valour and Arms,* an historical novel dealing with the Civil War around Vicksburg, by James Street (New York: Dial Press, 1944); *Royal Street,* a novel, dealing with Old New Orleans, by W. Adolphe Roberts (Indianapolis: Bobbs-Merrill Company, 1944.)

Articles of United States History

The articles bearing particularly on the Negro include: "The Scalawag in Mississippi Reconstruction," by David H. Donald (*The Journal of Southern History,* November, 1944); "Due Process of Law in 'Race' Cases," by Loring B. Moore (*National Bar Journal,* December, 1944); "The Negro and the Bar: The South," by Arthur D. Shores (*ibid.*); "Our Founder," a sketch of the career of Attorney George H. Woodson, by S. Joe Brown (*ibid.*); "An American Dilemma," by Frank Tannenbaum (*Political Science Quarterly,* September, 1944); "Caste or Democracy? An American Dilemma," by Mordecai Grossman (*Contemporary Jewish Record,* October, 1944); "Recent Events in Negro Union Relationships," by Robert C. Weaver (*The Journal of Political Economy,* September, 1944); "Problems of Race in Postwar Peace," by A. O. Bowden (*World Affairs Interpreter,* summer, 1944); "Negro Moves North," by David L. Kohn (*Atlantic,* November, 1944).

Articles treating the Negro along with other questions include these: "Abraham Lincoln Becomes a Republican," by Reinhard H. Luthin (*Political Science Quarterly,* September, 1944); "Jail Bird Immigrants to Virginia," by Charles Edgar Gilliam (*Virginia Magazine of History,* July, 1944); "A Transplanted Yankee in Mecklenburg County, 1880," by Millicent B. Rex (*ibid.*); "Can the Philippines Stand Alone?" by H. Foster Bain (*Foreign Affairs,* October, 1944); "William Penn's Experiment in Race Relations," by Thomas E. Drake (*The Pennsylvania Magazine of History and Biography,* October, 1944); "J. D. B. De Bow, the Man," by Otis Clark Skipper (*Journal of Southern History,* November, 1944); "Health and the Medical Profession in the South," by Martha Carolyn Mitchell (*ibid.*)

Books on Latin America and the West Indies

The most recent in this field include among others: *Brazil on the March,* by Morris Llewellyn Cooke (New York: Whittlesey House, 1944); *A Century of Latin American Thought,* by Rex Crawford (Cambridge: Harvard University Press, 1944); *The Rise of Fernando Cortes,* by Henry R. Wagner (Berkeley, California: The Cortes Society Special Edition, Limited, 1944); *To the South,* by Kurt Severin in collaboration with Lenore Sorsby (New York: Eagle Books, Duel, Sloane and Pearce, 1944); *Haiti, Our Neighbor,* a melodrama in two acts, by Henri C. Rosemond (New York: The Haitian Publishing Company, 1944); *Citizen Toussaint,* by Ralph Korngold (Boston: Little Brown and Company, 1944) *Argentine Riddle,* by Felix J. Weil (New York: The John Day Company, 1944).

ARTICLES ON LATIN AMERICA AND THE WEST INDIES

Some of the articles pertinent to the study of the Negro to the South of the United States include the following: "The Approach to Sir Conrad Reeves," by H. A. Vaughan (*The Forum*, Barbados, B. W. I, September, 1944); "The Growth of Liberty," by J. D. and P. F. (*ibid.*)

BOOKS ON AFRICA

The most recent works on Africa include the following: *Akokoaso: A Survey of a Gold Coast Village*, by W. H. Beckett (London: Humphries, 1944); *Ibibio Indigenous Judicial System*, by C. A. Ekere (West Africa Study Group Lecture); *Cape Town's Underworld*, by S. W. Lavis (Lovedale Press, 1944); *African Conversation Piece*, a picture of Ibo life, by Sylvia Leit-Ross (London: Hutchinson, 1944; *An Outline of Native Law*, by Julius Lewin (Johannesburg: R. L. Esson Company, 1944); *Hunger and Health in the Colonies*, by the Fabian Colonial Bureau (London: Fabian Publications, Ltd., 1944); *The Missionary Doctor: The Story of Twenty Years in Africa*, by Mary Floyd Cushman (New York: Harper and Brothers, 1944).

Of a political and administrative nature are the following: *Race and Politics in Kenya*, by Elspeth Huxley and Margaret Perham (London: Faber and Faber, 1944); *Minimum Standards of Social Policy in Dependent Territories*, by the International Labour Conference (Montreal: International Labour Office, 1944); *Soviet Light on the Colonies*, by Leonard Barnes (Middlesex: Penguin Books, 1944); *The British Empire*, Basil Williams (London: Oxford University Press, 1944); *Kenya—White Man's Country?* by the Fabian Colonial Bureau (London: Fabian Publications Ltd., 1944); *Report of the Social Security Committee and Report No. 2 of the Social and Economic Planning Council Entitled: Social Security, Social Services and the National Income* (Pretoria: Government Printer, 1944); *Colonial Policies in Africa*, by H. A. Wieschhoff (Philadelphia: University of Pennsylvania Press, 1944); *History of Nigeria*, an account of the people and their relation to the British Empire, by Allan Burns (New York: W. W. Norton Company, 1944); *Without Bitterness*, a warning from Africa that cruel exploitation must give way to new methods for education and social amelioration, by A. A. Nwafor Orizu (New York: Creative Age Press, 1944); *The Black Man's Burden*, by John Burger (London:

Victor Gollancz, 1944) ; *Empire in Africa,* by Alexander Campbell (*Ibid.*) ; *Our Colonies: A Challenge,* by H. M. Grace (London: Edinburgh House, 1944) ; *Maynier and the First Boer Republic,* by J. S. Marais (Cape Town: Maskew Miller, 1944).

ARTICLES ON AFRICA

Articles on Africa dealing with things scientifically include the following: "Médicine indigène et plantes médicinales au Soudan," by S. Ben Sai (*Notes Africaines,* January, 1944) ; Two Games from Africa from the Makua and Yao Tribes, by Paul G. Brewster (*American Anthropologist,* April-June, 1944) ; "Le 'Tuppal', Une cérémonie au Fouta Djallon," by Ousmane Diallo (*Notes Africaines,* January, 1944) ; "An Unusual Bantu Tale of the Little-Hare," by C. M. Doke (*African Studies,* March, 1944) ; "Chasse—Redevances dues au Propriétaire du fusil," by the President of Moba Territory (*Bulletin des Jurisdictions Indigènes et du Droit Coutumier Congolais,* March-April, 1944) ; "Studies in African Land Tenure," by Max Gluckman (*African Studies,* March, 1944) ; "Masai Women and Their Work," by Jane Fosbrooke (*Crown Colonist,* May, 1944) ; "L'industrie du sel dans la Subdivision de Grand-Popo," by R. Grivot (*Notes Africaines,* January, 1944) ; "Les trois pêcheurs bredouilles, conte bambara, by Amadou Hampaté Ba (*Notes Africaines,* January, 1944) ; "Magical Thought Pattern of the Bantu in Relation to Health Service," by J. D. Krige (*African Studies,* March, 1944) ; "Une baguette guerzée," by P. Lassort (*Notes Africaines,* January, 1944) ; "The Museum in the Royal Palace at Abomey, Dahomey," by Eva L. R. Meyerowitz (*The Burlington Magazine,* June, 1944) ; "The French Institute of Negro Africa," by Th. Monod (*Man,* May-June, 1944) ; "Coutumes et institutions des Barundi," introduction and first chapter treating religion and beliefs, and the second chapter the family, by Eugène Simons (*Bulletin des Jurisdictions Indigènes et du Droit Coutumier Congolais,* January-February and March-April, 1944) ; "Jeux Africains, en Afrique Occidentale Française," by Y Tounkara (*Notes Africaines,* January, 1944) ; "Native Paddy Cultivation and Yields in Zanzibar," by F. B. Wilson and G. E. Tidbury (*East African Agricultural Journal,* April, 1944) ; "Wanyakyusa Agriculture," by D. H. Thwaites (*ibid.*) ; "Katsina Ala as seen by an Ijaw," by V. A. D. Kemmer (*Nigeria* 22, 1944) ; "The Psychic Element in

African Sickness," by Neil Macivar (*South African Outlook,* January, 1944); "The Progress of Art in Nigeria," by K. C. Murray (*Nigeria Review,* January and February, 1944); "Significance of Descent in Tale Social Structure," by M. Fortes (*Africa,* July, 1944); "Joking Relationship In Tanganyika," by R. E. Moreau (*ibid.*); "Nutrition in East Africa, by G. M. Culwick (*ibid.*); The Nkumu of the Tumba, Ritual Chieftainship on the Middle Congo," by H. D. Brown (*ibid.,* October, 1944); "Native Courts and British Justice in Africa," by Julius Lewin (*ibid.*); "Notes sur les Groupements Ethniques en Afrique Equatoriale Française," by Médécin Général A. Sice (*ibid.*); "Figurines Used in the Initiation Ceremonies of the Nguu of Tanganyika Territory," by A. Cory (*ibid*).

Articles bearing mainly on matters administrative include the following: "The Olu of Itsekiris, and Obi, Oputa of Aboh," by R. L. Bowen (*Africa,* July, 1944); "The Congo in 1945 and After," by R. Godding (*Message,* 29, March, 1944); "British East Africa: A Balanced Picture," by Geoffrey Hunter (*Crown Colonist,* May, 1944); "East Africa, its Difficulties and Possibilities," by Geoffrey Hunter (*African Affairs,* July, 1944); "The Oil Palm in the Belgian Congo," by L. Tobback (*Message,* 28, February, 1944); "Law and Justice in Ethiopia," by Norman Bentwich (*Contemporary Review,* May, 1944); "Partnership in Nigeria," by Bernard Bourdillon (*Journal of the Royal Society of Arts,* April, 1944); "The Sudan Past, Present and Future," by Angus Gillan (*African Affairs,* July, 1944); "The Role of Cooperation in Colonial Development: Far-reaching Plans in Southern Rhodesia," by the International Co-operative Alliance (*Review of International Cooperation,* April-May, 1944); "French Cameroons Has Progressed" (*West African Review,* May, 1944); "Labour Legislation in the French Cameroons," by the International Labour Office (*International Labour Review,* April-May, 1944); "Organisation of the Nigerian Labour Department," by the International Office (*ibid.,* March, 1944); "Social Security in South Africa," by J. R. (*Bulletin of International News,* June 24, 1944); "Broadcast Talk on East Africa," by H. S. Scott (*East Africa and Rhodesia,* June 29, 1944); "Broadcast Talk on Demobilization Problems in Kenya," by G. A. Tyson (*ibid.*); "Political Reforms in Ibadan," (*West African Review,* May, 1944); "Opobo To-day," by K. C. Murray (*African Affairs,* July, 1944).

PERSONAL

JAMES ALBERT BRAY

James Albert Bray died all but suddenly from a stroke at Little Rock, Arkansas on September 1, 1944. He was born in 1870 at Carnesville, Georgia, the son of Andrew Jackson and Margaret Frances Bray. Young Bray worked on his father's farm and studied in the rural schools of Franklin County Georgia. He completed his secondary work at the high school of Athens, Georgia, and then entered Atlanta University where he completed the course leading to the degree of Bachelor of Arts. Later in life he took special courses at both Chicago and Harvard. Atlanta University conferred upon him the degree of Master of Arts and Wilberforce that of Doctor of Laws.

Bray began his career as a teacher. His first important position was that of principal of the Negro High School in Athens, Georgia, which he developed into the first accredited secondary school of the Negroes in that State. From this post he arose to the presidency of Lane College in Jackson, Tennessee, and later to that of Miles Memorial College in Birmingham.

As an educator he made a favorable impression, but earlier in his career he entered the ministry. He was ordained by Bishop L. H. Holsey and received as a member of the Georgia Conference of the Colored Methodist Episcopal Church. His first important service as a clergyman was the pastorate of the Trinity Church in Augusta, Georgia. Next he became a presiding elder in Alabama. In 1914 he was appointed as General Secretary of Education of the Colored Methodist Episcopal Church. In this service he was the first to succeed in interesting educational boards to the extent of securing from them appropriations for the schools of his denomination. In 1934 he was elevated to the bishop's bench and was assigned to areas which required direction and supervision of religious work in Michigan, Wisconsin, Northern Indiana, Illinois, Eastern Missouri, Arkansas and Southern Louisiana.

Bishop Bray was a brilliant orator and a fearless leader. He had the courage to battle for what he considered to be right. At the time of his death he had just completed a term as the head of the Fraternal Council of the Churches in America, an interdenominational effort to unite the religious forces of the country to advance

108

the cause of the Negro. In all educational matters, religious efforts, and civic affairs respecting the Negro he could be counted on to take an active part. In most of these efforts, too, he had to work without pay and often without the gratitude of some whom he served. His achievements under these circumstances place him in the ranks of the useful men of his time.

He was a man with family ties. His first wife was Mattie Davis who died early leaving one daughter, now Mrs. Ella Clark, the wife of Dr. E. B. Clark. Later the churchman married Miss Mattie Childs of Marion, Alabama. She bore him a daughter who died some years ago.

JOSEPH SIMEON FLIPPER

Joseph Simeon Flipper died on October 10, 1944. He was born in Atlanta, Georgia, the slave of Ephraim G. Ponder on February 22, 1859. He was the son of Festus and Isabella (Buckhalter) Flipper. He was too young to experience all the horrors of slavery which was abolished when he was a small lad. He was sent to a missionary school in the Bethel African Methodist Church in 1867 and later to Storrs School, the forerunner of Atlanta University. When this higher institution opened its doors in 1869 Flipper was one of the first students to enroll. He applied himself diligently there until 1876 when he went to Thomaston Georgia to teach. The following year he went to Thomasville to which his parents had moved. There he was converted and joined the St. Thomas African Methodist Episcopal Church. He taught further in Thomas County in 1877 and 1878. In 1879 Governor Alfred H. Colquit commissioned him as captain to raise a company to constitute a part of the State Militia. In 1879 Flipper taught at Groversville in Brooks County and, although he had decided to follow another profession, he taught at Cairo and Whigham, Georgia, in 1883.

During the years following his conversion in 1877 the young man showed inclination toward the ministry. While teaching at Groversville in 1879 he was licensed to preach and was recommended for the Georgia annual conference. In 1880 he was received into the itinerant ministry of the Georgia conference at Americus, and was assigned to the Groversville circuit. He was sent to the Boston circuit in 1881. His rise then became rapid. He was ordained deacon in 1882, and was appointed to Darien. That year, moreover, he was elected secretary of the Georgia conference and trustee of Morris Brown College. In 1884 he was ordained elder at Valdosta and appointed to Quitman where he served until 1886.

Flipper received his first important charge when he was transferred to the North Georgia Conference and assigned to the Bethel African Methodist Episcopal Church in Atlanta where his parents had attended and where he as a boy began his education. He appreciated the opportunity and made the most of it. During the four years of his service at this post he greatly increased the membership of the church and established a record for raising money that no other pastor exceeded for twenty-five years. He was desired longer in Atlanta, but the regulations of the African Methodists forbade a longer stay. He was sent in 1889 to Athens where he served three years, at the expiration of which he was appointed presiding elder in 1892. In 1895 he was assigned to the St. Paul African Methodist Episcopal Church in Atlanta.

Having served long as a teacher, he could not abandon the school room altogether. In 1903 he was called to the deanship of the Theological Department of Morris Brown College, and the following year he was made the head of the entire institution. Here again he made a fine record of enrolling the largest number of students in the history of the school and of elevating considerably the tone of that atmosphere during his four years of administration. His ability thus made manifest enabled him to reach the office of bishop for which he was chosen at the general conference of the African Methodist Episcopal Church in Norfolk in 1908. Assigned to the ninth Episcopal district, he did constructive work in both Oklahoma and Arkansas. He was next assigned to the sixth district which embraced his native home in Georgia. He showed his efficient leadership again in securing funds to build a new boys' dormitory at Morris Brown, in establishing Central Park Normal and Industrial Institute at Savannah, and in the purchase of ten acres of ground for Payne College at Cuthbert, Georgia. These he united as one system entitled Morris Brown University. He served also as bishop of the Florida diocese and of South Carolina.

While thus busily engaged with specific tasks Bishop Flipper served the Church and race in several other capacities. The most important of these wider activities were the chairmanship of the Episcopal Committee for four years and membership on the Financial Board for eight years. To stimulate his people toward thrift and economic independence he set the example of encouraging among them various enterprises. He was a stockholder of the Standard Life Insurance Company and both a stockholder and a director of the Atlanta State Savings Bank. In recognition of these services Allen University conferred upon him the degree of Doctor of Divinity in 1893 and Wilberforce University the degree of Doctor of Laws in 1906.

In 1880 Bishop Flipper married Amanda Slater of Thomasville, Georgia. One of his sons, the Reverend Carl F. Flipper is a prominent minister in the African Methodist Episcopal Church. Bishop Flipper was a brother of H. O. Flipper, the first Negro to be graduated by the West Point Military Academy.

WILLIAM JASPER HALE

William Jasper Hale was born at Retro, Tennessee, September 26, 1876 and died in New York City, October 5, 1944. He had been retired in 1943 as president of the Agricultural and State College, Nashville, Tennessee. He was educated in the local public schools of his community and at Maryville College in Tennessee. Until within the last generation this college, founded by mountaineers of the Scotch-Irish type, who became abolitionists in 1841 and did much to stimulate Unionism in East Tennessee during the Civil War, admitted Negroes. This school was somewhat like Berea College in Kentucky where state laws, as in Tennessee, later excluded Negroes.

Hale's first important service as an educator was as principal of the St. Elmo High School in Chattanooga, Tennessee. From that position he was called to be the president of the Agricultural and Industrial State College in Nashville. When he took charge the plant consisted of only a few frame buildings. Under his direction it developed into an institution of a score of modern buildings on 200 acres of land with provision for teaching the practical things of life in all their varying aspects. In fact, the plant became recognized as the pride of Nashville, one of the best equipped among the Land Grant Colleges of the country.

In view of his success as a builder of this modern educational plant he was called on at times to serve in various capacities such as president of the Conference of the Negro Land Grant Colleges, vice-president of the National Business League, honorary president Tennessee Association of Teachers in Colored Schools, chairman of the executive committee of the National Association of Teachers in Colored Schools, vice-president of the Citizens Bank and Trust Company of Nashville, and member of the local Negro Board of Trade. In 1930 he was awarded a medal by the Harmon Foundation in recognition of his services as an educator. As indicated by these posts at which he served he became an outstanding citizen of considerable means, and his cooperation was sought by all organizations interested in the advancement of the Negro.

Hale's important contribution was as a builder of the school over which he presided for almost two generations. He was not a scholar in the strict meaning of the word, but he had the vision to build in Nashville a plant which scholars may use to advantage in the years to come. Several times in his career he was attacked by those who found unbecoming conduct in his administration, but until 1943 they failed to muster enough influence to dislodge him from the position as head of the Agricultural and Industrial State College. Whatever these charges were they are not sufficient to overbalance the good which Hale accomplished at the post at which he so long served.

In 1912 Hale married Hattie Hodgkins who bore him three children: William J. Jr., Gwendolyn, and Edward, by whom he is survived.

JOSEPH SAMUEL CLARK

Joseph Samuel Clark, president emeritus of Southern University, died October 27, 1944. He was born in Sparta, Louisiana, June 7, 1871. He was the son of Philip and Jane Clark. On December 29, 1901 he married Octavia Head who bore him a son, Felton Grandison Clark. He succeeded his father as the head of Southern University.

Joseph Samuel Clark began his education in the Public Schools of Bienville Parrish and spent some time also studying privately in the same district. He studied at Coleman College, Bishop College, and finally attended Leland College from 1896 to 1901 when he received there the degree of Bachelor of Arts. He did some special work at Chicago and Harvard. Selma University, Leland College and the Arkansas Baptist College conferred upon him honorary degrees.

Clark spent most of his active life in education. He did not tarry long in the schoolroom before his ability as an administrator became manifest. In 1901 he was made head of Baton Rouge College and functioned thus until 1912. In 1913 he was called to the presidency of Southern University, the Negro Land Grant College of Louisiana at Scotlandville, and there he labored successfully until 1940 when he retired in favor of his son, a scholar who has already made a favorable impression in his field.

Joseph Samuel Clark was called to Southern University to undertake a new program in the education of the Negro in Louisiana. Under State Superintendent T. H. Harris, one of the first Southern white educators to take a stand for equal educational facilities for both races, Clark found the opportunity of his life. Appropriations large enough to offer qualified teachers salaries somewhat commensurate with their ability and to build a plant with modern equipment followed. The cooperation of the Rosenwald Fund with the State in building rural schoolhouses and securing better trained teachers for them helped to build up a more advanced school population on which Southern University could draw. The appropriations for the schools for the two races were not equalized, but the allowances allocated to Negro education were brought within closer proximity of equality than ever in the history of Negro education in the South. With the aid of Federal funds Southern University has been recently rebuilt as one of the most modern schools of its type in the United States. From a plant of two buildings worth about $100,000 the school has grown into modern institution with about forty buildings dotting 500 acres and about 60 instructors in charge of the varied activities of the school.

During these busy years Clark functioned as more than an educator. He was always active in fraternal and business circles and served in various capacities the agencies with which he became identified. Among the more important organizations with which he became identified were the National Business League, the Interracial Commission, the National Urban League, and the People's Life Insurance Company. In 1932 he was made president of the New Capitol Insurance Company of New Orleans. In all these extra efforts, however, Clark adhered to his calling as an educator and devoted most of his time and energy to the furtherance of educational work. He reorganized the Louisiana State Colored

Teachers Association and served it as president for eight years. He served for a year as president of the National Association of Teachers in Colored Schools and devoted both time and means to the development of this organization. In 1931 he was offered the position of Minister to Liberia, but declined the proposal because he preferred to continue his work at Southern University.

JAMES FRANKLIN LANE

On December 11, 1944 pasesd from this life James Franklin Lane, the president of Lane College at Jackson, Tennessee. He was born on February 18, 1874 the son of Isaac and Francis B. Lane, in the same city in which he died. At that time his father, the late Bishop Isaac Lane was engaged in the development of the Colored Methodist Episcopal Church in which he figured as an outstanding pioneer. The father founded in Jackson in 1879, Lane College of which the son was president when he died. The father lived more than a hundred years, but the son did not advance far beyond three score and ten.

James Franklin Lane began his education at Lane College. He completed the high school course offered there and next the normal course. He then finished at Walden College in Nashville the course leading to the degree of Bachelor of Arts which was awarded him in 1891. He later did some work at Harvard College in 1897. Walden awarded him the degree of Master of Arts in 1903. The young man began his career as teacher. He served as principal of the Panola High School in Sardis, Mississippi in 1896. He went to Lane College as an instructor in mathematics, but soon thereafter was appointed as the head of its department of education. He became president of the instution in 1907 and continued in this capacity until he died.

For years Lane College was mainly a high school with some theological and college work for the few students thus advanced, but as such it was for many years the largest school maintained by the Colored Methodist Episcopal Church. James Franklin Lane did much to improve the status of the school and to restrict it to the main purpose for which it was established—higher education. He found time also to travel considerably and wrote two works entitled *My Second Trip Abroad* and *Much in Little*.

MRS. FRANCES BOYCE

Recently the Association for the Study of Negro Life and History received $250.00 from the estate of Mrs. Frances Boyce who died June 7, 1943. Another small sum is expected from the distribution of the surplus from this estate. The staff is thankful that this lady, following the example of her late pastor, the Rev. Francis J. Grimké, remembered the Association as an undertaking deserving perpetuation. Mrs. Boyce's late husband, Stansbury Boyce, was likewise interested in the Association. One of the first things he did on moving from Jacksonville, Florida, to Washington, D. C. just before the First World War, was to connect himself with the Association as a life member. After his passing Mrs. Boyce manifested similar interest by making annual appropriations to the Association. It was fortunate that she and her companion had worked together successfully in Baltimore where they first started their career and later in Jacksonville, Florida, where as merchants they accumulated a small fortune. They had no children. With a considerable portion of their wealth they aided causes projected for the good of humanity.

Mrs. Boyce was active not only as a giver but as a participant in the various efforts of philanthropic agencies. She served for a long time as chairman of the committee charged with the affairs of the Phillis Wheatley Branch of the Young Women's Christian Association in Washington. She gave some attention also to the National Association for Advancement of Colored People. She was especially generous in her support of the Fifteenth Street Presbyterian Church of which she was a most faithful member.

THE JOURNAL
OF
NEGRO HISTORY

Vol. XXX—April, 1945—No. 2

THE UPGRADING OF THE NEGRO'S STATUS BY SUPREME COURT DECISIONS[*]

The first recorded issue of color in the social order came with the emergence of Christianity, and we seem never to have been able to free ourselves from its overwhelming influence from that time until the present. In the revelation of St. Peter at Joppa, it was declared that all races were of equal standing:

"Whom God hath cleansed, call not thou common or unclean."

This is the first statement of the doctrine of equality in terms of race.

In America, as in no other country of the world, the impact of two races of different color living together in large numbers developed forces that play upon and determine the conduct, behavior, attitude and philosophy, not only of the individual, but the state and nation, and these have been vitally important influences in developing national character as a whole from a political and social point of view.

For many years, therefore, so many in fact, we of the Negro race almost despaired of a change, it became almost

---

[*]Delivered by Raymond Pace Alexander, member of Philadelphia Bar, former President National Bar Assn., at the Annual Meeting of the Association for the Study of Negro Life and History on Sunday, October 29, 1944, in Faneuil Hall, Boston, Massachusetts.

117

an established fact that if America had any general policy
of race relations at all, it was one of racial segregation and
discrimination. This policy had its roots and background in
that soul destroying institution of slavery, a malignant
growth in democracy which, like the deadly disease that it
was, left its cancerous influences to spread to other parts of
the national body to cast up its ugly and poisonous head
in the civic, political and social life of America with increasing frequency.

Since 1865, the Negro people of America, and thousands
of their liberal and courageous white friends, have insisted
that a true democracy could be achieved for all people, regardless of color, and that there should be no citizens of
the "second class." But all of us know, regardless of how
we may try, that there are millions of people in America,
many of them of considerable wealth and influence, many
of whom occupy high places in our state and national government, and I deeply regret to say, in our churches, colleges, social welfare organizations and the like, who are still
unwilling to believe that democracy in America should em-
brace in theory *and practice* the Negro. We believe that the
frontiers of America consist of more than its physical geographical limits of land, from the Atlantic to the Pacific,
made up of mountains and valleys, forests and plains, rivers
and lakes. We believe that America has as well, a democratic frontier springing from its very national constitution and
its Bill of Rights which embraces its underlying socio-politi-
cal philosophy, which, by its very words and their inescapable meaning, were made to include all people regardless of
race or color.

It is the assault on these democratic frontiers that has
occupied the minds and attention of the leaders of Negro
life and actions, the organizations and associations for their
social, economic and political advancement, and, as concerns the subject of this paper particularly, the Negro lawyers of America.

That there has been a change, however, in the "conduct, behavior, attitude and philosophy" in the field of interracial relations and, in the last two decades, a pronounced advance and upgrading in the social, economic and political status of the Negro, there can be no denial. To what forces and influences may be credited this upgrading, and in what manner the field of law, the common law, federal statutes and federal directives contributed to this happy advance in race relations, may be answered in part in the following analysis.

It should be understood at the outset that what we call the great American Constitution, the body of laws adopted in 1787, does not mention civil rights at all. It was not until 1789, two years later, that what we familiarly call the Bill of Rights (the first ten Amendments to the Constitution) was adopted. The Declaration of Independence, which was preliminary to both the Constitution and the Bill of Rights, was in reality a Proclamation of Freedom; a Declaration from Englishmen in America against other Englishmen in the British Isles that they no longer could suffer the long series of abuses heaped upon them by the British Crown which acted as a tyrant, and that they therefore had the right, even the duty, to throw off such a yoke of government which was so oppressive and set up a new social order for the future of themselves and their posterity.

In 1787 when the discussion of the Bill of Rights (the first ten Amendments) was at its height, the delegates were concerned about the encroaching of the Federal Government on the power of the States. This was entirely natural because of the unhappy experiences of these men under the rule of the British Crown just recently shaken off. These ten Amendments therefore protected the *individual* against *government* or *federal* usurpation of power. Thus began, to the Negro's great loss and detriment, the theory of states' rights so frequently imbedded in the early laws and judicial decisions.

No one ever seemed to realize that the *individual* would soon need protection *against* the action of the *states* whose laws and acts were later designed to deny many millions of persons, the Negro people within their borders, the basic rights of citizenship.

For all practical purposes, because of the very small number of free Negroes in the United States at the time of the adoption of the Constitution and the Bill of Rights, it can be stated that the Negroes were not considered as a special class or any sizeable minority as such. After the War of Independence and the following period of adjustment, came the twenty years of heated sectional disputes between the North and the South on slavery and abolition, ending with the Civil War, the Emancipation Proclamation, and the three great War Amendments, the 13th, 14th and 15th, to the Federal Constitution.

The 13th Amendment, adopted in 1865, abolished slavery as well as involuntary servitude throughout the country. The 14th Amendment endowed the Negro with citizenship in the United States and the several states in which he resided. The 14th Amendment was passed in 1866. The 15th Amendment (passed in 1870 when the Ku Klux Klan was at its height) provided that it was unlawful for any state to deny the citizen the right to vote.

Now began the long struggle of a nation of people of one color, representing roughly 10 per cent of the population, within a nation of people of another color, representing the other 90 per cent of the population for social, economic and political adjustment between these two groups.

To whom did these newly created citizens look for the protection of these newly created rights, who just yesterday were held in bondage as chattels by the laws and customs of the states in which they lived? To the states? Manifestly not, but to their new creator of these rights, the Federal Government. Then suddenly, these great sons of early patriots, whose forefathers a few generations previously had fought a bloody war to free themselves from the very yokes and obstacles to freedom, the like of which these new citizens of color were seeking, used all sorts of devices, tenuous and specious arguments to deny these new freed men the privileges and immunities of citizenship which were so recently accorded them.

The path to advancement and upgrading of the American Negro was a long and arduous one fraught with the drama of hopes fulfilled to be later destroyed by one device or another by acts not alone of the legislatures of the former slave-holding states, but by the federal legislature and the courts themselves.

Without going into detail to support the last mentioned statement because of the length of the subject, there were five statutes passed by Congress after the war known as the Civil Rights Bills which were enacted to strengthen the 13th, 14th and 15th Amendments and the enforcement of the same by an elaborate program of federal supervision designed to protect the freedmen in all their basic and fundamental civil and political rights.

The first decision of the Supreme Court of the United States interpreting the 14th Amendment of the Constitution was in the famous Slaughterhouse Cases, The Butchers' Benevolent Association of New Orleans *versus* the Crescent City Livestock Company, et al, 83 U. S. 36 (1872). This decision showed how quickly the *Supreme Court* attempted, and successfully so, to whittle away the protection that was so valiantly fought for and incorporated in our Constitution and Bill of Rights after a great and bitter struggle. In this divided opinion by a none too learned justice, Mr. Justice Samuel F. Miller, the court gave the narrowest possible construction to the 14th Amendment and held that this Amendment protected rights springing from Federal citizenship, and the decision held that *Federal citizenship* was different from *state citizenship* and *rights* inherent in *State citizenship* were not subject to the protection of the 14th Amendment.

The facts of this case did not even directly or indirectly have anything to do with the Negro. It was solely and exclusively the construction of a statute of the State of Louisiana granting a monopoly to one corporation for the slaughtering of animals over a wide area. The court held that the state had enforced a valid exercise of its police power in protecting the health of the people of the state. It would seem, as professors of this branch of the law have stated time and again in trying to understand this decision, that the 14th Amendment was not even involved in this case. Mr. Justice Miller wrote the opinion for the majority of five, but a most brilliant, able and very exhaustive dissenting opinion was filed by Mr. Justice Fields, in which the Chief Justice Salmon P. Chase and Mr. Justices Bradley and Swayne joined. These Justices attacked the reasoning of the majority as "tenuous and specious." This was the era termed by the Negroes "Knocking at Closed Courtroom Doors."

Gradually, by narrow construction mostly on the opinions of a divided court, especially in the famous Civil Rights cases in which Negroes brought prosecution in their various states for discrimination on the railroads, in theaters, hotels, etc., the Supreme Court held these and like statutes unconstitutional, thereby taking from the purpose of these fine enforcement acts the very vitals and underlying reasons for which these great equalitarian laws were passed, over the hostile objections of a large minority in the Congress. (See the "Civil Rights" cases, viz. U. S. *vs.* Stanley (Kentucky), U. S. *vs.* Ryan (California), U. S. *vs.* Nichols (Missouri), U. S. *vs.* Singleton (New York), Robertson *et. ux. vs.* Memphis & Charleston Railway (Tennessee) 109 U. S. (1883). The majority opinions in the Civil Rights cases were written by Mr. Justice Bradley, who held that the Civil Rights cases were unconstitutional.

There was a single minority opinion by the great and learned Justice John M. Harlan. This opinion reads like the present majority opinions of the brilliant Justices of the Supreme Court as it is composed today, and would do justice to the great legal philosopher now among the departed, the late Mr. Justice Oliver Wendell Holmes, and the other two members of that brilliant triumvirate of dissenters, the late Mr. Justice Louis D. Brandeis and Mr. Justice Benjamin N. Cardozo.

Mr. Justice Harlan stated the following: "I cannot resist the conclusion that the substance and spirit of the recent Amendments to the Constitution have been sacrificed by a subtle and ingenious verbal criticism. . . . Congress has power to enforce by appropriate legislation the provisions of this Article. . . . Was it the purpose of the nation simply to destroy the institution of slavery and then remit the race, heretofore held in bondage, to the several states for such protection, in their civil rights, as those states, in their discretion might choose to provide? . . . I insist that the National Legislature may, without transcending the limits of the Constitution, do for human liberty and the fundamental rights of American Citizenship, what it did, with the sanction of this court, for the protection of slavery and the rights of the master of fugitive slaves." (Justice Harlan was obviously referring to the case of Dred Scott (Dred Scott *vs.* Sandford, 60 U. S. 393) (1856.).

It seems to be conclusive and inescapable, therefore, that the safest and most certain guaranty of justice is the personality of the judge or judges who pass on the merits of a particular case. His intellectual and spiritual honesty and integrity and his moral courage are the tests upon which the future of the people, state or nation, may eventually depend. With the decision just mentioned and the legion of cases following, there was but a single voice in the deep wilderness, growing weaker as the strain of years bore heavily upon him, that spoke up in support of the then five mil-

lion people of the darker races for whom the majority of
Congress framed the 13th, 14th and 15th Amendments in
order that they might achieve and enjoy the full rights
of American citizenship. That was the voice of Mr. Justice
John M. Harlan. It was not until a new voice ascended to
the Supreme Court bench that a new philosophy of thought
began to find utterance in behalf of the under-privileged
and the minorities of all races, colors and creeds in this
great commonwealth of states. That voice was the voice of
the great judicial scholar and philosopher, the late distinguished jurist, Oliver Wendell Holmes of Massachusetts.

During the earlier years of Mr. Justice Holmes' tenure
on the bench, Mr. Chief Justice White and Mr. Justice Day
were often heard in brilliant decisions in support of the
issues about which the subject of this paper treats. This
was the era of "Cracking the Courtroom Doors."

THE RIGHT TO VOTE

It was not until about the year 1918 that the Negro began to obtain a favorable audience and a sympathetic ear in
our Federal Supreme Court. The first successful case was
that involving the attack on the famous Grandfather
Clauses in the southern states, notably the case of Guinn vs.
United States, 238 U. S. 347 (1915) in an opinion by Mr.
Chief Justice White. The facts of the case are briefly as
follows: In the year 1910 the Constitution of Oklahoma was
amended, restricting the franchise or the right to vote by
what is known as a "Grandfather Clause," which provided
that no person could be registered unless he was able to
read and write. In addition, the clause provided that should
a person be denied the right to vote because he could not
read or write, if he lived in some foreign country prior to
January 1, 1866, or if he was eligible to register prior to
that date, or if his lineal ancestor was eligible as of that
date, then he was exempted and could register and vote. Of
course, before 1866 Negroes were not eligible to vote at all,

so the law very definitely and pointedly disfranchised the Negroes. As a result of the failure to allow Negroes to vote, certain of the election officials were indicted under the Constitution provision. Eventually the case reached the Federal Supreme Court at a time when several other states had similar cases pending covering the very same type of Grandfather Clauses. The decision in the instant case was decisive of all cases awaiting judicial interpretation. Mr. Chief Justice White, writing for the majority of the court, outlawed this statute as clearly unconstitutional with the following biting words:

". . . While this piece of legislation contains no express words of an exclusion, from the standard which it establishes, of any persons on account of race, color or previous condition of servitude prohibited by the 15th Amendment, . . . *the standard itself inherently brings that result to existence since it is based purely on a period of time before the enactment of the 15th Amendment and makes that period the controlling and dominant test of the right of suffrage.*"

This ended for quite a long while the attempts on the part of the various southern states to deny Negroes the right to register and vote at the primary and in the general election. It was not until some years later, which I shall discuss in a moment, that the famous Texas Primary Cases came before the Supreme Court with varying results until a most recent case which outlawed as unlawful and a violation of the Federal Constitution all such attempts to deny the Negro his right to vote.

Cases Involving Neighborhood Segregation

The right of people of color to purchase property and freely enjoy the rights of citizenship in a city or state by building or owning property and living therein in the various sections of a city or state without discrimination or segregation has always been one in which the Negro has encountered great difficulties. A particularly important decision in the United States Supreme Court involving this very question was the case of Buchannan *vs.* Warley, 245 U. S. 16 (1917), known as the "Louisville Segregation Case." The facts briefly are as follows:

A colored man by the name of Buchannan bought a piece of property in the City of Louisville, Kentucky, and when the seller refused to settle when Buchannan tendered his money, he filed a bill for specific performance for the contract of sale. The defendant stated that Buchannan was a Negro and by virtue of an Ordinance of the City of Louisville he would be unable to occupy the land in a white block. Buchannan stated that the Ordinance was in conflict with the 14th Amendment of the Federal Constitution, but the Court of Appeals of Kentucky held that the Ordinance was valid on the ground that the Ordinance prohibited whites from living in Negro neighborhoods and Negroes from living in white neighborhoods, and any violation was punishable by criminal prosecution.

The Supreme Court of the United States in an opinion by Mr. Justice Day reversed the Court of Appeals of Kentucky and held:

"As we have seen, this court has held laws valid which separate races on the basis of equal accommodations in public conveyances, the courts of high authorities have held enactments lawful which provide for the separation in public schools of white and colored pupils where equal privileges are given. But in view of the right secured by the 14th Amendment of the Federal Constitution, such legislation must have its limitations, *and cannot be sustained where the exercise of authority exceeds the restraints of this Constitution.*

"We think these limitations are exceeded in laws and ordinances of the character now before us.

". . . It is said that such acquisitions by colored people depreciate property owned in the neighborhood by white people. But property may be acquired by undesirable white neighbors or put to disagreeable uses . . . with like results.

"We think this attempt to prevent the alienation of the property in question to a person of color was not a legitimate exercise of the police power of the state, and it is a violation of the fundamental law enacted in the 14th Amendment of the Constitution preventing state interference with property rights except by due process of law. The Ordinance cannot stand."

This was the old equal but separate theory. While the Negro was very happy to get this decision from the Supreme Court outlawing this Louisville Ordinance, nevertheless there was much danger in the phraseology of Mr. Justice Day, particularly in the first paragraph just mentioned. ". . . This court has held laws valid which separate the races on the basis of equal accommodations in public conveyances . . . and for the separation in the public schools of white and colored pupils. . . ." These statements of the learned justice came back to haunt the Negro in later appeals to the Supreme Court in cases involving the separation of races in public conveyances and the separation of white and colored pupils in public schools, and gave to a none too willing majority judicial excuse for the support of much discriminatory legislation.

RIGHT OF FAIR TRIAL

Following the decisions of our highest court, in chronological order, in order that we may more easily trace the development of sentiment in the upgrading of the Negro in his quest for the full rights of citizenship, the next important case in his long and hard fight for citizenship through judicial interpretations and judicial fiat was the famous Elaine, Arkansas, Riot Cases (Moore *vs.* Dempsey, 261 U. S. 86 (1923). The opinion of the majority was rendered by Mr. Justice Oliver Wendell Holmes. A group of Negro farmers were holding a meeting in Philips County, Arkansas, for the purpose of organizing and pooling their means as well as their thoughts to obtain a better price for their crops. They were meeting in a colored church at Elaine, Arkansas, in October, 1919. During the course of the meeting they were fired upon by a group of white men from the outside. As a result of the clash a riot took place, many of the Negroes fighting back for the protection of their own lives, and in the course of the melee some whites were killed.

Seventy-nine Negro men were arrested and tried for murder. It was only after a great deal of difficulty and the presence of United States Troops that a great mob of people who had marched to the jail for the purpose of lynching these men, were prevented from so doing under a promise by members of a local committee who called themselves the "Vigilantes" that, "if the mob would refrain from their attempts to lynch these men, they would execute those found guilty in the form of law." There were many Negro witnesses who were ready to testify in behalf of their fellowmen, but the mob had whipped them so and placed them under such fear of their lives that they agreed to testify against the men if they were given their freedom.

These seventy-nine men were brought to trial in an atmosphere completely controlled by mob violence, under the threat to lynch these defendants if the jury did not convict them. The court appointed counsel for the men, which counsel failed to ask for a change of venue and called no witnesses in defense of the Negroes, and only one of them was placed upon the stand by their counsel. The trial of the entire seventy-nine men lasted less than one hour, and the jury brought back a verdict in five minutes after it had received instructions, finding all of the men guilty of murder; twelve were sentenced to death and sixty-seven were sentenced to long prison terms.

The Supreme Court of Arkansas sustained the conviction and then an appeal to the United States Supreme Court followed.

Mr. Justice Holmes, in reversing the opinion of the Supreme Court, had this to say:

"In Frank vs. Mangum, 237 U. S. 309 (the famous Leo Frank Case) . . . it was recognized . . . that if in fact a trial is dominated by a mob so that there is an actual interference with the course of justice, there is a departure from due process of law; and that if the state supplying no corrective process, carries into execution a judgment of death or imprisonment based upon a verdict thus produced by mob domination, the state deprives the accused of his life or liberty without 'due process of law.' . . . If the case is such that the whole proceeding is a mask that counsel, jury and judge were swept to the fatal end by an irresistible wave of public passion, and that the state courts failed to correct the wrong, neither perfection in the machinery for correction nor the possibility that the trial court and counsel saw no other way of avoiding an immediate outbreak of the mob, can prevent this court from securing to the petitioners their constitutional rights.''

In chronological order again, the Supreme Court, in the famous New Orleans Segregation Case (Harmon *vs*. Tyler, 273 U. S. 668 (1926), reversed in a per curiam decision the attempt on the part of the City of New Orleans to set up segregated districts for colored people in which only colored could live and white districts in which white only could live, on the authority of Buchannan *vs*. Warley, above referred to.

I have already referred to the devious methods by which the southern states attempted to deny the Negro the right to vote in their various Democratic primary elections in discussing the Oklahoma Grandfather Clause Cases. The first famous Texas primary case was that of Nixon *vs*. Herndon, 273 U. S. 536 (1927) in which Mr. Justice Holmes denied the right of the state of Texas to refuse a Negro, Doctor L. A. Nixon, the privilege of voting and participating in a Democratic party election held in the State of Texas. Of course, the Supreme Court of Texas sustained the right of the election board to refuse Dr. Nixon. He carried his case to the Supreme Court, and this is what Mr. Justice Holmes had to say:

''The Statute of Texas in the case referred to assumes to forbid Negroes to take part in the primary election, the importance of which we have indicated, discriminating against them by the distinction of color alone. States may do a good deal of classifying that is difficult to believe rational, but there are limits, and it is too clear for extended argument that color cannot be made the basis of a statutory classification affecting the rights set up in this case.''

There followed in 1930 a per curiam decision sustaining the Supreme Court of Virginia in outlawing a Richmond

Segregation Case of the same type discussed heretofore in the Louisville and New Orleans Segregation Cases. This was the case of the City of Richmond *vs.* Deans, 281 U. S. 704 (1930), and it is refreshing to know that the Supreme Court of Virginia decided that the Richmond Ordinance was unconstitutional.

Not to be outdone by the first Texas primary case, the State of Texas promptly passed a new statute empowering the State Democratic Committee to set up its own limitations in primary elections, immediately after the decision of the Federal Supreme Court in the famous case of Nixon *vs.* Herndon, supra. The State of Texas Executive Committee of the Democratic Party adopted the resolution "that all white Democrats who were qualified under the Constitution and Laws of Texas . . . and *none others* shall be allowed to participate in the primary elections of the State of Texas." Dr. Nixon, also determined not to be outdone by this devious method of circumventing the decision of the highest court of the land, again presented himself to the election officials in his district to qualify to vote in the Democratic primary. Being refused this privilege, he immediately brought suit for damages in the federal courts under the Civil Rights Statute. The case was dismissed in the lower court and taken to the United States Supreme Court, and it is to be noted that four members of our Federal Supreme Court, Justices McReynolds, VanDevanter, Sutherland and Butler, dissented from the opinion of the majority, thereby making the voice of one lone person on the Supreme Bench the determining factor in deciding whether or not State Democratic Committees in the Southern States should disfranchise nine million Negroes within their borders. Mr. Justice Cardozo, speaking for the majority of the court, in the customary beautiful and brilliantly turned phrases of which he was an acknowledged master, said the following:

"Barred from voting at a primary, the petitioner has been, and this for the sole reason that his color is not white. The result for him is no different from what it was when his cause was here before. The argument for the respondent (Texas Democratic Committee) is, however, that identity of result has been attained though through essential diversity of methods. We are reminded that the 14th Amendment is the restraint upon the state and not upon private persons unconnected with a state. . . . With the problem thus laid bare and its essentials exposed to view, the cases seem to be ruled by Nixon vs. Herndon. . . . Delegates of the states . . . have discharged their official functions in such a way as to discriminate invidiously between white citizens and black. The 14th Amendment, adopted as it was with special solicitude for the equal protection of members of the Negro race, lays a duty upon the court to level by its judgment these barriers of color."

The Right to Be Called for Jury Service and The Right of Representation by Counsel

A most important series of cases were argued in the Supreme Court on the right of the Negro to serve on both the trial jury and the grand jury in the various states in the south. Perhaps the most important of these cases was the famous "Scottsboro Case" (Powell vs. Alabama, 287 U. S. 45 (1932).

In this case the fundamental questions of the right of an accused to be represented by counsel was thoroughly considered by the Court. The Supreme Court held that the right to counsel meant the right of the accused to have an opportunity to confer with his counsel, the right to subpoena witnesses and compel them to appeal at trial, the right to have an adequate opportunity to prepare his case for trial and to be heard both by himself and his counsel in the latter's right to address the court and jury in his behalf.

In the second trip of this same case to the Supreme Court the questions of the continuous and systematic exclusion of Negroes from service on the grand and petit juries of the state of Alabama came up for review. This court, in 1935 (Norris vs. Alabama, 294 U. S. 587, 55 S. St. 579, and the companion case of Paterson vs. Alabama, 294 U. S. 600; 55 S. Ct. 575) declared such practice to be illegal restraint

upon these constitutional rights and a denial of due process
to the Negro defendant, and again reversed the conviction
of the court of Alabama. (See Strauder *vs.* West Virginia
(1879) 100 U. S. 339; Neal *vs.* Delaware (1880), 103 U. S.
370.)

FREEDOM OF SPEECH AND ASSEMBLY

In the case of Herndon *vs.* Lowery, 301 U. S. 242, decided in 1937, the question of the constitutionality of an old
Georgia statute against insurrection was called in question.
Here, a young Negro named Angelo Herndon was charged
with distributing literature of the Communist Party in a
rural Georgia town in which literature he urged the Negro
farmer and share-cropper to organize for their protection
and to attend meetings sponsored by the Communist Party.
He was tried and convicted under the old Georgia insurrection statute and sentenced to life imprisonment. The United States Supreme Court held this statute unconstitutional
as an unreasonable limitation to freedom of speech and assembly in violation of the due process clause of the Federal Constitution, in that the statute was too vague and
failed to furnish a sufficiently ascertainable standard of
guilt.

THE TEXAS PRIMARY DECISION
UPHOLDING THE WHITE PRIMARY

The State of Texas finally achieved a victory in its attempt to disfranchise the million Negroes within its borders
in the case of Grovey *vs.* Townsend, 295 U. S. 45, decided
in 1936. This victory, however, as disastrous as it was in
the pursuit of the Negro in his march to full citizenship,
was, happily for the cause of American democracy, only a
temporary one. It did last, however, eight years, from 1936
to April, 1944, when the recent case of Smith *vs.* Allwright
et al (decided April 3, 1944) was handed down by a strong
majority opinion of 8 and only one dissent.

The Supreme Court in the Grovey Case, in an opinion

by Mr. Justice Owen W. Roberts, sustained the right of the Texas State Democratic Committee to set up qualifications of persons to vote in the Democratic Primary Election. It made no difference whether these persons were to vote in State or Federal elections. The Court said that the Texas Democratic Convention was not a State agency, and though the laws of the State of Texas provided how and when State Primaries would be held, yet this did not make the Texas State Democratic Convention a State agency, and that it could, similarly to a private club, regulate who should be admitted as members.

The case of Jeff Hollins (Hollins vs. Oklahoma, 295 U. S. 204 (1935)) presented another issue of the Right to be Represented by Counsel on the second trial of this case. The facts are very interesting and can be briefly stated as follows: The defendant, Hollins, was convicted December 29, 1931, at a trial which was held in the basement of the prison in Sapula, Oklahoma. He was charged with rape. There was no lawyer appointed for him and none to advise him on his rights and none to represent him at trial. He was found guilty of murder and sentenced to death. A stay of execution was had three days before his scheduled execution. The Supreme Court of Oklahoma reversed this conviction and sent it back for a new trial.

At the second trial of the case, the question was raised in the lower court and argued in the United States Supreme Court on the question of a systematic exclusion of Negroes from service on the jury panel to try this defendant. The Supreme Court in a per curiam decision on the basis of earlier decisions declared this to be a denial of due process and therefore the conviction to be void.

Forced Confession of Defendants by Physical Violence

The extortion of confessions by force, physical torture, threats and violence upon defendants charged in criminal cases has given rise to a long series of cases in the various southern states, many of which have been appealed to the highest federal tribunal. The most noteworthy of these cases, and the one that has given a strong admonition to the states that have been guilty of such conduct, is the case of Brown, Ellington and Shields *vs.* State of Mississippi (297 U. S. 278 (1936)). In this case the defendants were indicted for the murder of one Raymond Stewart in April of 1934. They entered pleas of not guilty. The court appointed counsel to defend them and they were found guilty and sentenced to death.

The only evidence that the state had against these defendants was an alleged confession which it was shown was obtained through force and physical torture. When these defendants were arrested and denied the crime, the sheriff hanged one of the defendants by a rope to a tree, and then when he was released just before strangulation, he was tied to the tree and severely beaten. When he refused to "confess," he was permitted to return home, but was later seized and whipped severely until he agreed to "confess." This confession was used at the trial and was the only evidence against the defendants. At the time of the trial Ellington stated he was tortured and produced evidence, showing the marks of the rope around his neck which were still visible at the time of the trial. The sheriff admitted the whipping of Ellington and very boldly stated that he "did not think he had whipped him too much for a Negro and not as much as I would have done if it were left to me." Other witnesses admitted that they had beaten the defendant into submission, but the Supreme Court of Mississippi affirmed the judgment of death.

Mr. Chief Justice Hughes, however, speaking for the United States Supreme Court, said the following in reversing the Supreme Court of Mississippi:

"The rack and torture chamber may not be substituted for the witness stand. It would be difficult to conceive of methods more revolting to the sense of justice than those taken to procure the confessions of these petitioners, and the use of the confessions thus obtained as the basis for a conviction and sentence was a clear denial of due process.

"The duty of maintaining the constitutional rights of a person on trial for his life rises above mere rules of procedure and whenever the court is clearly satisfied that such violations exist, it will refuse to sanction such and will apply the corrective."

In Hale *vs.* Kentncky (303 U. S. 613 (1938)), the Supreme Court, in a per curiam decision, sustained the right of a Negro on trial for his life in Kentucky to have members of his own race called for service on the jury selected to try him for a criminal offense. In this case the defendant proved that the jury commissioners had demonstrated a long continued, unvarying and wholesale exclusion of Negroes from jury service in that county on account of their race and color, and for no other reason. He was convicted of murder and sentenced to die. The Supreme Court of Kentucky affirmed the appeal, but the United States Supreme Court reversed the decision which re-established the principle that a systematic and arbitrary exclusion of Negroes from jury service, solely on account of their race and color, constituted a denial of the equal protection of the laws guaranteed by the 14th Amendment.

THE EQUAL RIGHT TO EDUCATION IN STATE SUPPORTED UNIVERSITY

Perhaps one of the most important and far-reaching cases in the history of the fight of the Negro for a full citizenship status that has ever been carried to the Supreme Court, is the famous case in the State of Missouri, in the matter of Missouri, *ex rel.* Gaines *vs.* Canada, *et al.* (Lloyd Gaines *vs.* University of Missouri) (305 U. S. 337). Lloyd Gaines was a young Negro with excellent qualifications who attempted to enter the University of Missouri Law School, but was refused solely because of his race or color. Asserting that this refusal was a denial by the state of Missouri of the equal protection of the laws in violation of the 14th

Amendment, he brought an action of mandamus to compel
the University to admit him. He was urged by the University of Missouri officials to accept a scholarship that the
state was willing to offer, to send him outside of the State
of Missouri for study. This he refused to do. Then the University defended on the ground that the local Negro University (Lincoln University) offered a law course which was
then in preparation and would be ready in the very near
future. The lower court as well as the Supreme Court of
Missouri dismissed the petition for mandamus. The Supreme Court, however, in a decision by Mr. Chief Justice
Hughes, from which there were two dissenting opinions, reversed the Supreme Court of Missouri and held the action
of the University of Missouri to be a denial of due process.
The dissenting Justices were Mr. Justices McReynolds and
Butler. The majority opinion of Chief Justice Hughes
stressed the following points:

"The basic consideration is not as to what sort of opportunities
other states provide, or whether they are as good as the State of
Missouri, but as to what opportunities Missouri itself furnishes to
white students and denies to Negroes solely upon the ground of
color. The admissibility of laws separating the races and the enjoyment of privileges afforded by the state rests wholly upon the equality of the privileges which the laws give to the separated groups
within the state. The question here is not of a duty of a state to
supply legal training or the equality of training which it does supply, but of its duty when it does supply such training to furnish it
to the residents of the state upon the basis of an equality of right.
By the operation of the laws of Missouri, a privilege has been created for white law students which is denied to Negroes by reason
of their race alone. The white resident is afforded legal education
within the state. The Negro resident, having the same qualification,
is refused this and must go outside of the state to obtain it. That is
the denial of the equality of legal right to the enjoyment of the
privilege which the state has set up and the provision for the payment of tuition fees in another state does not remove the discrimination.

"Here, the petitioner's right is a personal one. It was as an individual that he was entitled to the equal protection of the laws, and
the state was bound to furnish him within its borders facilities for
legal education substantially equal to those which the state there

afforded for persons of the white race, whether or not other Negroes sought the same opportunities.''

This was one of the most brilliant, courageous and forceful statements supporting the fundamental purpose of the 14th Amendment that has ever been declared by our Supreme Court.

OPENING OF COURTROOM DOORS

Following this case the complexion of the Supreme Court radically changed. It was shortly after this case, through the death and resignation of several of these Justices of the Supreme Court, that the hand of the present Chief Executive was strongly felt in placing new, younger and liberal minds on the bench of our highest tribunal. With the elevation of Mr. Chief Justice Stone and the appointment by President Roosevelt of Justices (1) Reed, (2) Black, (3) Frankfurter, (4) Murphy, (5) Jackson, (6) Douglas and (7) Rutledge, with the sole remaining conservative being Mr. Justice Roberts from Pennsylvania, there is at present a group of Justices to whom the Negroes of America can look for the most sympathetic, broad and liberal construction of not only the Amendments to the Constitution for whose benefit they were passed, but to a favorable construction of the remaining Civil Rights Statutes and all cases affecting the political, civil, social and economic rights that the Negro and all minorities may from time to time present to this court for interpretation. The fears of the Negroes as to how Mr. Justice Black would decide cases involving their fundamental rights were immediately dispelled upon his filing the now famous opinion in the case of Chambers *vs.* Florida, 309 U. S. 227 (1940). In this case four Negroes were charged with murder and convicted. Their cases were appealed five times to the Supreme Court of Florida. After the fifth appeal, the case was carried to the United States Supreme Court. Mr. Justice Black, on behalf of the United States Supreme Court, reversed the conviction of these men on the ground that the confessions used to convict them were extorted by force and violence. In his opinion, Mr. Justice Black stated:

". . . Today, as in ages past, we are not without tragic proof that the exalted power of some government to punish manufactured crime dictatorially is the handmaid of tyranny. Under our constitutional system courts stand against any winds that blow as havens of refuge for those who might otherwise suffer because they are helpless, weak, outnumbered, or because they are non-conforming victims of prejudice and public excitement. Due process of law . . . commands that no such practice as that disclosed by this record shall send any accused to his death. No higher duty, no more solemn responsibility rests upon this court, than that of translating into living law and maintaining this constitutional shield deliberately planned and inscribed for the benefit of every human being subject to our constitution, of whatever race, creed or persuasion."

Several cases involving the civil rights of Negroes were decided within a year or two after the elevation of the above-mentioned Justices to the Supreme Court bench, and all were decided favorably to the cause of the litigants. These cases were Canty vs. Alabama, 309 U. S. 629 (1940) in which the Supreme Court reversed a decision of the lower court of Alabama and its Supreme Court, ordering a new trial for the defendant charged with murder, thus voiding a death sentence of the State of Alabama because of irregularities in the trial of the lower court.

White vs. Texas, 309 U. S. 631 (1940). The Supreme Court granted a writ of certiorari and reversed on authority of previous cases, the conviction and sentence to death from the State of Texas.

RESTRICTIVE COVENANTS RESULTING IN RESIDENTIAL SEGREGATIONS

Earlier we have seen that the Supreme Court has outlawed residential discrimination by city ordinances (Buchannan vs. Warley, 245 U. S. 60 (1917).

In the case of Lee vs. Hansberry, U. S. 61, S. Ct. 521, 70 L. Ed. 969 (1940), the respondent, Hansberry, a Negro, bought some land in Chicago's so-called restricted area. This property was covered by a restriction against use by colored persons by a covenant or contract signed by a large majority of the adjoining property owners. The Illinois Supreme Court ruled the covenant to be valid and that the Negro purchasers could not occupy the land in question. The Federal Supreme Court reversed the Illinois Court and held that the Negro purchasers were not bound by this agreement to which they had not been a party, and to hold them so bound was a denial of due process.

(It should be stated here, however, that the flat issue of the validity of such contracts or restrictive covenants was not altogether before the court and therefore not squarely and satisfactorily settled.)

RAILROAD DISCRIMINATIONS

The case of Congressman Mitchell *vs.* Chicago, Rock Is. & Pac. Ry., U. S. 61 S. Ct. 873, 85 L. Ed. 811 (1941), deserves attention here. It will be recalled that former Chief Justice Hughes, then an Associate Justice, in the case of McCabe *vs.* Atchison, Topeka and Santa Fe R. R., 235 U. S. 151, in 1914, said in supporting the separate coach law of a state, that whenever the case came before this Court of an exclusion of the Negro travelling interstate from service on sleeping cars, parlor cars on dining cars, even where the demand for such service was too small to make profitable equal facilities, the court would grant relief.

Congressman Arthur Mitchell, Negro Democratic representative from Illinois, gave the Supreme Court the opportunity to fulfill that statement of Mr. Justice Hughes, made in 1914. And the Supreme Court did not fail to adhere to its promise. The facts in this case disclosed that the Negro Congressman was denied Pullman accommodations on a trip from Chicago to Hot Springs, Arkansas after the train entered Arkansas and was made to leave the Pullman and go into a 2nd class Jim Crow coach provided for colored passengers only. Mr. Chief Justice Hughes said for the Court:

"This was manifestly a discrimination against him in the course of his interstate journey and admittedly that discrimination was based solely upon the fact that he was a Negro. The question whether this was a discrimination forbidden by the Interstate Commerce Act is not a question of segregation but equality of treatment. The denial to appellant equality of accommodations because of his race would be an invasion of a fundamental right which is guaranteed against state actions by the 14th Amendment."

In Ward *vs*. Texas, 316 U. S. 547 (1942), Mr. Justice Byrnes, since retired from the bench, set aside a conviction of the lower court of Texas on the ground that the confession admitted in evidence, allegedly signed by the accused, was the result of force and violence.

JURY EXCLUSION

In Hill *vs*. Texas, 316 U. S. 400 (1942), Mr. Chief Justice Stone reaffirmed the principle that "equal protection of laws is more than an abstract right. It is a command which the state must respect for benefits of which every person may demand. Not the least merit of our constitutional system is that it safeguards and extends to all—the least deserving as well as the most virtuous." This was a case involving the systematic exclusion of Negroes from the jury panel in the county where this case was tried.

In the United States *vs*. Adams, Bordenave and Mitchell, 319 U. S. 312 (1943), Mr. Justice Black, on a question raised by the three defendants who were members of the armed forces of the country, sentenced to death under an alleged crime on a civilian woman within the camp confines of Camp Claiborne, Louisiana, reversed the conviction of these men on the ground that the federal courts of the State of Louisiana had no jurisdiction and released these three defendants from the custody of the civilian authorities to the army for further proceedings as the case warranted.

The last decision of the Supreme Court affecting the Negro's civil rights was decided on April 3, 1944, and this is the now famous case known as the Texas Primary Case, Smith *vs.* Allwright, *et al.*

Eight of the nine Justices of the Supreme Court decided in favor of the voter, Dr. Loney E. Smith, the single dissent, being by Mr. Justice Roberts, who wrote the opinion of the Supreme Court in the Grovey *vs.* Townsend case just referred to, allowing such denial of right to vote. This case began in Houston, Texas, in 1941 and was an action for damages for the refusal to permit qualified Negro voters to vote in the Democratic primary election in Texas. The case was based upon a violation of the 14th and 15th Amendments and the Federal Civil Rights Statutes. As was expected, the lower Texas court ruled against Dr. Smith. The United States Circuit Court of Appeals sustained the lower court, but the Supreme Court of the United States overruled its former decision by expressly stating so, and for all times declared the case of Grovey *vs.* Townsend, which sustained the State of Texas in its attempt to outlaw Negro voters, to be void. Mr. Justice Reed stated:

"The United States is a constitutional democracy. Its organic law grants to all citizens a right to participate in the choice of election officials without restrictions by any state because of race. This grant to the people of the opportunity for choice is not to be nullified by a state through casting its electoral process in a form which permits a private organization to practice racial discrimination in the election. Constitutional rights would be of little value if they could be thus indirectly denied."

Civil Rights Prosecution

A new section of the Department of Justice known as the Civil Rights Section has given light to the remaining Civil Rights Statute and has actively engaged in the enforcing of the conspiracy section in these various codes, particularly all cases involving the interference of the right to vote and anti-peonage laws.

The United States *vs.* Classic, 313 U. S. 299, and United

States *vs.* Saylor, decided May 22, 1924, and Taylor *vs.* Georgia, 313 U. S. 25, and Pollock *vs.* Williams, decided April 10, 1944, are all cases in which the Civil Rights Unit in the Criminal Division of the Department of Justice actively prosecuted, as a result of which our Supreme Court decided that Labor Contract Statutes of Georgia and Florida, which lean towards peonage conditions and involuntary servitude, were declared unconstitutional. These cases placed the right to freedom from involuntary servitude on such a broad base, that the way had been opened to an attack on the "enticing labor" and "emigrant agents" statutes, and some of the vagrancy statutes and "work or fight" orders, which experience has proved to be in reality, indirect means of enforcing involuntary servitude, especially against Negro farmhands and laborers.

ECONOMIC ACTION AT LAW

I have deliberately removed from the chronological order involving the Negro a very interesting and far-reaching case that represented the first case involving the attempt by Negroes to force businesses that have many customers among Negroes, to employ Negroes among their personnel. This was the case of the New Negro Alliance *vs.* Sanitary Grocery Co., 303 U. S. 552; 58 S. Ct. 703, decided in 1938. Here, an association of individuals, organizing themselves together as a group interested in seeking to uplift themselves economically and provide jobs at the time of widespread unemployment for their members and the Negro people generally, tried to bargain with the owners of the Defendant Company, unsuccessfully, by peaceful conferences. In order to implement their demands that this Company, operating stores all over the District of Columbia, should employ Negro salesgirls and clerks at its store in the thickly populated Negro district, some of the members, by peaceful and quiet means, picketed the particular store with signs.

"Buy where you can work."

"This store refuses to hire colored clerks and salespeople."

It worked. Not a colored purchaser entered the store, and as a consequence the owners brought suit in the courts of the District of Columbia to enjoin these picketers from parading their complaint in front of their stores to the damage of their business. It would seem that the old adage "That you may hire whom you please to work" would carry the case over. The lower court and the District of Columbia Court of Appeals so held, but the Supreme Court, in a 7-2 opinion (Justices Butler and McReynolds dissenting), thought differently and upheld the right of picketing in a brilliant opinion by Mr. Justice Roberts. The whole case turned on the interpretation of the Norris-LaGuardia Statute governing labor disputes and the restraint placed upon the courts of the country by that Act to issue injunctions against labor in its right to strike, and to force employers, by peaceful means, such as picketing, to bargain with them.

The majority of the Court said that an association of individuals of a particular race, in seeking to uplift itself, may properly organize and seek out a particular business, firm or company with which this group of people does business, to do business, in turn, with them, by hiring or employing members of that particular race of people, and such falls within the definitions of labor disputes as contemplated by the Act. The dissenting Justices, Butler and McReynolds, were bitter and denunciatory of the majority opinions.

EQUALIZATION OF TEACHERS' SALARIES

This most important class of cases which has meant so much to the colored teachers throughout the South was brought on the first instance in the Federal Courts for the District of Maryland. The original case was Walter Mills *vs.* Board of Education of Anne Arundel County, Maryland,

30 F. Supp. 245 (D. Md. 1939). (See also Mills *vs.* Loundes, 26 F. Supp. 792, 801: (1940) 53 Harv. Law Rev. 669.) In this case, evidence disclosed a systematic practice engaged in for years by the State of Maryland and all the Southern states, allowing one scale of salaries for white teachers serving the same class of students as colored, and another scale of salaries for colored teachers, the latter, performing the same kind of services, fulfilling the same standards and requirements for employment, but receiving from 25 to 40 per cent less compensation than their white fellow workers. The lower court found race discrimination to be a fact, and that the only reason for the difference in pay was based on discrimination on account of color alone, and held that the colored teacher was unconstitutionally discriminated against in the practice of his profession by the County of Arundel, Maryland, the defendant, and issued the injunctions sought by the school teachers. Judge W. Calvin Chesnut of the U. S. District Court of Maryland wrote the opinion of the lower court in such a sweeping and able manner that the defendant school board took no appeal therefrom.

See: Alston *vs.* School Board of the City of Norfolk, Virginia, C.C.A. 4th Cir. (1940); 112 F (2nd) 992.

THE FIGHT AGAINST DISCRIMINATION BY LABOR UNIONS

Just before going to press the Supreme Court, in a far-reaching decision by a unanimous court, on December 18, 1944, declared that the Railway Labor Act (48 Stat. 1185), 45 U. S. C. sec 151 et. seq., imposes on a Labor Union which assumes to act as the exclusive bargaining agent of a class of railway employees, the duty to represent all the employees of the craft and this agent, in its bargaining with the employer, cannot make contracts, which result in discrimination against certain members of that craft because of their race or color, and when such violations of duty on the part of such bargaining agent appears, the courts will step in and enjoin such violations of duty which the statute above referred to clearly imposes on such union representative.

The facts and history of this case (Bester W. Steele *vs.* Louisville and Nashville R. R. Co., Brotherhood of Locomotive Firemen and Enginemen, *et al.*, No. 45 U. S. Sup. Ct., Oct. Term 1944) are important for a clear understanding of the significance of the issues involved.

For a quarter of a century prior to 1930 almost all the trains in the South, both passenger and freight, were "fired" by Negro locomotive firemen. With the improvement in design of locomotives and their use of automatic stokers and ash removers, and particularly with the introduction of Diesel and oil burning locomotives, there was an increasing demand for the jobs as firemen by white railway workers. Gradually Negro workers were eased out of the better runs and placed on long-hour night and holiday freight runs and shifting engine jobs about the yards—the most unsatisfactory and least-paying jobs. The brotherhood had worked out plans that would ultimately force out of the employ of the southern railroads all their Negro employees in this craft (locomotive firemen). The Brotherhood of Locomotive Firemen and Enginemen could not be appealed to by the Negro workers, who were in fact a large minority of this class of workers, because the union expressly, by their ritual, refused membership to Negro workers. Therefore, Steele, petitioner in the case, took his case to the court and asked for relief under the theory that the respondent Brotherhood, as a labor organization, was, under sec. 2 of the Act (supra) the exclusive bargaining agent of the craft of firemen, was so recognized by it, and as such, the order of the Brotherhood (respondent) of March 28, 1940, notifying some 21 Railroads that the proposed new collective bargaining agreement designed to exclude ultimately *all* Negro firemen from the 21 southern railroads service, was illegal and of no effect. No notice was served on the Negro firemen nor was any opportunity given them to be heard on the agreement submitted to the respondent railroads; and in fact the orders were put into effect before their existence was disclosed to the Negro firemen. The petitioner showed that he and his fellow workers, for whom he asked leave to sue, were performing their service satisfactory.

The Supreme Court of Alabama took jurisdiction of the case, but held that no cause of action was shown. The Supreme Court of the United States, in an opinion written by Mr. Chief Justice Stone, held that "Congress, in enacting the Railway Labor Act and authorizing a labor union chosen to represent the craft, did not intend (it) to sacrifice the rights of the minority of the craft without imposing on it any duty to protect the minority."

The Court held that since the Negro workers were barred from membership in the union, "the Act required, in fact *commands,* the bargaining agent to act for them, and, citing the order of the National Mediation Board in the case of Employees of St. Paul Union Depot (No. R. 635), once a craft or class has designated its representative, such representative is responsible under the law to act for *all* employees—members as well as those who are not members." The court therefore enjoined the Brotherhood from enforcing such a flagrant and violently discriminating order.

Mr. Justice Murphy, in a concurring opinion, felt compelled to say the following regarding the underlying issue of race prejudice which was so pregnant throughout this case.

"The economic discrimination against Negroes practiced by the Brotherhood and the railroad under color of Congressional authority raised a grave constitutional issue that should be squarely faced.

"The utter disregard for the dignity and the well-being of colored citizens shown by this record is so pronounced as to demand the invocation of constitutional condemnation. To decide the case and to analyze the statute solely upon the basis of legal niceties, while remaining mute and placid as to the obvious and oppressive deprivation of constitutional guarantees, is to make the judicial function something less than it should be.

"The constitutional problem inherent in this instance is clear. Congress, through the Railway Labor Act, has conferred upon the union selected by a majority of a craft or class of Railway workers the power to represent the entire craft or class in all collective bargaining matters. While such union is essentially a private organization, its power to represent and bind all members of a class or craft is derived solely from Congress. The act contains no language which directs the manner in which the bargaining representative shall perform its duties. But it cannot be assumed that Congress meant to authorize the representative to act so as to ignore rights guaranteed by the Constitution. Otherwise the Act would bear the stigma of unconstitutionality under the Fifth Amendment in this respect. For that reason I am willing to read the statute as not permitting or allowing any action by the bargaining representative in the exercise of its delegated powers which would in effect violate the constitutional rights of individuals.

"If the Court's construction of the statute rests upon this basis, I agree. But I am not sure that such is the basis. Suffice it to say, however, that this constitutional issue cannot be lightly dismissed. The cloak of racism surrounding the actions of the Brotherhood in refusing membership to Negroes and in entering into and enforcing agreements discriminating against them, all under the guise of Congressional authority, still remains. No statutory interpretation can erase this ugly example of economic cruelty against colored citizens of the United States. Nothing can destroy the fact that the accident of birth had been used as the basis to abuse individual rights by an organization purporting to act in conformity with its Congressional mandates. Any attempt to interpret the Act must take that fact into account and must realize that the constitutionality of the statute in this respect depends upon the answer given.

"The Constitution voices its disapproval whenever economic discrimination is applied under authority of Law against any race, creed or color. A sound democracy cannot allow such discrimination to go unchallenged. Racism is far too virulent today to permit the slightest refusal, in the light of a Constitution that abhors it, to expose and condemn it wherever it appears in the course of a statutory interpretation."

(See the remarks of the same Justice in his dissenting opinion in the case of the Removal of Japanese citizens from their Pacific Coast Homes under the war evacuation program, (*In re* Fred Toyosaburo Korsmatsu, decided Dec. 18, 1944.) The court held in a majority opinion written by Mr. Justice Hugo L. Black, to which there were three dissents, that the constitutional rights of the Japanese-American citizens were not violated. Mr. Justice Murphy again expressed grave fear over the rise of racism, saying that "such expulsion goes over the very brink of constitutional power and falls into the ugly abyss of racism."

This case closes for the present (Jan. 3, 1945) the struggle of the Negro for economic, civic and political freedom and his effort, so bravely and courageously fought over a half century, for full citizenship in the framework of American Democracy, through the most difficult of all methods, that of "citizenship through judicial fiat."

It is important to note, and emphasis should be placed on the fact, that in almost every leading case related in this article, the cases were initiated, appealed and argued exclusively by Negro attorneys. An enormous amount of credit should be given to the National Association for the Advancement of Colored People, and their staff of attorneys throughout the country, and particularly their former Chief Counsel, Charles H. Houston, Judge William H. Hastie and their present chief counsel, Thurgood Marshall, and their various associate counsel, for their monumental work and unusual success in their frequent appearances in our Federal Supreme Court.

CIVIL RIGHTS

In recent years there has been a marked change, both in the attitude of Congress and the Courts towards the strengthening and the protection of civil rights. How much may be achieved in any litigation attempting to force employment relations and to upgrade the Negro worker from unskilled positions in industry, or to force his employment in a particular industry which had heretofore failed to employ him and discriminated against him in all lines of employment, is open to great question. Undoubtedly remedial legislation from Congress would be necessary to guarantee the right of employment in industry in peace time. Some steps have been taken, and much progress has been made in this field by the passage of such Legislation as the National Labor Relations Act and the Fair Labor Standards Act. However, these Acts go but little distance in the ultimate aim of travel of the Negro worker, and this means more than six millions of peacetime employables among the Negroes of America. Whether the Negro must await the results of his present efforts to have the Congress pass a permanent Fair Employment Practice Bill to supplement the war measure, a purely temporary and, as yet, unenforceable one, (Executive Orders Nos. 8802 and 9346) or continue to resort to the tremendously slow and unsatisfactory "judicial fiat" method explored in this article depends on America's answer to the challenge of its vaunted ideals of democracy, everywhere so proudly expressed, but no where so proudly practiced. It depends on the answer to the question, "Does America in fact and in truth acknowledge the democratic belief in the dignity and rights of all men regardless of race or color?"

RAYMOND PACE ALEXANDER
Member of the Philadelphia Bar

JAMES BOON, FREE NEGRO ARTISAN

In sketching the life of a particular personality, the student of history finds himself face to face with some of the most serious and dangerous problems in connection with the reconstruction of the past. There is the danger that the writer may oversimplify the period in which his subject lived and thus mislead his readers into thinking that they can understand all the forces that shaped the history of the period by becoming acquainted with one person. There is the great danger, moreover, of becoming too biased and thereby painting the subject as a hero or a villain when he is neither. One must keep in mind the fact that sweeping generalizations based on the life of one person are neither good history nor good biography. It must be remembered, further, that the same psychological, sociological, and environmental factors that defy reduction to rules and laws in society serve to render almost impossible the establishment of generalizations in the sequence of human movement based on individual performances.

Despite the fact that such an undertaking is fraught with dangers which may prove disastrous to one undertaking to sketch the life of a person, there are factors which by their very nature are so persuasive that one is willing to assume the risks involved. So often, the reconstruction of the past is done with such artful evasion of personalities that it is completely and irrevocably dehumanized. After all, the history of a group or a nation is made up of the stories of the lives of its constituents; and so long as one realizes that the individual element in the past is less important than the communal element, it is an acceptable procedure to humanize and enrich our history by studying the personalities that have been a part of the past. This view is not to be interpreted as a surrender to the so-called "great man theory of history." It is merely the assertion of what seems to be an obvious fact, namely, that history can be vitalized and, in some instances, clarified by studying the fortunes of personalities who, in their own way, have helped to make the heart of a group or a nation pulsate.

A study of the life of a free Negro—in this instance, James Boon—has value for several significant reasons. In the first place, it is not common to find sufficient historical materials bearing on the life of a free Negro to reconstruct it to any appreciable degree. He was generally inarticulate, due often to illiteracy and sometimes to his dissociation of himself from life about him. His preoccupation with the struggle for survival seldom left him the time or the energy to express his views or to preserve the records which were a part of his experiences. Like many others, however, of similar political, social, and economic circumstances, the average free Negro kept no records, perhaps because of the feeling that posterity would not concern itself with the fortunes and misfortunes of the "little man." In the second place, one way of studying the relationship of the free Negro to the larger community and of observing the difficulties involved in his struggle is to evaluate the impact of the forces at work on the life of a member of that group. The student of history, however, must resist the temptation to claim that his subject is representative or typical of the group. One must be satisfied with the belief that the forces that affected his subject perhaps affected countless others as well. Finally, the study of the life of a free Negro is of sufficient vitality and humanity to remind one that people— of varying statures, of innumerable races, and of diverse characteristics and circumstances—make up history; and through people one can gain a valuable insight into the forces that shape history.

The parentage and early life of James Boon are somewhat obscure. A later reference to him as a "free born boy of color" suggests that at least his mother was a free

Negro, though it sheds no light on the status of his father.[1] He was born in 1808, and there is a great likelihood that he was born in or near Louisburg, North Carolina, where he spent most of his life.[2] Free Negroes were generally immobile in ante-bellum North Carolina, because of their impecunious circumstances and because the whites did not, as a rule, welcome strange free Negroes into the community. It would have been safe, therefore, for Boon to have remained in the community where he was born.

The earliest record of Boon is the unsavory account of his implications in a fight. In 1825, when he was perhaps seventeen years old, he was ordered to appear before the county court "to answer in an indictment . . . against him for involvement in a fight and an affray."[3] On September 15, Boon appeared "and entered his submission whereupon the Court ordered he be fined $5 and costs."[4] The records do not indicate either the circumstances of the fight or the other parties involved.

In 1827 Boon became an apprentice under the law of the previous year which empowered the county court "to bind out the children of free Negroes or mulattoes, where the parent, with whom such children may live does not or shall not habitually employ his or her time in some honest industrious occupation."[5] There is no indication that proof was offered to show that Boon came under the law, and there is

[1] Minutes of the Court of Pleas and Quarter Sessions for Franklin County, June 16, 1827.

[2] The Minutes of the Court of Pleas and Quarter Sessions for Franklin County record Boon's age as twenty-one years in September, 1829. Since he was eighteen years old in June, 1827, his birthday must have fallen between June and September.

[3] Minutes of the Court of Pleas and Quarter Sessions for Franklin County, September 13, 1825.

[4] State v. Boon, "affray and assault and battery," Minutes of the Court of Pleas and Quarter Sessions for Franklin County, September 15, 1825.

[5] Laws passed by the General Assembly of North Carolina, 1825-1830. (Raleigh, 1831), 15.

no record of parental objection. On June 16, 1827, the following order was entered:

Ordered that James Boon a boy of Colour about the age of Eighteen years be bound to William Jones untill he arrive at the age of 21 years to learn the Carpenters Trade—the said Jones entering to the Bond according to Law by giving for security James H. Murray who is approved by the Court.[6]

The indenture covering the apprenticeship of Boon is not available, but under the law of 1762 all masters of apprentices were required to provide "Diet, clothes, Lodging, Accommodations, fit and necessary; and teach [their wards]."[7] Boon learned the trade of a carpenter and it is assumed that his treatment by his master was satisfactory to the court; but although the requirement of teaching free Negroes to read and write remained an integral part of North Carolina's apprenticeship law until 1838,[8] Jones did not teach Boon to read or write. In all of the papers where his signatures were required, he signed with the mark of an unlettered person in the presence of witnesses.[9] For James Boon, the inability to read and to write was to prove to be a distinct handicap because of his innumerable business transactions which would doubtless have been facilitated by at least a rudimentary knowledge of the written language.

Boon remained under the care of William Jones for two years and three months. In 1829, at the September term of the Franklin County Court of Pleas and Quarter Sessions, he requested a release from his apprenticeship. The court

[6] Minutes of the Court of Pleas and Quarter Sessions for Franklin County, June 16, 1827.

[7] Walter Clark, ed., *The State Records of North Carolina* (Winston, 1905), XXIII, 581.

[8] In 1838, when portions of the apprenticeship law were rewritten, the requirement to teach apprentices to read and write was confined to white wards, *Laws, 1838-1839.*

[9] In this connection it is interesting to observe that the "X" mark of James Boon has been cut out of almost all of his papers which are in the North Carolina Department of Archives and History.

granted his prayer and entered the following order in its minutes:

James Boon a boy of Colour who was bound by this Court came before the Court at this term and made it appear that he was twenty-one years of age and was thereupon ordered to be liberated.[10]

Thus after twenty-seven months Boon was "graduated" from North Carolina's apprentice system, the principal educational institution for free Negroes and many whites. In some instances it was not a benevolent system, and not infrequently the wards suffered from various kinds of mistreatment at the hands of their masters. For a goodly number of free Negroes, however, it was an opportunity to learn a skilled trade and to become sufficiently close to one or more white persons to have a sponsor on which to rely in a more or less hostile community. For James Boon it meant that he had acquired the skill of a carpenter and that he had in William Jones a source of protection and support that was to stand him in good stead in the years that lay ahead. If in twenty-seven months James Boon could become a finished carpenter—as he certainly did—it is perhaps both because he had an ample amount of aptitude and initiative and because his master taught him with considerable diligence and faithfulness. Through the years, Boon was to demonstrate the fact that he had learned his trade well and that he had much for which to thank William Jones.

For several years after his release from his apprenticeship, Boon did odd jobs around Louisburg, building up a reputation as an able and reliable carpenter. It seems that during this period his tasks consisted mainly of making

[10] Minutes of the Court of Pleas and Quarter Sessions for Franklin County, September 16, 1829. A copy of this release is also in the papers of James Boon, North Carolina State Department of Archives and History, hereinafter called Boon Papers. "And set free" is an additional phrase on Boon's copy which was signed by the Clerk of the Court. It was doubtless used as an identification by Boon.

repairs in homes and public places. Already, however, he had made an impression on the leaders in the community. In 1835 he was engaged to make some much-needed repairs on the County Court House, for which he was paid the sum of $21.12.[11]

Boon's ingenuity was not confined to the mere matter of engaging in the trade of carpentry himself, but extended into the field of contracting jobs and hiring others to assist in the execution of them. In 1834 he had secured a job which was too large for him to do, and had engaged two hands to help him. For three weeks, during the summer, Boon and his men worked for Benjamin Avery of Louisburg and secured seventy-five cents per day and board.[12] Boon's serious efforts in the field of setting up a labor pool from which he could draw for his own jobs out and of which he could assign men to others began in 1839. During the next fifteen years, Boon had more than a score of men in his employ. On one occasion he had nine men working for him on one job.[13]

At least three of Boon's assistants were free Negroes, two of whom had come up through the apprenticeship system. One former apprentice was William Dunston who was thirty-one years old when he began to work for Boon in 1838.[14] The other was Boon's brother, Carter Evans, about nine years younger than Boon, who had been the apprentice of Nathaniel Dunn and Simon Williams.[15] Another free Negro, William Mitchell, appears on the pay roll of Boon with Evans in 1839. From that time until about 1855 these three men were the most regularly employed helpers of

[11] Minutes of the Court of Pleas and Quarter Sessions for Franklin County, March 13, 1835.

[12] See the account of Boon's work for Benjamin Avery, July and August, 1834. Unless otherwise specified, the manuscript materials quoted hereafter are in the Boon papers.

[13] See Boon's account of work for D. Cosby, September 8, 1849.

[14] For an account of Dunston's apprenticeship see the Minutes of the Court of Pleas and Quarter Sessions for Franklin County, September, 1822.

[15] *Ibid.*, March, 1826 and March, 1833. For a discussion of Boon's family connections, see page 176.

James Boon.[16] Perhaps the majority of the other employees of Boon were free Negroes, but their status cannot be conclusively established. It is interesting to observe, however, that Boon did not confine his staff of workers to free Negroes; for there are several instances where he hired the slaves of white men to work for him. In 1841 the slave of one Webb was working on one of Boon's jobs in Louisburg.[17] In 1848 Hilley, the slave of B. M. O. Gaines, was working for Boon.[18] W. Y. Collins' slaves, Adam and Granville, worked for Boon thirty-seven days in 1850.[19] While in Raleigh, Boon used George W. Mordecai's slave, Lunsford, for many weeks, and even carried him to Louisburg to work on a job.[20] Boon's use of the slaves of white men indicates both the willingness of the slaveholders to hire their slaves out to anyone who could pay for them and their faith in the integrity of James Boon.

By 1843 Boon owned one slave himself. When and how he acquired the slave is not known. It may have been merely an act of benevolence, as was the case of much of the slaveholding by free Negroes. It must be said, however, that on occasions Boon used his slave boy as chattel. In 1843, 1851, and 1852 the "Negro boy Lewis" was a part of the property which Boon conveyed in deeds of trust to insure the payment of his debts.[21] When the boy was old enough, Boon used him as a laborer on his jobs.

With the manpower which was at Boon's disposal, it is only natural to expect that he could undertake jobs of varying proportions and requiring varying degrees of skills. During the twenty-year period in which Boon was active as

16 See, for example, Benjamin Jones to James Boon, Dr., June 10, 1839 and Carter Evans to James Boon, March 6, 1848.

17 Memorandum of March 9, 1841.

18 The bill for the work done by Hilley is dated August 23, 1848.

19 Collins' receipt for Boon's payment for their hire is dated February 2, 1850.

20 Mordecai's receipt is in the Boon Papers, September 1, 1850. See also Cosby & Company to James Boon, 1850.

21 See page 171.

a carpenter and contractor in Louisburg, Wilmington, and
Raleigh, almost every conceivable type of repair and construction job was undertaken by him and his helpers. He
was constantly in demand for repairing doors, padlocks,
window sills, and the like.[22] He could undertake such jobs
alone or send one of his more reliable workers out on them.
Replacing and repairing woodwork in homes was one of
Boon's specialties. In 1846 he made extensive repairs in the
home of Mrs. Elizabeth Yarbrough in Louisburg.[23] In 1849
he repaired the porch, floors, panels, blinds, and molding in
the home of Augustus Lewis.[24]

On the more difficult jobs and those which required
rapid work—such as those in public places—Boon used several helpers. He and three workers remodeled the interior
of the store of Augustus Lewis and put new shingles on it
in less than a week.[25] Among the things which Boon had to
do on a job for Ballard, Harris, and Davis were to put new
shelves in the store, make new drawers, and put new legs on
a display stand.[26] Among the more tedious jobs on which
Boon worked were turning stairs, making bedsteads, and
the making of benches, chairs, and stools. Of his versatility
in the field of working in woods, there can be no doubt.

It seems, also, that Boon did some painting on his jobs.
Although his papers contain no bills to debtors for painting
jobs done,[27] there are many accounts which indicate that he
purchased large quantities of paint and painting equipment;
and one is led to the conclusion that he was also a painter.
For example, in 1838, he purchased a gallon and a half of
chrome green and a paint brush on one occasion and a few

[22] See, for example, James Boon to Tho. D. Fleury, June 28, 1839.

[23] Bill for Mrs. E. R. Yarbrough, March 9, 1846.

[24] Bill for Augustus Lewis, June 1, 1849.

[25] James Boon to Augustus Lewis, March 22, 1847.

[26] James Boon to Ballard, Harris, and Davis, April-May, 1849.

[27] Very often, the bills merely indicated that work had been done and did
not give an intimation of the nature of the work performed.

days later he purchased a varnish brush and a training brush from the same merchant.[28]

On the job, Boon gave every indication of a man of superior ability and capacity for direction. The records suggest the fact that once he undertook a given job, he assumed the full responsibility of getting it done. There was hardly any detail that was not attended to by him. In most instances he purchased all the materials that would be needed, and had their cost placed on his account. His papers are filled with accounts of his purchases of building materials from merchants in the town where he worked. On one day in 1845 he purchased $36.25 worth of lumber from A. L. Perry of Louisburg. The principal items included in the list were railings and planks of various dimensions and weatherboarding.[29] Boon kept an account with Patterson and Dent, prominent merchants of Louisburg, and there are many purchases of railing, posts, shelving, and planks.[30] He also purchased new tools from time to time. Among his papers, for example, are the following items purchased on one occasion in 1848: one drawing knife, two chisels, one adze, four files, a plane iron, and two augers.[31] For these tools Boon paid cash.

Having purchased the materials and tools with which to work, Boon often assumed the responsibility of transporting them to the scene of the job and charged the costs to his employer. Sometimes it involved hiring the conveyance, such as the occasion in 1840, when he hired a wagon and a driver from Young Patterson, the clerk of the county court.[32] While working for Augustus Lewis in 1847 and 1849, Boon transported the building materials to the job

28 William Haywood to James Boon, May 7 and May 28, 1838.

29 A. L. Perry to James Boon, November 9, 1845.

30 Patterson and Dent to James Boon, February-December, 1848, March-September, 1849. Other stores at which Boon purchased materials were Stith and Co., Macon and Wilson, and F. and S. T. Patterson, all of Louisburg.

31 James Boon, Bought of James Anderson, April 29, 1848.

32 Receipt of Young Patterson to James Boon, March 28, 1840.

and charged the cost to Mr. Lewis.[33] Boon may not always have been able to hire the means of conveyance with ease. In 1851 he carried a note from W. D. Powell to Mrs. Delia Herring which requested that she permit him to use her vehicle. In part, it said:

The boy James Boon wishes to hire some vehicle of you to go to Raleigh. He will I have no doubt take good care of it should you let him have it.[34]

For hiring a wagon in 1851, Boon paid $1.25 for the use of it for two and one-half days. There is reason to believe that he took full advantage of the opportunity to make extra money when he hired a wagon to haul the materials to his job. There are several instances, among his papers, where he hauled materials for other people, and at times one gets the impression that he was in the drayage business. In 1837 he hauled eight loads of wood for one Vaughan, for which he was paid $2.04.[35] In 1850 Boon charged one employer $1.75 for hauling logs for one day.[36]

Not only did Boon secure the job, purchase and transport the materials to it, and engage a staff of assistants, but he also collected the wages for all the men who worked on the job. Whenever he presented bills to his employers, they included the wages for the labor of the men whom he had hired to work for him as well as for himself. As the contractor and, presumably, the most skilled person on the job he received the highest pay. Once he had established himself as a reliable artisan, he never received less than $1.25 per day for his labors. The pay of the other men, apparently, depended on their skills and ranged from fifty cents to one dollar per day. In 1848 he and William Dunston worked "50 and ¾ days" for William Jeffreys. For that

[33] Augustus Lewis to James Boon, March 22, 1847 and March-June, 1849.

[34] W. D. Powell to Mrs. Delia Herring, April 19, 1851.

[35] James Boon to Vaughan, December 20, 1837. Boon usually charged his employers 25c per load for transporting materials to the job.

[36] James Boon to W. T. Fentress, February 16, 1850.

period, Boon collected $76.25 for himself, while he collected for Dunston $50.75, averaging $1.25 and $1.00 per day, respectively. He collected $49.75 for the labor of Thomas Hall for "49 and 3/4 days."[37] Boon seemed to have had his men carefully classified according to skills, and the pay which he collected for them indicates the meticulous care with which it was done. For example, on one occasion he collected 78 cents per day for the work of Henry Dunce and 93¾ cents per day for the work of Lewis Boothe.[38] On another job, he collected 62½ cents per day for the work of Henderson Tyler for part of the time and 62.2 cents for him for the remainder of the time.[39]

In at least some instances, Boon made a profit from the labor of some of his men. When he was working on a job for one Benjamin Jones he collected 75 cents per day for the labor of William Mitchell,[40] while the rate of Mitchell's pay which he received from Boon was 69 and 1/10 cents per day for the same period.[41] In other words, in addition to the pay which he received from his own labors, he sometimes made a profit of several cents per day on his laborers. The justification for such a policy is to be found not only in the fact that Boon apparently took the initiative in securing and managing the jobs, but that in many instances he supported these men during periods of unemployment.[42]

The wages which Boon received for himself were somewhat less than the prevailing wage for carpenters during the period. At the end of the decade of Boon's last years, the average wage for carpenters in North Carolina was $1.56 per day,[43] while there is no record of Boon's having

37 James Boon to William Jeffreys, May 1, 1848.

38 James Boon to Augustus Lewis, March 22, 1849.

39 James Boon to Mr. Mead, October 8, 1849.

40 James Boon to Benjamin Jones, June 10, 1839.

41 William Mitchell to James Boon, January 6, 1840. There is a reference in the statement to work done by Mitchell during the previous June.

42 See page 167.

43 See the tabulated wage scale in Guion Griffis Johnson, *Ante-Bellum North Carolina* (Chapel Hill, 1937), 70.

ever received more than $1.25 per day. Boon's lower wages were hardly the result of his inferior workmanship or his willingness to depress the wages of his trade. In all probability, they were the result of the determination of his employers to distinguish between his status as a free Negro and the status of white artisans. Because he was a free Negro, he was forced to satisfy himself with a wage below the prevailing standard. There was general hostility toward free Negro artisans throughout North Carolina,[44] and although there is no record of Boon's becoming the special victim of the ire of the whites, his status as an artisan was doubtless affected by it. There is every reason to believe that as a free Negro he was at a disadvantage not only in the matter of wages, but also as far as jobs themselves were concerned. His lower wages, it seems, are symbolic of his degraded position in society.[45]

Boon's employers were among the most respected men in the communities in which he worked. It appears from the records that he did more work in places of business than in private homes. Much of his work was for merchants from whom he could collect in kind if not in cash. Ballard, Harris, and Davis of Louisburg employed Boon fairly regularly. This was one of the leading businesses in the village.[46] Augustus Lewis, another merchant of Louisburg, employed Boon frequently, while his records also reveal employment

[44] John Hope Franklin, *The Free Negro in North Carolina, 1790-1860* (Chapel Hill, 1943), 136 ff.

[45] It is difficult to make any comparison between the wages of Boon's assistants and the prevailing wages. Seldom were they classified according to the type of work they were doing, and one must be content merely to observe that he made careful distinctions among them and that in all probability they too received less than the prevailing wage. An additional observation can be made, however, that whenever Boon hired slaves to work for him he always paid their owners one dollar per day per slave.

[46] See the tax lists of Franklin County, 1840-1850. See also the Minutes of the Court of Pleas and Quarter Sessions for Franklin County, 1840-1850. Members of this and other firms for which Boon worked often filled public positions of trust and responsibility.

by Paterson and Dent, and John G. King and Company, of Louisburg, and D. Cosby and Company, of Raleigh.

Through the years, Boon built up an enviable reputation as a carpenter and business man, and the recommendations of his employers are the best testimony to his efficiency and general reliability. Boon was shrewd enough, it seems, to request his employers to write a word in his behalf, and many of them complied. This was an especially wise procedure for a free Negro. In a community which was hostile to him the word of a respected white man would go far in the effort to secure work, and in especially difficult circumstances might conceivably serve as a protection for a free Negro. Some of Boon's employers may have refused to write recommendations for him, while others may have written ones which were not favorable. Those that have been preserved, however, are so generally full of praise that it is difficult to conceive of his not having been liked by practically all who employed him. In 1843 N. W. and B. W. Edwards wrote:

This is to certify that James Boon a coloured man has been at work for me during the last twelve months, during which term his conduct has been of the strictest propriety. I believe him to be an honest straightforward hard working man. In short he is in my opinion a gentleman.[47]

In 1847 Brian Green of Penny Hill, Wake County, North Carolina, gave Boon the following recommendation:

This is to certify that the bearer James Boon has worked for me some two or three months and that He has given me to believe that He is a pretty faithful workman and therefore deserves to be patronized.[48]

A semi-literate white man by the name of A. Kornegay not only thought highly of Boon, but was willing to assume the responsibility for his conduct. In 1848 he wrote:

James Boon is a free man and under my protection and wishes to pass about where his business may cale him at eny time unmo-

[47] November 14, 1843.
[48] December 2, 1847.

lested and rec'd fair treatment as a honable free man of culer. I hereby recommend as such.[49]

One employer referred to Boon as "an excellent carpenter and a man who has uniformly conducted himself with the utmost propriety."[50] All of the recommendations were without qualification except one which said:

The bearer Jim Boon has been in my Employ for some time and but for liquor would have done very well. he is a good workman.[51]

Despite the fact that Boon was usually highly recommended by his employers, work was not always easy to find. For a man of Boon's energy and initiative, there can be no doubt that periods of unemployment were unbearable. He, therefore, risked molestation and humiliation at the hands of whites by going into strange communities in search of work. Armed with a recommendation from one of his former employers, he left Louisburg in 1839 and went to Littleton, North Carolina. He secured work with the person to whom his communication was addressed.[52] He worked between Littleton and Louisburg for more than two years, and added one more name to his growing list of sponsors. When he finally left Littleton early in 1842 for Halifax, he carried with him the best recommendation that he ever received. In part, it said:

This will be handed to you by James Boon a free man who has been in my imployment as a carpenter for some time—At his instance and as an act of justice I write this to say to you or to any other person who may wish to get his services that he is an orderly and well behaved man and attentive to his business. His work is executed better and with more taste than any persons within my knowledge in this section of the country. Should you want his services my impression is you cannot do better than imploy him.[53]

To be sure, this was as much as Boon could have wanted in the way of an introduction, but through it Boon was not able

[49] March 7, 1848.
[50] Statement by Will O. Jeffreys, March 22, 1848.
[51] Dabney Cosby to whom it may concern, October 27, 1850.
[52] Will Plummer to Richard H. Mosby, October 8, 1839.
[53] R. H. Mosby to Isaac Fanecon, Halifax, N. C., February 22, 1842.

to make satisfactory connections in Halifax. Within a few months he was back in Louisburg, where he remained for several years.

When Boon went to Wilmington early in 1848 in search of work he carried with him not only the usual recommendations, but also several men who had worked with him in Louisburg. His brother, Carter Evans, and several others with whom Boon was associated were already there. It was Evans who urged Boon to come to Wilmington. In a letter written in January, 1848, Evans said:

> Dear Brother
> I take great Pleasure in wrightting yo a few lines to inform yo that I am well and hope theas few lines will find yo enjoying the Same. the Boys are all well and are tolerably well satisfide only they want to here from thier famerlys as often as posebl. wee have bin doeing tolerable good bisness only wee are affraid. I know that it is going to be dull. Yo will Pleas es Mr. Duke harrison and get him write Mr. Jeffrey and get him to bee there protector as my Protectr dont appear as he wants to be botherd with them. I offered to pay him but he wont act. Pleas write me as soon as poseble concerning it and State in your letter when yo will be down. I would like very much for yo to come down if yo dont stay but 3 days.[54]

Despite the urgent nature of the letter Boon did not answer. His silence seemed to annoy Evans, who wrote him again in March:

> Dear Bother,
> I am very sorry to think that you should loose confidence in me. . . . William Mitchell will be in Louisburge before you come if you do not come soon, as you have lost so much confidence in me that you can not write to me. . . . if you wish William Dunson write to me and i will send him. if you will take $10 more wages in the year than you pay him i will keep him the whole year. the boys all say that you shall come as soon as you can. . . . the espence of

---

[54] Carter Evans to James Boon, January 20, 1848. For a long time, Wilmington had led the State in restricting the freedom of free Negroes. As early as 1785 free Negroes were required to register, secure a protector, and wear an arm band with the word ''Free'' on it. See Franklin, *Free Negro in North Carolina*, 59-60.

bringing your tools will be very little if you come shortly. We have at preasent about $70 worth of work.[55]

Apparently the prospect of work in Wilmington was sufficiently great to attract Boon. Within two weeks after receiving this letter he was in Wilmington. He carried the letter from Duke Harrison to William Jeffreys which Evans had requested in January. He then persuaded Jeffreys to write him a letter of recommendation, realizing that a word in his behalf from a local man would have greater weight in Wilmington that the word of a resident of Louisburg. Thus, on March 22, 1848, William Jeffreys wrote:

> The bearer of this James Boon (a free man of color from Franklin County, N. C.) comes highly recommended to me by persons whom I know well. . . . I would recommend him to the favorable consideration of the community and he will refer to me in all cases where it may be necessary. This will also be considered as a pass during all lawful hours.[56]

Jeffreys must have been impressed with Boon for he gave a job to him and two of his helpers which lasted for fifty days. Boon was back in Louisburg late in the summer, but his brother, Carter Evans, remained in Wilmington. Two others apparently stopped in Goldsboro en route to Louisburg. In September, 1848, Carter Evans wrote Boon a letter which sheds considerable light on the employment problems of free Negroes at that time:

> Brother—I drop yo few lines to inform you that I am well at presant hoping these few lines may fine you the same. Your man Thomas (Thos) Hall has come from Golds Borough to me for something to doo but I hav notthing for him to Doo and the rest of the hands at Golds Borough are at nothing. TOm says William[57] hav taken his tools and giv them to some other work man to work with. I will keep Tom hear untill I hear from yo so I want you to

[55] Carter Evans to James Boon, March 6, 1848.

[56] Boon Papers, March 22, 1848.

[57] This is William Dunston, a free Negro carpenter, who had worked regularly with Boon in Louisburg and who worked on the Jeffreys job in Wilmington.

write fourth with as I hav nothing to doo. . . . Times is verry dull at present. . . .[58]

Wilmington, with its peculiar hostility to free Negroes and its lack of work was no place for Boon, and he did not return. He worked in Louisburg during the following winter. In the summer of 1849 he went to Raleigh and was joined there by the group he had left in Wilmington. Immediately he secured work in Raleigh on which he was able to employ seven other men.[59] Jobs came rapidly in Raleigh, and for the next few years Boon worked alternately in Raleigh and Louisburg. He took up temporary residence in Raleigh in 1849, and by 1852 he considered it his home.[60] His rovings were over. Even if James Boon was not satisfied with the capital of the North State, he had perhaps tired of moving. At any rate, Raleigh was about as good as any town he had found, and what was more it was not too far from Louisburg, where his property and family were.

Because of Boon's reputation for reliability his credit was good, and he used it extensively. He made heavy purchases regularly at a large number of stores in Louisburg, Wilmington, and Raleigh. In his papers are many statements from Yarbrough and Perry; Gaston Utley; Haywood Little and Company; A. L. Perry; Patterson and Dent; P. I. Brown; Ballard, Harris and Davis; John King; and Richard F. Yarbrough and Company. He also frequented auctions where he purchased goods.

Items purchased by Boon can be classified into three groups: materials used in connection with Boon's work; food and clothing for Boon and his family; and various items for the men who worked for him. The following is a typical account of Boon's purchases of building materials:

58 Carter Evans to James Boon, September 10, 1848.

59 James Boon to D. Cosby and Company, September 8, 1848.

60 See Registers Book No. 19, Wake County, North Carolina, 388. On August 31, 1852, Boon was referred to as a resident of Wake County.

JAMES BOON DR. TO A. L. PERRY, NOVEMBER 9, 1845

47	weatherboarding	16½ ft. long	7	inches wide	$4.52
20	"	15½ " "	7¾	" "	2.00
29	"	16 " "	8	" "	3.09
102	Railin	12 " "	3	" "	3.06
128	"	12 " "	3	" "	3.71
62	"	16 " "	3	" "	6.20
91	"	12 " "	3	" "	2.65
14	Plank	16 " "	12	" "	2.24
107	Railin	16 " "	3	" "	4.30
10	"	16 " "	3	" "	1.00
13	Plank	16 " "	10	" "	1.69
3	"	16 " "	12	" "	.48
8	"	10 " "	15½	" "	
7	"	14 " "	13½	" "	1.35

$36.28

Boon's accounts with Ballard, Harris, and Davis are typical of his purchases of items for himself and his family. Among the purchases are the following commodities: molasses, meat, salt, meal, sugar, coffee, whiskey, calico, muslin, "pant stuff," lining, hooks and eyes, and thread.[61] Among those who made purchases on Boon's accounts were Hilliard Boon,[62] Hillary Dunce,[63] Lewis Booth,[64] and William Mitchell.[65]

With irregular employment and the responsibility of maintaining a family and the men who worked for him, it is not surprising that he experienced many difficulties in trying to remain solvent. Boon's employers were not always regular in their payments. His frequent absence necessitated by the search for employment doubtless caused him to overlook some matters to which he would have attended had he been in Louisburg. It must be added, moreover, that his accounts reveal here and there a tendency to spend, rather

[61] Ballard, Harris, and Davis to James Boon, January to September, 1849.
[62] Yarboro and Perry to James Boon, November 15, 1834.
[63] Ballard, Harris & Davis to James Boon, August to December, 1848.
[64] Ibid., January to September, 1849, and R. F. Yarbrough and Company to James Boon, January to October, 1849.
[65] W. W. Jones to James Boon, April to June, 1849.

recklessly, and this certainly added to his financial worries. From the time he began work as a carpenter and contractor until the end of his career, he was hard pressed to meet his financial obligations. His debts fell into three categories: those to his employees, those to merchants, and those to persons who lent him money. In Boon's papers are several items which indicate that sometimes he owed his employees for long periods of time, and in at least one instance an employee resorted to suit in order to recover his wages.[66]

Boon almost always had outstanding bills with the merchants with whom he did business. At times his accounts would run for a year without any settlement whatever. For example, he began an account with Patterson and Dent of Louisburg in February, 1848. He made purchases almost every month until December. It was not until June of the following year that the account was settled.[67] In August, 1848, he began trading with Ballard, Harris, and Davis. In January of the following year, he had not paid anything, and was carried over into the new year. His purchases continued. In May of 1849, he made a small payment on the account, and in August Boon gave the merchants his note for another part. In January, 1850, almost a year and a half after the account was opened, Boon was still in the arrears by more than $40.00.[68]

Boon's credit with merchants, good though it was, could be stretched to the breaking point and on the occasions when the snap seemed imminent he borrowed money. Then, too, there were certain situations when cash, not credit, was what was needed. In those cases, Boon borrowed money. The amounts ranged from two dollars to more than one hundred. Typical is the occasion when he borrowed $5.00

66 William Mitchell vs. James Boon, January 6, 1840.

67 Patterson and Dent to James Boon, June 13, 1849.

68 Ballard, Harris, and Davis, August, 1848 to January 1, 1850. See also his accounts with R. F. Yarbrough and Company, January to October, 1849, for other illustrations of Boon's difficulties with merchants.

from R. H. Yarbrough in 1849.[69] Sometimes the need was apparently desperate, as in the case when he borrowed $53.00 from Dr. A. S. Perry of Louisburg for one day.[70]

Boon owned some real property in and near Louisburg which was a source of income, at times; and it doubtless helped him in meeting his obligations. There is no lack of clarity in the records of the manner in which he acquired the property,[71] but there is no question concerning his ownership of both town lots and some land in the country.[72] In 1843 he was described as ''the owner of some small property in this neighborhood [Louisburg].''[73] In the same year he is credited with owning about an acre of land near Louisburg,[74] while in 1855 he owned a lot on Court House Street in Louisburg.[75] In 1847 his house and lot was rented to Joseph I. Harper, and in 1848 he leased it to W. H. Furman for a year at the rate of five dollars per month.[76] From time to time he sold timber off his land,[77] and on one occasion in 1840 he sold $35.23 worth of ''rails.''[78]

Boon's income from his labor and his property and the money which he borrowed from time to time were insufficient to satisfy the demands of his creditors, and frequently he was pushed to extreme measures in order to escape serious consequences. The schemes which Boon devised to remain solvent were almost ingenious for a man who was illiterate and who doubtless enjoyed only a limited amount of

[69] Boon Papers, April 16, 1849.

[70] Boon Papers, January 1, 1851.

[71] The Books of the Register of Deeds for Franklin County shed almost no light on the subject. They show disposition of property by Boon without showing acquisition.

[72] See page 171.

[73] Richard Noble's recommendation of Boon, July 10, 1843.

[74] Deed Record No. 28, Franklin County, p. 379. January 2, 1843.

[75] Deed Book No. 31, Franklin County, North Carolina. July 4, 1855.

[76] Contract between James Boon and W. H. Furman, February 8, 1848. Furman owned land adjoining Boon's property.

[77] W. W. Jones to James Boon, February 18, 1850.

[78] Receipt given to Wiley Clifton, April 7, 1840.

legal counsel. A favorite method of Boon's was to cover his debts with a note to his creditors when a request for extension of time failed. In 1849 when he opened a new account with R. F. Yarbrough and Company, he satisfied an old account of $128.27 by giving the firm a note for the amount.[79] Four days later, he gave the same firm another note for $35.07.[80] Apparently the merchants were satisfied with Boon's house as collateral, for on each of the notes there are indications that during this period the rent from Boon's house was paid directly to R. F. Yarbrough and Company. Boon handled his account with Patterson and Dent in much the same way. In the same year, he gave that firm a note for $125.00 to cover outstanding debts with them.[81] Although these were only temporary measures and merely postponed the day when payment of his debts would finally have to be made, they at least satisfied his creditors, for the moment, and gave him a breathing spell during which he could search into his resources for other techniques of maintaining solvency.

When Boon was especially hard pressed for money with which to pay his debts, he resorted to the method of turning his land over to a person by making out a deed of trust to him. If his debts were not paid within a certain time, the trustee was empowered to sell the property and use the funds to pay Boon's creditors. On three occasions, Boon executed deeds of trust to insure the payment of his debts. The first was in 1843 and was made in order to redeem three notes held by Richard F. Noble having a total value of $200.[82] The second was executed in 1851 and was for the purpose of insuring the payment of debts totaling $407.61

[79] Note in Boon Papers dated January 18, 1849.

[80] Ibid., January 22, 1849.

[81] Ibid., September 5, 1849. See also his note to Ballard, Harris, and Davis, August 19, 1850, and the one to John Skinner, January 18, 1851.

[82] James Boon to Davis Young, Trustee, Deed Record Book No. 28, Franklin County, North Carolina, January 2, 1843, p. 379.

which Boon owed to eleven creditors.[83] After Boon took up permanent residence in Raleigh he found it necessary to execute a third deed of trust. Because it is symbolic of the kind of business difficulties which Boon had, it merits quotation:

This indenture made and entered into this 31st day of August ... 1852 between James Boon of the first part, and Charles G. Scott of the Second part, and Alfred Williams and Henry Mordecai of the third part, all of the county of Wake and State of North Carolina—witnesseth, that whereas the said James Boon stands justly indebted to William R. Poole in the sum of six hundred and twenty five dollars ($625) by his promissory note ... bearing date the 26th day of August 1852, and to which said note so due and payable ... Alfred Williams and Henry Mordecai are his securities, which said note ... James Boon honestly desires to pay and to indemnify and save harmless his securities from any loss on account of their Suretyship—Now in consideration of the premises and in further consideration of the sum of five dollars ... paid by the said Charles G. Scott ... James Boon hath bargained and sold ... to the said Charles G. Scott ... the following property to wit: a certain lot or parcel of land lying and being in the County of Franklin near the town of Franklin [a description of the land follows] ... containing about one acre ... also one negro Slave a boy by the name of Lewis about eighteen years of age—To have & to hold the aforesaid lot of land and negro slave Lewis to him the said Charles G. Scott ... provided nevertheless ... That the said Charles G. Scott shall and may on the failure of the said James Boon to pay off the said debt of Six hundred and twenty five dollars due ... as aforesaid ... whenever he may be so required to do, sell for cash after first giving twenty days notice ... the aforesaid property and the monies arising from said sale to pay off the ... debt and interest, and the overplus of any he shall pay to the said James Boon. ...

his
James X Boon
mark

Witness: Joseph Jones   Charles G. Scott[84]

Apparently Boon was always able to pay his debts before his trustee was forced to sell his property, for he used the

[83] James Boon to James H. Yarbrough, Trustee, Deed Record Book No. 30, Franklin County, North Carolina, January 20, 1851, pp. 362-364.

[84] James Boon to Charles G. Scott, Trustee, Registers Book No. 19, Wake County, North Carolina, August 31, 1852, p. 388.

same lot and slave in all three of the deeds of trust which he executed.[85]

Another method which Boon used in trying to remain solvent was to assign the debts owed him to his creditors, when this was agreeable to them. In 1834 Boon asked his employer, Benjamin Avery, to pay his creditor, James Moss, the amount of $25.00 which Avery owed him.[86] In 1848 he asked two employers to pay the amount they owed him to another of his creditors.[87] Boon had the feeling, perhaps, that the additional pressure of his own creditors would force his employers to pay him more quickly. It was a means of impressing his creditors, moreover, with the fact that his negligence of his obligations was due in no small degree to dereliction on the part of those who owed him.

With all of Boon's efforts to pay his debts before his creditors resorted to legal means, there were times when he was unsuccessful, and was forced to answer in court for his failures. On several occasions his creditors turned his accounts over to a justice of the peace for collection. His experience in 1847 is typical:

State of North Carolina   M. F. Sykes
Franklin County   vs
                                                    James Boon

To any lawful officer to execute and return within thirty days from the date hereof (Sundays excepted).

You are hereby commanded to take the body of James Boon and him safely keep, so that you have him before me or some other Justice of the Peace for said County to answer the complaint of M. F. SYKES for the non payment of the sum of six dollars due by oath. Herein fail not. . . .

G. Lewis, J. P.

Judgment granted against the defendant for five dollars and

[85] It may be said, however, that in 1849 Boon's property was up for sale for debts according to a notice issued September 4, 1849. Apparently he satisfied his creditors' claims before the date of sale.

[86] James Boon to Benjamin Avery, July and August, 1834.

[87] James Boon to B. Hawkins, February 27, 1848.

51 cents. A just jury hast ordered him pay the sum and forty cents cost given in Court. March 11, 1841.[88]

The question may well arise as to whether or not Boon's financial straits arose out of an unwillingness to fulfill his obligations. There is nothing in the records which suggest any evasion of responsibility born of faithlessness or the lack of honor. Everything seems to point to the fact that Boon was a serious person with a keen sense of honor. His notes, his overdue accounts, and his other papers which reflect the almost impossible task which confronted him of remaining solvent are balanced by the many indications in his records that even if he was not always prompt, he usually satisfied his creditors by finally paying his bills. Scores of receipts indicate that he purchased items on a cash basis, while many others show that he busied himself in the redemption of notes and the payment of bills which were out against him. These receipts run from 1830, the year after he was released from his apprenticeship, down to 1857, the last year in which there is any extant record of him in any connection. They cover the entire range of his transactions, from the purchase of the most insignificant items to the purchase of large quantities of building materials running into the hundreds of dollars.[89] Each of the deeds of trust which he executed described the transaction as an effort on the part of Boon "to make safe and secure" his outstanding debts or that he was "honestly desirous to secure the payment of the claims." The description of Boon by those who recommended him as a "sober steady man," as "a honable free man of culer," and one whose "conduct has been of the Strictest propriety" would not suggest that he was a man without honor or a sense of responsibility.

Boon lived during a period when the hostility toward

[88] M. F. Sykes vs. James Boon, March 11, 1841. A similar judgment was rendered in the case of Willy Jones vs. James Boon for $16.09, January 21, 1851.

[89] Among these are receipts for poll taxes paid in Raleigh, for a blind mare which he purchased in 1849, for house rent paid for himself and for others, and for many other transactions. See his papers, 1830-1857.

free Negroes was mounting steadily. He represented a
group whose very presence was not wanted. In dozens of
different ways, through the practice of local customs, he
was isolated and made to suffer the hardships which were
directed to all free Negroes. The success of Boon in maintaining himself as a respectable man in several communities
becomes more amazing when his life is set against a background of the increasing antagonism toward the group. It
must be remembered, also, that he was completely without
training, one who could not even sign his name. How was he
able to get along as well as he did? How is the meticulous
care with which he attended to his business and entered innumerable transactions to be explained?

Boon was a shrewd and clever business man. There is
not a single record among his papers which does not suggest a rather remarkable aptitude for understanding business and the many transactions in which the business man
engages. One is led to believe that Boon, without any help
or advice whatever, could have made a creditable showing
as a carpenter and contractor, if he could have led a normal
existence as a free, unmolested, and unintimidated human
being. In ante-bellum North Carolina, a free Negro's existence was infinitely easier if he was fortunate enough to have
a white friend who could protect him from the attacks of
the hostile community and who could give him honest and
sound advice when it was needed. James Boon found such a
friend in the white man to whom he had been bound as an
apprentice in 1827. William Jones may not have taught
Boon to read and write, as he should have done, but he
proved to be his friend in a number of ways. Since Boon
was illiterate, it was necessary to have someone to keep his
books and accounts for him. William Jones was doing this
in 1840 for $5 per year.[90] Since they were so closely asso-
ciated for the next ten years Jones, in all probability, continued to perform this service. In view of the fact that
Boon's business ran into the hundreds of dollars each year

[90] William Jones to James Boon, November 4, 1840.

and that there were the tedious tasks of keeping a check on the various men in his employ and on his many purchases, a fee of five dollars per year does not seem exorbitant.

During Boon's long periods of absence from Louisburg, it was William Jones who looked after his interests in his home town. He attended to the matter of renting Boon's house and collecting the rent for him. His general interest in matters affecting Boon can be clearly seen in the letter which Jones wrote to him in 1850 when he was in Raleigh:

Mr. James Boon
Dear Sir

I received your letter of the 10th Inst. requesting me to attend to some business you omited to tell me of which I will do with plesure. You stated to me you heard that Mr. Waddell had rented out your stalls to Mr. Stallings which I suppose to be so—I received your letter today and have not had time to see Mr. Stallings to know on wat terms he has rented them out of Mr. Waddell. So as soon as I can have the opportunity of seeing him I will have the matter aranged. You also spoke of my making an inquiry of Mr. Jones to know how much timber Mr. Taylor used of your and I went to see him about the matter and he said none of your timber was used that he knew of. I have not found any person to rent your shop yet. Thing is going about the same, if anything acurs where your are concerned and I can not adjust it I will write to you.

Your Friend
William Jones[91]

Jones demonstrated his friendship for Boon in other ways. He wrote letters for Boon and mailed them. When Boon was away, Jones would advance Mrs. Boon money if she needed it. On several occasions in 1840, she called on Jones for cash, which Boon repaid upon his return.[92] He also advanced Boon money on occasion.[93] When it was necessary, in 1849, for Boon to secure a co-signer on a note to James Dent for $125, it was William Jones who placed his signature on the paper. It was men like William Jones, master carpenter, counsel, and benefactor, who did much toward making life bearable for free Negroes when the laws and the community were equally determined to exterminate

[91] William Jones to James Boon, February 18, 1850.
[92] William Jones to James Boon, August 14, 1840, and November 4, 1840.
[93] William Jones to James Boon, December 26, 1850.

them in order to create a social system in which there would be no group whose very existence constituted a threat to the institution of slavery.

Boon's family circle was small. There is no indication of his having more than a brother, a wife, and a son. One may well question the relationship of him to Carter Evans, in view of the fact that they had different surnames. The regularity with which they addressed each other as brother in their correspondence, however, and the fraternal affection which is easily discernible, lead one to believe that they actually were brothers. They may have been the sons of different fathers or they may have been reared in different homes; but they recognized each other as brother throughout their lives, and worked together harmoniously for more than twenty years.

Boon's wife, Sarah, was the slave of Maria Stallings of Louisburg. She was an intelligent, semi-literate woman whose owner obviously gave her privileges which amounted to virtual freedom. She was extremely interested in his business ventures, and undertook to do what she could in his behalf during his absences from Louisburg. When he was away in 1849, she was attending to at least part of his business. She wrote:

> Your wishes have been attended to, as far as they were in my power. I sent to Mr. Hawkins immediately after the reception of your letter to know if he intended to haul the rails he had promised but he has not done it. I sent also to Mr. Taylor to know if the pen should be put up, but he said it could not be put up now, it would be too much in his way, but that he would leave weak after next and then I would do as I pleased. . . . Jack Thaw said he would buy the rails if Mr. Hawkins did not have them hauled before then. I think it would be better for you to come home if you can stay only one day for your hogs are running wild and I fear they will be destroyed for I can do nothing. . . .
> I remain your devoted wife
> Sarah Boon[94]

Sarah Boon not only demonstrated her interest in her husband's business affairs, but she also manifested a deep

[94] Sarah Boon to James Boon, November 27, 1849.

devotion to him and a real concern for his personal welfare. When he was ill in Raleigh in 1850, she wrote in a tone of genuine alarm:

> I was truley sorey to hear that your health was bad. I wish you to let me no if you should get down sick and I have no doubt but what my owners would let me come and stay with you.

At the same time, Sarah Boon was also alarmed over what she felt to be her husband's infidelity. She had heard of an alleged connection between him and another woman. She was furious and criticized his conduct severely. Then, in a moment of tenderness, she added:

> My dear Husband I frealy forgive. I have no doubt that you will find it in the end that I was rite. I wish it to be banished from our memorys and it never to be thought of again and let us take a new start and work on together as we have binn doing for many years. Miss Marian has give T me great concorlation but before that I was hardly able to creep. I hope you will concider my fealings and give me the sentiments of your mind in ancer to this letter. I think it would be better for you to wind up your buisness in Raleigh if you could conveantley and come some where clost about me witch would be a great prise to me than all the money you could make. . . . I do not think it is rite to me for such a long absence frome me if I cant come to you. You can come to me. . . . I remain your affectnate wife untill Death
>
> Sarah Boon[95]

Although Boon returned to Louisburg for short periods, he never went back to live. During the following months, his visits became more infrequent. In 1851 he rented a house in Raleigh.[96] In 1855 Boon sold his property in Louisburg to E. L. Stegal for $425.[97] His relationship with his wife after that time is unknown.

The status of Boon's son remains vague. Since his mother was a slave, it is assumed that the boy was also a slave. Yet, he was with Boon in Raleigh in 1849, and one has the impression that he moved about as a free person. In 1849

---

[95] Sarah Boon to James Boon, July 11, 1850.

[96] Contract between A. B. Humphrey and James Boon, December 31, 1851.

[97] Deed Record Book, No. 31, Franklin County, North Carolina, July 4, 1855, p. 663. The deed was not registered until January 30, 1857.

Sarah Boon wrote her husband, "Give my love to my son and tell him I hope he is doing well and attends preaching regularly."[98] In the following year, he was not with his father, and his mother was worried about him. She wrote "I have not heard from our little son since he left but expect to hear soon and I will let you know as soon as I can."[99] Boon may have purchased his son from the Stallings family. It may be that the Stallings family emancipated him, as an act of benevolence, though the court records do not reveal such a transaction. Finally, he may have been accorded virtual freedom without any legal transaction having ever been made. At any rate, he seemed to have been a substantial bond between his father and mother, and his very existence may well have had the effect of preserving the semblance of a family organization when forces were at work to destroy it.

In observing the habits and tastes of James Boon, one gets the impression that he had a formula for living and that he enjoyed it as much as circumstances would permit. He seemed to be a restless, sensitive soul who was always in search for something—security, happiness, respectability. Those were extremely elusive things for a free Negro in the ante-bellum South. In the absence of them in tangible form, Boon escaped to a fanciful world which permitted him to revel in make-believe. He seemed especially fond of fine clothes, and the records indicate that he had more than a man of his means would ordinarily have. He purchased suits, hats, and shoes frequently. On one occasion when he bought a complete outfit, he paid $10 for a hat.[100] In 1848 he paid $4 for a beaver hat in Wilmington.[101] In

---

[98] Sarah Boon to James Boon, November 27, 1849.

[99] Sarah Boon to James Boon, July 11, 1850.

[100] Yarboro and Perry to James Boon, November 15, 1834.

[101] Myers and Baucum to James Boon, July 5, 1848. Boon also had a gold watch that was of sufficient value to be one of the items which he conveyed in a deed of trust in 1851. Deed Record Book, No. 30, Franklin County, North Carolina, p. 363.

1850 he purchased two dress coats and one "frock coat" at one place and on the same day purchased a "fine silk hat" and a "fine plush cap" at another.[102] Later in the same year, he placed an order with William Green, shoemaker, for a pair of "furestrate boots."[103] In addition to these examples of superior merchandise, there are many indications that he bought ordinary clothes regularly.

One gets the impression that in his later years Boon drank rather immoderately. In 1848 he purchased a barrel of brandy in Wilmington and had it shipped to Louisburg.[104] While there is some evidence of his having sold a portion of it,[105] there is no reason to believe that a man of Boon's tastes retailed the entire barrel. In 1849 he purchased wine or whiskey monthly, usually in half-gallon measures, during April, May, and June.[106] On each of his statements from Ballard, Harris, and Davis, whiskey is among the items purchased. It was perhaps the tendency toward immoderateness that led Dabney Crosby to state that Boon was a satisfactory worker, except "for liquor."[107]

Boon never enjoyed robust health, it seems. On several occasions after 1843, he was ill enough to require a visit from his physician. Between 1844 and 1849 the physician called on him seven times. There were many other occasions during the same period when Boon went to the physician for medicine. The many prescriptions which Boon received of blue pills, liniment, cough medicine, calomel, and quinine

[102] E. S. Harding to James Boon, March 13, 1850; J. Creech to James Boon, March 13, 1850.

[103] William O. Green to James Boon, May 21, 1850.

[104] D. Johnston to James Boon, July 5, 1848.

[105] Boon sold two gallons to Lockward Alford on August 15, 1848. There is no record of his having received a permit to retail liquor from the county court.

[106] W. W. Jones to James Boon, April-June, 1849.

[107] October 27, 1850. There was agitation against the sale of liquor to free Negroes during this entire period, but a law preventing such sale was not enacted until 1859. Franklin, *Free Negro in North Carolina*, 80-81.

tempt one to speculate concerning his maladies, and the temptation is resisted with considerable difficulty.[108]

The last record of Boon's activities is dated 1857. At that time he was only forty-nine years old. Despite the fact that he was still in the prime of life, it is doubtful that he lived long after that. It is difficult to believe that a man of his vitality and business initiative could have continued to live without intruding his name into the records of the community. For our purposes here, James Boon ceased to exist when his record for posterity came to a close.

That James Boon lived for at least forty-nine years has great significance for the student of ante-bellum history. To have the opportunity to know rather intimately the life of a person of his capabilities and his adroitness is a privilege which is too frequently denied us by the scarcity or inadequacy of the records. James Boon reminds us once more that the history of a nation is to be found not only in the records of victorious battles or in the lives of the notable personages but also in the lives of the most humbly born, the most consistently despised, and the most miserably improvident. The life of James Boon may not have been typical of the lives of most free Negroes of North Carolina and the South, but one cannot escape the conclusion that it reflects, in a measure, the common experiences, the fortunes, both good and ill, which all free Negroes had. Finally, the disparity between the theory of free Negro-white relations of the ante-bellum period and the reality of Boon's relatively respectable existence in an ostensibly hostile community serves as a warning against the formulation of conclusions regarding societal relationships based entirely on theoretical formulas.

JOHN HOPE FRANKLIN
North Carolina College for Negroes

[108] See the statement from Boon's physician, Willie Perry to James Boon, October, 1844, to January 18, 1851. Unfortunately, a part of the statement is mutilated and no light is shed on the condition of Boon's health after 1851.

AMERICAN SLAVERY AS SEEN BY BRITISH VISITORS, 1836-1860*

In the shadow of the Capitol stood a slave mart. To more than one Briton this gave the living lie to the imposing declaration, "All Men Are Created Free and Equal."

The principle of human bondage was repugnant to most Englishmen. To J. S. Buckingham, former Whig Cabinet Minister, it seemed as if democratic America assigned exactly the same reason for enslaving Negroes, as did the Sultan or the Czar for withholding from their subjects those very political ideals of which America was so proud.[1] Certainly, the existence of slavery in a land dedicated to freedom furnished a paradox that merited investigation.

The recent abolition of slavery in the British colonies gave a timeliness to the topic. So did the Texan Question, which Englishmen regarded as hinging on the matter of slavery. The occasional clashes between American slave smugglers and British patrols off the African coast also kept the topic in the foreground.

The traveller's interest, already awakened, was further whetted by the abolitionist controversy. *Uncle Tom's Cabin* spotlighted the subject in the 'fifties, and became a by-word in Both Europe and America.

*English travellers who visited the United States during the quarter-century preceding the Civil War were a motley lot. They included authors, journalists, lecturers, scientists, businessmen, clergymen, soldiers, politicians, artists, promoters, actors, songwriters, and sportsmen—to mention but a few. The total number of Englishmen who came to visit America during these years can never be estimated accurately, since no statistics of this type were kept by either the British or American governments. However, the number appears to have been quite large. Of these, approximately two hundred and thirty published accounts of their travels. They came for many reasons and saw many things, their travel accounts naturally reflecting their special interests. But practically all of them paid a visit to the South, if for no other reason than to see its "peculiar institution" at first hand. See Max Berger, *The British Traveller in America, 1836-1860* (Columbia University Press, 1943), for a brief description of each traveller, and a critical evaluation of his travel account.

[1] J. S. Buckingham, *America*, II, 464-465.

181

Hence, no trip to America was complete without some personal investigation of the problem. Even though the visitor might not be able to include an extended tour of the South, at least a side-trip over the Mason-Dixon line was almost inevitable.

In his naive eagerness to discuss the matter and secure first hand information, the traveller often ran into trouble. William Thomson, a sickly Scot coming to Virginia to visit his brother, argued with his ship captain as to the evils of slavery. Upon landing, word spread that he was an abolitionist. Only the quick intervention of his brother, a slaveowner, prevented his being tarred and feathered.[2] Ironically, Thomson returned to England an ardent champion of slavery. As early as 1837, Buckingham had noticed that any discussion of slavery was taboo in the South. In Savannah, he was surprised to learn, the word "abolitionist" was more terrible than the name of any murderer.[3] W. E. Baxter, an English businessman, claimed that a marked change had taken place by 1854 in that the subject was no longer taboo in the Southern press, and that many people, though supporting slavery in public, no longer did so in private. He attributed this change to the quiet propaganda supposedly spread by New England merchants and teachers living in the South.[4] Evidently, belief in this very factor, plus the increasing bitterness of the slavery controversy, made Southerners suspicious of all strangers. English visitors travelling through the South in the 'fifties often felt that they were under surveillance. James Stirling, for example, while quietly conversing with a woman about slavery, noticed an old gentleman change his seat in the coach so that he could overhear the conversation.[5] From such experiences, visitors learned to keep their eyes open, and their mouths shut.

2 William Thomson, *A Tradesman's Travels in the United States and Canada*, 168-170.

3 J. S. Buckingham, *Southern or Slave States*, I, 131.

4 W. E. Baxter, *America and the Americans*, 194.

5 James Stirling, *Letters from the Slave States*, 200.

The visitor had no need to be told when he entered slave territory. The transition was painfully obvious. In the North, all was energy, activity, and enterprise. In the South, ill-built houses going to ruin, fences out of repair, dilapidated railroads, impassable roads, and dirty inns provided a sharp contrast. As compared to the bustling cities of the free states, even Charleston seemed no better than a third-rate town on the banks of the Ohio.[6]

Nor was the difference between the two sections due to soil and climate alone. The Yank flourished in Georgia as well as in Maine, in New Orleans no less than in Boston. Whenever an improvement was seen in the South, the traveller professed to believe that it was the work of a Northerner.[7] Georgia, to which many Yanks had emigrated, was sometimes called the most progressive state in the South. Sir Charles Lyell, the renowned geologist, told of some New England farmers settled in Virginia who had raised the value of their land from $5 to $40 per acre by employing white labor.[8] Obviously, Englishmen concluded, the difference between the two sections was explicable only on the basis of that peculiar institution, slavery.

A visit to a slave plantation became, therefore, a "must" so far as most travellers were concerned. Riding through the fields, where blacks of both sexes clad in dingy ill-fitting clothes could be seen pausing in their work for a moment to stare at the stranger, the visitor came to the main house. Its appearance was always disappointing to those who had conjured up visions of luxurious mansions. The slave quarters, however, did live up to expectations. The typical slave cabin consisted of one room, twelve by fifteen, with a rude wooden bedstead and moss blankets. Sometimes two families resided in one cabin, its earthen floor littered with fire-

[6] Baxter, *op. cit.*, 175; Charles Mackay, *Life and Liberty in America*, II, 36.

[7] Baxter, *op. cit.*, 175.

[8] Sir Charles Lyell, *Second Visit to the United States*, I, 274.

wood and shavings. In cold weather, half-naked children crouched 'round the smouldering embers. Poultry walked everywhere. An open ditch took care of the sewage.[9] Small wonder that Harriet Martineau called the slave quarters "something between a haunt of monkeys and a dwelling place of human beings."[10]

Working conditions for the slaves varied widely. Household slaves were well-treated and well-dressed. Even abolitionists would admit as much. A personal bond existed between servant and master. Moreover, a nice-looking staff of domestics was a credit to the house. But the field hands were worked for all that could be gotten from them. Conditions were worst in the far South. In the coastal swamps of Georgia, the slaves worked from dawn to dusk, six days a week. A peck of Indian corn a week was the sole food allowance for a grown man, Buckingham reported. A woolen jacket and trouser in winter, and a cotton trouser in summer, was their only clothing.[11] Britons were horrified to hear that on the sugar plantations of the Gulf Coast, Negroes would be worked to death in six or eight years, since it was held to be cheaper "to work them off" in that time than to improve working conditions and lower the output. Women worked the same as the men, even to ploughing.[12] In the event of childbirth, the woman had to be back in the fields within three weeks. Excess slaves were hired-out by their masters. In the case of artisans, especially in the border states, it was customary to give the slave a share of his salary, sometimes as much as fifty per cent.[13] The new master, however, was apt to squeeze the last ounce of work from the Negro in whose welfare he had no property in-

[9] F. A. Kemble, *Journal of a Residence on a Georgian Plantation, 1838-1839*, 31.

[10] Harriet Martineau, *Society in America*, I, 224.

[11] Buckingham, *op. cit.*, I, 133.

[12] Martineau, *op. cit.*, I, 224.

[13] R. B. Allardice, *An Agricultural Tour in the United States and Canada*, 93-94.

terest. Rich planters in good times fed their slaves well. But the smaller, poorer proprietors bought broken-down Negroes at a low price, fed and housed them poorly, caring little about them since they could easily be replaced.[14] The model plantations, cited by Ulrich B. Phillips and J. D. B. DeBow, in which the field slaves were protected from over-work by the strict regulations laid down by paternalistic masters,[15] were never visited by English travellers. The latter would doubtless have been surprised to learn of such scientific and humane management on a slave plantation.

So far as British visitors were concerned, professional medical attention for the slaves was unknown. Shortly after her arrival on her husband's plantation, Fanny Kemble paid a visit to the infirmary. Its earthen floor was strewn with wretched women clad in rags. Smoke from a defective chimney filled the room. The shutters were closed, and the room was almost pitch dark. "The poor dingy supplicating sleepers upraised themselves as I cautiously advanced among them; those who could not rear their bodies from the earth raised their piteous beseeching hands."[16] Not even a blanket was available. Medical attention was left to an old Negro woman who acted as nurse.

It was in such surroundings as this that the old worn-out Negro awaited his end. Fanny Kemble's portrait of the death of an old slave was in sharp contrast to the kindly paternalism depicted by pro-slavery propagandists. The old Negro lay there;

His tattered shirt and trousers barely covered his poor body. . . . He had nothing under him but a mere handful of straw . . . and under his head, by way of pillow for his dying agony, two or three

---

[14] Sir E. R. Sullivan, *Rambles and Scrambles in North and South America*, 186.

[15] Ulrich B. Phillips, ed., *Documentary History of American Industrial Society*, I, 112-115; J. D. B. DeBow, ed., *The Industrial Resources of the Southern and Western States*, II, 330-333.

[16] Kemble, *op. cit.*, 215.

sticks. . . . The flies were all gathering around his mouth and not a creature was near him.[17]

James Stirling had accepted slave-owners' tales as to the happiness of their slaves until one day in Kentucky he overheard the screams of a female mulatto servant being lashed by his inn-keeper for failing to serve Stirling's break-fast on time.[18] Yet not all slave-owners were cruel. Though she was an ardent abolitionist, Miss Martineau admitted that ''the thoughtfulness of masters, mistresses, and their children about, not only the comforts, but the indulgences of their slaves, was a frequent subject of admiration to me.''[19] She went on to tell of a wealthy South Carolina master who had refused to leave his plantation during a cholera epidemic, and had nursed his slaves all day with his own hands.[20] But although instances of this kind were not infrequent, most visitors felt that they had only limited significance since contrary examples could also be cited. Visitors were shocked by the heartlessness of such an-nouncements as, ''To be sold immediately, a Negro woman and a case of damaged Marseilles soap.''[21] Charles Dickens listed a series of newspaper advertisements illustrating the harsh treatment of slaves.

Ran way the negress Fanny. Had on an iron band about her neck. . . . Ran away a negro woman and two children. A few days before she went off, I burned her with a hot iron on the left side of her face. . . . Was committed to jail, a negro man. His back very much scarred by the whip; and branded on the thigh and hips in three or four places. The rim of his right ear has been bit or cut off.[22]

Who could maintain that slaves were well-treated in the face of such evidence? Francis Wyse, author of a widely read emigrants guide, went even further. He gave extracts

[17] Kemble, op. cit., 246.
[18] Stirling, op. cit., 49.
[19] Martineau, op. cit., II, 107.
[20] Ibid., II, 408.
[21] Lady E. C. E. M. Stuart-Wortley, Travels in the United States, 121.
[22] Charles Dickens, American Notes, 418-419.

from Southern law codes to show what the slave could expect. He cited one section to the effect that seven slaves or more found together on a road without the presence of a white man would be liable to twenty lashes apiece; another stating that should a Negro use any but "the most usual route" between two points, he would receive forty lashes.[23] If the slaves were as happy and contented as Southerners claimed, why was there need for such regulations? Why, also, did slaves run away? And why should there be need for bloodhounds on large plantations? Travellers rarely saw a slave actually being punished. But Baxter, a businessman, insisted that in New Orleans one could watch the whipping of naked, chained slaves as freely as one could enter a reading room or a playhouse.[24] "Shall we whimper over legends of the tortures practised on each other by the pagan Indians and smile upon the cruelties of Christian men?" protested Dickens.[25]

Slave auctions had a strange fascination for British visitors. Some, like the abolitionist preacher Ebenezer Davies, deliberately sought them out. Practically all visitors tried to attend one. Southerners did not look upon their presence with favor. When C. R. Weld presented a letter of introduction to the editor of *The Richmond Enquirer,* he was welcomed most cordially. But when he requested to be taken to a slave mart, the editor refused on the ground that the spectacle was too revolting to him. Weld accepted this excuse at its face value, and went alone. He found about fifty prospective buyers present. The slaves were led out for inspection from a jail-pen in which they were kept. The men were stripped naked and examined carefully. "Marks were criticized with the knowing air assumed by horse-dealers and pronounced to be the results of flogging, vermin and scrofula." The women were examined on the hands,

[23] Francis Wyse, *America; Realities and Resources,* II, 55-56.
[24] Baxter, *op. cit.,* 185.
[25] Dickens, *op. cit.,* 428.

arms, legs, bust, and teeth. If they claimed to have had no children, their bosoms were carefully fondled to check on this. After these preliminaries, the bidding commenced. The opening figure was $500. Bidding was frequently interrupted while the Negro was walked up and down, and further examined "precisely like a horse." Finally, there came a mulatto woman with one babe in her arms and two others about three or four years old hanging on to her skirt. Her master (the father of her children) had decided to sell her. The mother and children were put up as a unit at a minimum price of $2,500. When only $1,100 was bid, they were removed from the auction block. Bystanders informed Weld that the woman alone would have brought more, but there was a strong aversion against purchasing white children.[26]

The slaves, themselves, did not seem to mind being sold, and appeared apathetic to their fate. Not infrequently one would call out, "Buy me, master, I am a good field hand and can work at anything."[27] In Virginia, domestics were sometimes given the opportunity of finding their own new masters. Robert Russell, the well-known naturalist who lectured at the Smithsonian Institution, overheard one Negro woman plead for special privileges from a prospective master. She demanded that her friends be allowed to visit her. Unable to gain this concession, she nevertheless finally consented to look over the house of her prospective master to see how she liked it.[28]

The break-up of families, the sale of children apart from their parents, the separation of man and wife were extremely revolting to British visitors. Though none but Fanny Kemble had actually seen such a separation, they regarded such occurrences as both frequent and inevitable. This was

[26] C. R. Weld, *A Vacation Tour in the United States and Canada*, 302-304.
[27] Robert Russell, *North America*, 277.
[28] *Ibid.*, 151.

one of the chief evils that they believed to be inherent in the slave system.

The disregard for morality was equally revolting to them. Slaves, it appeared, were bred like animals. The aged James Madison nonchalantly informed Miss Martineau that slave women bore as many children as possible, the average being fifteen.[29] In the northern tier of slave states, and especially in Virginia, where cotton culture had declined, visitors reported that the plantations were used as breeding grounds for the slaves needed farther south. Women of less than thirty had ten children. Fanny Kemble, a plantation mistress herself, affirmed rather wildly that "not a girl of sixteen on the plantation but has children, nor a woman of thirty, but has grandchildren."[30] Frequently, masters and overseers cohabited with Negro women, and sold their offspring. Weld had been present at one such sale in Richmond. Sir Edward Sullivan witnessed a similar occurrence at New Orleans, where he saw slaves auctioned who were as fair as himself.[31] Fanny Kemble knew an overseer's wife who had the driver string up and lash three women for several days on end, within a month of childbirth, because they had permitted her husband to seduce them.[32] Another planter's wife bitterly informed Miss Martineau that she was but "the chief slave in the harem."[33] A popular tale with travellers was the case of the planter who had several daughters by a slave. He sent them to Europe for their education, and raised them as ladies. His sudden death led the heirs to liquidate his property. It was then discovered that he had never legally manumitted his daughters, and so they were sold into prostitution.[34] Even though the traveller often considered the Negroes an inferior race, he

[29] Martineau, *op. cit.*, II, 118.
[30] Kemble, *op. cit.*, 58, 182.
[31] Sullivan, *op. cit.*, 190.
[32] Kemble, *op. cit.*, 227-228.
[33] Martineau, *op. cit.*, II, 118.
[34] T. C. Grattan, *Civilized America*, II, 441.

saw no justification for such conduct. Jefferson was denounced by Tory visitors as "a wretch" on the ground that he had illegitimate children by his slaves, children whom he allowed to work on his plantation.[35] This baseless calumny was pounced upon by critics happy to demonstrate by his example that "licentiousness and tyranny have met together; democracy and slavery have kissed each other."[36] Nor could most Britons understand why it was socially permissible for a white man to have children by a Negro woman, while for a Negro to cohabit with a white girl would be cause for lynching.[37]

Cases of the latter occurred infrequently, but often enough to come to the traveller's attention. While Harriet Martineau was in Mobile, two Negroes were burned alive over a slow fire for the attempted rape of a white woman.[38] Local newspapers made no mention of the incident, but she saw to it that the story was circulated when she returned to the North. Some months later another Negro lynching, this time in St. Louis, also came to the attention of visitors. These rather isolated cases received attention out of all proportion to their frequency.

Aside from actual lynchings, however, slavery was accused of breeding irresponsibility and lawlessness on the part of the dominant white race. The frequency of dueling, the ever-ready pistol, the deadly bowie knife, the hard-drinking, hard-gambling desperadoes were all regarded as largely the off-shoots of the slave system. The economic backwardness of the South was also laid at its door. How could the South improve its economic condition when production was entrusted to the hands of stupid, slow, shiftless Negro slaves? As a system, it inevitably brought about "disorder, slovenly negligence, stereotyped adhesion to old

---

[35] Sullivan, *op. cit.*, 192; Capt. Frederick Marryat, *Diary in America*, first series, III, 55; Mrs. Felton, *American Life*, 56.

[36] Felton, *op. cit.*, 56.

[37] Buckingham, *op. cit.*, I, 241.

[38] Martineau, *op. cit.*, I, 372.

methods, disregard of all improvements, costly and unnoticed expenditure and general impoverishment in all that pertained to the cultivation of the soil.''[39]

Other evils of slavery were enumerated *ad infinitum.* It had led to internal dissension between the sections that threatened to end in civil war and disunion. It had led to ''Bleeding Kansas,'' with its border ruffians intent upon one object—''the extermination of every Free-Soiler.''[40] It had led to complications in foreign affairs, causing among other things the Texan Revolt and the Mexican War. Furthermore, it was creating friction between England and America because of clashes between British patrols and American slavers off the African coast.

Legally, of course, the importation of slaves from Africa had been prohibited since 1808. British visitors pointed out that this trade was being continued clandestinely. The clipper ships, they stated, were particularly suitable for this purpose. Francis Wyse, a businessman, had been aboard a number of clipper ships in New York harbor which were ''notoriously intended'' for black ivory. Such ships sailed under American papers to Havana where the crew was changed. Then the American captain took her to the African coast, and loaded her with slaves. On the return voyage, just before approaching Cuba, he would turn over the ship to another captain sailing under Portuguese papers secured in advance. Thus the slaver had the protection of the American flag on the high seas against British interference. From Cuba the slaves were easily smuggled into Florida and Texas.[41]

Comparison with former slave conditions in the West Indies was inevitable. The general verdict declared American conditions to be worse. But the reasons given to justify this opinion were seldom better than Grattan's naive asser-

[39] T. H. Gladstone, *An Englishman in Kansas*, 219-220.
[40] *Ibid.*, 125-126.
[41] Wyse, *op. cit.*, II, 69-74.

tion that "no well-bred Englishman would dare be a harsh master."[42]   Perhaps the fact that Grattan was British Consul to Boston was partially responsible for this gallant reflection. Although American masters were declared to be more cruel, no adequate evidence of this was ever given, even by men such as Ebenezer Davies and J. M. Phillippo who were familiar with West Indian conditions.[43]

Yet, despite their condemnation of Negro slavery on almost every conceivable basis, English travellers were overwhelmingly opposed to abolitionism. Those who openly favored the latter were so few as to be counted on one's fingers. Joseph Sturge helped runaway slaves to escape on the Underground Railway;[44] Harriet Martineau defied public opinion by speaking from an abolitionist platform in Boston; Francis Wyse, denouncing the Gag Rule as "a duplicity and a crime," urged emigrants to support the abolitionists. But these three stood almost alone.

In fact they were outnumbered by those visitors who looked upon slavery with favor. One of these, naturalist Amelia Murray, had expressed abolitionist sympathies when she had landed in New England in 1854. But a sojourn in the South changed her views. "We should bestow our compassion on the masters instead of on the slaves,"[45] she affirmed. Far from being mistreated, the Negroes were the merriest, the most contented people she had ever seen. They were only grown-up children. A domestic in Lynchburg had told her, "Missus, we very like monkies." She had heard a Negro woman who had been offered her freedom take it as an insult and reply, "I know what the free niggers are, missus, they are the meanest niggers as ever was; I hope never to be a free nigger." Obviously, then, Miss Murray concluded, *Uncle Tom's Cabin* was a libel upon the slave-

[42] Grattan, *op. cit.*, II, 417.

[43] Ebenezer Davies, *American Scenes and Christian Slavery*; J. M. Phillippo, *The United States and Cuba.*

[44] Joseph Sturge, *A Visit to the United States.*

[45] A. M. Murray, *Letters from the United States, Cuba, and Canada*, 195.

owner. Far from being evil, slavery actually established "permanent and therefore kind relations between labour and capital."[46] A free Negro in Florida, awaiting passage to Liberia, had assured her that the mass of slaves were unfit for freedom, and that the African slave trade should be reopened so that more could be brought away and improved. To abolish slavery because an occasional master was cruel, declared Miss Murray, would be as logical as to destroy free labor because some bosses were hard. As for free Negro labor, that was as practical as English constitutional government in Ashantee.[47]

William Thomson, the Scotch weaver who had narrowly escaped mob violence as a suspected abolitionist when he had first arrived in the South, became another champion of slavery. He denied that the slave-owners broke up families. On the contrary, Thomson insisted, they went out of their way to maintain them. When slave families were separated, it was chiefly because slaves deliberately married off their own plantation in order to have an excuse for visiting friends after working hours. The slaves were not overworked, not even the field hands.

Truth, then, compels me to say that the planters in general treat their slaves with great humanity. . . . Would to God the aristocracy (of England) would interest themselves half as much to improve the physical condition of the factory slave in England.[48]

Thomson had seen children of ten and twelve in British factories, working twelve hours a day till their hands bled, and he had seen these children whipped when their emaciated limbs could no longer support them to their work. "There is not a planter in America whose blood would not rise and whose arm would not be lifted up to defend even the Negroes from such cruelty," affirmed Thomson.[49] Happy, therefore,

[46] *Ibid.*, 203.
[47] *Ibid.*, 195-205, 264.
[48] William Thomson, *op. cit.*, 191.
[49] *Ibid.*, 193.

was the slave! He had no responsibility, no fear of his children starving, no worry of neglect in sickness or old age—"whereas the labouring men of this boasted country [England] have all the care and responsibility of freemen and none of their valued privileges."[50] Allardice, a well-known English athlete, agreed with Thomson. He charged that there were many instances of English parish apprentices receiving treatment "the atrocity and horribleness of which would draw tears from the eyes of any slave-owner in Virginia."[51] Both men were won over to slavery by its paternalism.

Other factors also played a part in winning pro-slavery adherents. Sir Charles Lyell, whose aristocratic background naturally predisposed him to favor the aristocratic social system of the South, told Lord Acton that he thought well of American slavery because it had done more to elevate the minds of the slaves than had been done by the free North for its poor.[52] Lyell claimed to have seen schools for Negro slaves in Virginia, Kentucky, and Tennessee, an assertion which Northern friends heard with incredulity. In any case, he felt that the evils of slavery had been grossly overdrawn. The break-up of families, in his opinion, was rare. He, himself, had seen buyers refuse to bid on a woman who had been put on auction with her child. He had known of a widow, with five daughters, who refused an opportunity of moving to Richmond solely out of reluctance to turn over the slaves on her isolated farm to the mercies of a strange overseer.[53] Such instances, of course, were exceptional, but Lyell professed to believe the contrary.

Mrs. Maury, an Englishwoman who had great difficulty with the servant problem in New York, found slavery to be the solution to her troubles. "I like the disposition, I like

50 William Thompson, op. cit., 195.

51 Allardice, op. cit., 94.

52 J.E.E.D. Acton, "Lord Acton's American Diaries," Fortnightly Review, CX, 917; Lyell, op. cit., I, 129-130, 274.

53 Lyell, op. cit., I, 275, 278, II, 286.

the service, I like the affection of the slave; I like the bond which exists between him and his master; the union of interests, and the companionship which death alone destroys."[54] When she had spoken to Calhoun about the sale of slaves, "an involuntary shudder passed over his frame. 'The sale of a slave,' said he, 'I could not look upon'."[55] Small wonder, then, that she admonished the abolitionists to worry about their own poor rather than the Negro. Mrs. Houstoun, another aristocratic woman troubled by the servant problem, came to the same conclusion. She threw back the Northern plea of humanitarianism by charging that ninety per cent of all cases of undue severity towards slaves were traceable to ex-Yankee masters. Next she turned upon British abolitionists and pointed out that the English mills would be the first to suffer from the cotton shortage that would inevitably result from liberation.[56]

All pro-slavery adherents agreed with Brothers' statement that to liberate the slave would inflict a curse upon him rather than a blessing. What would be his status as a freeman? Brothers told of the mobs he had seen march through the Philadelphia Negro quarter, rioting for three days and nights, tearing down forty houses, looting, and murdering. All of this, he informed his countrymen, had occurred with the full knowledge of the city authorities.[57] Alfred Bunn, former manager of the Drury Lane Theatre, carried this argument still further. He testified that Negroes had been barred even from a concert given by a Negro singer, the Black Swan, at the Metropolitan Opera House in New York.[58] What better indication could be offered as to the dreadful fate awaiting the liberated Negro? Was he not far better off under the paternalism of slavery?

[54] Mrs. S. M. Maury, *An Englishwoman in America*, 193.

[55] *Ibid.*, 245.

[56] Mrs. M. C. J. F. Houstoun, *Hesperos*, II, 202-212.

[57] Thomas Brothers, *The United States of North America as They Really Are*, 198.

[58] Alfred Bunn, *New England and Old England*, 61.

But it remained for D. W. Mitchell, who after ten years in the South returned to England and wrote an apology for the Southern viewpoint in the Civil War, to expound the extreme pro-slavery argument. Paraphrasing Dew, Harper, and Fitzhugh, he assured Englishmen that the Negroes were an inferior race whom slavery had raised from savagery. "From the lazy, murdering, thieving, fetish worshipping African, he has been converted into one of the most useful and productive of the world's laborers."[59] Mankind was not born free, nor equal; neither did it have any inalienable rights. Abolitionism was sheer hypocrisy. Which abolitionist would not see his daughter rather dead than married to a "genuine nigger"—however well-dressed or well-educated? Had the Constitutional Fathers succeeded in their ill-advised attempts to abolish slavery, the entire South would still be an Indian hunting ground. Slavery, he insisted, was a beneficent institution. In his opinion, Britain would do well to establish it in India if she wished to make that area as prosperous as the South.[60]

But these arguments fell on deaf ears so far as the vast majority of English travellers were concerned. They hated slavery as the plague. Why then did they object to abolitionism? Chiefly because they felt it to be an impractical and extremist approach to the problem. Immediate manumission without compensation would be obviously unjust, and would ruin the South. Small wonder, agreed most Britons, that with their fortunes at stake, slave-owners fought liberation tooth and nail. It was easy for those without any financial stake, and far removed from the scene of vast Negro populations, to talk abstractedly of the moral righteousness of immediate liberation. The unreasonableness and the

[59] D. W. Mitchell, *Ten Years in the United States*, 230.

[60] *Ibid.*, 182, 216, 227-251. Although English travellers who upheld slavery paraphrased the doctrines expounded by such Southern apologists as Dew and Harper, they made no direct mention of these men. Anti-slavery travellers likewise failed to mention them. Evidently visitors were unfamiliar with the importance of these apologists in formulating the pro-slavery argument.

violence of abolitionist agitation had unified the slave-owners into presenting a common front. Therefore, far from
hastening the ultimate end of slavery, said most Britons,
abolitionism had simply tightened the collar 'round the
slaves' necks.[61] For every visitor like Johnston who thought
that abolitionism had its value in arousing dormant public
opinion,[62] there were a score of others who regarded abolitionist efforts as misdirected zeal which retarded the day of
emancipation. The extent to which abolitionism had solidi-
fied the South behind slavery, it was charged in 1844, could
be measured by the fact that Calhoun would not have dared
to call slavery "a glorious institution" twenty years earlier.[63] Abolitionist pressure was regarded as responsible for
the slavocracy's change from the defensive to the offensive.
Capt. Frederick Marryat stated in 1838 that he had found
many Southerners favoring liberation.[64] But in the 'fifties,
scarcely a slave-owner would admit as much to a traveller.
Britons held the abolitionists alone responsible for this
hardening of hearts. Not only had the abolitionists arrested
the anti-slavery movement in the South, but they had inten-
sified sectional bitterness and caused the shedding of blood
in Kansas. "It is wonderful," said Baxter, a man who
hated slavery with all his soul, "that men who revere their
Bible can listen to the Parkers and Garrisons."[65]

Not only were the abolitionists intemperate and unwise,
Englishmen added, but they were hypocrites as well. Until
they gave evidence of regarding Negroes as human beings
by removing the disabilities against them in the North,
"abolitionism was a delusion and a snare."[66] What could
the visitor think when that great abolitionist champion,
John Quincy Adams, in discussing the role of Desdemona,

[61] Alexander Mackay, *The Western World*, II, 106.
[62] J. F. W. Johnston, *Notes on North America*, II, 486.
[63] J. R. Godley, *Letters from America*, II, 73.
[64] Capt. Frederick Marryat, *Diary in America*, first series, III, 64.
[65] Baxter, *op. cit.*, 191.
[66] William Chambers, *Things as They Are in America*, 359.

assured actress Fanny Kemble with a most serious expression of sincere disgust that he considered "all her [Desdemona's] misfortunes as a very just judgment upon her for having married a nigger."[67] Instead of ranting at the South, said the Briton, let the abolitionists prevent the shameless violation of the rights of the free blacks in the North. Though the status of the free Negro had improved somewhat in New England by the 'fifties in that he was no longer barred from the regular railroad coaches,[68] yet "if a negro had the intellect of a Newton—if he were clothed in purple and fine linen, and if he came fresh from an Oriental bath and as fragrant as Araby's spices—a Northerner would prefer sitting down with a polecat."[69] In the free states, a Negro dare not show his face outside the gallery set aside for him in the theatre; if sick, he was never admitted to the white man's wards; when praying he must do it in a white man's church; on most trains he was compelled to ride in the filthy Negro car; when dead, gold could not buy him the privilege of being buried in a white man's cemetery. Knowing this, how could abolitionists heap abuse upon the South, where the social position of the Negro was far better? Physical repulsion to the Negro was certainly stronger in the North, asserted visitors. Newspaperman Charles Mackay remarked that those who talked loudest of liberty and political equality, turned up their scornful noses at the slightest possibility of contact with a Negro.[70] In the South, on the other hand, mothers did not hesitate to suckle their babes at the breast of a Negress, nor even to have pet pickaninnies sleep like puppies in their very bedchambers. For that matter, almost every planter admitted one or more female slaves to the intimacy of his bed.[71] So far as the British traveller could see, the

---

[67] Kemble, *op. cit.*, 86.
[68] Stirling, *op. cit.*, 53.
[69] H. A. Murray, *Lands of the Slave and the Free*, 208.
[70] Charles Mackay, *op. cit.*, II, 43.
[71] Kemble, *op. cit.*, 23.

Negro was treated like a dog in both sections, with the difference that "in the South he is sometimes a pet dog, whereas in the North he is always a cur, kicked and booted on every occasion."[72]

If not abolitionism, what was the solution to the slavery question? On this the visitor was hazy. He regarded it as inevitable, however, that sooner or later slavery would be eradicated.

There appeared to be little likelihood that the whites, either North or South, would ever accord full equality to the Negro. Colonization in some tropical clime appeared, therefore, to be the most logical alternative. The efforts of the American Colonization Society and of a number of border states to accomplish this evoked a sympathetic interest. In 1834 Maryland had granted a subsidy of $200,000 for the creation of a Maryland in Liberia, at Cape Palmas. A decade later this colony controlled 1,000 miles of territory, but had only 600 Negro colonists. Despite this poor showing, some Britons still remained hopeful.[73] Most of them, however, viewed the project pessimistically. Harriet Martineau opposed the entire scheme as unjust and unwise. The Negro birthrate, alone, she showed, was greater than the number that could be deported. Southerners favored the scheme, she declared, because it offered an easy means of getting rid of clever and discontented Negroes. Let slavery be kept from expanding further, Miss Martineau urged, and it would ruin itself. This in turn would lead to manumission, after which, she trusted, both Negro and white would learn to live amicably with each other.[74] Buckingham took a similar view, though he doubted that social equality would be possible for a long time to come.[75] The paucity of the number transported to Liberia became even more notice-

[72] Sullivan, *op. cit.*, 192.

[73] Godley, *op. cit.*, II, 216-217; Chambers, *op. cit.*, 363.

[74] Martineau, *op. cit.*, I, 356. Later she became an abolitionist, and demanded complete immediate emancipation.

[75] Buckingham, *op. cit.*, I, 574-575.

able as time passed. By 1850 the American Colonization Society had transported a total of only 6,653 Negroes, of whom about seventy-five per cent had been liberated solely for that purpose. States like Maryland continued to subsidize their colonization projects. Johnston, a British agricultural expert, thought the figures spoke for themselves. Not only was the plan a failure in regard to numbers, but he could see no justice in deporting men from the land of their birth, usually against their wishes.[76] James Stirling added still another criticism. He pointed out that in the event the project should succeed, the South would thereby lose its sole labor supply.[77]

The colonization project was evidently not practical. What solutions were? Stirling placed his hope in a gradual raising of the economic and intellectual level of the Negro. This would decrease prejudice, and prepare the slave for emancipation.[78] Just exactly how this was to be done, he did not say. Religious-minded travellers, especially clergymen, placed their faith in some mystic process of emancipation brought about by "the influence of Christian faith."[79] Most Britons were so convinced of the superiority of free over slave labor that they felt the South had only to be convinced of this also in order to have it voluntarily give up slavery. However, the method of persuasion, and the fate of the manumitted slave remained enigmas.

Other visitors were not so optimistic. J. R. Godley was certain that if the colonization scheme failed, insurrection would be inevitable.[80] Capt. Marryat was equally positive that sooner or later by desertion, insurrection, or manumission, the slaves would join the Indian tribes in the West. He only prayed that England would keep clear of any servile

[76] Johnston, op. cit., II, 358-361.

[77] Stirling, op. cit., 237-238.

[78] Ibid., 239-245.

[79] Baxter, op. cit., 195; F. J. Jobson, America and American Methodism, 394.

[80] Godley, op. cit., II, 216-217.

war that might develop.[81] Alexander Mackay, who otherwise disagreed with everything Marryat said, also pictured a slave insurrection as inevitable, to be followed by the ultimate expulsion of the slaves from the Continent.[82] No visitor, not even those writing on the eve of the Civil War, believed emancipation to be imminent.

Thus, if the slavery question troubled the minds of Americans, it was a problem for which the British visitor could offer no ready answer. But the solution must be found, and found soon, became more and more evident. As early as 1836, C. A. Murray had warned that unless slavery were shortly remedied its "gangrene would spread beyond the reach of medicine."[83] In the next quarter-century the gangrene did spread, until slavery became, in the eyes of the traveller, the most momentous question affecting the United States.[84] Would it lead to the dissolution of the Union? In 1845 Major Warburton had stated that the South would risk everything rather than surrender on this question.[85] Five years later, Johnston, noting the growing strength of the North, replied that America would never stand for dissolution. Should any attempt in that direction occur, said he, the majority would "resist such separation by force of arms and compel the adhesion of the refractory states," regardless of the constitutional questions involved.[86] The tentacles of the cancer spread steadily over an ever-widening area. In 1856 Stirling remarked that the issue was no longer centered on the position of the Negro, but on the social and economic differences between the North and South. On the even of the war, William Tallack, a Quaker minister and abolitionist sympathizer, and Hugo Reid, a Southern sympathizer, both agreed with Stirling

[81] Marryat, op. cit., first series, III, 78-80.
[82] Alexander Mackay, op. cit., II, 141.
[83] C. A. Murray, Travels in North America, II, 204.
[84] Grattan, op. cit., II, 409.
[85] G. D. Warburton, Hochelega, II, 256.
[86] Johnston, op. cit., II, 343.

that sectionalism, which had taken on the guise of the slavery question, was now the real and deadly issue.[87] One traveller summarized the situation succinctly:

The South seems to be in that mood of mind which foreruns destruction: there is a curse upon the land. . . . The whole South is like one of her own cotton steamers . . . filled from the hold to the topmost deck with the most inflammable matter; everything heated up to the burning point, a furious draught blowing from end to end, and a huge high pressure boiler in her belly pressed to bursting.[88]

Secession appeared inevitable.

MAX BERGER

Chairman, Social Studies Department
Manhattan High School of Aviation Trades
New York City

[87] Stirling, *op. cit.*, 70; William Tallack, *Friendly Sketches in America*, 227; Hugo Reid, *Sketches in North America*, 205, 221.
[88] Stirling, *op. cit.*, 59.

BOOK REVIEWS

My Happy Days. By Jane Dabney Shackelford. (Washington, D. C.: The Associated Publishers, Inc., 1944. Pp. 121. Price $2.15.)

The story of the development of the Negro family in America is one of varied and intricate ramifications and wide social implications. It covers the entire period of American history from the time the first slaves were landed on the soil of Virginia in 1619 until the present day. That the earliest Negro family life of which there is any record was, of necessity, and because of the disruptive forces of the slave system, unstable and wretched cannot be gainsaid. But the fact remains, nonetheless, that there was a modicum of permanence to it in spite of the cruel and heartless treatment meted out to the helpless victims of the slave system.

Little heed was given to the emotional needs and normal instincts of the slaves. Family relationships were arbitrarily set up at the whims of the master class and were as easily disrupted with little or no consideration for the spiritual sufferings or wretchedness endured by the hapless objects of these whims. And yet, despite the initial lack and later instability of early Negro home life, its misery and its heartbreak, during the slavery period, the record of its survival is of major interest and importance. Certainly it can be safely said that no other ethnic group in the history of civilization has been compelled to undergo such sudden and violent changes, where family life and stability are involved, than has the Negro in America in the past 300 years. And the fact that a major degree of permanence has now been achieved is one of the evidences of the inherent stamina of this people.

Scholars have developed at length and in detail the story of the Negro family in the United States. Its survival through the periods of slavery and reconstruction, its adjustments during the migrations from the rural to the urban centers, its endurance in the face of disease, poverty, and social insecurity in the present time, write an epic of Homeric proportions and give incontrovertible evidence of the progress of the minority tenth of American citizenry.

One author, William F. Ogburn, in his study of *Recent Social Trends,* has stated that the American family has lost or is losing its historical functions: economic, educational, recreational, health, religious, and protective. On the other hand, he finds that it still retains three of its most significant attributes: affection, rearing of children, and the informal education of its members. And certainly these latter points are applicable to the Negro family in America.

Early biographical records of the slave era left by such former slave notables as Frederick Douglass and his contemporaries, bear witness to the pattern of the home life of that day. Douglass, in writing of his own childhood, described how the hardships and miseries of the wretched life in "the quarters" and the cabins were softened by the tender devotion of the slave mother (and when possible—of the slave father too) toward the little ones. In later years when he had achieved freedom and established a home and family of his own Douglass wrote with enthusiasm and tenderness about his own fine children in whose welfare and development he and his wife showed such pride and interest.

Numerous other records have come down to us of the family life of the great and near great of the race, whether slave born or free, and the patterns of "in-family" education, affection, and child guidance, referred to by Ogburn are persistently present in these family chronicles.

Today there is before the American reading public a new record —a child's story of a Negro boy and his small sister in a typical Negro home and family situation, a story which has never before been told quite so completely or so wholesomely, though it represents a large segment of middle class family life in today's America. Already it has attracted nation-wide attention, and gives promise of being one of the most important pieces of documentary evidence produced to date—evidence that, given equal opportunity for growth and development, the average Negro family can be as happy, and complete, and inspiring a unit as any in present day life.

The book is called *My Happy Days* and gives in simple fashion in the words of the child himself, the day-to-day experiences of a wide-awake youngster who is happy because he *has* these normal, happy, every-day experiences—in home, in school, and in the community—which are the boon and birthright of unfettered childhood in Twentieth Century America.

That he is a Negro child is not important per se. The importance of that fact, however, lies in its implications. It is significant only because it is a *new*, a different portrayal of Negro life and childhood, quite contrary to the old stereotypes, the old patterns of the Topsies and little Black Sambos so common in current literature for children.

Beautifully illustrated with photographs depicting each incident mentioned, the book in its 121 pages describes a home in which intelligent, thrifty, and progressive young parents recognize the spiritual needs, the human dignity of the young lives committed to their keeping and in wise and wholesome fashion shape and mould these youthful personalities, with love and tenderness, understanding and sympathetic companionship as their major tools for building.

Though called "a book for children" it might better be termed a hand-book for parents, for certainly no adult whose task it is to "bring up" a family today could find a better guide than this attractive, beautiful little volume called *My Happy Days*.

From still another angle the book is significant. Perhaps it was not the intent of the author to do so (though one would hesitate to make such a statement without equivocation, for Jane Dabney Shackelford is wise with the wisdom that abides in teachers of youth and mothers of children of their own), but she has produced a document which, in the field of race relations in present-day America, will go far toward furthering understanding and respect between the majority and minority groups so torn and biased by prejudice, misunderstanding and fear at the present time. For this book portrays *Childhood* in wholesome, average situations, and any reader, old or young, white or black, cannot miss the impact of these facts: that average human beings, in normal every-day situations, react in the same way, regardless of pigmentation, to the same stimuli, enjoy with equal pleasure the happy experiences of life, and grow to a full and rich appreciation of the things about them which make life beautiful, *when given the incentives and the opportunities for so doing*.

ESTHER POPEL SHAW

Deep River. By Henrietta Buckmaster. (New York: Harcourt, Brace and Company, 1944. Pp. 481.)

This is a novel that concerns itself primarily with life among the mountain folk of Georgia in the years just before the Civil War. It is a story of those people who, because of isolation and inarticulation, have received little attention either from historians or novelists. Around them hangs none of the glamor and romance that have so frequently been associated with the people who lived on the big, "prosperous" plantations of the rich coastal plains and river bottoms. They were a slaveless people, eking out their existence with the labor of their own hands on the sides of hills and in the all-too-small vales between the mountains. But some of them had been nourished on the philosophies of Thomas Jefferson and Tom Paine, and some of them loved human liberty and scorned those who held slaves.

Henrietta Buckmaster's hero, Simon Bliss, loved the mountains that had made him what he was. He realized, however, that life in the mountains could be bearable only if he went into the low country and fought slavery and the political power of the slave holders, who oppressed poor people, black and white alike. A high-spirited wife from the plantation, Negro-exploiting world increased his difficulties immeasurably; and his first task, which he finally completed, was to win her over to the point of view of him and his people. Before this was accomplished, however, their personal relationship typified the struggle between his people and hers.

The moving story of these two young Southern whites is painted against a rich background of life among the mountain folk, planters, slaves, and free Negroes; and the incongruity of the existence of several distinct worlds within each other is sharply portrayed. The story carries the reader swiftly through the crucial events that transpired in the two years preceding the outbreak of the Civil War. The power of the slaveholders is clearly seen in the manner in which they controlled the legislature and the convention which, despite the opposition of men like Bliss, finally voted Georgia out of the Union. The struggle between the people of the mountain and those of the plantation increased in intensity as the time for decision approached. In depicting the struggle, Miss Buckmaster has succeeded in making striking character delineations and in drawing exciting scenes of conflict. With secession, the comrades of

Bliss, lovers of freedom and the Union, lost; but in defeat they seemed to realize that they were to win the final victory.

Miss Buckmaster has done a satisfactory job of combining the fiction of the characters she has created with the reality of the times in which they live. To enliven and to convey an atmosphere of authenticity, the author has dealt acceptably, if not always accurately, with actual historical characters and events. Alexander Stephens, Charles Sumner, Hinton R. Helper, Robert Toombs, and many other figures of the period either appear in the pages of the narrative or are discussed. The result is an altogether pleasing treatment of a period that has not received the most careful attention of the historians that have dealt with it.

One's imagination is strained only in a few instances. When Savanna Door Bliss becomes so convinced of the evils of slavery that she helps slaves to escape from the plantation of her family, with whom she is still friendly, she achieves a love for freedom that, in all probability, seldom existed among her kind in the ante-bellum South. There is the possibility, moreover, that the hatred of the mountain folk for slavery was seldom accompanied by the respect for all mankind, including the blacks, that characterized the attitude of Simon Bliss and his people. Even in these instances, however, the characters and circumstances are not unreasonably overdrawn, but simply emphasize the emotional and spiritual chaos that was so much a part of the Old South. In combining in a thoroughly satisfactory manner history and fiction—two areas frequently not wholly unrelated—Miss Buckmaster has achieved a difficult task.

JOHN HOPE FRANKLIN

North Carolina College for Negroes

The Rising Wind. By Walter F. White. (New York: Doubleday, Doran and Company, 1945. Pp. 322. Price $3.00.)

The appearance of this book itself marks an epoch in the development of the Negro toward freedom and equality. The book was made possible by the permit from the United States Government authorizing the visit to the front of a man at the head of an organization advocating the full measure of citizenship for the Negro. The military authorities made it possible for the author to see and hear the things about which he has written. A trip of this sort could not have been made during the First World War.

There was so much fear that the Negro might demand some of the democracy for which he had fought in Europe that only Negroes certified by Thomas Jesse Jones and his imperialistic coworkers were allowed access to the Negro soldiers abroad. This book is evidence of the gradual break-up of the machine for Negro control in the United States.

In the book itself the author does not tell us much which we have not gleaned already from notices appearing in the press. The author has rendered the public a service, however, in bringing these facts together in a useful volume and so organized as to justify important conclusions and recommendations. We have long since known of the reluctance to send Negro soldiers to the front except to do drudgery in the capacity of members of the Engineer Corps, or in plain language, as labor battalions. Only in a few cases when so urged or in dire necessity have the military authorities permitted Negroes to fight shoulder to shoulder with white soldiers. Negroes in the camps have been kept there so long in inaction that they have grown as tired of the monotony as men when actually imprisoned. They have had no opportunity to express openly their feeling because the restrictions in military circles have made this course impracticable. Nevertheless, this fact has become widely known through the very movements and assignments of the troops themselves. A secret of this sort discloses itself.

One eloquent fact reported by the author and well substantiated by a number of white soldiers and officers returning from the front is that wherever the troops of both races have served in the same divisions facing the same enemy and experiencing the same fears and dangers a feeling of comradeship has sprung up between them which bids fair to assure the success of the much desired try-out of democracy in our military forces. The author expressed himself to General Eisenhower, as advocating further brigading of the soldiers of both races, and the Commander-in-Chief was not insulted at the suggestion. Several officers have gone as far as subordinates can go in thus urging democracy even to the extent of mixed units in the military forces, and one officer has in process of manufacture a book in advocacy of this bold stand.

The author of *Rising Wind* sees trouble ahead if we do not learn quickly to deal with colored people as with other elements of the world population. The United States Government will find itself in an impossible position in trying to dictate the rule of the rest of the world with its large majority of colored people when the United States is permitting subordination of the Negro element of this country to their exploiters who deny them social, economic and political rights in their own native land. The failure of the country to wipe out race distinctions at home will place it in the position of a suspect who cannot be trusted to interfere with free peoples of other parts of the world. The Negroes of the United States are no longer without friends abroad, and in foreign circles their case will naturally arise to torment those who will die for democracy abroad and die to crush it at home. If a change does not come trouble lies ahead, and wars without end will follow from the array of the whites against the colored peoples.

The warning as to the rising wind does not carry as much force as it would have in a book of this type published earlier in the present war when the outcome was more uncertain. At present Japan, long since self-styled as the champion of the colored peoples of the world, seems to be on the way to a crushing defeat which will turn back the wheels of progress there for at least a hundred years. India, once manifesting evidence of self-assertion, has played a losing game in the present international conflict. East Africa and the Northern littoral are safely subordinated to the economic imperialists. Native West Africa is talking much about natural rights but at present has no means for translating thought into action. Native South Africa in the tentacles of racial proscription seems to have no hope except through a volcanic eruption. Yet, the author is justified from history in believing that man cannot calculate the incalculable, and the social order always contrives in some way to redeem itself.

C. G. WOODSON

Education of Teachers for Improving Majority-Minority Relationships. By Ambrose Caliver, Senior Specialist in the Education of Negroes in the United States Office of Education. (Washington, D. C.: United States Government Printing Office, 1944. Pp. 64. Price 15 cents.)

The purpose of this study is to focus attention on the need for improved relationships among all varying elements of the population of the country. In order to do this we must emphasize the previously unrecognized potentialities of both individuals and groups, we must change the attitude of minority groups toward themselves and the majority group, and we must change the unfavorable attitude of majority toward the minority groups. The important minority groups in this country are the Negroes, Indians, Chinese, Japanese and other nonwhites. This problem, then, is an educational matter. The first task is to prepare the teaching corps for this special effort and then proceed to work with the students. The demands of the situation cannot be met in any other way.

A brief survey of the curricula of the schools and colleges show that the teachers turned out by them are not prepared to function in this capacity because the courses offered them are not adequate for this purpose. Schools and colleges offering courses on Latin America, the Far East, Africa, and the like are concerned mainly with the relations of this nation with those parts. Indians are studied mainly in the prehistoric sense and by regions rather than in the broad sense in which we take into account the Greek, the Roman and the Teuton. In Negro schools some attention is given to the study of their own background, but they neglect the history of the Indians with whom the past of the Negro in the United States is closely interwoven and give little or no thought to other minority groups. The author concludes from the results of his study that in "some instances large geographic areas have been hardly touched; in other instances institutions are making but little use of the excellent facilities at their command for intercultural purposes; and in too few is the kind of approach being made that the importance of the subject demands."

The schools must rise to the occasion. It is the function of education to improve majority-minority relationships. Schools must study minority groups to promote national unity and assure a lasting peace. There can be no permanent peace unless race prejudice is reduced. Prejudice is not inherent and through proper education may be removed. The approach, however, must not be sentimental. The procedure must be by scientific method. There must be an enrichment of the materials used in the effort and the method employed must be systematized and thorough. The problem, moreover, must be viewed as an international rather than as local affair which a few millions in one corner of the universe may handle to suit themselves. Science has brought all nations together as one large family and what ails one ails all. The race problem in the United States is a manifestation of a world problem which claims the attention of the rulers in Africa, Asia, Australia and the islands of the sea. All the peoples in these once distant parts must study these closer relationships and the groups now thus indissolubly linked for the common good. History does not offer any other course for clearing up misunderstandings and removing those antipathies which have drawn the so-called civilized world into an all but self-exterminating world conflict.

JEROME HILL.

The Negro Artist Comes of Age. A National Survey of Contemporary American Artists. Foreword by John Davis Hatch, Jr. Introduction, "Up Till Now," by Alain Locke. (Albany, New York: Albany Institute of History and Art, 1945. Pp. 85.)

This work is a catalogue of an exhibit of Negro art set up by the Albany Institute of History and Art. The aim is to lift the Negro artist from the patronizing sphere of a group set off by itself and regarded as Negro artists rather than as artists who happen to be Negroes. The very exhibit itself left upon one of the artists invited to participate this very undesirable impression and for that reason he refused to exhibit. Whether he is standing in his own light or blazing the way for a new hearing for Negro artists is not clear. Negro artists, like all other Negroes of merit, receive recognition only occasionally and in some cases not at all. How then can the Negro of merit present his case to the public? By exhibiting his productions in separate and distinct shows, or by keeping his works in his studio until the barriers of caste are broken down? History shows the former has been the wiser course. Henry O. Tanner began his career by exhibiting his paintings before gatherings in Negro churches and schools. Next he advanced to the one-man show among Negroes and sympathetic whites. In this way he realized sufficient from his works to go abroad where he distinguished himself. Negro singers have traveled the same hard road. Marian Anderson and Roland Hayes began their careers by singing in Negro churches for from five to ten dollars an engagement.

This survey, although emphasizing distinctly Negro artists, is intended to show that the Negro artists have come of age. They are making a real contribution to our national art. The Albany Institute believes that their contribution is equal to that of their more popularly recognized contemporaries in music and literature. These friends of Negro artists believe that they should be no longer appraised by special standards as a group, "but as individuals among the greater body of creative artists of our country." The Institute has discovered as many as forty-one deserving such recognition and expresses disappointment at the failure of *Who's Who in American Art* to include more than twelve of this number.

Any one interested in the esthetic development of the Negro will do well to secure a copy of this work. The introduction by Alain Locke gives in concise form what he has said in extenso in his other works in this field and thus makes available at a low price a treatment which otherwise would cost much more. In the catalogue, too, appear sketches of a number of painters and sculptors who are not yet widely known. When we mention the Negro in art we inevitably think of Richmond Barthé, Aaron Douglass, Palmer Hayden, Sargent Johnson, William H. Johnson, Lois M. Jones, Archibald J. Motley, James A. Porter, Meta Vaux Warrick Fuller, William Edouard Scott, James L. Wells and Hale Woodruff; but recently have developed in this sphere a number of others who have shown evidence also of measuring up to the highest standards. We have taken notice of William Artis, Henry W. Bannern, Eloise Bishop, Elizabeth Catlett, Jacob Lawrence, Eldzier Cortor, Horace Pippin, and Vernon Winslow; but knocking at the door also for recognition are Romare Bearden, Selma Hortense Burke, William Carter, Claude Clark, Ernest Crichlow, Joseph Delaney, Fred C. Flemister, Rex Goreleigh, Ronald Joseph, Norman Lewis, Edward L. Loper, Frank W. Neal, Marion Perkins, Charles Sebree, Hughie Lee Smith, Thelma Johnson Streat, Charles White, Ellis Wilson, John Wilson, and others.

C. G. WOODSON

Unsung Americans Sung. Edited by W. C. Handy. (New York: Handy Brothers Music Company, 1944. Pp. 236.)

This book is an effort to bring together in one volume the thoughts and expressions of as many as thirty-eight contributors who in prose, poetry, or music have paid tribute to Negro makers of history in this country and abroad. Among so many contributors there are naturally varying qualifications and consequently they present productions ranging from the serious and significant to the trivial and unimportant. These thoughts on the lives selected are not well expressed in prose; and the poetry, with the exception of a few specimens like the beautiful tribute paid William Monroe Trotter by James William Henderson, does not rise to the level of the music to which it has been set. Throughout the book appear a number of verses which may be properly styled as jingle. In the rather brief and inadequate accounts of careers appear mistakes like those on page 78 about Frederick Douglass's selected birthday and his learning to read.

It is unfortunate that there should creep into the book such a thing as an illustration of a bogus picture of Crispus Attucks which was made to order for a few dollars some years ago by a man in Washington, D. C. No one knows how Crispus Attucks looked, and in paintings of the Boston Massacre artists have been honest enough to indicate merely the death of a loyal black hero without defining in detail his looks. We have no paintings of Crispus Attucks by himself. Photography was unknown here at that time. The only thing we know about his looks appeared in the advertisement of him as a runaway in 1750, saying that he was a mulatto six feet two inches high, with short curled hair, and knees closer together than common.

The work fails also to distinguish between the famous and infamous and therefore includes considerable material which might have been appropriately rejected. It does not impress the reading public favorably to see the few Negro heroes of the present war given space to the exclusion of those Negroes who have achieved fame in art, literature, science, and public service. Children and many adults without any foundation on which to base a systematic study of the Negro may be thereby misled in trying to grasp the meaning of the Negro in history.

When the reader observes among the contributors Langston Hughes, Alain Locke and George W. Schuyler he cannot resist the wish that one of these had given the ensemble an editorial checking before the volume was printed.

Yet in spite of all its demerits this book must be considered a commendable undertaking. It marks an epoch in the thinking of the Negro. The race is now conscious of the heroism of the noble men and women who have led it thus far out of the wilderness. These toilers and fighters for opportunity and recognition of the worthwhile achievements of the race must now be honored. The whole story has not been told in this one volume. Several productions of this type will be required to complete the narrative and to celebrate in song the heroism of its martyrs. Music herein drawn upon, as the author states in the preface, has a distinct service to render in this dramatization, and the panorama with its aid will leave a more lasting impression. W. C. Handy has made the initial effort, and others in the years to come will follow in his footsteps.

C. G. WOODSON

Frederick Douglass: Selections from His Writings. Edited with an introduction by Philip S. Foner. (New York: International Publishers, 1945. Pp. 95. Price 35 cents.)

This is by far the most informing and the most valuable brief treatment of the career of Frederick Douglass hitherto published. In the larger works dealing with the career of the great abolitionist many phases of his life find a more detailed treatment, but no author has put into such limited space so many valuable comments and suggestive observations on Douglass and the men and measures of his time. The book is more of a brief biography of Douglass than a collection of his writings. About half of the space is devoted to the introduction in which the author presents Douglass as the tribune of his people and the selections from his writings follow this illuminating story in such useful arrangement as to serve as a prolongation of the author's story of this Negro statesman. The booklet may be appropriately styled a brief biography of Frederick Douglass.

In writing this story the author did not depend altogether on *The Life and Times of Frederick Douglass* which has served as the boundary of most authors who have taken up this man's career. The author of this booklet made considerable use of the editorials of the *North Star* or *Frederick Douglass's Paper* and examined a number of his letters and other unpublished productions. The story constructed on this broader basis of the general interests of the Negro reformer makes a very interesting and informing account. We learn therefrom more about Douglass's relation to the Abolitionists both in this country and abroad, more about his handicaps within the circles of his friends and blows from his enemies from without, more about his relations with outstanding national figures like Gerrit Smith, John Brown, Abraham Lincoln, and Andrew Johnson. Illuminating also is Douglass's concern for the economic uplift of the Negro to assure his political power. The connection of the reformer with the labor leaders, the advocates of woman suffrage and the extension of freedom and opportunity in their broad aspects to men of all classes and conditions is emphasized in this brief narrative.

In the account of the development of Douglass gradually to the stature of a leader the author unconsciously ranks him as a statesman above the level of Wendell Phillips and William Lloyd Garrison. The mind of Douglass had such potentiality that he could not be restricted to a narrative of his life in slavery while others gave the philosophy justifying the extermination of the system. Douglass, after listening to the arguments advanced by his friends, discovered that he reasoned better than they; and much to their displeasure he branched out with his own philosophy in exposing the evils of the system and using moral suasion to set the public mind against it. Douglass was not deterred by those who wanted to hush him for the reason that he spoke so eloquently and so convincingly that the public would not believe that he had been held as a slave.

Furthermore, while Garrison and Phillips denounced the Constitution as proslavery and would have nothing to do with slavery or the government which supported it, Douglass was wise enough to distinguish between dealing with slaveholders and dealing with slaveholding. Douglass had hopes for the conversion of the slaveholders just as he believed that by making the reform element a factor in politics the United States Government might some day be changed from a proslavery to an antislavery regime. Douglass went into politics in order to register on the Government as far as possible the will of those opposed to slavery while the Garrisonians held themselves aloof crying out, ''No union with slaveholders.'' Douglass saw that, if the union with slaveholders were broken, slavery would be thereby secured rather than weakened, and abolitionism would have no ultimate purpose. Time has shown that Frederick Douglass was right. History, then, as the whole truth tends to get a hearing, will crown this man as one of the greatest statesmen of his time. Not only a great Negro, but a broad-minded, far-sighted humanitarian interested in the improvement of all mankind and daring to battle for his convictions when others sought his destruction.

This useful booklet may be improved by adding a short index. Should the work pass to a second edition, as it doubtless will, *Hugh Garnet* on page 25 should be corrected to read *Henry Highland Garnet* and *Governor Andrews* on page 34 to read *Governor Andrew.*

C. G. WOODSON

The Role of the Supreme Court in American Government and Politics. By Charles Groves Haines (Berkeley: University of California Press, 1944. Pp. xiii, 697. Price $6.00.)

Because of the traditional sacredness of justice and the courts from which it emanates we dislike the idea of associating the courts with politics in the general use of the term. Politics considered as the science of government, however, sounds better to the sensitive admirer of modern institutions when reference is made to courts. Yet it must be admitted that courts do become political in the sense of conforming to or trying to influence public opinion, and persons insisting on maintaining the administration of justice above the level of chicanery have denounced our courts on this account. The most striking example of this was the Dred Scott decision and the supposed collusion between the executive and the judiciary in that unpopular mandate. In his inaugural address in March, 1857, James Buchanan referred to the slavery controversy as a matter soon to be settled by the United States Supreme Court, and a few days thereafter Chief Justice Roger B. Taney came out with the decision that since the Negro was not a citizen of the United States he could not sue for freedom or anything else in a federal court. Public opinion rebelled against that decision and brought on the Civil War which countermanded that verdict.

The author of this volume deals with the United States Supreme Court on a higher level. He endeavors to correct what he considers to be an error of historians who have paid too much attention to the Federalist views which dominated the national tribunal long after that party had been overthrown. Just as much attention, he believes, should be directed to the views of the Anti-Federalist or States' Rights-Republican views which by constructive opposition contributed greatly also to the development of the role of the United States Supreme Court. These opponents objected to the nationalistic tendencies of the tribunal and arrayed themselves against judicial review of matters so important to their program for the democratizing of the institutions of the United States. To ignore their efforts or to fail to evaluate them properly in producing the legal history of the United States, the author believes, is an error which historians should now correct.

In this work, however, the author writes more like a theorist than an historian or a practical lawyer. On paper what he says makes a deep impression, but when the facts of the case appear in the picture his words lose much of their weight. In the first place, the term democracy is misused. The States' Rights party impeded rather than promoted democracy. This doctrine is responsible for fastening the Negro in chattel slavery and the poor whites in economic slavery. This party denied the poor whites representation, the right of suffrage and access to civic honors. The Democratic party which emerged from the States' Rights-Republican affiliation preached one doctrine and practiced another. Thomas Jefferson, the distinguished philosopher of that faith, is considered one of the great presidents of the United States; but the justification for thus estimating his administration is based almost solely on those things which he did in going contrary to the doctrines which he advocated —acquiring the Louisiana Territory without authority from the representatives of the people, and setting up therein a government with all but dictatorial powers, waging war on the Barbary States to compel respect for our rights on the high sea, passing the Embargo and the Non-Intercourse Acts which killed New England commerce and forced that section all but to the point of secession. Andrew Jackson the next outstanding exponent of the same party did not seem to have any clear views by which he might be classified as a loose or close constructionist. He wanted to hang the South Carolinians for trying to nullify the tariff law, but he would not enforce the mandate of the United States Supreme Court which declared unconstitutional a law of Georgia by which Samuel A. Worcester was convicted and imprisoned for its violation in going without a license from the Governor to reside among the Cherokees after March 1, 1831. Jackson also firmly supported slavery which rested upon states' rights as its sure foundation.

The objection raised by the Democratic party to the nationalizing decisions of the Supreme Court came largely when these decisions did not advance their political cause. The Democratic party did not object to the Dred Scott decision by which slavery was to become nation-wide. In the early history of the country, moreover, there was no sharp distinction between loose constructionists and close constructionists of the Constitution. Parties were built mainly around popular leaders as today. The average partisan does not know when he is drifting in one direction or in another. The Republican Party of today, for example, is now in the same position where the Democratic party was in 1860. The Democratic party of today is building up a strong central government at the expense of the governments in the states, and in order to return to power the Republicans have taken up their old doctrine of states' rights. At the same time there are in both parties strong minorities favoring the doctrines advanced by their opponents.

C. G. WOODSON

The United States, 1865-1900: A Survey of Current Literature with Abstracts of Unpublished Dissertations. Edited by Curtis Wiswell Garrison. (Fremont, Ohio: The Rutherford B. Hayes and the Lucy Webb Hayes Foundation, 1944. Pp. 453. Price $1.00.)

This work is the result of the effort to make available to the public a digest of the historical literature treating the period during which Rutherford B. Hayes and the measures he championed influenced the history of the United States. The editors, as the title indicates, looked in both directions for an evaluation of what has been actually produced and for notices of scholarly works which are soon to appear. These reviews, as far as practicable, are classified for the convenience of the student. In order appear those designated as political and constitutional, economic and social, educational and intellectual, and finally those bearing upon religion, literature and art. Other reviews of the volume are classified according to regions and states. A section is devoted to recent textbooks, surveys and popular histories, and still another to abstracts of unpublished dissertations accepted in 1943 relating to American History. It is inevitable, of course, that these lines of demarcation become tortuous inasmuch as one work may bear upon practically all these phases of history. The effort at classification is commendable and will save the busy student much time in arriving at what the volume evaluates.

It is unfortunate, however, that the Editor and his associates are not sufficiently enlightened or broadminded to evaluate more works bearing on the Negro. To say that they did not know of any more such works is not a plausible excuse. Scholars have the ability to find out things, or they who do not have such ability are not scholars. Some of the volumes on the Negro made available to the staff, moreover, were not reviewed as, for example, the four volumes of the works of the late Francis J. Grimké. The administration of Rutherford B. Hayes touched more vitally the Negroes of the United States than any other element of the American population, and it is difficult to write any comprehenisve history of the country during this period without noting this fact. It seems then that if this board of editors mean to evaluate this history as it should be they must place on their board some Negro scholar who will take the time to look into matters about which most of them do not know very much. Among their editors they have Dr. Charles H. Wesley listed. The position, however, is probably one of mere recognition, although he did write one of the reviews. As the head of Wilberforce University he hardly has the time to give to such details, and the volume as it now stands was hardly published with his approval as an adequate digest of the historical literature which appeared between September, 1942 and September, 1943.

A mere glance at this survey will show how lacking it is with respect to works bearing on the history of the Negro from 1865 to 1900. Julian H. Lewis's *Biology of the American Negro*, Rackham Holt's *George Washington Carver*, Robert M. McDill's *Early Education of the Negro in America*, James A. Porter's *Modern Negro Art*, and Marion Thompson Wright's *New Jersey Laws and the Negro* receive attention. Hugh Morris Gloster's and Nancy Bullock Woolridge's works on the Negro in fiction are outlined, and likewise Emma Corinne Brown Galvin's treatment of the *Lore of the Negro in Central New York State*. In addition appear estimates of some magazine productions. This inadequate treatment does the literature of the Negro a great injustice which should be remedied by a more conscientious and scholarly staff.

C. G. WOODSON

NOTES

BOOKS OF AMERICAN HISTORY

Two Men and a Bargain is a reprint from the Spring 1943 Number of *South Today* published by Lillian Smith at Clayton, Georgia. It is being distributed as a paper-bound pamphlet of twelve pages by the National CIO Committee to Abolish Race Discrimination. The work gives the story of the understanding between the rich man and the poor white in the South to keep the Negro down.

The Abolition of Industrial Slavery, a paper-bound booklet published privately by the author, Lilly A. Perry, at 1427 Perry Place, Northwest, Washington, D. C., presents the effort toward this end by promoting justice in industry and all human relations, by quickening "humanity's consciousness to the recognition and practice of justice, righteousness, unity, universal brotherhood and peace."

Divide and Conquer, by Allan Sloane and Bob Russell, with a foreword by Howard Fast, is a playlet for children for combatting race discrimination. When first produced in the Amityville Primary school the newspapers gave it publicity and friends of tolerance began to order it. The first orders for hundreds led to orders for thousands. The work is now distributed through the Green Publishing Company, Box 283, Amityville, New York, for 15 cents a copy.

Negro Churchmen Speak to White Churchmen is a demand for the "Open Church," for the Church of Christ, not the church of races and nations which accepts some human beings and rejects others, but the Church as conceived and launched by Jesus of Nazareth. This statement was prepared at the request of the Federal Council's Commission on the Church and Minority Peoples by a Committee of its Negro members consisting of Benjamin E. Mays as chairman, Channing H. Tobias, Charles H. Wesley, and Olivia P. Stokes. It is signed by 106 clergymen and laymen who thereby urge that all churches admit to full and active membership all persons without regard to race, color or national origin; for, if democracy cannot be practiced in the Church, it will have no hope through other institutions.

A Monthly Summary of Events and Trends in Race Relations for December 1944, published under the direction of Charles S. Johnson for the Rosenwald Fund, gives in digested form what has happened recently in advancing or retarding the effort to bring the races together in helpful cooperation. While most of what appears in this number may be remembered as recent news, the summary supplies these facts in handy and useful form.

Whites Look at Negroes and Negro Problems is a report of a survey made in this field by the National Opinion Research Center of the University of Denver. In this mimeographed production of seventy-five pages are summarized the findings from data of thousands of questionnaires seeking opinions on four important matters: The treatment of Negroes in the United States, Negro education, Negroes and jobs, and social contacts of Negroes. Samples of the answers obtained from the various sections of the country indicate that the Negroes have made some progress toward fairness and justice but the people of the United States are about equally divided as to granting Negroes equal economic opportunity and recognizing them as citizens.

The Black and White Rejections for Military Service is the report of an investigation made by the American Teachers Association through a committee consisting of Martin D. Jenkins, Francis A. Gregory, Howard H. Long, Jane E. McAllister, and Charles H. Thompson. The report shows that conisderably more selectees were rejected for educational reasons in the South than in the North and West, that fewer white selectees have been rejected for educational reasons in the North and West than in the South; that almost invariably a larger percentage of Negro selectees have been rejected for educational reasons in each of the 28 states for which data have been made available than in the case of white selectees in these states and that a smaller percentage of Negro Selectees in New York City, Illinois, Massachusetts, Indiana, Michigan, West Virginia, Ohio, Kentucky, California, and Pennsylvania have been rejected for educational reasons than white selectees in Georgia, Virginia, Alabama, South Carolina, Arkansas, Texas and North Carolina. The committee does not consider very convincing the hypotheses that the tests used are not valid for estimating the knowledge of persons of subcultural environments, that different methods of applying the test may have produced differences in the results, and that some men deliberately made low scores to evade the draft. The committee is rather of the opinion that the chief explanation lies in the lack of schooling and in poor cultural background. It is recommended that the facilities of the education be improved; and, since the states have not the revenue adequate to this demand, the Federal Government should change its policy and subsidize education.

Small Farm and Big Farm, by Carey McWiliams, is Public Affairs Pamphlet, No. 100. The author examines briefly all types of farms but does not advocate the multiplication of any special type, "for no one type has monopoly of economic or social efficiencies. Our chief aim should be that of maintaining democracy in agriculture. What is important is not the size of the farm, but what happens to the people who work the land." In the development of this thought the author shows that Negro farmers have been neglected and that organizations projected to ameliorate the condition of farmers have restricted or excluded Negroes.

Books dealing with other matters but giving some thought to the Negro include these: *Journal of a Southern Student, 1846-1848*, letters of a student of a college in South Carolina, by Giles J. Patterson (Nashville: Vanderbilt University Press, 1944); *Rochester in the Civil War*, edited by Blake McKelvey (Rochester, New York: Rochester Historical Society, 1945); *Jefferson Davis and His Cabinet*, by Rambert W. Patrick (Baton Rouge, Louisiana: University of Louisiana Press, 1945); *Growing up with Chicago*, by Carter H. Harrison (Chicago: Ralph Fisher Seymour, 1944).

Books which concern the Negro especially include the following: *Black Boy, a record of Childhood and Youth*, by Richard Wright, the author of *Native Son* (New York: Harper and Brothers, 1945); *Were You There When They Crucified My Lord?* a Negro spiritual in 39 illustrations, by Allan Rohan Crite (Cambridge, Massachusetts: Harvard University Press, 1945); *Complete Equality*, democracy and the Negroes, by Max Bedacht (New York: International Workers Order, Inc., 1945); *Trends in Federal Policy toward the Negro*, by A. A. Taylor, being a reprint from the Annual Report of the American Historical Association for 1942; and *Democracy Begins at Home*, the Tennessee Poll Tax Fight, by Jennings Jerry (Philadelphia: J. B. Lippincott Company, 1944).

Closely connected with problems of all minorities are the thoughts in the following: *Born Free and Equal,* a story of Japanese-Americans, by Ansell Adams (New York); and *Prejudice: Japanese-American: Symbol of Racial Intolerance,* by Carey McWilliams (Boston: Little Brown and Company, 1944).

ARTICLES OF AMERICAN HISTORY

Articles of general political importance include these: "William Yancey's Transition from Unionism to States' Rights," by Austin L. Venable (*Journal of Southern History,* August, 1944); "Politics in Maryland during the Civil War," by Charles B. Clark (*The Maryland Historical Magazine,* December, 1944); "Opposition to Lincoln in the Elections of 1864," by Leonard Newman (*Science and Society,* Fall Number, 1944); "The Army of Northern Virginia," by R. H. Woody (*South Atlantic Quarterly,* January, 1945); "The Price Paid for Disfranchising Southerners in 1867," by William A. Russ, Jr. (*ibid.*); "Between Slavery and Freedom," by William Linn Westermann (*American Historical Review,* January, 1945).

The following have a more direct bearing: "Prudence Crandall," by E. W. Small (*The New England Quarterly,* December, 1944); "The Jerry Rescue," by W. Freeman Galpin (*New York History,* January, 1945).

Of mainly social and economic importance are the following: "Negro Episcopalians in Ante-Bellum North Carolina," by John Hope Franklin (*Historical Magazine of the Protestant Episcopal Church,* September, 1944); "Negro Secret Societies," by Edward Nelson Palmer (*Social Forces,* December, 1944); "Changing Patterns of Religious Thought among Negroes," by Thelma D. Ackiss (*ibid.*); "Tobacco Belt of North Carolina," by Franklin C. Erickson (*Economic Geography,* January, 1945); "Tenancy in the United States: A Consideration of the Validity of the Agricultural Ladder Hypothesis," by La Wanda Fenalson Cox (*Agricultural History,* July, 1944); "Automobile Unions and Negro Labor," by Lloyd A. Bailer (*Political Science Quarterly,* December, 1944).

Of a strictly legal nature are the following: "Enforcement of Civil Rights," by Victor W. Rotnem (*National Bar Journal,* March, 1945); "The White Primary and the Supreme Court, by Sidney A.

Jones, Jr. (*ibid.*); "The South's Challenge to the Negro Lawyer," by Charles W. Anderson, Jr. (*ibid.*); "Peonage or Debt Slavery in the Land of the Free," by William Henry Huff (*ibid*).

Books on the West Indies and Latin America

Books of varying significance in this field include the following: *The South*, the intimate aspects of Latin-America, by Kurt Severin (New York: Dual, Sloan and Pierce, 1945); *The Virgin Islands and Their People*, by Antonio Jarvis (Philadelphia: Dorrance and Company, 1944); *Mexico: Magnetic Southland*, by Sydney A. Clark (New York: Dodd, Mead and Company, 1944); *Argentine Riddle*, by Felix Weil (New York: The John Day Company, 1945); *Britain and the Independence of Latin America*, by C. K. Webster (Oxford); *Economic Problems of Latin America*, edited by Seymour E. Harris (New York: McGraw-Hill Book Company, 1944); *Brazilian Literature*, by Erico Versisimi (New York: The Macmillan Company, 1945); *Sintesis Historica de la Cubanidad en los Siglos XVI y XVII*, a lecture by Elias Entralgo (La Habana: Molina y Compania, 1944).

Articles on the West Indies and Latin America

The important recent articles dealing with the people in these parts are: "Quatro seculos de civilizaçao devidos aos negros escravos," by Alvaro Gonçales (*Cultura Politica*, Rio de Janeiro, January, 1944); "Los negreros del Caribe," by Alberto Miramon (*Bol. Hist. Antig.*, January, 1944); "The Slave Trade in Mexico," by Gonzalo Aguirre Beltran (*Hispanic American Review*, August, 1944); "The Negro Race in Mexico," by Joaquin Poncal (*ibid.*); "The Slave Trade and the Negro in South America," by Fernando Romero (*ibid.*); "Saco's History of Negro Slavery," by D. C. Corbett (*ibid*).

Of social and economic significance are the following: "The Belief System of the Haitian Vodun," by George Eaton Simpson (*American Anthropologist*, January-March, 1945); "West Indian Market for Dominican Products," by Rafael Espaillat (*Bulletin of the Pan American Union*, February, 1945); "Guatemala's New School of Agriculture" (*ibid.*); "Haiti's Five Year Plan," by Elie

Lescot (*ibid.*); "Race Relations in Puerto Rico and the Virgin Islands," by Eric Williams (*Foreign Affairs,* January, 1945).

BOOKS ON AFRICA

Books on Africa dealing mainly with economic and social matters include the following: *Half Past When,* by Hassoldt Davis (Philadelphia: J. B. Lippincott and Company, 1945); *Labor Problems of Africa,* by John A. Moon (Philadelphia: University of Pennsylvania Press, 1945); *Soviet Light on the Colonies,* by Leonard Barnes (London: Penguin Books, 1944); *The Bantu in South African Literature,* by Edgar H. Brookes (Johannesburg: South African Institute of Race Relations, 1944); *The Future of Colonial Peoples,* Lord Hailey (Oxford University Press, 1944); *Inside Our Prisons,* by F. E. T. Krause (Johannesburg: South African Institute of Race Relations, 1944); *Revenge or Reformation?* by H. P. Junod (Lovedale: The Christian Council of South Africa); *Land Hunger in the Colonies,* by C. W. W. Greenidge (London: Unwin Brothers, 1944); *Ourselves and Empire,* by H. W. Foster (London: Macmillan Company, 1944).

ARTICLES ON AFRICA

Articles of a scientific bearing include the following: "Notes on Form and Structure in Bantu Speech" by E. O. Ashton (*Africa,* January, 1925); "Preliminary Note on a New Series of Pottery Figures from Northern Nigeria," by Bernard Flagg (*ibid.*); "Religious Beliefs of the Akan," by Edwin W. Smith (*ibid.*).

Articles dealing mainly with the economic or political situation are the following: "Native Farm Labor in South Africa," by James G. Leyburn (*Social Forces,* December, 1944); "The Mauritius Riots of 1943," "The West African Cocoa Control Scheme," "The Future of the Rhodesias and Nyasaland," "Abyssinia," "The Native in Parliament," (*The Anti-Slavery Reporter and Aborigines' Friend,* January, 1945); "Vanishing Lands and Migrant Labour," by Maurice Webb (*Race Relations,* Numbers 3 and 4, 1944); "Some Economic Aspects of Changing Native Policy," by R. H. Smith (*ibid.*); "The African Village after the War," by A. G. Dickson (*ibid.*); "The Soviet Approach to Colonies," by George Sacks (*ibid.*); "The Legal Plight of the African Woman," by Dawn

Wentzel (*ibid.*); "Changing Conditions in the Protectorates" (*Race Relations News*, Johannesburg, September, 1944); "African Soldiers Abroad" (*ibid.*); "Reform of the Pass Laws" (*ibid.*); "The Natives' Representative Council Debates" (*ibid.*, October, 1944); "Farm Labour" (*ibid.*); "No Solution of the Indian Problem" (*ibid.*); "Police and Prisons" (*ibid.*); "Scholarships for African Girls" (*ibid.*); "Race Relations Overseas" (*ibid.*); "Pensions for the Aged and Infirm" (*ibid.*, October, 1944); "Youth Serves" (*ibid.*); "Welfare of Colored People" (*ibid.*); "Thrift" (*ibid.*); "Native Education" (*ibid.*); "Africans to Build Own Homes" (*ibid.*); "A Race Riot and Its Causes" (*ibid.*, December, 1944); "Inability to Pay" (*ibid.*); "Our Crowded Prisons" (*ibid.*) and "The Indian Crisis" (*ibid.*).

PERSONAL

John Henry Manning Butler

The Filipinos owe a debt of gratitude to the Negro soldiers who helped to free their country from the stranglehold of Spain and made possible their recent development toward independent status. They owe a similar debt to the Negro teachers who volunteered to go to that crude country immediately after pacification to give the people a modern language and develop their minds unto modern stature. The names of these Negro teachers would make a long list of workers—the most important of whom were W. H. Holder, and J. F. Hart from Kansas City, Caldwell from Texas, Thomas Shaffer from Kentucky, May Fitzbutler from St. Louis, Frederick Bonner from Connecticut, and C. G. Woodson from West Virginia. The outstanding among them all, however, was John Henry Manning Butler.

Butler was born in Elizabeth City, North Carolina, and was educated at the Plymouth Normal School. He taught at the Normal and Industrial School in Elizabeth City from 1891 to 1894 while serving the institution as vice-principal. From 1896 to 1900 he taught at the Agricultural and Technical College in that state. After spending these years there in education he went to the Philippine Islands in 1902 as an organizer and inspector of schools for the Filipinos. His first important work was the establishment and development of the school at Alaminos in the Province of Pangasinan. There his grasp of the educational needs and his efficiency in vocal music made him an outstanding figure. He was so successful in securing the cooperation of the natives and in enlightening both adults and their children that the school of Alaminos was estimated among the best in the province.

In 1903 Butler brought over his wife whom he had married prior to his departure for the Philippines. She did not like the situation so well and later returned to the United States to live. Butler came back to this country several times to visit but spent the rest of his years at this post in the Philippines. He later made a contribution in simplifying books adapted to the capacity of the Filipinos and published several texts of original stamp. His fine record entitled him to promotion. He was appointed as Acting Superintendent of

243

Public Schools in the Province of Isabela in 1921. In 1927 he was made the Superintendent of Public Schools of both Isabela and Cagayan. In 1928 his burdens were lightened by restricting him to the superintendency of Cagayan alone. From this position he was retired on a pension on September 25, 1933, when he reached the age limit. He served thereafter in the department of education of National University in Manila, a private institution. There he was when the Japanese took the country. The crisis was too much for him, a man of three score and six; and for some unknown reason he succumbed January 10, 1944. He deserves credit for being not only a representative Negro but a distinguished American citizen who made a contribution to the modernization of the Philippines.

WALTER HOWARD LOVING

One other distinguished Negro left on the Philippines a more lasting impression than even some of the Americans sent there as governors. He was Major Walter Howard Loving, the director of the Philippine Constabulary Band which he made famous throughout the civilized world. He too was caught in the Philippines by the Japanese conquest, and recently was reported killed in the fighting incident to the reconquest of the archipelago by the American Army.

Loving was born in Washington, D. C., December 7, 1872, and was educated in its public schools. He worked for some years as a printer and studied music locally. When the Spanish-American War broke out he volunteered and served in the Eighth United States Volunteer Infantry. While thus engaged he organized from crude materials a band which was acclaimed as the best ever thus developed in the service. When the volunteers were mustered out at the close of this war of only 121 days, Loving entered the army as a regular and went to the Philippines with the force consisting of the 48th and 49th Infantry. There he again applied himself to the development of another military band which became the idol of the army and the people of Manila. When these United States forces had served their time and had to leave the Philippines according to schedule, Loving had so endeared himself to the whole country that Filipinos and Americans prevailed upon the War Department to release him for organizing such a band among the Filipinos. With the support of the Insular Government, headed at that time by William Howard Taft, Loving admirably succeeded. The Philippine Constabulary Band not only charmed the people at home but went on a tour of the Orient and came to the United States, showered with praise wherever it appeared.

The first chance Americans had to hear this famous musical aggregation was in 1904 when it was featured as an outstanding attraction of the Saint Louis World Fair. The Band figured later as an attraction also on the Million Dollar Pier in Atlantic City, New Jersey, one summer. The Band made a tremendous hit and received a great ovation at the Pan American Pacific Exposition in San Francisco in 1915. Loving retired with the rank of major and left the Band in the hands of a Filipino as his successor who suffered the aggregation to lose ground. Upon the urgent request of friends and the chief men of state he returned to revive it, and retired to the United States again. At the request of the late Manuel Quezon, the president of the Philippine Commonwealth, Loving returned again to restore the Band to its former standing. There the war overtook him.

As a bandmaster Major Loving admitted no superiors. Philip Sousa, a great bandmaster himself, said that the Philippine Constabulary Band was the greatest musical aggregation of a military nature that he had ever heard. The passing of Major Loving was a great loss to the Philippines and to the United States.

FREDERIC BANCROFT

In the death of Frederic Bancroft on the 22nd of February, research in the field of Negro History lost a great friend. He was born in Galesburg, Illinois, October 30, 1860, and passed his early life there. He completed his college education at Amherst in 1882 and from there he went to Columbia University to specialize in history, working toward the degree of Doctor of Philosophy which he received in 1885. He then went abroad and studied at Götingen in 1883, and in Berlin, Frieburg and the École des Sciences Politiques in Paris from 1885 to 1887. Knox College, in Galesburg, Illinois, early impressed with his scholarship, conferred upon him the degree of Doctor of Laws in 1900 and much later Amherst the degree of Doctor of Humanities in 1932.

His first and only important employment was as Librarian of the United States Department of State from 1888 to 1892. While devoting most of his time to research he lectured in the field on political history of the Civil War and Reconstruction at Amherst in 1888; on the political and diplomatic history of the United States from 1898 to 1899 at the same institution. He lectured also at Johns Hopkins and at the University of Chicago on the political history of the United States; and at Lowell Institute in Boston from 1902 to 1903 on "Life in the South." For a long time he served on the staff of the New York *Nation*. He was sent as a delegate to the Congress of Historians in Paris in 1900.

In his early efforts he deeply invaded the field of American History as it had been influenced by the Negro. His first product was *The Negro in Politics* in which he showed the reconstruction views of most students of the Department of History and Political Science of Columbia University at that time. This work appeared in 1885. In cooperation with William A. Dunning he published in 1900 the life of William H. Seward in two volumes. In 1908 Dr. Bancroft published *The Public Life of Carl Schurz* and in 1913 *The Speeches, Correspondence and Public Papers of Carl Schurz* in six volumes. In 1927 he produced *The Mission of America and Other War Time Speeches of Edgar A. Bancroft*, his brother, who died while serving as United States Ambassador to Japan. In 1928 appeared Dr. Bancroft's *Calhoun and the Nullification Movement in South Carolina*. Near the end of his career Dr. Bancroft became interested in the study of slavery and in 1931 brought out his epoch-making work entitled *Slave Trading in the Old South*. In this monumental work he exposed so many fallacies of writers like Phillips, Craven and Lloyd that they have been discredited as authorities on slavery.

Dr. Bancroft welcomed the first appearance of the JOURNAL OF NEGRO HISTORY in January, 1916 and through reading this magazine became acquainted with its editor. Concerned with his many tasks, Dr. Bancroft could not devote time to any effort in this special field, but he encouraged the undertaking as timely and worthwhile. In 1932 he decided to give some stimulus to the work by providing annually for four history prizes: a first prize of one hundred dollars for the best article contributed to THE JOURNAL OF NEGRO HISTORY during the year, and a second prize of fifty dollars for the next best article contributed to this magazine during the same year. Also a first prize of fifty dollars for the best book review contributed to the JOURNAL OF NEGRO HISTORY during the year, and a second prize of twenty-five dollars for the next best book review contributed to this magazine during the same period.

It was fortunate that in making his will he thought well enough of the Association for the Study of Negro Life and History to provide that from the fund which his estate will go to establish, this organization will be paid two hundred and twenty-five dollars annually for five years for prizes with the understanding that one hundred dollars of this amount must be used as a prize for the best article contributed to THE JOURNAL OF NEGRO HISTORY every year. The Association will designate these as the Bancroft History Prizes in memory of the distinguished historian.

Dr. Bancroft was a man of high ideals. He insisted on honesty in his relations with all men. In his own circle he fearlessly attacked those using their positions to exploit the public for selfish purposes. He had no patience with those so-called historians who used facts on one side of a question and ignored other data to the contrary. He spent much of his time and considerable means in exposing such whitewash and propaganda. In his independent position as a man of wealth and professional standing he accomplished much for the advancement of historical research. Humanity suffered a great loss in the passing of such a servant of the truth.

A COMMUNICATION

Port au Prince, Haiti,
March 12th, 1945.

Dr. Carter G. Woodson,
Editor of "The Journal of Negro History"
Washington, D. C.

Dear Sir:

I must thank you very gratefully for your kind appreciation in "The Journal of Negro History" of January 1945, of my last book *La Fondation de la Republique d'Haiti par Alexandre Pétion.* That would be sufficient to tell you, if there were not some little mistakes which it is necessary to point out for American readers.

First mistake.—You say: "The achievements of Pétion, like those of other leaders, however, must be recorded exactly as they were and with adequate documentation to inspire confidence in the account." This is just what I did. All my documentation is quite adequate, because all was taken from the first great historians of Haiti, each historian being compared and controlled by the others. Perhaps, you don't know them, because their works are very rare. All the documents of Haitian history can be consulted in the two libraries of Port au Prince, at Seminaire College St-Martial and at St Louis College. So that I can sincerely say that my documentation is *quite* adequate and *must* inspire confidence in my account. All opinions, pro and contra, are quoted and thoroughly discussed, so that there is no place for fancy. Fustel de Coulanges said: "The best historian is the one who remains closest to the text, who writes and thinks only according to the text." This is what I did.

Second mistake.—You say: "The work under review is based mainly upon secondary authorities." The contrary is true, because all authorities I quoted are the best known as first class in Haiti and abroad. If what I say is not true, you are then obliged to prove the contrary by the enumeration of all those of the best I did not quote. I know pertinently that you cannot, because there are none better, because I have read all first class matter on the history of Haiti.

Third mistake.—You say: "The historians must do more than merely correct certain erroneous impressions received from the misinforming treatments on Haiti published by Americans and Europeans.'' I indeed illuminated all dark points in the events of the first years of independence of Haiti, by taking similar examples in general history, by comparing *all* documents on such events. So that I can say that my account gives satisfaction of the best critics of modern historiography, because I have been studying historiography, historical method, *for many years*. In reading my book, I think any one will see it is not merely a eulogistic personal account, but an historical account of the events concerning the foundation of the Haitian Republic. You know well the important part played by great men in history. It is impossible to forget the man who did a great deed whose influence was good for his country. Biography gives the explanation of many historical deeds. Mace, p. 291, speaks of the ''ethical value of studying historical persons.''

Fourth mistake.—You say: ''Dr. Dalencour was trained in medicine, not in history.'' That is a fancy, because you don't know my student life. I have been studying the history of my country, Haiti, from my youth up, and I never gave up the studying of history, even when attending to medical science and practice, so I can say that I have always been in contact with History, and I did not study only the History of Haiti, but very much ''historical method,'' ''historiography,'' as if I were following lessons in a University. I have studied very thoroughly historical methods in French, German, English and American authorities. I am well acquainted with the three best American authors: Mace, *Method in History*. Johnson, *The Historian and Historical Evidence*. Fling, *The Writing of History*. And I intend to translate into French the best book on Historical Method of the German Professor, Ernst Bernheim: *Text Book of Historical Method*.

You will then see that I have had a good training in modern historiography. I was then well prepared to write the history of my country. Not only I studied historical method, but knowing that political economy is indispensable to the historian for the understanding of historical events, I studied also that science. I think that scientifically I did my best to be able to write on the best conditions the history of my dear country.

Now, when you say: ''It is desired that from the Haitian youth may come historians who with scientific objectivity will tell the story anew to an uninformed world,'' it must be understood that it is not a question of *historical romanticism* as Nazism and Fascism which have been given to mankind in building up certain false tendencies as historical data.

I cannot think that you would make such a mistake. But, what I can tell you with the most complete accuracy, is that *the history of Haiti has already been well written by our greatest historians whose works are complementary, help each other,* and that only some secondary events want to be more detailed in biograhphies and monographies. As you know, in History there is the principal part, and the accessory part.

I beg to thank you again for the opportunity you gave me to inform American public opinion on a better understanding of the history of Haiti, and on a more accurate account of my book.

You will be very kind to publish my letter in extenso in the next issue of "The Journal of Negro History."

With my best thanks and my kindest regards,

Yours very sincerely,

DR. FRANÇOIS DALENCOUR.

THE JOURNAL
OF
NEGRO HISTORY

Vol. XXX—July, 1945—No. 3

ANNUAL REPORT OF THE DIRECTOR

The year ending June 30 has not been exactly one of marking time, inasmuch as some important objectives of the Association have been attained. On account of war conditions, which no individual or organization can control, however, it has been necessary for the Association to direct its attention to whatever the exigencies of the crisis permit.

The work has been aided somewhat by income from new sources. The late Mrs. Frances Boyce bequeathed the Association $250 which has been paid and also a part of the residue from her estate which will probably amount to an additional $750 or $800, which has not been paid. Dr. Frederic Bancroft who died on February 22, 1945, provided in his will that the $225 which he has annually contributed for History Prizes since 1932 shall be paid from his estate for five years after his death.

A decided stimulus was given the work by the appeal of the members of the Phi Delta Kappa Sorority, headed by Mrs. Gertrude Robinson. The members raised among themselves in subscriptions and contributions the amount of $349 which was presented by Mrs. Marion H. Bluitt, the grammateus, at one of the Negro History Week celebrations in Washington. From several persons who have completed their life membership payments a considerable sum has been obtained. Among these should be mentioned Mrs.

Mary McLeod Bethune, Attorney Louis R. Mehlinger, Attorney Raymond P. Alexander, Miss Nannie H. Burroughs, and Dr. Charles H. Wesley.

The brief summary of the financial report of the Secretary-Treasurer given below will be further informing as to the income of the Association and the sources from which it has been obtained.

FINANCIAL STATEMENT

July 1, 1944-June 30, 1945

RECEIPTS		DISBURSEMENTS	
Subscriptions to the JOURNAL	$1,883.30	Printing and Stationery	$6,358.45
Active Membership Fees	750.00	Accounting and Stenographic Service	2,197.14
Contributions	6,019.70	Salaries	3,000.00
Publications	2,278.84	Traveling Expenses	1,307.13
Subscriptions to the BULLETIN	4,198.48	Rent	500.00
Newsstand Sales	680.68	History Prizes	225.00
Life Membership Fees	570.00	Taxes withheld	67.90
Advertising	100.00	Postage and express	200.00
History Prizes	225.00	Sundry Expense	225.59
Sundry Income	195.28		
	$16,901.28		$14,081.21
Bal. on hand July 1, 1941	549.47	Bal. on hand June 30, 1945	3,369.54
Grand Total	$17,450.75	Grand Total	$17,450.75

Respectfully submitted,

L. R. MEHLINGER,
Secretary-Treasurer

RESEARCH

It has been impossible to carry forward the projects of research of the Association. During recent years the Director himself has given much attention to the study of materials on Africa in European archives. Inasmuch as these points are still inaccessible, the Association has been concentrating on simplifying and adapting the data collected. Schools are now becoming alive to the duty of studying all peoples whom they have long neglected and are now giving more attention to the Negro, not only in the United States but throughout the world. However, what the schools require is not strictly scientific or monographic studies in their original form but adaptations of these serious productions to the capacity of students.

This effort has already borne some fruit. In cooperation with Dr. W. B. Hambly, of the Chicago Natural History Museum, the Association has helped to make possible the publication of his well illustrated book on handicraft entitled *Clever Hands of the African*. This work is intended for children in the 5th grade. The same sort of assistance has been given Beatrice J. Fleming and Marion J. Pride in producing their forthcoming book entitled *Distinguished Negroes Abroad*. Departing from the usual procedure of mentioning only those Negroes who became famous in Europe, these authors have sketched a number of prominent, though less known, persons of African blood in the West Indies, Latin-America and Asia. The Association cooperated also with Mrs. Geneva C. Turner and Mrs. Julia H. Roy in compiling their new work entitled *Negro Pioneers of Long Ago*. They, too, had to undertake considerable research which the Director of the Association supervised.

Others engaged in more serious tasks have also been assisted by the Association. Dr. L. D. Reddick has had the assistance of the Director in his effort to collect the works of Frederick Douglass. Dr. Philip S. Foner, of New York City, likewise drew upon the services of the staff to make it possible for him to consult the records of the Douglass Home in Anacostia, D. C., and his recent work on the Abolitionist shows that the author profited by the opportunity. The Association has rendered aid also to Dr. John Hope Franklin in his study of George Washington Williams, the outstanding historian of the Negro race in the Western Hemisphere. Minor services which are rendered from day to day are not mentioned in this brief summary.

EDUCATIONAL WORK

The educational work of the Association during the present crisis with restrictions on travel has to be carried on mainly by correspondence and through the ever increasing number of persons in various parts who are now becoming sufficiently informed on the Negro to help those around them. Schools, which once had professors taking pride in the declaration that they had paid no attention to the Negro as such and did not care to discuss the race in their classes, now have scientifically trained teachers who, in treating the Negro as a constituent factor in world progress along with others who have helped to make the present civilization, have put such self-confessed ignorance to shame. In some cases, as noted heretofore, there is so much interest in the Negro and such an earnest desire to impart the new truths recently unearthed that the temptation is to dwell upon the Negro exclusively rather than teach the Negro about himself in relation to others and others about themselves in relation to the Negro. An important objective of the Association is to guard against the extremity in either way in order that students thus directed will have a balanced view of these forces at work in the making of our civilization.

Another precaution also been necessary. Many of the clubs and classes directing attention to the long neglected study of the Negro have had to be cautioned not to become completely absorbed with the problems of the present war. The Association has urged the leaders of these groups to pay sufficient attention to the past to understand the underlying causes of this conflict and the extent to which racialism, bigotry, caste and race prejudice, long at work in the past, have brought upon the people of this generation this world-wide calamity. Since such a study naturally leads to suggestions for obviating the recurrence of this catastrophe the historian becomes the source for information required in the race-problem-solving circles. Here again the Association has had to warn historians against developing into professional race leaders. The function of the historian is to serve the truth rather than agitate. In this way much has been done to direct the work along the proper channels and to keep it on the level of publishing the truth rather than participating in propaganda.

NEGRO HISTORY WEEK

Negro History Week still grips the nation as a national celebration. In the remote parts of the country this observance takes predecence over any other week celebrated in Negro schools and in mixed schools with a considerable Negro enrollment. Schools which are not alive to the situation and pay no attention thereto are not regarded as progressive, and they find little pleasure in boasting of ignoring this celebration. Even some Southern schools which Negroes cannot attend observe in a certain way the celebration, and the occasion is growing upon them from year to year. Among all thinking people the Negro is a factor to be reckoned with, and students must be educated with this as an objective. Even in the extreme North and West where few, if any, Negroes are found the tendency to study this large element of the national population is receiving some emphasis. Canada and the West Indies report considerable activity.

The Association in the midst of these manifestations must direct the celebration along the right path. In the first place, there are the charlatans who take up almost anything which will bring them before the public, and there are exploiters who stage so-called celebrations for personal gain or for movements whose work is foreign to that of the Association for the Study of Negro Life and History. Then there are the politicians who try to use Negro History Week as a means to an end. They go to the mayors of cities and governors of states and induce them to issue proclamations calling upon the people to observe Negro History Week without doing anything to further the study of the Negro in the schools where the proclamations are made. On paper the proclamation helps a man in public life to show his interest in Negroes when he is looking for their votes. The national officers of the Association have never sought such political cooperation. These manifestations have come altogether from local leaders who are playing some sort of political or publicity game. If these public functionaries desire to further the study of the Negro let them send messages to their councils and legislatures urging them to incorporate into the curricula of their schools the systematic study of the achievements of the Negro along with their courses on the Hebrew, the Greek, the Latin and the Teuton. Those who do not actually study the Negro have nothing to celebrate during Negro History Week. The objective of the celebration of Negro History Week is an educational effort.

What is said herein, however, must not be construed as a complaint against a general misuse of Negro History Week. The large majority of people, especially the teachers and their students, understand the objective of the celebration and cooperate willingly in reaching this end. The Director is merely warning the public against the undesirable participants who should be silenced as soon as possible. The Association notes with much satisfaction the increase in the numbers of those seriously approaching the study of the Negro and their wise use of the celebration of Negro History Week in arousing those who have not as yet been moved to action. To these earnest and unselfish workers seeking thus to advance the truth should go the plaudits of their race and nation. They are not only studying the Negro but are raising money to aid the national staff to prosecute the work more successfully. Among these deserving friends of the truth should be placed high on the roll of honor F. D. Moon in Oklahoma, Harvey C. Jackson and Sylvia M. Tucker in Detroit, W. F. Savoy in Columbus, Wilhelmina M. Crosson in Boston, Mrs. C. C. Bannister in the District of Columbia, Mrs. Myrtle Brodie Crawford in Louisville, Luther Porter Jackson in Virginia, and E. P. Southall in Florida.

THE JOURNAL OF NEGRO HISTORY

The Journal of Negro History desires to move forward more rapidly than it is permitted to go. The subscriptions have had a normal increase and even more could be obtained if the Association made the effort, but the restrictions on paper make such an undertaking impracticable at this time. The magazine is not allowed to increase its circulation during this crisis, and it has had much difficulty in devising ways to supply those already subscribing. Even without any special effort some increase has embarrassed the management. It has been necessary to supply new subscribers from the number reserved for binding at the end of the year. At first 200 copies in sheet form were set aside for this purpose. Early in the year, however, the manager had to divert twenty-five of these to new subscribers; later the number thus used had to be increased to fifty and finally to seventy-five, leaving only one hundred and twenty-five copies in reserve for binding and to supply European libraries as soon as war restrictions are removed. The circulation of the magazine is now 1,550, and the indications are that it must be increased beyond that point, or we shall have to turn down new subscriptions.

On the other hand, active members of the Association, who are also subscribers to the *Journal,* have decreased. Many of these were called to serve in one capacity or another during the war and cancelled their subscriptions for the duration of the conflict. Others who might have joined failed to act accordingly because of the uncertainty of their status. This same sort of loss was sustained earlier in the war among subscribers abroad. They have been likewise compelled to cancel their subscriptions. The circulation of the *Journal,* however, is still far above the average because of supplying it to all persons and agencies contributing as much as $5.00 a year. In this case contributions actually represent subscriptions, although they are not reflected as such in the number of persons reported as actually subscribing to the *Journal*. These contributors are schools and colleges in which are now found persons especially interested in the promotion of the work of the Association.

The Negro History Bulletin

The Negro History Bulletin has suffered from all the handicaps met with by the *Journal of Negro History*, and in addition others peculiar to its own status. The paper restriction became more of a problem in that it was rationed so as to prevent the staff from bringing out the *Bulletin* on time. The printer could not secure the paper until he could assure authorities that the work requiring it was at hand, and because of the shortage of labor in the plants the paper could not be delivered on time. Consequently the *Bulletin* could not be printed on time. Inasmuch as the periodical is planned for educational work and should be in the hands of teachers and students by the first of each month the magazine, delivered as a rule during this crisis as late as the middle of the month, could not be thus used, and some cancelled their subscriptions accordingly.

The same thing happened in the case of the newsstands. A magazine for this use should be delivered to them five days before the first of the month for which it is published, but during this crisis the *Bulletin* could be delivered to them not earlier than two weeks later. This allowed for sale at these stalls only half of the time heretofore taken, and the circulation through this channel correspondingly dropped. The amount reported from newsstands this year, however, is larger than that of the fiscal year ending twelve months ago, but this is due to the collection of large outstanding accounts on what had been sold the previous year.

This decrease in bulk subscriptions, however, is not discouraging. There has been an increase in subscriptions among individuals more widely distributed rather than among persons concentrating on special uses of the *Bulletin*. An increase in the subscriptions from West Virginia and Missouri indicate the tendency toward a more national circulation of the *Bulletin* among individual subscribers. Other interest expressed in several quarters in the West Indies and in Latin America encourages the staff in this expectation. The present indication is that the number lost will be regained as the Association and its coworkers readjust their program for invading new fields. The circulation of this periodical is still between 8,000 and 9,000 but there is no reason why it should not be doubled in the near future.

SLAVERY AS A DIPLOMATIC FACTOR IN ANGLO-AMERICAN RELATIONS DURING THE CIVIL WAR

The diplomatic axiom that domestic conflict produces foreign difficulties was certainly true during the American Civil War. It was natural that foreign governments would view with peculiar interest the American scene as many of the great powers were doubtful of the permanency of a democracy. The role played by Great Britain, however, was unique not only because other European nations would doubtless follow her leadership but also because both the North and the South felt a claim to British interest. The North thought that England would sympathize with her since they were in accord on the injustice of slavery; whereas the South felt that England would aid her as she deemed American cotton essential to Britain's economic existence. Since the North looked to England for sympathy, her diplomacy centered around keeping the Mother Country neutral; and since the South felt that England depended upon her for cotton, her negotiations emphasized English recognition of her independence and intervention. Although many factors are involved in the efforts of both sides to accomplish their objectives, this study will be limited to one, namely, slavery. It is the aim of this paper to show the influence of slavery as a diplomatic factor in Anglo-American relations during the war between the sections.

The election of Lincoln in 1860 on the platform of "no extension of slavery" was pleasing to the British press and public. "We rejoice," said the *Times,* . . . that it (the election) has ended in the return of Mr. Lincoln. We are glad to think that the march of Slavery, and the domineering tone which its advocates were beginning to assume . . . has been at length arrested and silenced."[1] The *Times* led and other leading periodicals followed in moralizing tones to

[1] The *Times*, November 21, 1860, cited in E. D. Adams, I, 38.

condemn the South. Up to the time of the secession of South
Carolina neither official England nor the press believed that
a break was about to take place between the North and the
South. When it came, however, British opinion believed in
and hoped for a speedy and peaceable settlement. Until
war became inevitable, the South was adversely criticized
by the press as seeking the preservation of an evil institution. The April 1861 issue of the *Edinburgh Review* charged
the whole difficulty to slavery. It "asserted that British
sympathy would be with the anti-slavery party, yet advanced the theory that the very dissolution of the Union
would hasten the ultimate extinction of slavery since economic competition with a neighboring free state, the North,
would compel the South itself to abandon its beloved 'domestic institution.' "[2]

The trend of events in America caused English opinion
to become uncertain and wonder if there were just basis for
its sympathy. Many who voted for Lincoln on a platform
opposing the further territorial extension of slavery would
have renounced any plan to take active steps toward the extinction of slavery where it already existed. Lincoln not
only took the stand that the terms of his election limited his
action but also that it was highly desirable to keep the border states, Maryland, Kentucky, and Missouri, all of which
had many slaveholders, in the Union. Therefore, as secession developed he centered his attention upon the preservation of the Union.

Between Lincoln's election and inauguration grave problems confronted President Buchanan who floundered in a
sea of indecision. Congress tried in vain to devise a plan of
reconciliation and the proposed constitutional amendment
making slavery inviolable in the states where it was established passed by the necessary two-thirds in each House by
February 28, but was ratified by only two states. Mean-

[2] Ephraim D. Adams: *Great Britain and the American Civil War*, Vol. I,
p. 45.

while the Confederacy had been organized on February 4 in Montgomery, Alabama. Finally, when Lincoln in his inaugural address declared: "I have no purpose, directly or indirectly, to interfere with the institution of slavery in the States where it exists. I believe I have no lawful right to do so, and I have no inclination to do so,"[3] many liberal Englishmen were in a quandary and wondered if the future of slavery in America were at stake.

The English public was not well enough informed on internal affairs to know that the slavery issue tied Lincoln's hands at home. The administration preferred to run the risk of not winning the anti-slavery sympathy of England rather than to hazard forfeiting the support of many voters in the North and still more in the border states. Thus, gradually after the secession of South Carolina the London press was changing front so that soon after Lincoln's inauguration the Southern tone was marked. The *Times,* the *Saturday Review,* and the *Economist* were conspicuous in their change of attitude. The press might not have been so caustic if W. H. Russell, an unusually able and objective war-correspondent who abhorred slavery, had not been recalled. In spite of the fact that Delane, editor of the *Times,* favored the South, and that Russell's description of Bull Run in the *Times*[4] was the beginning of Northern antipathy to him, Russell, as early as September, 1861, wrote Delane privately that it was obvious that the North would succeed in reducing the South.[5] Ardent friends of the North continued to insist that slavery was the real cause of the conflict and four outstanding periodicals remained pro-Northern: the *Spectator,* the *Westminster Review,* the *Daily News,* and the *Morning Star.* As war clouds hovered over America, the British government became concerned in regard to how

[3] John G. Nicolay and John Hay: *Abraham Lincoln*—Vol. II, p. 328.
[4] The *Times,* August 5, 1861.
[5] Worthington C. Ford: *A Cycle of Adams Letters* (1861-1865), Vol. I, p. 141.

the country would fare and what would be its policy in case actual conflict ensued.

In the meantime the South was pressing its case in Great Britain. Difficult as the task of Northern diplomacy appeared, the job of the South was even harder. The North as a recognized nation could hold formal diplomatic conversations but the South as a belligerent could use only indirect methods. Her first commission, however, consisting of William L. Yancey, Pierre A. Rost,[6] and A. Dudley Mann arrived in England before the fall of Fort Sumter. In their unofficial interviews with Lord Russell, May 3 and 9, they made a plea for recognition in accordance with their instructions. Though negative the main inducement which Secretary Toombs offered England was that she could not get cotton unless she came after it; in other words, unless she could break any attempted blockade. One point on slavery was included in Toombs' instructions. The commissioners were authorized to assume obligations for all treaties in existence between the United States and Great Britain except the one for the suppression of the slave trade. This instruction read: "The only exception is in reference to the clause of the treaty of Washington . . . which obliges the United States to maintain a naval force on the coast of Africa for the suppression of the African slave trade. It is not in our power to comply with this obligation. We have prohibited the African slave trade, and intend . . . to prevent it in our country. But we are not prepared . . . to aid the rest of the world in promoting that object."[7]

Russell asked about a Southern plan to revive the African slave trade, but Yancey and Rost denied the rumor and said that they had prohibited it and did not intend to revive it. Russell's report to Lyons stresses this point but the report of the Commissioners to Toombs on May 21 does not.

[6] Rost spent considerable time in France.

[7] James D. Richardson: *Messages and Papers of the Confederacy*, Vol. II, p. 8.

They do, however, say that they think that slavery delays their much desired recognition. In the meantime, in a dispatch dated May 18 Toombs informs the Commissioners that the Congress on May 6 passed a law recognizing the existence of war between the United States and the Confederate States. His statement in regard to slavery is significant to us: "It is obvious, therefore," says Toombs, "that, however it may be concealed under the guise of patriotism and fidelity to the late Federal compact, the real motive which actuates Mr. Lincoln and those who now sustain his acts is to accomplish by force of arms that which the masses of the Northern people have long sought to effect — namely, the overthrow of our domestic institutions. . . .[8]

Since policies are being developed in May, the sources are replete with diplomatic correspondence. Russell in his formal instructions to Lyons gives advance notice of the Cabinet's decision to recognize the belligerent rights of the South but advises him not to tell Seward. Lyons expresses to Russell his strong sympathy with the North but adds that he refrains from expressions of sympathy as he does not want to encourage the Northern Cabinet in its plan of prosecuting war.

A significant day in this month is the thirteenth, for on this day Charles Francis Adams, the newly appointed minister to the Court of St. James, is startled upon his arrival to see published in the *Gazette*[9] the Queen's Proclamation of Neutrality. With the exception of the *Spectator* and a few provincial papers, the English press strongly favored the Proclamation and the English public was surprised that neither the North nor the South was pleased. Adams was confronted immediately with a knotty problem as the philosophy underlying the recognition of the belligerency of the Confederacy was a far cry from the philosophy under-

[8] *Ibid.*, p. 30.
[9] James T. Adams: *The Adams Family*, p. 255.

lying the foreign policy of his chief, Secretary of State Seward. Seward held that as the sovereignty of the United States had not been overthrown, the acts and purposes of the Confederates and the question of slavery were purely domestic affairs which could be ignored or brought to the fore, as public sentiment and military interests required. So in his first instructions to Adams he said: "You will not consent to draw into debate before the British government any opposing moral principles, which may be supposed to lie at the foundation of the controversy between those (the Confederate) States and the Federal Union."[10]

Adams, an able diplomat and peculiarly fitted by nature and training to represent his country in England, soon understood the English point of view in regard to the Proclamation of Neutrality as well as the American "border states" policy. He regretted, however, that neither side understood the other on these points at the time and summed up the British opinion as to the cause of the war in a letter to his son, Charles Francis, Jr.: "People do not quite understand Americans or their politics. . . . They do not comprehend the connection which slavery has with it, because we do not at once preach emancipation. Hence they go to the other extreme and argue that it is not an element in the struggle."[11]

The publicity given to the victory of the South in the Battle of Bull Run, July 21, by the British press caused the commissioners to feel that this was an opportune time to present their case to Lord Russell. He sidestepped their request for an informal interview, however, and asked that they present a written statement. This paper dated August 14 reviewed the arguments in favor of recognition which they had presented May 3 and 9 and emphasized the power of the Confederacy as well as its military successes. It also

[10] *Diplomatic Correspondence*, 1861-76. Cited in Bancroft: *Seward*, II, 317. (Source not checked.)

[11] *A Cycle of Adams Letters*, I, 14-15.

attempted to resist the anti-slavery sentiment of England and to urge that slavery was not an issue in the struggle raging in America. Russell in his reply to this request on August 24 stated that England could not pass judgment upon the issue of the conflict and that he hoped that an adjustment would be made which would be satisfactory to both sections.

The rapid growth of Confederate military prestige in the summer of 1861 caused the question of slavery to be almost forgotten by foreigners, while the Union policy was permitting the development of public opinion abroad that might lead to the early recognition of the Confederacy. In the fall of 1861 both Schurz and Bigelow warned Seward of the situation and attempted to show him that the moral anti-slavery issue would popularize the cause of the North in Europe. Seward was not convinced at first as noted in his replies, but in a confidential dispatch to Adams, February 17, he made it plain that, although the policy of the administration was not distinctly anti-slavery, the results were.[12] On February 21, Adams wrote Seward urging "a Northern declaration in regard to slavery in order to meet in England Southern private representations that, independence won, the South would enter upon a plan of gradual emancipation to be applied 'to all persons born after some specific date.' "[13]

However, it was not until May 28 that Seward removed the restriction against discussing the meaning of the war in relation to slavery. Recurrent rumors of mediation caused Adams to show the dispatch to Russell on June 20. Seward said that the North would be forced to aid in an uprising of the slaves against their masters if foreign nations intervened or mediated in favor of the South. This threat of a "servile war" if Great Britain aided the South would

---

[12] Frederic Bancroft: *The Life of William H. Seward*, Vol. II, p. 328.

[13] State Department Eng., Vol. 78, No. 119. Cited in E. D. Adams, II, 98. (Source not checked.)

place her in an embarrassing position. Less than one month after Adams had presented the "servile war" threat policy of Seward to Russell, he advised Seward that the distinct acknowledgment of an anti-slavery object in the war would counteract the arguments for foreign intervention and that the North should be prepared to meet an offer of mediation from Europe "by declaring that if made to extinguish slavery such mediation would be welcome."[14] This plan Adams thought would probably put an end to mediation as well as strengthen our position among the great powers.

In a further effort to influence British opinion against the seceding states, Seward signed a treaty with Great Britain on April 7, giving mutual right of search for the suppression of the African Slave Trade.[15] Coming at this time, however, it did not alter England's attitude, as the Admiralty was not particularly interested in the suppression of the African slave trade. Furthermore, it was viewed as a feeble bid for English sympathy.

Meanwhile the Confederacy made a change in its diplomatic personnel. The South's diplomatic job was extremely arduous and the Commission had accomplished little during the year. Thus, in December 1861, Jefferson Davis appointed James M. Mason of Virginia as special envoy to Great Britain. Mason decided to lay aside the recognition claim and to urge European renunciation of the blockade. His unofficial interview with Lord Russell on February 10 ended in disappointment to him. On March 10 in a speech in the House of Lords Lord Russell upheld the legality and effectiveness of the blockade and said "that if England sided with the South in any way the North would appeal to a slave insurrection."[16] Mason was surprised to find his

[14] E. D. Adams, *op. cit.*, II, 99.

[15] U. S. Messages and Documents, 1862-63. Pt. I, p. 65. Cited in E. D. Adams II, 90. (Source not checked.)

[16] Cal. Deb., Ser. 3, Vol. 165, pp. 133-43. March 10, 1862. Cited in F. L. Owsley: *King Cotton Diplomacy*, p. 248. (Source not checked.)

loyal, conservative friends, Seymour Fitzgerald and Lord Donoughmore, and his liberal Confederate champion, Spence, fixed in their hostility to slavery.

As a part of their propaganda program, the Confederate State Department sent Henry Hotze as "commercial agent" to England about the same time as Mason. His method at first was to obtain the insertion in the large metropolitan dailies of editorials which he thought would be useful to the Southern cause. Not satisfied with these results, Hotze started a Confederate newspaper, the weekly *Index,* in May, 1862.[17] In his zeal to please Englishmen, Hotze frequently displeased his own fellow-countrymen. His skillful handling of the slavery question did strengthen the prevalence of anti-Northern feelings but did not help recognition.

Although Mason was unable to have official interviews with Russell, the foreign minister himself was devising a mediation plan which at first met with the approval of both Palmerston and Gladstone. The march of military events, particularly the Northern victory at Antietam, vigorous opposition within the Cabinet, and Gladstone's Newcastle Speech, contributed to a deviation from the original forthright plan for mediation and recognition. Russell's memorandum on America, circulated October 13, contained three major points the last of which stated that the emancipation proclamation was but an incitement to a servile war. He "urged that the Great Powers ought seriously to consider whether it was not their duty to propose a 'suspension of arms' for the purpose of 'weighing calmly the advantages of peace.' . . . Appended to the memorandum were the texts of the emancipation proclamation, Seward's circular letter of September 22, and an extract from the *National Intelligencer* of September 26, giving Lincoln's answer to Chicago

[17] Pickett Papers, Hotze to Secretary of State, Nos. 7 and 8, April 23 and May 15, 1862; O.R.N., Ser. 2, Vol. III, pp. 399-401; 423-24, respectively. Cited in Owsley: *King Cotton Diplomacy*, p. 170 (Source not checked).

abolitionists.''[18] Of the various memoranda circulated, the
October 17 reply of Sir George Cornewall Lewis to Russell
was significant. Although there were other English memoranda as well as a French proposal suggesting an armistice
of six months including a suspension of the blockade, England, in the final analysis, made no change of policy. This
action was most fortunate for the United States as Russell's
mediation plan was the most dangerous diplomatic crisis
that confronted Charles Francis Adams. Had it been
adopted probably war would have ensued between England
and the North. Whatever its results in other respects the
independence of the South would have been established and
slavery would have received fresh impetus by British action. Since all parties in the cabinet agreed that Lincoln's
emancipation proclamation was but an incitement to servile
war, this edict played no part in the final decision.[19]

Though probably slightly influenced by Charles Sumner,
chairman of the Senate Committee on Foreign Relations,
Lincoln soon saw the gradual emergence of emancipation as
a war problem and approached it gradually through legislative and administrative acts. Lincoln's carefully worked
out plan of emancipation and his first proclamation should
be considered as domestic measures. There is slight evidence for believing that Lincoln was convinced that the
proclamation would improve foreign relations. Seward
linked emancipation with servile insurrection for he became
convinced that national interests alone would determine the
attitude and action of Great Britain. Beginning in February 1862, he had been using the threat of a servile insurrection as a deterrent upon British talk of intervention. He
wished to use emancipation as a threat of servile insurrection, but did not desire emancipation itself for fear that it
would cause intervention.

On July 14, the day following Seward's first knowledge

[18] Palmerston, M.S. Cited in E. D. Adams, II, 49. (Source not checked.)
[19] E. D. Adams, op. cit., II, Chapter XI, pp. 33-74.

of Lincoln's planned emancipation proclamation, he sent to
his agents abroad a copy of the bill that was introduced into
Congress that day embodying Lincoln's plan for gradual
and compensated emancipation. Though sent without material comment, this method of emancipation would fit in
with his philosophy of slavery in relation to foreign powers
much easier than a definitive proclamation of emancipation.
Still fearful of the effects of emancipation abroad, Seward
on July 24 said in a private dispatch to Motley: "Are you
sure that today, under the seductions and pressures which
could be applied to some European populations, they would
not rise up and resist our attempt to bestow freedom upon
the laborers whose capacity to supply cotton and open a
market for European fabrics depends, or is thought to depend, upon their continuance in bondage?"[20] Motley's answer beginning, "A thousand times No,"[21] gave fresh impetus to what the most intelligent United States representatives in Europe had been saying for nearly a year about a
forthright anti-slavery policy. Adams repeated his plea for
a moral issue and on September 25 met Seward's "material interests" argument by showing that in the case of
Great Britain the chief difficulty in the cotton situation lay
in uncertainty rather than scarcity.[22]

Meanwhile on September 22, five days after the battle of
Antietam, Lincoln issued the Proclamation of Emancipation and Seward immediately sent a circular, with a copy
of the proclamation, to all the diplomatic and consular officers of the United States in foreign countries. In his instructions to Adams, September 26, he presented his philosophy of what had transpired and what was to be done.
Although Seward acquiesced in the "high moral purpose"
argument in the emancipation proclamation, the "material

[20] MS. Archives. Cited in Bancroft: Seward II, 336. (Source not checked.)
[21] Motley to Seward, August 26, 1862. Seward MSS. Cited in *Ibid.*
[22] U. S. Messages and Documents 1862-'3, Pt. I, p. 191. Adams to Seward.
Cited in E. D. Adams, II, 99. (Source not checked.)

interests'' of Great Britain were still in his thoughts judging from the readiness with which he grasped at an emigration plan for liberated slaves. Although there was much diplomatic correspondence between September, 1862, and March, 1864, on a scheme to transport to the West Indies or to any of the British colonies the slaves about to be emancipated, the plans never materialized.

Since the British public strongly associated servile war with emancipation, it is not surprising that in the fall of 1862, the proclamation was more vigorously denounced than any other one situation in the Civil War. ''It was received by the government with disfavor, by the press with contempt, and by the public, even the friends of the North, with apprehension.''[23] But as no servile uprising occurred, public opinion in December began to turn in favor of the proclamation. Soon emancipation became popular. Jefferson Davis issued a counter edict on December 23 which meant death to the slave fighting for his freedom, even as a regular soldier in the Northern Army.[24] Official opinion is not quickly changed. Lyons hoped that neither proclamation would be enforced and Russell regarded the January 1 proclamation as a questionable war measure.[25]

The British anti-slavery public, though, was aroused. It at last had a moral issue. Emancipation societies were formed and frequent public meetings were held in the larger cities of England and Scotland. Jordan noted forty-four meetings in February in England and Scotland and nearly as many in March and April each.[26] The most important of all the demonstrations in favor of emancipation was the mammoth meeting held in London at Exeter Hall on January 29. The audience, estimated at ten thousand,

[23] E. D. Adams, *op. cit.*, II, 114.

[24] Messages and Papers of the Confederacy, *op. cit.*, I, 273.

[25] James Ford Rhodes, *History of the United States*, Vol. IV, p. 357.

[26] Donaldson Jordan and Edwin Pratt: *Europe and the American Civil War*, p. 151.

was composed of the lower middle and of the working classes. "The group that favored the Emancipation Proclamation was weak among electors, very weak in Parliament and in society, but strong in numbers and self-consciousness, and possessed of a leadership and organization which rendered its weight even greater. Political Dissenters, skilled laborers, and a large section of the younger 'intellectuals' constituted this class."[27]

The South was sensitive of any mention of slavery by outsiders as she had been held up as a horrible example for so long. The reply to this European hostility to slavery was naturally made about this time and was embodied in a circular sent to all the agents, January 15, 1863, in which Benjamin instructed them to decline any negotiations which in any way related to slavery. "This Government," wrote Benjamin, "unequivocally and absolutely denies its possession of any power whatever over the subject, and cannot entertain any propositions in relation to it."[28]

The hostile attitude of Europe and the need for soldiers caused the Confederacy to alter its policy in regard to the discussion of abolishing slavery. In fact, knowledge of the universal hostility of Europe to slavery and the frequent warnings that Europe would never recognize a slave power were just as important factors in the Confederacy's decision to begin the emancipation of slaves as military necessity at home. In execution of this new policy Benjamin on December 27, 1864, sent Duncan Kenner, chairman of the Ways and Means Committee, as special envoy to England to take his dispatch and to act with Mason should negotiations ensue. In this dispatch Benjamin puts the question squarely up to England as to whether slavery was and had been the obstacle to recognition. If slavery proved to be the

[27] *Ibid.*, p. 163.
[28] Messages and Papers of the Confederacy, *op. cit.*, II, 404.

"objection," the commissioners were authorized to propose the emancipation of the slaves.[29]

The Confederate press and the *Index* in the meanwhile were preparing both the American and European public for such a move. Early in 1863 as a counter stroke to the emancipation proclamation, the Confederate lobby in Europe began to discuss the emancipation of the slaves and their enrollment in the army. During 1863 a rumor was spread abroad that the South planned to arm 500,000 slaves and give them their freedom. Therefore, when the South proposed to arm and free the slaves both from military and diplomatic necessity, Hotze was ready to advocate the idea. However, before Kenner arrived both Hotze and Mason were practically convinced of the futility of offering emancipation as the price of recognition. In his interview with Palmerston Mason attempted to appeal to British interests by emphasizing the threat of a reconstructed Union.[30] In this last supreme effort in which she "laid all upon the altar" the South failed.

It is to be noted that the large majority of the rich and many among the professional classes in England sided with the South, whereas the working class, at least half of the middle class, together with many men of intellectual distinction, favored the North. It was not unnatural for the upper classes to favor the Confederacy as the two groups were bound together socially and economically. The plantation aristocracy of the South resembled closely the landed aristocracy of England. Neither does one have to look far for a reason for the North's sympathizers. The emigration of hundreds of thousands of Englishmen to the North had caused the masses to consider that region as the haven of free labor and democracy. The masses soon thought that they had a stake in the American debacle. The great dem-

[29] *Ibid.*, 694-97. Although these are Slidell's instructions, a note on p. 694 says (A large portion of this dispatch was sent Mr. Mason.)

[30] Owsley: *King Cotton Diplomacy*, Chap. XVIII, pp. 551-61.

onstration meetings held in England after the issuance of the second emancipation proclamation were marked by demonstrations of democratic strength. The spectacular gathering of the Trades Unions of London at St. James' Hall on March 26 was, according to Ephraim D. Adams, the most notable one in support of the North held throughout the whole course of the war, as well as "the most notable one as indicating the rising tide of popular demand for more democratic institutions."[31]

Henry Adams in reporting that meeting said that the group showed no faith in the existing English government and that every antagonistic reference to the "privileged classes" was greeted with cheers, whereas applause greeted allusions to American democratic institutions.[32]

A final evaluation of the influence of slavery in Anglo-American relations during the American Civil War brings a few points into bold relief. Of peculiar significance is the fact that the policy of both the North and the South in regard to slavery as a diplomatic factor changed during the struggle. Due to the domestic situation frequently called "political expediency," the North disavowed the slavery issue but as her representatives kept urging a definitive anti-slavery purpose to avoid English recognition of Southern independence Seward enunciated the "servile war threat" policy. Although evidence does not show that the Proclamation of Emancipation was designed to aid foreign relations, it proved to be a master stroke in Northern diplomacy. The South, realizing England's antipathy to slavery, attempted at first to avoid the issue, but when she was

[31] E. D. Adams, II, 133. See p. 14 above in which the writer accepts Jordan's view on the most important meeting for the Northern cause. Jordan agrees with Adams on the significance of the St. James meeting to the cause of democracy but differs from him in regard to its significance to the Northern cause.

[32] State Dept., Eng., Vol. 82, No. 358. Adams to Seward, March 27, 1863, enclosing report by Henry Adams. Cited in E. D. Adams, II, 293. (Source not checked.)

pressed denied that slavery was an issue, using Lincoln's statements for their purpose. As a last resort she promised the emancipation of the slaves in exchange for recognition of independence.

This changing status of slavery as an issue brings to our minds these questions: What would have been the role of slavery in Anglo-American relations if the North from the beginning of the conflict had avowed an anti-slavery purpose? What part would slavery have played in Anglo-American relations if the South in the early days of secession had promised to grant the slaves gradual emancipation in return for recognition from England? Adequate answers to these questions are extremely difficult to make after brief study, but one general statement seems obvious: namely, that in either instance, the war would have been short lived. In the first place, public opinion which was with the North after Lincoln's election would doubtless have remained on that side, becoming so powerful as to strengthen the morale of the North and to weaken that of the South. Under these circumstances the South could not have held out long. In the second, the South might have won a speedy victory as she not only organized for war sooner than the North but she won the early victories.

In the mere prolongation of the war we view the slavery factor negatively, but in the results produced by delay epoch-making changes occurred in the United States and Great Britain. Time gave the voteless working man in England the opportunity through far-seeing leadership to mould public opinion in his favor. Not until after the emancipation proclamation did the adherents of democracy become vociferous. Meanwhile the battle for democracy in England was being fought in America. Herein lies the role of slavery in Anglo-American relations during the war between the sections.

SADIE DANIEL ST. CLAIR

Miner Teachers College

NEGROES AND MULATTOES IN EIGHTEENTH-CENTURY FRANCE

Since the late 1400's Negroes had gradually been making their way to France. During the 1600's their numbers were far from inconsiderable, and in Orleans a street and college were named after them *rue* and *Collège des Africains*. It was at Paris above all that one found them. Most were in menial positions, but certain of them claiming high birth in Africa were rendered homage at court and by the French aristocracy.[1] Throughout the first several decades of the eighteenth century there was an accelerated influx, due primarily to the increase of slavery in the colonies and the growth of opulence among the planters. For though a few of the Negroes came directly from Africa, the vastly greater number were from the French colonies of the New World.[2] Most of them were brought as servants, their owners being planters, colonial administrators, sea captains, or army officers; others were imported for service in the army (many

[1] J. Mathorez, *Les étrangers en France sous l'ancien régime: histoire de la formation de la population française* (Paris, 1919-21, 2 v.), 387-95; Charles Woolsey Cole, *French Mercantilism, 1683-1700* (New York, 1943), p. 104.

The historical literature on Negroes in France (as also source material) is scanty, the treatment by Mathorez (I, 387-404) being the only study of significance. Next in importance is Maurice Besson's "La police des noirs sous Louis XVI en France," *Revue de l'histoire des colonies françaises*, XXI (Paris, 1928), 433-46, an article given largely to the quotation of French legislation concerning Negroes. The legislation is also to be found, sometimes in abridged form, in Isambert's *Recueil général des anciennes lois françaises depuis l'an 420 jusqu'à la Révolution* (Paris, 1822-33, 28 v. and table). Discussion of the legislation on slavery early in the Revolution, and of the agitation pro and con, is well set forth by Mitchell Bennett Garrett in *The French Colonial Question, 1789-91* (Ann Arbor, 1916), 167 p. *The Black Consul* (New York, 1935), by Anatolii Vinogradov, presents many pictures of Negro and mulatto life in Paris during the period of the Revolution but they are of doubtful accuracy.

[2] Mathorez, *op. cit.*, I, 397-98; Martin-Doisy, *Dictionnaire d'économie charitable* . . . III [forming tome VII of the Abbé Migne's *Troisième et dernière, encyclopédie théologique*] (Paris, 1856), 1058; Eugène Fieffé, *Histoire des troupes étrangères au service de France, depuis leur origine jusqu'à nos jours et de tous les régiments levés dans les pays conquis sous la première république et l'empire* (Paris, 1854, 2 v.), I, 281.

of them from Africa); a few were sent by their owners or fathers for education; a small number came as visitors. During the Revolution certain ones came as political representatives to the parliamentary assemblies. It was to the cities, and above all to Paris, that these migrants went; there is no reference to a Negro being engaged in agriculture in France during the 1700's.[3] At Brest quite a number of Negroes were resident in 1763, the servants of persons who had bought them.[4] Bordeaux in the early 1790's had a Negro quarter and a Negro street.[5] Toulouse had its Black Virgin.[6]

In France as also in England during the eighteenth century it was fashionable in aristocratic and bourgeois circles to have Negro servants, commonly dressed in livery and sometimes carrying a parrot, monkey, or gay parasol.[7] Madame du Barry possessed a Negro boy named Zamore, given her as a present by the Prince de Conti. Dressed in velvet and silk, he carried the train of his mistress's gown,

[3] Mathorez (''Les éléments de population orientale en France,'' *Revue des études historiques*, année 83 [Paris, 1917], 180) mentions Ethiopians along with Moors, Tartars, Russians, Turks, Circassians, and Bosnians as having been slaves in Roussillon in the 1200's, engaged in ''cultivation of the soil.''

[4] *Inventaire-sommaire des archives départementales antérieures à 1700. Ille-et-Vilaine*, C 72. Technically slavery did not exist in France, but actually the slave owner appears to have enjoyed rights of possession over his slave. Cf. Maurice Besson, *op. cit.*, *Revue de l'histoire des colonies françaises*, XXI, 433.

[5] Quartier de Terre-Nègre and Chemin de Terre-Nègre. Marguerite Castel, ''La formation topographique de quartier Saint-Seurin,'' *Revue historique de Bordeaux et du département de la Gironde*, XV (Bordeaux, 1922), 310 with n. 1.

[6] It was an object of special veneration in the Eglise de la Daurade. During the severe flood of 1727 it was carried in procession through the streets. Ernest Rochach, ''Etudes historiques sur la province de Languedoc,'' *Histoire générale de Languedoc*, XIII (Toulouse, 1876), 1006; Shelby T. McCloy, ''Flood Relief and Control in Eighteenth-Century France,'' *The Journal of Modern History*, XIII (March, 1941), 3-4.

[7] Mathorez, *Les étrangers en France*, I, 400-01; A. S. Turberville, ed., *Johnson's England: An Account of the Life and Manners of His Age* (Oxford, 1933, 2 v.), I, 342. Dr. Johnson had a Negro servant named Francis.

served her and her guests with refreshments, and entertained them at tumbling on a rug and in various other manners. Madame du Barry spent large sums on him. She
engaged one or two artists of the day to paint him at her
side. At the outbreak of the Revolution he left her, and
at her trial in 1793 gave evidence against her. Later that
year he, too, was arrested.[8]

The pirate Dulain, granted amnesty by the French government, brought to Nantes in 1729 fifteen Negro slaves,
reckoned as worth 1,000 livres apiece in France. One of the
Negroes falling sick was taken to the Hôtel-Dieu (municipal
hospital); the others were placed (evidently for safekeep-
ing, awaiting disposal) in the Château de Nantes.[9] Rocham-
beau in November, 1796, had with him in France a mulatto
aide-de-camp brought from Santo Domingo, though not as
a slave since the Convention had abolished slavery in all
French colonies on 16 pluviôse an II (February 4, 1794).
The Tascher de la Pagerie family owned a devoted female
servant named Marion, who accompanied Josephine to
France and was her maid there.[10] Not infrequently those
bringing slaves to France gave them their freedom.[11] Such
an instance was the manumission of the Negro Jean Bap-

8 Mathorez, op. cit., I, 401; Erhard Breitner, Madame du Barry, tr. by
Lord Sudley (London, 1938), pp. 123, 173, 175, 182. Alexandre Dumas, in his
Memoirs of a Physician, has many references to him.

The Duke and Duchess of Chartres had three Negro servants in 1777:
Aladdin, aged thirty-five; Scipio, seven; and Narcissus, age not given, a slave
whom they treated as though free. Besson, op. cit., Revue de l'histoire des
colonies françaises, XXI, 434-35.

9 Léon Vignols, ''La piraterie sur l'Atlantique au XVIIIe siècle,'' An-
nales de Bretagne, V (Rennes, 1889-90), 373-74. Breton ships are said to have
been heavily engaged in the slave trade. Most of the 11,833 Negroes transported to Martinique during the years 1714-21 are said to have been carried in
Breton vessels, and above all in those from Nantes. Ibid., V, 244. Large numbers of Negroes were to be seen on the streets of Nantes. Mathorez, op. cit.,
I, 400.

10 E. A. Rheinhardt, Josephine, Wife of Napoleon, tr. by Caroline Frederick (New York, 1934), pp. 3, 9, 14, 30, 35.

11 Mathorez, op. cit., I, 399.

tiste Batoche, aged twenty-five, native of Guadeloupe, by his master, Dugommier, general-in-chief of the army of the Eastern Pyrennees, June 13, 1793. The act was signed before a notary in Paris, and the slave granted full liberty.[12] Sometimes a Negro freed in another European state made his way into France, as did Job Ben Solomon, Pholey Negro liberated in Holland by his sea-captain owner.[13] That there were occasional runaway slaves is attested by the declaration of a Parisian wholesale merchant, Alexandre Etienne Pierre Boulonnois de Saint-Simon, that a Negress whom he had purchased in Martinique at 3,000 livres and brought to France as a servant had taken leave and was at liberty. He protested before the police on April 2, 1791, because of the monetary loss involved.[14]

A few Negro and mulatto youths were sent to France by their owners or fathers for education or religious training. One such, educated at Paris, was the Haitian mulatto insurgent, Jacques Vincent Ogé, broken at the wheel in 1791 because of his part in the first phase of insurrection in Santo Domingo. He belonged to a free family and after his education served for a time in the French army abroad, rising to the rank of lieutenant colonel.[15] During the Revolution a special school in France was opened for Negroes, and to it Sonthonax (French commissioner) and Toussaint L'Ouverture sent Negro and mulatto youths from Santo Do-

[12] J. Adher, ''Les colons réfugiés d'Amérique pendant la Révolution,'' *Bulletin de la Société de Géographie de Toulouse*, année XXXIV (Toulouse, 1915), p. 164.

[13] Elizabeth Donnan, ed., *Documents Illustrative of the History of the Slave Trade to America* (Washington, 1930-35, 4 v.), II, 416.

[14] A. Tuetey, ed., *Répertoire générale des sources manuscrites de l'histoire de Paris pendant la Révolution française* (Paris, 1890-1914, 11 v.), II, 184, no. 1743.

[15] See the biographical article in *Nouvelle biographie générale . . .*, ed. by Jean C. F. Hoefer (Paris, 1855-72, 46 v.), XXXVIII, 550; also the sketch by Vinogradov, *op. cit.*, pp. 25-40.

mingo to be educated at state expense.[16] Toussaint's sons, Isaac and Placide, were sent to Paris for this purpose. Josephine frequently entertained them at meals.[17] In 1801 Dessalines, fiery general under Toussaint, married a Negro woman "of remarkable beauty and intelligence, the former mistress of a planter who had given her a good education."[18] Occasionally Negro rulers in Africa sent their sons to England and France to do the "Grand Tour" of European aristocratic scions and acquire some polish in manners. John Currantee and Coffee Yango, two Fanti chiefs (caboceers), sent their sons to France for this purpose around 1750, and in 1751 the kings of Anisham and Fetu made preparations to send their sons to England. In 1749 two black princes of Anamaboe had spent some time in London, the Earl of Halifax taking them in custody and educating them. As was common in such instances, they were "received in the higher circles, and introduced to the king." In their

[16] C. L. R. James, *The Black Jacobins: Toussaint L'Ouverture and the San Domingo Revolution* (New York [1938]), pp. 142, 216.

A French-born and educated mulatto who attained eminence in the medical profession was François Fournier de Pescay (1771-c. 1833). A native of Bordeaux (his family having come from Santo Domingo) and educated there, he was army surgeon for several years in the 1790's, later founded a medical school at Brussels, again after 1806 was army surgeon, for a time was physician to the Spanish King Ferdinand VII, in 1814 was chosen secretary to the Council of Health of the French armies, and from 1823-28 was representative of France on a diplomatic mission to the Negroes of Santo Domingo. Louis XVIII in 1814 conferred on him the cross of the Legion of Honor, and certain of his writings (chiefly on medical topics) achieved distinction. See biographical sketch in *Biographie universelle, ancienne et modern* . . ., ed. by J. L. and L. G. Michaud (Paris, 1811-62, 85 v.), LXIV, 385-86.

[17] *Ibid.*, p. 219. Vinogradov portrays them (*op. cit.*, p. 321) as studying at the military school in Paris and arrested on Napoleon's order. Later they were sent by Napoleon on the Leclerc military expedition to subdue Toussaint, being asked to carry a message of good will to their father. For details of their reception and actions in the island, see James, *op. cit.*, pp. 249-51, and Vinogradov, *op. cit.*, pp. 353-65.

[18] James, *op. cit.*, p. 214. Vinogradov (*op. cit.*, p. 345) presents one Jacob Dessalines, friend of Ogé in the Negro circle at Paris. He is not to be confused with the general, Jean Jacques Dessalines, later Governor-General and Emperor Jean Jacques I of Haiti.

reception of such youths the French and British governments were anxious to obtain the favor of the African chieftains.[19]

Proneness to curry favor with African chiefs paved the way for a hoax on the court of Louis XIV by a slave from the Ivory Coast, named Aniaba. Given as a present in 1687 to two French Dominicans by the chief of Assini, the Dominicans sent him to France with a letter in which he was designated as heir to the throne of the kingdom of Assini. In France he was treated with honors befitting royalty. He was baptized by no less a person than Bishop Bossuet, and Louis XIV acted as his godfather, giving him the name Louis. For his first communion he was instructed by the Cardinal de Noailles, and on that occasion placed "his kingdom" under the protection of France and the Virgin. Later he was made a cavalry captain. At length in 1700 news came to France that the king of Assini was dead; whereupon Louis XIV sent him on a warship to claim his throne. On arrival it was found that the natives had already selected a successor and were not minded to accept as king a former slave. The commander of the vessel accordingly ridded himself of Aniaba and set about soliciting concessions from the new Assini chieftain.[20]

This was not the only instance in which the French were the victims of deception by Negroes. There is the celebrated case of Louise Marie Theresa, the "Mooress" (designated by Mathorez as a Negro woman), who claimed to be none other than the natural daughter of Louis XIV. Many writers of the time, including Saint-Simon, tell of her. Some authorities would have her the legitimate daughter of Louis XIV by Marie Theresa, who due to shock or envy bore a colored child. The laws of biology, however, do not explain Negro births in terms of shock and envy. According to other authority, the "Mooress" was the daughter of Louis XIV

[19] Donnan, *op. cit.*, II, 4-5, n. 2.
[20] Cole, *op. cit.*, p. 104.

by a Negro woman who was servant to his mother, Anne of Austria. Louis in his youthful amours displayed fondness for this woman, by whom the child Louise Marie Theresa was born in 1656. Voltaire, who saw the "Mooress" in 1716, says that she resembled Louis XIV. From 1695 until her death in 1732 she resided in a convent at Moret, on a royal pension of 300 livres a year, and there is ground for believing that she enjoyed this pension for some years prior to her adoption of the religious life. Madame de Maintenon manifested an interest in her, making several visits to her at the convent. These marks of royal favor did not leave unspoiled the nun, who exhibited a haughty spirit of which her superiors complained. On one occasion she referred to Monseigneur, the dauphin, as her brother. To this day the story has its mystery. The one thing certain in it is that Louis XIV and Madame de Maintenon showed a remarkable interest in the woman.[21]

In 1792 a case of alleged imposture was brought before the Paris police by Pierre Philippe de Grouchet, planter from Santo Domingo and wearer of the cross of Saint-Louis, against a mulatto girl, aged seventeen, whom he had brought to France as a child. After some years of service this girl had left him, and now claimed to be his natural child by a free Negro woman. She demanded of him 20,000 livres by way of support. Grouchet insisted that she was only his slave and was trying to blackmail him.[22] The outcome is not reported.

Certain Negroes and mulattoes ran afoul of the law and were imprisoned. In 1784-85 two Negroes were arrested by royal order for vagrancy or begging and placed in the *dépôt de mendicité* (compulsory workhouse) at Soissons.[23] In October, 1790, one Demarest, a former farmer-general,

---

[21] Mathorez, *op. cit.*, I, 394-96.

[22] Tuetey, *op. cit.*, V, 318, no. 3088.

[23] [Abbé Montlinot] *Etat actuel du dépôt de mendicité de la généralité de Soissons. IV. comte. Années 1784 & 1785* (n.p., n.d.), p. 3, chart.

complained to the police in Paris of "some malversations" made by the Negro servant of Sieur de Combe, to whom he had rented an apartment.[24] About the same time two French citizens denounced as a swindler one Sieur Bengala, a Negro servant of the Duke of Orleans, who had come illegally into possession of a bank note (*billet*) signed by the Duke de Biron.[25] At length on 20 floréal an II (May 9, 1794) a former Negro servant of the Duke of Orleans (evidently another Negro than the one just mentioned), named Edouard, later captain in the French army, was arrested, imprisoned, and reportedly executed by order of the Committee of General Surety.[26] Doubtless an examination of the police records in French archives would reveal other instances. This merely means that Negroes like other elements in the French population had difficulties with the police.

To others France was indebted for military service. Maurice de Saxe, famous French marshal in the War of the Austrian Succession, had a regiment of which he was particularly proud, called the Saxe Volunteers, composed of Negroes, Turks, Tartars, and Roumanians. One brigade was of Negroes from Guinea, Senegal, the Congo, Santo Domingo, Arabia, and Pondicherry. It was mounted on white horses and under the immediate charge of one Jean Hitton, a *sous-brigadier,* who claimed to be the son of an African king. This brigade fought in all the campaigns of the war directed by Maurice, and afterwards, from 1748 until his death in 1750, was stationed with him at Chambord. The Negroes were allowed to take as wives either French women or those of their own color, who by this time had re-

---

[24] Tuetey, *op. cit.,* II, 154, no. 1451.

[25] *Ibid.,* II, 205, no. 1931.

[26] *Ibid.,* XI, 532, no. 2028. H. Castonnet des Fossees (*La perte d'une colonie. La Révolution de Saint-Dominque* [Paris, 1893], p. 176) mentions, interestingly enough, a Negro named Edouard, formerly a servant of the Duke of Orleans, as being an aide-de-camp to General Desfourneaux in Santo Domingo in 1796. Either the Duke of Orleans had had two Negro servants named Edouard or the reported execution must be erroneous.

joined the men. Despite the Marshal's request in his will
that the brigade be kept intact and pass under the control
of his nephew, the government broke it up, distributing the
Negroes as kettle-drummers among the various cavalry
regiments. This action, it is said, was due to representations made to the government by the colonial planters
against the military training of Negroes, inasmuch as the
latter outnumbered them in the colonies.[27] Shortly later
the great influx of Negroes into France was to create fears
for those that were racial purists, and the return of Negroes
from France to the colonies to create trouble for the planters. Some restrictive legislation which resulted will be described later.[28]

During the period of the Revolution Negroes served in
the French army. In 1792-93 Alexandre Davy de la Pail-
leterie Dumas, mulatto, father and grandfather of the two
French writers Dumas of the nineteenth century, was lieutenant colonel of a corps of Negro and mulatto troops. He
won distinction after distinction in the army, and by September, 1793, was a general.[29] His prodigious physical
strength and his reckless courage gave rise to stories bordering on the mythical.[30] He served under Napoleon in his
First Italian and Egyptian campaigns, a valorous feat in
the former winning for him the sobriquet of "Horatius
Cocles of the Tyrol." Napoleon however took a violent dislike to him, whether for his race or his republican opinions,
and after Dumas's return from the Egyptian campaign
(and a two years' imprisonment in Southern Italy) he was
released from the army and spent his last years in sickness
and poverty. On November 22, 1792, he married Marie

[27] Mathorez, *op. cit.*, I, 403; Mathorez, *op. cit.*, *Revue des études historiques*, année 83, pp. 201-02; Fieffé, *op. cit.*, I, 280-81.

[28] Martin-Doisy, *op. cit.*, III, 1058-59; *Inventaire-sommaire* . . . *Bouches-
du-Rhône*, C 2561; *Inventaire-sommaire* . . . *Ille-et-Vilaine*, C 1171.

[29] *Nouvelle biographie générale*, XV, 163-64.

[30] These are related at some length by Francis Gribble, *Dumas, Father and
Son* (New York, 1930), pp. 15-35.

Elizabeth Labouret (white), the daughter of a Villers-Cotterets innkeeper, by whom Alexandre, author of *The Count of Monte Cristo,* was born (1802).[31]

On Napoleon's return from Egypt in 1799, Kléber, left in charge, purchased a large number (*une grande quantité*) of Negro slaves from Ethiopian caravans and made soldiers of them. The Twenty-first Half-Brigade of Light Infantry was so formed. It required only a short while to train them, and they were free from prejudices held by Moslem troops. In his victory over the Turks at Heliopolis in 1800 they had a part.[32]

Of Negro sailors in French service in the eighteenth century there appears to be no record. In an earlier period, however, Negroes had been used as galley-slaves. It was found that they did not stand up well in the service, being prone to die of tuberculosis.[33]

During the Revolution Negroes and mulattoes figured more prominently in France than at any earlier period of the century, due to the legislation and troubles over slavery. Among the Negroes and mulattoes in France at this time were representatives of the Negro and mulatto population in the West Indies to the parliamentary bodies in Paris and certain insurgent military leaders. Negroes who had been slaves sat in the Revolutionary parliaments.[34] At the outset of the Revolution the whites in the West Indian colonies sent representatives of themselves alone. This led to a letter of protest to the National Assembly as early as No-

[31] *Ibid.,* pp. 26, 34.

[32] Fieffé, *op. cit.,* II, 49. In 1802-03 a battalion of Negro and mulatto troops was formed of dischargees from English prisons, and attached to the engineering corps of the French army. The Negro officer in charge was one Hercules, who had distinguished himself in Italy and Egypt. With his account (*ibid.,* II, 54-5) Fieffé presents an illustration of the uniform worn by this battalion.

[33] Some Iroquois chiefs from Canada also were condemned to the galleys but their tribes rose in insurrection, forcing their delivery. Albert Rambaud, *Histoire de la civilisation française* (Paris, 1887, 2v.), II, 242.

[34] James, *op. cit.,* p. 204.

vember 23, 1789, in which certain mulattoes who designated themselves "Commissioners and deputies of the colored citizens of the French isles and colonies" demanded that the Negroes and mulattoes of Santo Domingo, Guadeloupe, and Martinique be represented as well as the whites.[35] They had not been seated by March 3, 1791, when another letter from the same parties was read before the Assembly requesting that they be allowed to take their seats. The Assembly at first decided to let them be seated when their credentials had been verified by its president, but on the next day countermanded this action by referring the matter to the Colonial Committee, where it died.[36] Throughout the early 1790's agitation for the emancipation and representation of Negroes was made in Paris by the *Amis des Noirs,* organized there in 1787 by Brissot, the Abbé Grégoire, and others, including certain mulattoes. Counter-agitation was made by the colonial planters through their Club Messiac. On February 4, 1794, the former group won the victory, with the seating of the Negro and mulatto representatives and the abolition of slavery throughout French possessions. On the reception of the Negro and mulatto members from Santo Domingo, the president of the Convention kissed them on each cheek.[37] During the Directory Negroes and mulattoes from the colonies continued to sit in the parlia-

[35] Those signing the letter were Ogé, *jeune;* Raimond, *ainé;* De Joly; Du Souchet de Saint-Réal; Honoré de Saint-Albert; and Fleury. Their letter was read before the Assembly at its seance of November 28, and is printed in *Archives parlementaires de 1787 à 1860,* ed. by J. Madival, E. Laurent, and others, série 1 (Paris, 1862-1913, 82 v.), X, 329-33. Garrett (*op. cit.,* p. 10) gives the names of the eight self-styled deputies.

[36] *Ibid.,* XXIII, 644. The Colonial Committee was controlled by West Indian planters and their friends. Garrett, *op. cit.,* pp. 46-7; cf. *ibid.,* p. 2.

[37] The delegates were Bellay, a former slave; Mills, mulatto; and Dufay, a white. James, *op. cit.,* pp. 112-13. According to Priestley (*op. cit.,* p. 325), the victory had been gained in part through the efforts of two colored deputies, Delacroix and De Levasseur. In the "wild enthusiasm" following the vote, these two deputies "embraced each other before the tribune, and each deputy gave them a fraternal kiss."

mentary bodies.[38]   In 1795 Toussaint L'Ouverture sent a
deputation to the French government "to attest his loyalty."   In the following spring Raimond, a mulatto, was
one of a commission of five sent by the French government
to Santo Domingo.[39]

Among the colonial insurgent leaders in France during
this period was Alexandre Sabès Pétion, distinguished
quadroon general, later twice president of Santo Domingo.
He came to France in 1800 but returned in 1801 with Leclerc's expedition.[40]

Walter Geer, historian of the Bonaparte family, states
that the wife of General Beauharnais's brother married a
colored man named Castaing, a widower with four children.   This was just after the Reign of Terror (1793-94),
when she was released from prison.   Her husband, the Mar-
quis François de Beauharnais, had fled from France as an
émigré.   The wife had been placed in prison during the Terror and narrowly escaped execution.   On being released,
she was without resources.   Her daughter, Emilie de Beauharnais, was taken in charge by Josephine after the latter's
marriage to Napoleon (March 9, 1796) and placed in Madame Campan's school for girls along with Josephine's
own daughter, Hortense.[41]

Throughout most of the eighteenth century there was

[38] The names of seven delegates from Santo Domingo in 1796 are given by
H. Castonnet des Fosses, *La perte d'une colonie. La Révolution de Saint-
Domingue* (Paris, 1893), p. 174.   Laveaux and Brothier were sent to the
Council of the Ancients; Thomacy, Sonthonax, Periniaud, Boisrond, and Mentor, to the Five Hundred.   All save Sonthonax appear to have been Negroes or
mulattoes.   A picture of E. V. Mentor is reproduced by James, *op. cit.*, facing
page 152.   Mentor had been born in Martinique.

[39] *Ibid.*, pp. 132, 140.   Raimond was wealthy, educated, and a resident in
France since 1784.   Garrett, *op. cit.*, p. 2, n. 6, 134-35.

[40] He was well educated, moderate, and endowed with capacity.   He is not
to be confused with Pétion de Villeneuve (1753-94) of Convention fame.
Biographie universelle, ancienne et moderne, 474-77; *The Century Cyclopedia
of Names*, ed. by Benjamin E. Smith (London and New York, 1904), p. 799.

[41] *Napoleon and His Family: the Story of a Corsican Clan* (New York,
1927-39, 3 v.), I, 70.

miscegenation in France, as also in the colonies. Until the 1760's there appears to have been little if any racial feeling, the Negro being regarded as a curiosity from a far-off land. A taste for the exotic was paramount in Europe during this age of the Rococo, and the Negro appears to have carried an attraction even as did the "learned" Chinese and the simple or "natural" American Indian. Nevertheless during the 1760's some racial feeling arose, as revealed by the fact that a royal declaration of June 30, 1763, ordered all Negroes to leave France for the colonies whence they had come. This evoked protests both from the slaveowners traveling in France and from the Negroes themselves, some of the latter (evidently free Negroes) asserting that age and infirmities made it impossible for them to earn a living in the colonies. The protests had their effect, and on March 19, 1764, permission was given for them to remain.[42]

In the 1770's the question again came to the fore. Letters patent of September 3, 1776, and a royal declaration of August 9, 1777, charged that there were too many Negroes in France, that cultivation of land in the colonies suffered in consequence, that the "sojourn" of Negroes in French cities (and above all in Paris) caused "the greatest disorders," and that they returned to the colonies with a spirit of insubordination.[43] Consequently it was ordered

[42] *Inventaire-sommaire . . . Bouches-du-Rhône*, C 2561. Desire to get the Negroes back to the colonies for cultivation of the soil was another motive for the declaration. During the years 1763-65 France made strenuous efforts to send out more people to her colonies, the loss of Canada making her realize the need for such action.

[43] Isambert, *op. cit.*, XXIV, 105-06; XXV, 81-2. Part of the preamble of the latter runs as follows: ". . . nous sommes informé aujourd'hui que le nombre des noirs s'y [en France], est tellement multiplié, par la facilité de la communication de l'Amérique avec la France, qu'on enleve journellement aux colonies cette portion d'hommes la plus nécessaire pour la culture des terres, en même temps que leur séjour dans les villes de nôtre royaume, surtout dans la

by the latter enactment that, on the request of the inhabitants of the colonies, French ports would thenceforth be closed to the entry of Negroes, mulattoes, and other men of color. Colonists visiting France might bring one servant each to attend them during the voyage, but the latter must either be sent back from the port of entry on the first vessel returning to the colony or be placed in a *dépôt* (concentration camp) until taken or sent back home. In the latter instance, the master was liable for all expense of maintenance, to be paid at the admiralty office at the port before he should return; and by way of assurance he had to make deposit of 1,000 livres. To take a Negro, mulatto, or any other person of color, of either sex, into France in violation of these conditions made one liable to a fine of 3,000 livres. Ship officers were ordered not to receive on their vessels any Negro, mulatto, or other colored person unless they had definite orders from the proper French officials. Violation of this order would bring on them a fine of 1,000 livres for each Negro or mulatto transported, and suspension from their offices for a period of three years. In a repeated offense these penalties were to be doubled.[44] Persons already resident in France with Negro or mulatto servants prior to this declaration might retain their service on condition of registering them before admiralty officials or a royal judge in their locality within a month; this period passed, the servants might remain with them only of their own con-

capitale, retournent dans les colonies, ils y portent l'esprit d'independance et d'indocilité, et y deviennent plus nuisibles qu'utiles.''

For some time the colonists had protested against the training of Negroes as troops, lest they return to the colonies where they greatly outnumbered the whites.

[44] These regulations were not observed minutely by ship officers, with the result that a royal ordinance of February 23, 1778, demanded more explicit compliance. This ordinance is given in full by Besson, *op. cit., Revue de l'histoire des colonies françaises*, XXI, 444-45.

sent. All Negroes, mulattoes, and other colored persons not in service must register before the same officials, and on fulfilling this requirement might remain in France.[45]

This enactment was followed by an order of the council of state of April 5, 1778, forbidding marriage between whites and Negroes, mulattoes, and other colored persons. Any notary drawing up a license or contract for such a marriage was made subject to a fine, and the parties entering into such a marriage were to be expelled at once to the colonies.[46] The preamble states that this legislation was called forth by a number of instances in which such marriages were proposed, and in the opinion of the government "it would be against good order to tolerate" them. It appears that this legislation remained in force until the Revolution.

In 1789-91 much agitation with the chambers of commerce of the French port cities was undertaken with success by West Indian planters.[47] The Chamber of Commerce of Marseilles on September 2, 1791, by unanimous vote protested against the actions of the National Assembly on May 15 preceding, by which citizenship had been conferred on Negroes born free in the colonies.[48] Thirty-six merchants of Nantes called for revocation of the act.[49]

Racial feeling however, appears to have been limited to

---

[45] Isambert, op. cit., XXV, 82-4.

[46] Ibid., XXV, 257-58; Besson, op. cit., Revue de l'histoire des colonies françaises, XXI, 445-46. It is not clear whether the whites were to be sent to the colonies too: the word renvoyer (sent back) gives ground for argument that only the Negroes or colored people would be returned. The phrase runs: "Veut Sa Majesté que si aucun de ses sujets contrevient auxdites défenses, les contractans soient sur le champ renvoyés dans ses colonies."

[47] Garrett, op. cit., pp. 23, 93.

[48] Inventaire des archives historiques de la Chambre de Commerce de Marseille . . . (Marseille, 1878), BB, art. 19 (p. 315).

[49] Garrett, op. cit., p. 123. Citizens in Nantes, La Havre, Abbéville, Dunkirk, Rouen, and Dinant had written in advance to prevent passage of the act. Ibid., p. 94.

certain circles, notably the planters and their friends among the aristocracy and upper bourgeoisie. Throughout the second half of the century there had been a widespread movement, encouraged by the *philosophes,* toward abolition of slavery and the slave trade.[50] Forty-nine *cahiers* submitted to the royal government in early 1789 demanded the abolition of slavery.[51] Agitation toward this end was actively undertaken after 1787 by the Friends of the Blacks, and made rapid headway. With Jacobin rise to power victory was assured. On June 4, 1793, a group of colonials, chiefly Negroes, appeared on the floor of the Convention to ask for emancipation of slaves, and were warmly received. One of the deputation was "a colored woman aged 114 years," so feeble that she had to be supported as she walked. She was introduced as Jeanne Odo, of Port-au-Prince, Santo Domingo. In respect for her age the entire assembly stood, and the president gave her the fraternal kiss."[52] A few months later, on February 4, 1794, slavery was abolished by the Convention amid a burst of great excitement. One of the Santo Dominican colored representatives just seated made a pathetic speech exposing the sufferings of slaves in his country. On his conclusion, De Levasseur (representative from Sarthe) made a motion for the abolition of slavery in its entirety in the colonies. It was seconded by Lacroix (from Eure-et-Loir). Discussion was waived. The vote was taken and the entire assembly stood in support of the motion. Thereupon the president of the Convention proclaimed slavery abolished, to the cries of

[50] Cf. Edward D. Seeber, *Anti-Slavery Opinion in France during the Second Half of the Eighteenth Century* (Baltimore, 1937).

[51] Of these 17 came from the clergy, 11 from the nobility, 20 from the Third Estate, and 1 from the Third Estate and nobility jointly. Beatrice Fry Hyslop, *French Nationalism in 1789 according to the General Cahiers* (New York, 1934), pp. 276-77.

[52] *Archives parlementaires,* LXVI, 57.

"Vive la République! Vive la Convention! Vive la Liberté!" This abolition lasted until 30 floréal an X (May 20, 1802), when Napoleon as First Consul restored slavery in the French colonies. He also made marriages between whites and blacks once more illegal.[53]

Shelby T. McCloy

University of Kentucky

[53] *La grande encyclopédie*, art. "Abolition d'Esclavage." That strong excitement on the matter of emancipation continued after February 4, 1794, can be found in the report of a Negro celebration (*fête des nègres*) at Grenoble on 12 germinal an III (April 1, 1795), in connection with which a house was torn down by mob action. *Inventaire-sommaire . . . Isère*, L 145.

THE LEGAL STATUS OF JAMAICAN SLAVES BEFORE THE ANTI-SLAVERY MOVEMENT

The legal status of slaves in Jamaica was typical of their status in all the British West India Islands. Jamaica was not the first English colony to be faced with problems of law arising from slavery and her earliest slave legislation was patterned upon that of Barbados. Soon, however, Jamaica became the leading English Caribbean colony with a slave population greater than that of the rest of the British West Indies combined. As the natural leader of the British sugar colonies, her laws tended to be looked up to and copied by the other British West India governments.

Special legislation governing the slave population of Jamaica was early seen necessary. Principles of English Common Law could not apply to slaves. Negroes were a class apart, a servile class which possessed no natural nor civil rights within the community. The planters tended to manage the blacks solely from the standpoint of economic gain. The growth of the plantation system in Jamaica, characterized by large scale production, absentee ownership, and management of the slaves by overseers whose abilities were measured by the amount of sugar they produced, submerged humane considerations in the race for wealth. Many of the slaves proved unable to survive the physical labor and psychological strain produced by the change from the old way of life. The rest were kept under subjection only by a heavy hand and the constant vigilance of the whites.

The first complete Jamaican slave code was passed in 1696,[1] though as early as 1661 laws began to be passed dealing with special aspects of the slave problem. During the

[1] 8 William III, Cap. 2 (1696), ''An Act for the better Order and Government of Slaves,'' *Acts of Assembly passed in the Island of Jamaica 1681-1737* (London, 1738).

eighteenth century the slave act of 1696 continued to be the basic law of Jamaican slavery, supplemented by additional laws passed from time to time. By 1781 provisions relating to slaves were found in so many different statutes covering a period of eighty-five years that confusion and uncertainty prevailed, and the Jamaican legislature brought the different acts together in the codification of that year.[2] The Jamaican slave code of 1781 and the preceding acts, unlike later codes, were not passed with a view to conciliating anti-slavery sentiment in England. No widespread and effective criticism of West Indian slavery had yet come from England. The slave laws passed in Jamaica before 1788 were slightly if at all influenced by anti-slavery propaganda. These codes represent the true inclinations of the planters, not window dressing to mislead public opinion at home.

Jamaican slave acts had several purposes in view, but their guiding motive was fear of rebellion. A well-timed and coordinated uprising of the slaves on the island could by the overwhelming numbers of the blacks mean the complete annihilation of the whites. Such an insurrection was ever the nightmare of the English. To lessen the danger from rebellion, the planters tried to prevent communication between slaves on different plantations. The very first provision of the law of 1696 provided that masters were not to allow slaves to leave the plantation without a pass explaining the purpose of the journey and the time they were expected to be absent. The planters also took the precaution to forbid slaves on different plantations to assemble together where, according to the act of 1696 "they have taken liberty to contrive to bring to pass many of their bloody and inhuman transactions."[3] It was usual for the

---

[2] 22 George III, Cap. 17 (1781), "An Act to repeal several Acts and Clauses of Acts respecting Slaves and for the better Order and Government of Slaves, and for other Purposes," *Acts of Assembly passed in the Island of Jamaica from 1770 to 1783 inclusive* (Kingston, Jamaica, 1786).

[3] 8 Wm. III, Cap. 2, Sec. 34.

island legislators to throw out such phrases of moral indignation to describe the efforts of the Negroes for liberty.

Further restrictions were imposed after 1717 forbidding Negroes to assemble and beat drums or blow horns, thus after the manner of their native land transmitting signals "of their evil and wicked intentions" to confederates upon distant plantations.[4] Owners, however, were not to forbid their slaves meeting together "and diverting themselves in any innocent amusement."

More security against rebellion would have been obtained from a patrol system, and finally such a system was provided by an act of 1773. Three years later the act was repealed, however, as the shortage of white manpower rendered the measure too burdensome.[5]

With reason the planters desired all weapons kept out of the hands of slaves. Negroes found in possession of fire-arms, cutlasses, lances, or other weapons could be punished by death.[6] Slave owners were supposed to search the Negro houses every fortnight for "clubs, wooden swords and mischievous weapons."[7] Grog shops were prohibited from selling rum to slaves as the legislators believed that formation of conspiracies was aided by the potvaliant effects of intoxicating liquors.

"Out-lying slaves" as the phrase read, those slaves who had run away from their plantations but were not actually engaged in rebellion, were still considered very dangerous to the peace and safety of the island. Plantations deserted six months were ordered torn down lest they become a refuge for runaways.[8] Negroes recently off ship from Af-

---

[4] 4 Geo. I, Cap. 4, Sec. 8 (1717), "An Act for the more effectual punishment of Crimes Committed by Slaves," *Acts of Assembly passed in the Island of Jamaica 1681-1737.*

[5] 14 Geo. III, Cap. 19; 17 Geo. III, Cap. 29.

[6] 8 Wm. III, Cap. 2, Sec. 13.

[7] 4 Geo. I, Cap. 4, Sec. 7.

[8] 8 Wm. III, Cap. 2, Sec. 21.

rica were not punished by the civil administration for running away. The law tacitly acknowledged that to run away was only natural in the case of a recent arrival who had not yet established friends among the plantation Negroes or come to look upon the plantation as home. But if a slave who had been on the island three years disappeared and remained absent twelve months he was considered a bona-fide runaway, ready to engage in active rebellion if the chance presented itself, or to join with the Maroons in their raiding forays. He was ordered transported under the slave act of 1696; to be sold by the owner to any person who would take him off the island, preferably to a Spanish or French possession in the Caribbean or to the logwood cutters in Honduras. Later amendments defined a permanent runaway as a slave who had been two years on the island and absent six months.

Slave laws were difficult to enforce. The consensus of opinion on the island preferred that every slave should be responsible to his master alone. The state should actively interfere between owner and slave as infrequently as possible. No special enforcement agency existed to see that slave law regulations were obeyed. Many enactments, no doubt, remained upon the books unheeded until individual circumstances demanded some legal authorization to hold or punish a slave. Very infrequently were travelling passes required of slaves, it would seem, but at any time a suspected runaway or thief could be held for failing to possess a ticket until his identity could be checked. During periods of threatening rebellion this and other precautionary laws were no doubt strictly enforced.

Closely connected with security against rebellion was the further aim of slave legislation to preserve the proper subordination of the Negroes to the whites. Europeans by their color were sacrosanct, and except to protect his owner's life and property no slave was to offer any resistance to a white. The law threatened with death any slave who struck a white.[9]

Ownership of property by slaves was thought to elevate slaves above their proper humble position, and for reasons both of authority and security slaves were forbidden to possess "horses, mares, mules, geldings or asses."[10] Slaves did in fact hold various kinds of property, but had no right nor protection of ownership under law.

A discrimination was made in criminal procedure against slaves accused of serious offenses such as burglary, robbery or rebellion. Since the Africans should be made always to feel their inferiority, it was not considered desirable to allow them to enjoy the same judicial procedure and safeguards as the whites. Criminal cases were tried in a special slave court before two justices and three freeholders.[11] Jury trial was not allowed. Summoning a panel required time and occasioned delay, and justice to slaves should be swift and summary, believed the planters. The evidence of slaves was admitted against other slaves and against liberated blacks, but not against whites. Free Negroes could only testify in cases involving slaves or members of their own class.

Manumission was frowned upon in Jamaica. After 1774 no master was allowed to free a slave until he had given security to the churchwardens of the parish to provide the slave £5 annually during the remainder of the slave's life.[12] The legislators justified their action by the allegation that "the frequent manumission of Negro, mulatto, and other slaves by persons not making a provision for them, is a great nuisance to the community and promotes frequent

[9] 8 Wm. III, Cap. 2, Sec. 2.

[10] 4 Geo. I, Cap. 4, Sec. 12.

[11] 8 Wm. III, Cap. 2, Sec. 23; 22 Geo. III, Cap. 17, Sec. 28.

[12] 15 Geo. III, Cap. 18 (Dec. 24, 1774), "An Act for regulating the manumission of Negro, mulatto, and other slaves; and to oblige the owners to make a provision for them during their lives."

thefts.'' Edward Long, writing at the same time, strongly condemned the practice of certain avaricious owners who compelled slaves grown old and useless to shift for themselves.[13] From one point of view the Act of 1774 may thus be considered a protection for aged slaves. However, the measure bears strong resemblance to the more stringent laws of Barbados and Grenada absolutely prohibiting manumission. Slave owners disapproved of neighbors who freed their slaves or allowed slaves to purchase their freedom since it tended to make the other Negroes discontented. Laws impeding manumission express the hostility of the West Indian whites toward a large free-black population.

Free Negroes had also to be kept in due subordination to the whites. It was an affront to the European population and a bad example to slaves if free-blacks were allowed to meet the whites on equal terms. Regulations governing free Negroes formed a part of every slave code in Jamaica.

The feeling against the Negro as such was increasingly shown in legislation as the years advanced and the free Negro population grew larger. Mulattoes and Negroes were forbidden to sell any merchandise except foodstuffs by an act of 1735.[14] Probably this regulation was not rigidly enforced, but its presence acted as a deterrent and like many other laws relating to Negroes it remained always in reserve to be put into effect if the whites desired. The existence of free Negro retail merchants was one of those practices which the legislators lumped under the enigmatic and all-inclusive designation of causing ''great inconveniences to the utter Ruin of several Orphans, and other Inhabitants of this Island, and Decay of the Planting Interest.'' To prevent great wealth from falling into the hands of free Negroes, the legislature in 1761 forbade grants of over

---

[13] Long, Edward, *History of Jamaica*, III, 927.

[14] ''An Act to prevent hawking and peddling, and disposing of goods clandestinely.'' Act 106 of 1735.

£2000 value to Negroes or mulattoes not born in wedlock.[15]
"Such bequests," it was complained, "tend greatly to destroy the distinction requisite and absolutely necessary to
be kept up in this island between white persons and Negroes, their issue and offspring, and may in progress of
time be the means of decreasing the number of white inhabitants in this island." Another provision of the act of
1761 forbade any Negro or mulatto to purchase real estate
worth more than £2000.

No statute has been found expressly allowing slavery in
Jamaica nor declaring that the child of a slave should in-
herit the condition of his mother. It was considered necessary, however, to state in 1696 that no slave was to be free
by becoming a Christian.[16] All masters were supposed to
instruct their slaves in the principles of Christianity and to
fit them for baptism.[17] Except in isolated cases this clause
was completely disregarded.

A final class of enactments established a minimum of
fair treatment for the slave. These clauses for the protection of the slave are to be found in the earliest slave acts
and grew in number and humanity with the years. Their
underlying principle was that the condition of slaves should
not be made too desperate else discipline would be difficult
to maintain on the island. As the slave code of 1781 stated:

... nothing can contribute more to the good order and government
of slaves than the humanity of their owners in providing for and
supplying them with good and wholesome provisions and proper
and sufficient clothing and all such other things as may be proper
and necessary for them, during their being in a state of slavery...[18]

A new provision in the act of 1781 established in law the
customary practice on the island that every master allot his

[15] 15 Geo. III, Cap. 8, "An Act to prevent the inconveniences arising from
exorbitant grants and devises made by white persons to Negroes and the issue
of Negroes; and to restrain and limit such grants and devises."

[16] 8 Wm. III, Cap. 2, Sec. 40.

[17] 8 Wm. III, Cap. 2, Sec. 45.

[18] 22 Geo. III, Cap. 17, Sec. 2.

slaves sufficient land for them to grow their necessary food and allow them sufficient time to cultivate their plots. Previous to 1781 this well-nigh universal custom had not been made compulsory.

"For the better encouragement of slaves to do their duty," the code of 1696 obliged every slave-owner to provide proper clothing for their slaves: jackets and petticoats or frocks for the women, jackets and drawers for the men. Constables were to take care to bring negligent owners before the justices. In more general terms the code of 1781 stated that all owners should give "proper and sufficient clothing" as approved by the justices and vestry of the parish. Slaves were to be given holidays at Christmas, Easter and Whitsuntide, but for reasons of security were not to be allowed two holidays in succession.[19]

Official punishments decreed for slaves were always harsh. Cruel and extreme punishments were dictated from fear of the overwhelming numbers of the Negroes and the hope that harsh penalties would intimidate the slaves. As the years passed, punishments were gradually modified. Hans Sloane in the early years of the colony speaks of the punishment for rebellion as "nailing them down on the ground with crooked sticks on every Limb and then applying the Fire by degrees from the Feet and Hands, burning them gradually up to the Head, whereby their pains are extravagant." For lesser crimes, castration or chopping off half a foot was common.[20] During the eighteenth century this type of punishment became increasingly uncommon. An anonymous writer about 1740 remarked that some years before several Negroes were convicted of attempting to poi-

[19] 8 Wm. III, Cap. 2, Sec. 3; 46. 22 Geo. III, Cap. 17, Sec. 4; 11.

[20] Sloane, Hans, *A Voyage to the Islands of Madera, Barbados, Nieves, S. Christopher and Jamaica with the Natural History . . . of the last of those islands* (London, 1707), I, lvii.

son their mistress and were burnt alive as examples. He implies that this procedure was most unusual.[21]

A comparison of the slave laws passed between 1696 and 1781 reveals a progressive softening of the official punishments decreed for slaves. The penalty of dismemberment was removed from the law. Public whippings were limited to thirty-one or thirty-nine lashes. Whether death or some less drastic punishment than death should be imposed for felonies was with increasing frequency left to the discretion of the judges. Transportation off the island became a favored punishment because the value of the slave could be recovered at the same time that a dangerous individual was removed from the community. Separation of the Negro from his friends and family also brought in an element of retribution.

Yet when a frightful example was desired, or the whites were reduced to near hysteria by realization of their numerical weakness, the punishments meted out to slaves could be extremely barbarous. As late as 1760 one leader of a slave rebellion was chained to a stake and burned. Two others were hung up alive in irons for over a week till they finally perished.

As a general rule the state did not wish to interfere in the private relationship between master and slave. Plantation discipline was the sole concern of the owner in the early years of the colony, and slaves had no protection in law from inhuman punishments which the master might inflict. Later it was forbidden to dismember a slave. The code of 1781 coupled the word mutilation with dismemberment, thus in theory protecting the slave's eyes, ears and tongue as well as his limbs from the sudden anger of his owner. Thirty years earlier the House of Assembly, considering ways to restrain acts of cruelty by owners and overseers, had contemplated a bill to prevent castration or

[21] *The Importance of Jamaica to Great Britain, Consider'd* (London [1740]), p. 19.

other mutilation of slaves without the authority of the magistrates, but the opposition of the residents of the towns had shelved the bill.[22] A further amendment in the code of 1781, relating that it was necessary and proper for "the encouragement of slaves" that they be protected in their persons, prohibited the wanton or cruel whipping, beating, bruising or wounding of any slave.

These limitations upon plantation discipline perhaps afforded some protection to the slave from the fact that they were written into the statute books, but if the master chose to disregard them no one interfered. Should a slave happen to know when his legal rights were being infringed it was most impolitic for him to complain to a magistrate against his master. Neither he nor his fellow slaves could give evidence against any white person in court. Judge and jury in all cases involving ill-treatment of slaves were prone to find in favor of the white from apprehension that victory for a slave would lessen the awe which all slaves should hold for their masters.

By the severity of its discipline the slave code attempted to make sure the slaves would keep at a submissive and humble distance. Rigid treatment, it was hoped, would destroy all thought of liberty and make the slaves more docile. The security of the community, believed the lawmakers, demanded a severe regime. Too much indulgence to slaves raised the danger that they would be inspired to attempt the complete recovery of their liberty. On the other hand, it was recognized that extremely bad treatment might have the opposite effect. Life would become unbearable, and in desperation the slaves might revolt. For this reason clauses were inserted prohibiting extreme cruelty and endeavoring to guarantee proper food and clothing to the slaves.

Many of the provisions of the Jamaican code were seldom if ever enforced. The planters desired to have the law

[22] *Journals of the Assembly of Jamaica* (Jamaica, 1811-29), IV, 119-121.

in reserve, but except in extreme cases to allow each master to govern his slaves as he saw fit without any outside interference intruding between master and slave. The slave law does not show accurately the true relationship between the two races. The codes do present, however, the planters' ideal of slave discipline. They reflect their decision upon the proper relationship of black to white, the relationship which the island legislators deep in their hearts believed to be necessary when they looked upon the problems of slavery in a cold and dispassionate manner.

Robert Worthington Smith

Ohio State University

ANTHONY ADVERSE OR THEODORE CANOT?

Like millions of other people, I followed the literary trend a few years ago and read one of the much-heralded pieces of fiction. While perusing these twelve hundred pages and more, I concluded that Hervey Allen[1] relied upon the accounts of the slave trade to provide many details for his book—places and personalities which, I thought, offered the most intriguing portions of the novel.

Anyone who pursues the study of the slave trade will find an abundance of journals, written by slave traders, ship captains, ship surgeons, missionaries, and others whose work took them to Africa as early as the fifteenth century. Many of these are fantastic documents, written by adventurers who doubtless sought a large measure of approval from recording real or imaginary exploits. The reader of Allen's novel is entitled to wonder what journals, if any, constituted the sources of the novelist's material.

An exciting, thrilling, and romantic book of this kind is the life of Theodore Canot, a slave captain of the first half of the nineteenth century. After making and losing several fortunes in the slave trade, he was found broken in body but apparently not in spirit on the wharves of Baltimore. Here he formed an acquaintance with Brantz Mayer, a journalist of that day who, as Canot told his tales, recorded them in an exciting style. The Canot memoirs, as related to Mayer, were published in the fifties with a dedication to Nat Willis. Finally, in our own time, Malcolm Cowley[2] got hold of this choice document and, with some editing and a valuable explanatory introduction, gave it to the reading public, to too many of whom, I am sure, it has remained unknown.

No novelist can have his hero spend years on the African coast without providing him with a background in some of the more obvious elements in African culture. One such

---

[1] *Anthony Adverse*, Farrar and Rinehart, 1933.
[2] *Adventures of an African Slaver*, A and C. Boni, 1928.

item might be knowledge of the phenomenal ability of the members of the Kru tribe on the West Coast in constructing canoes and generally in adapting themselves to the hazards and pleasure of the seacoast. Neither can one scratch the surface of the slave trade without running into the general estimates of the qualities of Mandingoes, Foulahs, Hausas, and Senegalese which contributed to their desirability as slaves. The Middle Passage is known to all who have read of the trade, as are the commodities which were used by European and American traders in exchange for slaves.

In addition to these general factors, when the novelist has his principal character know not only the same places but the same people as are recorded in the diary of a slave captain, and then has them sail on ships of the same name, we are disposed to wonder whether there has not been a too literal reliance upon one document. Furthermore, it has the disillusioning effect of causing one to raise his mental eyebrow when the next best seller appears.

We can agree that lifting a document is not art. Interpreting it might be. The border line between these two realms can be determined only by critics and scholars. Significantly enough, both Adverse and Canot were on intimate terms with Carlo Cibo, a provisioner of Havana. Both refer to the Gallegos, the ship owners and financial agents of slave traders. In each case the hero sails on the *Aerostatica* and later on the *La Fortuna* to a destination which is rather vaguely identified as the Rio Pongo. Both have dealings with Ali Mami, a Foulah chief, through Ahmah-de-Bellah, his "nephew" in one instance and his "son" in another. In each case Ali Mami presides over the destinies of a section of Futa Jallon, a region which is not located in either document but which must have constituted the hinterland on the western end of the West Coast. Canot,[3] soon after he went to sea, put in at a Spanish port where, by mistaken

[3] *Ibid.*, p. 18.

identity, he was claimed by a mother and sisters as a long-lost brother and son, and named Antonio.

But these are merely some obvious details which Allen apparently borrowed from Canot to embellish the character and the exploits of his Adverse. An enumeration of them might begin with Canot's birth "in the interior of Italy" and of Adverse's within the boundaries of Liguria. They might end with Canot's ruin resulting from the burning of his plantation and with the burning of the great house on Adverse's estate in Louisiana. But more significant than the place of his birth is Canot's[4] sailing on a Dutch trader "under the command of two captains—male and female," while Adverse sailed for the first time under the command of Mr. and Mrs. Jorham[5] on the *Wampanoag* of Providence. Upon his arrival in Cuba, Canot[6] relates that Carlo Cibo received "me with unbounded kindness, welcomed me to his bachelor home; apologized for its cold cheerlessness, and ordered me to consider himself and his casa entirely at my disposal as long as I chose to remain" while Allen[7] enlarged the meeting with Cibo into a detailed description of semi-tropical luxury, sumptuous and leisurely living, the maintenance of a vast establishment, including the support of many children born out of wedlock. In each case Cibo was an important personage, whether he was selling slaves on commission, negotiating loans, or making the necessary "arrangements" with harbor officials for the clearance of vessels engaged in the slave trade. The manager of the slave factory at Bangaland, according to Canot,[8] was Mongo John, the son of an English slaver whose mother was the daughter of a native chief of the Rio Pongo. Allen introduces us to a factory by the same name, with the chief factor

4 *Ibid.*, p. 18.
5 *Adverse*, pp. 313-314.
6 *Op. cit.*, p. 59
7 *Adverse*, pp. 417-426.
8 *Op. cit.*, p. 78.

as Mongo Tom,[9] whose father was an English "renegade missionary."

Both our ship captain, Canot, and our fictional hero, Adverse, are able seamen and ship masters. Canot[10] found it necessary to assume responsibility for the *Aerostatica* in a serious storm. While he alienated the crew, he was successful in managing the ship. He showed comparable competence when he had a mutinous crew on his hands,[11] for, with the assistance of the cook and the boatswain, he was able to put down the mutiny and gain control of the ship. But storms at sea also constituted the principal hazards of the slave trade and Adverse,[12] despite his youth, demonstrated his prowess as a sailor. Furthermore, any detailed account of the slave trade presents not only the problems arising from a mutinous crew but, in the event of too much freedom, of the mutiny of the slave cargo. In keeping with the standards of romantic fiction, the novelist has his hero behave like a seasoned slave captain, even on his first voyage.[13]

In many accounts of the slave trade reference is made to the problems of assembling the slaves on the seacoast. Also, to the caravans which came down to the coast periodically with supplies of slaves, ivory, and other commodities. U. B. Phillips,[14] in a most imaginative way, gives us a vivid description of the caravan routes. Upon their approach to the factory at which the trading would be done, Canot[15] says that barkers would be sent forth to greet the caravan and to defer to the chiefs of the expedition. Adverse[16] had similar experiences in dealing with the caravans from the in-

[9] *Adverse*, p. 624.

[10] *Op. cit.*, pp. 63-65.

[11] *Ibid.*, pp. 65-68.

[12] *Adverse*, pp. 534-535.

[13] *Ibid.*, p. 545.

[14] *American Negro Slavery*, Appleton, 1918, p. 31.

[15] *Op. cit.*, pp. 87-88.

[16] *Adverse*, pp. 601-603.

terior. When the caravan chief took his departure, Canot[17] relates that ''we walked side by side for some miles into the forest'' and ''I promised, with my hand on my heart'' that I would visit his father in Futa Jallon. Allen had these same pleasant experiences befall his Adverse[18] who was to supply ''arms and ammunition'' to the chief in the interior and was promised, in return, ''an ample supply of slaves at home-prices.''

Of course, no record of slaving by an experienced slaver would be complete without an account of the devastating effects of African fever. Canot,[19] when afflicted with fever, was treated by a native doctor and nursed by Esther, the intelligent half-breed mistress, whose father had been a ''renegade missionary.'' Adverse[20] was nursed back to health by his half-breed mistress, Neleta,[21] whose father had been an English captain of one of Gallego's ships.

Both the ship captain[22] and the venturesome Adverse[23] of fiction are in agreement on the details for inspecting slaves at the time of their sale in Africa. On the matter of loading a cargo of humans on the African coast, again there is considerable agreement between the reports of Canot[24] and those of Adverse.[25] Canot reports that the departure was accompanied by an ''abundant feed,'' while Allen tells us it was a time of ''great feasting.'' In preparation for embarking, the slave captain tells us that ''nails are closely pared,'' the head ''is neatly shaved'' and each slave when taken aboard was ''entirely stripped,'' and ''their mouths are carefully rinsed out with vinegar.'' In the novel we are

[17] *Op. cit.*, pp. 96-97.
[18] *Adverse*, p. 605.
[19] *Op. cit.*, pp. 100-103.
[20] *Adverse*, p. 648.
[21] *Ibid.*, p. 562.
[22] *Op. cit.*, p. 98.
[23] *Adverse*, p. 606.
[24] *Op. cit.*, pp. 107-108.
[25] *Adverse*, p. 619.

told that in the departure of the slaves from Africa every head "was shaved smooth" that "fingernails were pared down to the quick" and that each slave was "stripped of every rag." Furthermore, "every slave was made to wash out his mouth with vinegar."

As we know, the slave trade was a tremendous gamble. Profits from one voyage could be easily wiped out in the next as a result of death or disease among the cargo, a delayed passage, capture of the ship, or one of a combination of many circumstances. Canot[26] reports the truly fabulous net profits of more than forty-one thousand dollars on one voyage, while Allen,[27] in embellishing an account which resembles Canot's, pegs his net profits for one voyage at more than sixty-four thousand dollars. In 1827 Canot sold 217 slaves for more than seventy-seven thousand dollars in Havana while Adverse disposed of his cargo of 221 for more than seventy-one thousand dollars. However, in their detailed financial statements, Adverse buys 227 "slave dresses" at $2.00 each while Canot buys 217 at the same price per garment. Canot reports "eighteen sailors' wages" at $1,972; Adverse, in his account, had "17 men before the mast" costing $1,872. Canot reports "wages advanced to captain, mates, boatswain, cook, and steward" as $440 while Adverse includes "wages advanced to captain, mate, boatswain, cook and steward" as $440. Canot records "provisions for crew and slaves" at $1,115 while Adverse includes items for "provisions for crew" and "for slaves (on return trip)" as totaling $1,345.11. Canot reports the payment of five per cent commission; Adverse paid ten per cent to Cibo. So, if one wants adventure and romantic details, why should it be necessary to go further than Canot's diary?

All of which means that in a considerable portion of his novel Allen has presented a faithful record of the slave

[26] *Op. cit.*, p. 107.
[27] *Adverse*, p. 686.

trade. Just as Canot[28] settled down to the ownership and operation of a plantation and was ruined when the plantation burned, so Adverse[29] acquired a plantation in Louisiana where he built the manor house which was destroyed by fire. However, all of the evidence points to the conclusion that Allen must have relied to a large degree upon the romantic reports of a slave captain whose memoirs deserve wider reading than has doubtless been accorded them.

JOHN A. KINNEMAN

Illinois State Normal University

[28] *Op. cit.*, p. 375.
[29] *Adverse*, p. 1136.

MASSACHUSETTS ANTI-SLAVERY SOCIETY

The records of the Massachusetts Anti-Slavery Society furnish a mass of material concerning the founding, aims, and achievements of the abolition movement. Since the work of any society is only that of the persons who constitute it, the records of the Massachusetts Anti-Slavery Society furnish the materials in the light of which the work of its prime leader, William Lloyd Garrison, may be evaluated.

Much has been written in recent years to discredit the work of Garrison. Great emphasis has been placed upon the extreme positions taken by him in his later years, to the extent of overlooking the part he played in the whole abolition movement. Careful examination of the facts, however, seems to reveal that the work of Garrison must loom large in the history of the abolition movement.

Evaluation of the abolition movement must be considered in terms of formulation of aims and policies, the execution of plans, and results achieved. If the entire program achieved success eventually, and if Garrison was a prime mover in this program, the work of Garrison must be evaluated in the light of this success.

I. BIRTH OF THE SOCIETY

With the appearance of the *Liberator* on January 1, 1831, William Lloyd Garrison began his violent attack upon the slaveholders of the South. Garrison's genius for organization soon rallied the support of anti-slavery elements in the East. These at first called themselves the "New Abolitionists" but were organized in 1832 as the New England Anti-Slavery Society. In order to concentrate the agitation of the entire country, Garrison, at a meeting in Boston on Monday evening, January 21, 1833, made a resolution for the formation of a national society. The American Anti-Slavery Society, as it was called, was founded at a conven-

tion held in Philadelphia on December 4, 1833.[1] With its
organization the states of Maine, New Hampshire, and Ver-
mont withdrew from the New England Society and formed
their own local state organizations. The residue of the New
England Society decided to limit its operations to Massachusetts. By 1834 it became, therefore, a state society, and
the name was changed from the New England to the Massachusetts Anti-Slavery Society.

The views and policies of the Society were so influenced
by Garrison that they may be said to be one and the same.
At least, any study of the attitudes of the Society is necessarily a study of the attitudes of Garrison. The Constitution of the Massachusetts Anti-Slavery Society, with its
demand for the immediate abolition of slavery, was merely
a repetition of Garrison's views. The first number of the
Liberator contained an address to the public which sounded
the keynote of the career of Garrison and the Society. He
determined to attack the system of slavery until "every
chain be broken, and every bondman set free."[2] He repudiated every plan for gradual emancipation and proclaimed
the duty of immediate and unconditional liberation of the
slaves.

Abolition meant to the Society not only freedom but the
eradication of all the incidents and results of slavery, including all the laws, discriminations, social customs, and
practices which bore against the Negro race. The abolitionists aimed to obtain for Negroes equal civil and political rights and privileges.[3]

The South was certain to oppose such attacks upon her
traditions. Having eliminated freedom of speech in the
slave states, the South sought to accomplish the same object

---

[1] New England Anti-Slavery Society, *The Abolitionist*, Vol. 1 (December,
1833), p. 177.

[2] *Liberator*, January 1, 1831.

[3] Massachusetts Anti-Slavery Society, *Constitution of the New England
Anti-Slavery Society*. Boston, Garrison and Knapp, 1832.

in the North. Such tactics caused fair-minded men in the North to become abolitionists on account of this crusade against the rights of white men quite as much as from their interests in the rights of Negroes. As the number of abolitionists increased, the determination of the South to suppress the movement grew apace.

There seems little foundation for Southern belief that there was a direct connection between the publication of the *Liberator* and the servile insurrection of Nat Turner which occurred during the following August, 1831. Garrison denied any connection, and he condemned the work of David Walker whose *Appeal,* a pamphlet calling on the slaves to revolt, caused widespread alarm in the South. Although the Society protested that no publications had been sent to the slaves, it was but natural, however, that the South should associate all abolition literature with slave revolts.

The legislatures of the Southern states were quick to condemn the abolitionists. Georgia offered a reward of five thousand dollars for the arrest, trial, and conviction of the editor of the *Liberator*.[4] South Carolina called upon the free states to suppress all abolition societies.[5]

During the winter of 1835-1836 the Governor of Massachusetts received these resolutions from the South. When a committee of the Massachusetts Legislature had been duly organized to consider the documents, the abolitionists requested the privilege of a hearing before the committee. Receiving no reply, they proceeded to formulate a statement of their case, but before they could publish it, they were invited to appear before the joint committee of the two houses. The public had been aroused by the issue and there was a large audience. The case for the abolitionists was stated by their ablest speakers, among whom was Garrison.

[4] Jesse Macy, *The Anti-Slavery Crusade.* New Haven, Yale University Press, 1919, p. 70.

[5] *Ibid.*, p. 71.

They labored to convince the committee that their publications were not intended to bring about insurrection. ''We ask attention to the fact, that although frequent insurrections among the slaves have taken place and a remarkable one in Virginia in 1831—yet, since the formation of the first Anti-Slavery Society in 1832, no such calamity has occurred. . . .''[6] The result was that the Massachusetts Legislature did not comply with the request of South Carolina.

However, it is not to be thought that the Massachusetts government gave any sanction to the abolitionists. As an evidence of the illiberality of Boston, it was with difficulty that any place could be obtained for the meetings of an abolition convention. Eight of the churches were applied for without success. After considerable hesitation, the New Jerusalem church was granted for one half day. The rest of the meetings were held in Julien Hall, which was not large enough to accommodate the assembly. A written request, signed by one hundred citizens, was presented to the City Government for the use of Faneuil Hall, but it was denied them. However, on August 21, 1835, Faneuil Hall, which had been refused a few weeks before to the anti-slavery convention, was thrown open to a meeting held for the purpose of protecting slaveholders.[7]

II. PROGRAM AND WORK OF THE SOCIETY

The abolitionists proposed to achieve their aims through three methods: moral suasion, political action, and direct aid to fugitive slaves. The main function of the abolitionist movement was to convince the Northern people that slavery was not only harmful to the South but contrary to their own interests. The Massachusetts Society attempted to do this by moral suasion, or, in other words, by arousing public

[6] Massachusetts Anti-Slavery Society, *A Full Statement Respecting Abolitionists and Anti-Slavery Societies*. Boston, Isaac Knapp, 1836, p. 4.

[7] Massachusetts Anti-Slavery Society, *Fourth Annual Report*. Boston, Garrison and Knapp, 1836, p. 29.

sentiment against the slaveholders. Such sentiment would, in turn, show the latter the necessity of emancipating the slaves. In the spirit of civil and religious liberty and by appealing to the Declaration of Independence, they exhorted the entire people to become an effective anti-slavery society.

In order to organize Northern public opinion against slavery in the South the abolitionists worked out a thoroughgoing system of propaganda. They used literature as a weapon; they sent out travelling agents; they held anti-slavery meetings in all sorts of places, from a stable-loft to a church or public hall. At meetings, escaped fugitive slaves were present to give addresses on their experiences of slavery. These experiences were usually put in written form by some member of the Society and circulated. The most famous of these fugitives was Frederick Douglass who was made an agent of the Society and who later set up an anti-slavery paper of his own, *The North Star.*

Among all the weapons of the anti-slavery conflict there were none more powerful than the anti-slavery presses, the most important of which was the *Liberator*. This paper contained harsh statements about slavery. Especially harsh were the editorials written by Garrison. Various epithets were used as descriptive of slaveholders, the most frequent one being "man-stealers." Many of the articles were written by individuals discussing the evils of slavery. Some of the matters which kept recurring were: "Facts Showing the Safety of Emancipation," "The Remedy for Slavery," and many others of a similar nature.

The influence of the paper was extended through quotations made from it by other newspapers. The immediate circulation of the *Liberator* was never large; it rose to about fourteen hundred in 1837 and was given up in 1865 when its work had been accomplished.

Garrison was not only a remarkable writer, he was an effective speaker, and for the same reason in both cases. He put his whole strength and vitality into his addresses, violently and often unfairly attacking foes and even friends, but hammering his principles home. This influence was greatly extended by occasional journeys. Toward the slave-holders Garrison was pitiless. He made no fine distinctions between the slaveholder who treated his slaves as beasts of burden and the conscientious man who recognized his responsibility to his slave household but did not see the duty of emancipating them.

The Society had some of America's best literary talents of that day. One of Garrison's warm friends was John Greenleaf Whittier, who was a member of the Massachusetts Legislature from 1835 to 1837. He was the author of various anti-slavery documents, but his chief service was as the poet of the anti-slavery cause. "The Farewell of a Virginia Slave Mother" is perhaps the best known. Longfellow also gave his aid to the cause by his verses, especially the "Poems on Slavery." Later to enter the cause was James Russell Lowell. In 1846 he wrote "The Bigelow Papers," in which he fused a fierce hatred of slavery with vigorous anti-slavery arguments against extension of slave territory.

The man who most resembled Garrison in the fierceness and mercilessness of his attacks was Wendell Phillips. At a meeting in December, 1837, held to protest against the murder of Lovejoy at Alton, Illinois, Phillips, then a law student, sprang into the forefront of the anti-slavery speakers.

It was many years before Garrison applied to the cause of abolition the peculiar doctrine of non-resistance and philosophic anarchy in such a way to separate himself and his followers from the great body of abolitionists in general. In the years 1833 to 1840 the Massachusetts Anti-Slavery Society did not keep itself aloof from the arena of political contention. They believed that political action was the right and duty of citizens. "When many men have a common object, one of the best means of attaining it, is to associate themselves together. . . . A large number of persons think that slavery ought to be abolished in the District of Columbia and the Territories, and that no new State ought to be admitted into the Union without providing against the toleration of slavery within its borders. They also think that the slave trade between the States ought to be abolished by Congress. Holding these opinions of the duties of the National Government, it becomes not only their right, but their duty to endeavor in every mode sanctioned by law and religion, to procure the action of Congress on these subjects.''

How was this to be done? The Society's answer was by diffusing information among the people and petitioning Congress. These were, no doubt, efficacious measures. But another, equally important, was to endeavor to send to Congress men who thought rightly on these subjects and to oppose others. The course recommended was the same which was pursued successfully by abolitionists in Great Britain.[8] They never became a political party, but merely by giving their support to only such candidates for parliament as were in favor of abolishing slavery, they finally succeeded in accomplishing their object.

The political action of the Society took several forms: petitions to state and national legislatures, speeches before legislative committees, and actual voting. Upon abolition petitions the General Court of Massachusetts in 1843 passed a joint memorial requesting Congress to take the preliminary steps towards an amendment of the Constitution, which should deprive slaveholders of representation on the basis of the three-fifths clause and place national representation upon the basis of the free population.[9] Petitions, signed by citizens, were referred to the Joint Special Committee asking the legislature to declare that Congress has the power and ought to abolish slavery and the slave trade

[8] Massachusetts Anti-Slavery Society, *Third Annual Report*, 1835, p. 16.
[9] Massachusetts Anti-Slavery Society, *Twelfth Annual Report*, 1844, p. 10.

in the District of Columbia, the territories of the United States, and the internal slave trade of the states of the Union. The influence of these petitions may be seen by the formulation of the last petition into a series of resolutions by the Massachusetts Legislature in February, 1860.[10] The abolitionists also brought pressure to bear so that in April, 1837, with the support of both major parties in the House and in the Senate, Massachusetts voted to restore to her statute books a law providing for trial by jury on questions of personal freedom.[11] So far as it affected fugitive slaves, the law was invalidated by the decision of the United States Supreme Court in the case of Prigg *vs.* Pennsylvania in 1842.[12]

The Society also used the right of petition in an attempt to alleviate the social discrimination against the Negro. The abolitionists worked for the repeal of an act forbidding persons of different color to marry. However, it would seem that not all abolitionists were agreed on this point. The Society was unable to obtain favorable action in regard to the bill forbidding Railway Corporations within Massachusetts to make distinctions because of color. Action was indefinitely postponed by a vote of one hundred and seventy-one to sixty-one after a long debate.[13] Some thought the time had not yet arrived, when the legislature was called upon to interfere, but that the point would be gained through the influence of public sentiment alone. This, according to the Society, was its only failure along this line.

Anti-slavery speeches were made at various times in the Massachusetts Legislature. On February 23 and 24, 1837, Henry Stanton condemned slavery to the legislature. He

[10] Massachusetts State House, "Report No. 33," *Documents Concerning Slavery from 1837 to 1850*, No. 16 (Feb., 1850), p. 10.

[11] Warren C. Shaw, *The Fugitive Slave Issue in Massachusetts Politics, 1780-1837.* Urbana, Illinois, University of Illinois, 1938, p. 14.

[12] *Loc. cit.*

[13] Massachusetts Anti-Slavery Society, *Twelfth Annual Report*, 1844, p. 7.

spoke against the resolution passed in Congress that no action would be taken on petitions, memorials, resolutions, propositions, or any paper relating in any way to slavery. Speeches of a similar nature helped to give the Massachusetts Legislature an anti-slavery nature.

Garrison summarized his views on voting in his *Address to the Abolitionists of Massachusetts*. "Do not stay away from the polls. Go and scatter your votes. This is the true way to make yourselves felt. Every scattering vote you cast counts against the candidates of the parties; and will serve as an effectual admonition to them, to nominate the next time, men whom you can conscientiously support."[14]

Garrison valued political action chiefly as a means of agitating the subject. To overthrow slavery all that was needed was to gain the ear of the people. This might be done by agitation, and never is agitation so thorough and effectual as when it begins in the halls of legislation.

The formation of a distinct political party would be dangerous, if not fatal, to the efficiency of the organization, according to Garrison. He declared, "If we were a political party, the struggle for places of power and emolument would render our motives suspected, even if it did not prove too strong a temptation to our integrity. If we were a distinct party, every member of it must vote for its candidates, however he might disagree with them on other important points of public policy. Experience seems to show, that under a free government, there cannot be at one time, more than two powerful political parties."[15]

The direct aid given to fugitive slaves, on the part of the Society, caused the people of Massachusetts to oppose national laws on the subject of slavery. The number of signatures appended to the Massachusetts and Great Latimer Petition was greater than had ever been obtained for any

[14] Massachusetts Anti-Slavery Society, *An Address to the Abolitionists of Massachusetts on the Subject of Political Action*, n. p., n. d., p. 15.

[15] *Ibid.*, p. 7.

legislative purpose. In this movement there was no distinction of party or sect, but persons of all descriptions united in their efforts to free the soil of Massachusetts from the polluting presence of the slave-hunter. A public meeting of the petitioners was held in Faneuil Hall on February 17, 1843, when the immense petition was delivered by Committee, which had it in charge, to Charles F. Adams. He presented it, on the same day, to the House of Representatives. The result of this petition was the passage of a law, with very few dissenting voices, making it a penal offense for any magistrate or executive officer of the State to assist in the arrest or delivery of any person claimed as a fugitive slave and prohibiting those having charge of the jails and other places of confinement to use them for his detention.[16]

Where the State could not openly aid the abolitionists, individual action was called upon. At an anti-fugitive slave law meeting in Faneuil Hall the Vigilance Committee was appointed to aid the fugitive slaves by all possible means. It was voted that an alarm be given by the ringing of bells whenever an attempt was made to arrest a fugitive.

The work of this Committee is a long story. A few highlights of its work have been reported by Austin Bearse, who was an official of the organization. The Committee's efforts were responsible for many fugitives escaping quietly into Canada. Their efforts in the widely publicized cases of Sims and Burns were in vain. United States Commissioner Loring handed down the decision that Anthony Burns should be returned to slavery in Virginia.[17] Burns was sent back to his owner, but he was the last. No fugitive slave was ever seized in Boston and returned after Anthony Burns in June, 1854. Three years before Sims had been given up to his doom of slavery in Georgia, and on the first anniversary of the day Wendell Phillips said, "Thomas

[16] Massachusetts Anti-Slavery Society, *Twelfth Annual Report*, 1844, p. 45.
[17] Austin Bearse, *Reminiscences of Fugitive Slave Law Days in Boston.* Boston, Warren Richardson, 1880, p. 13.

Sims is the first man that the city of Boston ever openly bound and fettered, and sent back to bondage.''[18]

That more than a hundred others, who were liable to the same cruel fate of Burns and Sims, escaped, was largely due to the Vigilance Committee, a group of over two hundred citizens of Boston. Bearse says, ''I was the doorkeeper of its necessarily guarded meetings held at the Meionaon, the 'lesser hall' of the Tremont Temple. It was my business to go around to their places and notify the members when a meeting was called, and I had to stand guard at the door to see that only the right ones went in. There were printed tickets of notice which I delivered to each member in person. . . .''[19]

The Fugitive Slave Law, which the Committee meant to resist and nullify by every possible means, was passed in September, 1850. The Vigilance Committee cheerfully braved the pains and penalties of the infamous law, the six months' imprisonment and one thousand dollar fine for each offense. The Committee harbored and concealed slaves.

The first actual arrest in Boston of a fugitive slave was that of Shadrach on Saturday morning, February 15, 1851. The warrant was served at the Cornhill Coffee House by a Deputy Marshal Riley and a Constable Byrnes, who went there on the pretext of getting breakfast. Shadrach, while unsuspectingly waiting on them, was seized as the property of United States Purser Debree of Norfolk, Virginia. He was hurried to the courtroom without even time to put off his waiter's apron. News got around that he was captured, and excitement spread like wildfire. In a few moments a crowd had assembled around the Court House. Five members of the Boston Bar, all members of the Vigilance Committee, volunteered for his defense; they were Samuel Sewall, Charles List, Ellis Gray Loring, R. H. Dana, Jr., and Robert Morris. They obtained a delay to prepare for

[18] *Loc. cit.*
[19] Bearse, *loc. cit.*, p. 15.

the defense. At the moment the case was adjourned, a crowd of sympathizing colored persons, at broad noon-day, pressed into the courtroom and fled with the prisoner. On that Saturday night, February 15, 1851, Shadrach started for Canada.

President Fillmore issued a special proclamation for the prosecution of all aiders of the Shadrach rescue. Arrests were made immediately, and persons were held to trial under heavy bonds. The Committee was prompt to aid such people financially and to defend them by counsel.

It is interesting to note in passing that Negroes played a part in these activities. Among the most prominent Negroes so engaged was Robert Morris, a lawyer and a member of the Vigilance Committee. Shadrach was rescued by the direct help of the Negroes themselves.

All the direct action of the Vigilance Committee in aiding the escape of fugitives to Canada was not as publicized at the time as was their defense of such fugitives in the courts. That the Committee contributed freely of its money for the purpose is testified to by Bearse who had been empowered by this organization to collect funds. Most of the Negroes held in conjunction with the deliverance of Shadrach were unable to pay for their legal defense. Committee members considered that they could spend their money in no better way than for the purpose for which it was used in the rescue trials. That some members contributed liberally is revealed by a report of the Finance Committee on May 6, 1851, listing the first subscriptions to the cause as follows:[20]

Charles Francis Adams	(Paid)	$100.00
S. C. Phillips	,,	100.00
Ellis Gray Loring	,,	25.00
Wendell Phillips	,,	100.00

While the abolitionists were defending the rescuers of Shadrach, the enforcement officers of the Fugitive Slave

[20] Bearse, *loc. cit.*, p. 22.

Law struck. On April 3, 1851, without a moment's warning, Thomas Sims was seized in Richmond Street on the pretext of theft. He was arrested by the police, who, disguised as city watchmen, violated the law of Massachusetts that forbade an officer of that State to aid in arresting a person claimed as a fugitive slave. Now on the alert to prevent a repetition of the Shadrach rescue, the enforcement officials were able to manage Sims' return to slavery. It is already noted that three years later in 1854 the return of Burns was similarly affected. Aside from these two instances, however, the work of the abolitionists was very successful in preventing the return of fugitive slaves from Massachusetts.

III. DIVERGENT VIEWS

As in most organizations there were bound to be differences of opinion, and so it was with the Massachusetts Anti-Slavery Society around 1840. Various charges were brought against Garrison personally. He was charged with having a "deliberate and well-matured design to make the anti-slavery organization subservient to the promotion of personal and sectarian views on the subjects of Women's Rights, ... Civil Government, the Church, the Ministry, and the Sabbath."[21] It was well known to Garrison's opponents in the Society that he was contemplating other reforms which he considered equal in importance to the anti-slavery movement. It was also known that Garrison held frequent consultations with his intimate friends to consider these other reforms. Such consultants were his brother-in-law, George W. Benson, Maria Chapman, the Misses Grimké, and others. These conferences, according to Garrison's enemies, led to the formulation of certain proposals concerning future policy. One plan was that Garrison would give up the *Liberator* or retire from its editorial care and

---

[21] Massachusetts Abolition Society, *The True History of the Late Division in the Anti-Slavery Societies.* Boston, David H. Ela, 1841, p. 6.

start a new paper. A second plan was to make a formal change in the *Liberator* and announce the fact that its leading object would no longer be the abolition of slavery but generic and universal reform, including the abolition of slavery as a part. Another plan would be to continue to hold out the abolition of slavery as the leading object of the paper, and then to sift in the other reforms as the people could bear them. This last plan, Garrison's enemies believed, was the one adopted. According to his opponents, great care was taken "to reiterate the assurance that anti-slavery is still its leading and distinctive object and the discussion of other reforms is merely incidental."[22] At the time that these accusations were made Garrison indignantly denied them. In spite of this denial, however, his enemies' beliefs were substantiated by Garrison's own earlier remark: "As our object is universal emancipation,—to redeem woman as well as man from a servile to an equal condition,—we shall go for the Rights of Woman to their utmost extent."[23]

In both 1839 and 1840 the Society was called upon to decide the question of Garrison's leadership and the use of the *Liberator* as an organ of anti-slavery. The question was decided by five hundred and sixty votes for Garrison and four hundred and fifty dissidents.[24]

One of the leaders of the group opposed to Garrison was a Mr. Torrey who instituted a vigorous correspondence to facilitate the establishment of a new anti-slavery paper in Massachusetts. He intimated that Garrison had become idle and negligent, that his paper was left to printers' boys or to other irresponsible persons. He urged the necessity of a new paper because "there was such a prejudice against the *Liberator*, that it was impossible to get it into sufficient

22 *Ibid.*, p. 16.

23 Editorial in *Liberator* (Boston, Mass.), December 16, 1837.

24 Albert B. Hart, *Slavery and Abolition, 1831-1841*. New York and London, Harper & Brothers, 1906, p. 201.

circulation, even to advertise the county meetings."[25] Torrey was supported by a Mr. Phelps and a Mr. St. Clair. In a letter written by St. Clair to Phelps the former stated the reasons why the *Liberator* was no longer sufficient and why a new paper was needed: "We want one so cheap that every abolitionist could and would take it, and we want one free from objectionable extraneous topics. The *Liberator* was two dollars and a half a year, and devoted just as truly to the woman question and the overthrow of human government, as to the abolition of slavery."[26]

These proposals for the establishment of a new anti-slavery organ were met with indifference by the Society. The Massachusetts Anti-Slavery Society, at a quarterly meeting, refused to pass any resolution condemnatory of the current organ. The Society disclaimed any responsibility towards the views of Garrison as advanced in the *Liberator*. It was stated that "The *Liberator* has never been the official organ of this or of any society. It is an independent paper, under the exclusive control of its editor, and for the management of which he claims to be wholly answerable."[27] However, as a result of all this, the Massachusetts Anti-Slavery Society ceased to defray the expenses of the *Liberator* from its treasury, although most of the members would have continued to do so. It was done out of respect to the minority, although the number, honestly opposed to the paper, was considered to be small. The Society concurred with Garrison that the interests of both the Society and the *Liberator* would be best served by the cessation of the pecuniary connection.

The same men who opposed the *Liberator* as the organ of the anti-slavery effort differed from the avowed political policies of the Society. Phelps and St. Clair formulated a

[25] Maria Chapman, *Right and Wrong in Massachusetts*. Boston, Dow and Jackson, 1839, p. 55.

[26] Massachusetts Abolition Society, *op. cit.*, p. 37.

[27] Massachusetts Anti-Slavery Society, *Ninth Annual Report*, 1841, p. 29.

plan of political action called the Fitchburg Resolutions which they, with Torrey's endorsement, submitted to the Society for consideration. These Resolutions declared that "Every abolitionist is in duty bound, not to content himself with merely refusing to vote for any man who is opposed to the emancipation of the slave, but to go to the polls, and throw his vote for some man known to favor it. When two candidates for Congress or State Legislatures are put in nomination, one for and other against the immediate abolition of slavery, he is duty bound to vote for the abolitionist, independent of all other political considerations; or, if neither candidate be of this description, then he is equally bound to go to the polls, and vote for some true man in opposition to them both, and do all he can, lawfully, to defeat their election.''[28] In effect, these Resolutions suggested the formation of a third political party if circumstances so warranted.

The Fitchburg Resolutions were rejected by the Massachusetts Anti-Slavery Society. Its opinion as to the inexpediency of a distinct anti-slavery political organization, which they had often expressed, remained unchanged. The Society believed that such an organization, under the most favorable circumstances, would be unwise and of evil effect. The Society declared, "We believe that our true policy is to make use of the existing political parties to do our anti-slavery work for us rather than to build up one for ourselves, the success of which must depend upon the extinction of one of the other two. We think we see the soundness of this philosophy illustrated in the legislative history of this State, which shows that we have obtained everything for which we have asked (with the exception of the railway bill) by the vote of members of both parties, without the expense of time and money involved in the inception and conducting of a third.''[29] On the subject of political action the Society

[28] Maria Chapman, *op. cit.*, p. 76.
[29] Massachusetts Anti-Slavery Society, *Twelfth Annual Report*, 1844, p. 21.

maintained that it constantly inculcated the doctrine that the anti-slavery question should be made paramount at the polls, to the sacrifice of all mere party considerations. This position of the Society was weakened, however, by the statement: "It does not make it a part of the anti-slavery creed to believe in the duty of every man to mingle or not to mingle in the political conflicts of the country."[30]

The minority group, receiving no satisfaction from the Massachusetts Anti-Slavery Society as led by Garrison, withdrew from the Society and established the Massachusetts Abolition Society. It was stated that "the difference between the old and the new anti-slavery organization is this: The new organization proposes to overthrow slavery by the use of means—the old, by simple truth."[31] Later in the year of 1840 this new society united with other organizations to form the American and Foreign Anti-Slavery Society and to found the Liberty Party with James Birney as the presidential candidate for that year.

Abolitionists generally rallied to the support of the new party forsaking Garrison's fold. The small group led by Garrison held to their old beliefs of political action within the framework of the two major parties. The abolitionists' ideal of supporting anti-slavery candidates was not foreign to the platform of the Liberty Party of 1840 and 1844, to the Free Soil Party of 1848, and to the Republican Party a few years later. Such support of political parties opposed to slavery is concrete evidence of the essential unity of the anti-slavery movement. The apparent lack of harmony was more like a family quarrel than it was a case of disunity in the face of a common foe.

Garrison's old guard remained the Massachusetts Anti-Slavery Society and was referred to as the "Old Society." Its members were few and its policy more extreme. It was, in fact, a brand-new society proclaiming doctrines and

[30] *Ibid.*, p. 53.
[31] Massachusetts Anti-Slavery Society, *Ninth Annual Report*, 1841, p. 6.

advocating policies in direct contradiction to those of the original organization. Probably not one in a hundred of even the New England abolitionists ever accepted the special views which the Garrison organization adopted after 1843.[32] The Old Society became extremely radical in its doctrines. Members pledged themselves to hold no office, the acceptance of which necessitated an oath to support the Constitution of the United States as long as the slavery clauses were retained in the document. On Thursday evening, January 25, 1844, Stephen Foster presented a ''Protest Against the Constitution of the United States.'' There followed a list of twenty grievances: existence of slavery, denial of petition in Congress, abrogation of liberty of speech and press in the South, war with the Seminole Indians (the main object being the recapture of fugitive slaves), taxing the North to support the Post Office Department in the South, and other complaints of a similar nature. Because of these reasons enumerated and others of similar import, the Society adopted, at this meeting, the following resolution: ''We now publicly abjure our allegiance to the Constitution of the United States and the Union.''[33] Foster was followed by Garrison who, after protesting just as violently against the Constitution, made the resolution that the compact between the North and the South should be overthrown by a moral and peaceful revolution.[34]

The new policies of Garrison's group caused the Massachusetts Legislature to denounce the members of the Old Society as radicals. Such opinions, as those expressed by the Old Society towards the Union and the Constitution, could find no echo in the Legislature. No member could entertain such thoughts without having committed perjury. The Legislature gave its adherence to the Constitution and

[32] Jesse Macy, *op. cit.*, p. 57.

[33] Massachusetts Anti-Slavery Society, *Twelfth Annual Report*, 1844, pp. 82-85.

[34] *Ibid.*, p. 87.

to the Union. In like manner, there was little national support for the views of the Old Society. It could even be said that the views of this small group contributed to the unpopularity throughout the country of the whole abolition movement.

SUMMARY

It can be said in retrospect that Garrison was the prime factor in founding the anti-slavery movement in Massachusetts and in promoting the spread of anti-slavery sentiment nationally. His programs and policies evolved with slight changes into the preponderance of abolition forces which were triumphant in the Civil War.

The evaluation of the work of Garrison and his Society must be judged in terms of the success or failure of avowed policies. The purposes were to crystallize anti-slavery sentiment by means of moral suasion, to check and defeat slavery by political action, and to give direct aid to fugitive slaves. It has been observed that sentiment in the State of Massachusetts became progressively liberal, as evidenced by the passage of laws against racial discrimination. Nationally, the progressive increase in the number of supporters of the abolition political parties is evidence of the same trend. Violent opposition to the Fugitive Slave Law of 1850, both locally and nationally, further shows evidence of the success of these policies. The numbers engaged in operating the Underground Railroad and the money expended for legal defense of fugitives testify to this end. The number of opponents of slavery actually elected to state and national legislature, in like manner, progressively increased.

Garrison's extreme actions of later years loom as of no great importance in the light of the successes of the abolition movement. The anti-slavery sentiments expressed on the platform and in the press had converted to the abolition cause many who did not ever understand Garrison's later peculiar views. He had already converted the masses, and although Garrison now adopted a radical set of views, they continued to follow along the lines of the original abolition crusade.

CONCLUSION

The life of Garrison and the story of the Massachusetts Anti-Slavery Society may be compared with that of Moses and the Exodus. Moses set the children of Israel upon the path straight for their goal. He built their ideologies and traditions; he directed their training and discipline, but he, himself, did not lead them into the land of Canaan. This was to fall to other leaders.

Garrison, like Moses, built the ground-work in the days of pioneering. He led the hue and cry which hounded the proponents of slavery at every turn. He watched the multitude swell behind him as battle lines began to form. The fact that Garrison turned a corner short of the goal must not be over-emphasized. The abolition movement rode forward to the end—rode forward on the principles and ideologies pioneered by Garrison. Abolition saw the achievement of its aims.

ELAINE BROOKS

Washington, D. C.

BOOK REVIEWS

The Negro in the Armed Forces: His Value and Status, Past, Present and Potential. By Seymour J. Schoenfeld, Lieutenant Commander (DC), USNR. (Washington D. C.: The Associated Publishers, Inc., 1945. Pp. 84. Price, $1.00.)

The unlovely story of race relations in America has been a matter of record for many years. In the past half decade, however, it has assumed major importance not only in national but in international circles. As one writer has expressed it the question of racial adjustment and understanding (or misunderstanding) in these United States has become "America's number one domestic failure and her number one international handicap." The eyes of the world are watching us for patterns and policies and procedures where the treatment of minorities—the Negro minority in particular—is involved. The "problem" has become a major weapon for our fascist enemies who have used it as a source of propaganda in order to stir up internal strife and to disrupt the war effort. Since internal unity and cooperation are as much a part of national defense as are battleships and fortifications, the importance of allowing no large minority group to feel arbitrarily excluded is obvious. Furthermore, the stresses of a wartime economy increase the interdependence of groups, not only in our own nation but in the entire world. And it must be shown that a nation can be administered without creating victims.

If the United States *is* "one nation, indivisible," and committed unequivocally to the high sounding principle of "liberty and justice for all," there can be no straddling of issues, no further acceptance of the reactionary policy of bi-racialism. A continuation of the viciously dangerous practices of segregation and discrimination can result only in failure. Segregation is a malignant growth in a democracy and the effort to maintain a dual racial system is stupid, costly, and stultifying. It is not only impossible but also impractical and wasteful. It makes a spiritual gap between the races, fosters in one a feeling of inferiority, in the other an equally dangerous complex of superiority. It violates the dignity of the human personality, the integrity of the human spirit. It breeds resentment, humiliation, suspicion and hatred, and serves to undermine the faith of the Negro in the very foundations of the democracy he is asked

331

to defend. Unless something is done, and done soon, to break down these attitudes and tensions, the whole issue of race will explode with disastrous consequences either in the very near future or during the not too distant post-war period.

To readers of the Negro press and the growing number of books and periodicals devoted to this problem, none of the facts mentioned are new. They have been reiterated with such frequency that they tend to become monotonous. Yet the dangers inherent in them must be and are recognized, and thoughtful people of both racial groups are attempting to do something about them.

The latest effort "to do something" is this book, just off the press, by Lieutenant Commander Schoenfeld concerning the Negro —specifically in the armed forces of America. There is nothing new in the book itself. A story told as often as this about the Negro's worth as a soldier, his heroism and his record of loyalty to his country in its several periods of emergency, in spite of discrimination and soul-searing humiliations, from the pre-Revolutionary period of American history to the present time, could have no new angles. But what is new, perhaps, and therefore *news,* is the fact that the story is being told this time by a United States Naval officer, a member of the so-called "dominant group" in America. And it is done with genuine sincerity and candor, with a view to converting other officers and service personnel as well as the lay reader to his enlightened way of thinking.

A significant statement appears in the foreword to the book—a foreword written by another high ranking officer of the armed services, Colonel Evans Fordyce Carlson of the U. S. Marine Corps. He says:

"This study should be required reading for all officers of the armed services and for all high school and college students. Our expanding influence in the world today imposes the responsibility for inspecting minutely our expression of the way of life we sponsor. We must mend the fences of our democratic society, and one of the gaps most in need of attention is the prejudice practiced in many communities against the Negro citizen. Education and understanding can correct this deficiency and Lieutenant Commander Schoenfeld has made an important contribution in this direction."

This is a point of view in which one can concur heartily after reading the book at hand. The presentation is thoughtfully objective. There is no sentimentality in approach and the handling of the context is adequate though brief. Eighty-four pages allow the author merely to scratch the surface but he has produced sufficient food for thought to spur the interested reader to delve more deeply into "the problem" for himself.

The chapter headings reveal the contents of this study. In the first the writer discusses the "Military History and Traditions of the American Negro." Chapter two is devoted to "Some Important Considerations of the Enviroment and the Characteristics of the Negro." This chapter outlines the social factors and forces which have made the Negro what he is today in America—a second-class citizen, not by choice but by circumstance, forced into unequal competition with his more favored but less understanding and largely unsympathetic and hostile "white" American brothers.

In chapter three we are told of the "Present Status of the Negro in the Armed Forces" and shown the methods used by the military authorities to "integrate" (in negative fashion) the Negro soldier into the fighting services of our country. That the "integration" is neither wholesome nor spiritually satisfying is obvious. And that it is responsible for a woeful, almost criminal waste of manpower, is not a pretty commentary on the policies of the United States military authorities.

The fourth and fifth chapters emphasize the "Potential Value and Status of the Negro: Improvements Possible under Present Military Policies and Organizations," and a suggested program for "Complete Integration Toward the Negro in the Armed Forces." They leave one hopeful that eventually the courage, forthrightness and sane thinking of Lieutenant Commander Schoenfeld will become contagious and serve to indoctrinate other service men, as well as civilians, with his fine feeling of fair play and good fellowship toward their darker brothers. When that happens one may be sure that a first and very significant step along the road to World Peace and Racial Understanding has been made. Until that day comes it remains unnecessary for the author to assure us, as he has done, that

"The opinions or assertions contained in this book are the private ones of the writer and are not to be construed as official or reflecting the views of the Navy Department or the Naval service at large."

That such a comment is necessary in this year of our Lord 1945 is sorry evidence that the road ahead is still a long and difficult one.

ESTHER POPEL SHAW

Washington, D. C.

One America, the History, Contributions, and Present Problems of Our Racial Minorities. Edited by Francis J. Brown and Joseph S. Roucek. Revised Edition. (New York: Prentice Hall, Inc., 1945. Pp. 717. Price $3.75.)

The subtitle of this study reveals its meaning and purpose to bring a previous investigation of 1937 up to date. The authors have employed native minority and racial scholars as well as some other writers to present the records of the various minorities and their roles in American life and culture. Criteria of minority differentiation are difficult in that they cannot be accurate. The legalistic and numerical conceptions frequently clash in the sociological analysis and defy exact definitions and meanings. Highly moot questions of race stalk throughout the extensive and abstruse attempts to explore diverse human elements and evaluate their contributions. Processes of acculturation and assimilation further complicate the melting pot of the infinitely complex American social composition that has no parallel in history.

The work gives a comparison of the old immigration from northern Europe with that of southeastern Europe in more recent times. Practically all of the national ethnic strains appear in the accounts of different immigrants. The ubiquitous problems of minorities, however, remain unclarified although citations of notables from every group appear in the accounts of their contributions to American civilization and progress. These are incomplete because assimilation has proceeded throughout the years and many individuals of every race and national group have deliberately or incidentally become absorbed into the complex American ethnic stream. There are some exceptions in the cases of orientals and, of course, Negroes whose conscious unlikeness to the majority of immigrant arrivals has remained distinct with some exceptions.

This volume gives considerable attention to the causes which have induced immigrants to come to America. These fall into the traditional religious, political, and ethnic restrictions and the urgent desires to share the fortunes of a new land. Some of these have survived in the maintenance of language and denominational organizations and social groups to preserve and transmit traditions. The foreign language press appears prominently in attempts to hold immigrants together. Such forces seem temporary in the accounts of most contributors because of subtle influences of the American public schools and the pressure of social conventions. Descendants of immigrant minorities have tended to forget parental traditions and to fuse themselves into the general pattern of American association and thought. Succeeding generations have gradually chosen to become Americanized and tended to discard their old world ties and ideals. The various authors indicate that this melting process has not yet been complete and that foreigners have left their institutional patterns upon communities where they have settled. The Scandinavian concepts of the social service state, for example, have appeared in communities of the central West where survivals of cooperatives, customs, and European traditions still prevail. In many cases modifications have come, but they have developed in response to the demands of the new American environment.

The tone and quality of *One America* appear dispassionate in that the writers have endeavored to present the claims of the minorities that they have described and cited some of the notable achievements of the various groups. Unquestionably each minority brought something from its native land which was adapted to America or which exerted influence in the development of the region of settlement. In this there is evidence that the free migrant had, first of all, certain enduring qualities which made him dissatisfied at home and ambitious to seek fortune abroad. Weaker and less adventuresome immigrants were at first contented to remain instead of attempting the hazards of a strange new land in America. Development of transportation made immigration easier to meet the demands of industry overseas. Growth of large-scale industry in America after the Civil War demanded ever increasing numbers of unskilled workers who found employment in mines, on railways, and in other types of work after the introduction of machinery and its subsidiary requirements of raw materials which the unskilled could help to provide. From practically every group of these Pilgrims the writers have found something worthy of citation.

Three chapters report the role of Negroes who are the "minority of minorities'' because of their general differentiation in physical appearance. Their full assimilation is out of the question in American history and tradition. The contributions of colored notables are restricted chiefly to areas of entertainment, music, some of the arts, and a literature which stresses dialect to a large extent or something else indicating a deviation from literature in general and restricting itself to colored themes. Two of the colored writers are literary scholars who conform to this pattern and the third is a distinguished sociologist who is so dominated by some of his former teachers that he discredits any inheritance of colored people from the African background. This is regrettable because many slaves had surviving qualities which enabled them to endure the midpassage which was far worse than that of any European immigrants. Such anthropologists as Herskovits have recently proved that the slaves brought to America vary much from their former habitats. While there was deliberate effort further to brutalize the slave victims and restrict them through over three centuries of enforced ignorance, it is regrettable (p. 451) that a colored scholar should accept the dictum that nothing survived from the African background. Cultural differentiation and assimilation of colored people have seemed so inconceivable that the majority of the writers report practically nothing for this greatest American minority. The attention which it receives in restrictions and restraints warrants more careful evaluation than this volume has given.

The value of this work, which is predominantly sociological and encyclopedic in its attempts to treat all minorities with detachment, except Negroes, is considerable. It appears at an opportune time when ''intercultural education'' has loomed into prominence with prospects of superseding ''interracial cooperation.'' While some good has been accomplished and further progress may be made, both of these movements warrant careful scrutiny by thinking colored people. Several otherwise unknown white persons have found careers for themselves in ''Negro affairs.'' The colored assistants to the white advisors in these fields have found fortune and opportunities as Quislings and participants in the exploitation of the jim-crow. In a larger sense, *One America* affords a sort of valuable panoramic view of immigration to the United States whose population is the most unique in history. Here is an illustration of the evolution of the ''American Way of Life'' which is infinitely more correct than the lip-service to Democracy, Christianity, and Freedom which end with the color line. Students of sociology and the general reader will find this an extensive though incomplete account of the peoples who have made America valuable.

WILLIAM M. BREWER

Miner Teachers College
Washington, D. C.

Black Boy: A Record of Childhood and Youth. By Richard Wright. (New York: Harper & Bros., 1945. 228 pp. $2.50.)

Much of *Black Boy* is for me reminiscent, in spots even nostalgic. Born in South Carolina six months before Richard Wright saw the light of his first Mississippi day, I know from my own childhood what life in the South of that day did to those who were black, yet who never once felt themselves inferior to any man. *Black Boy* is the story of all those unchildlike Southern children, who, black of skin, sensitive of mind, kind of heart, born in a jungle of hate and bigotry, eke out the endless days of their weary, bewildered youth bound in shallows and miseries. It is the story of thousands of Southern shanties on whose doorstep want is no stranger, and within whose walls life is one long cruel and inexplicable tragedy.

No doubt *Black Boy* will cause many Southern digestive disturbances, but it is nonetheless true. The grapes of Southern wrath are sweet to none of her native sons, white or black. In shockingly frank terms Wright documents for us as only he can, the dank, offensive miasma of the Southern swamp, where violence and brutality reign supreme and ignorance wears a diadem—where the Negro's daily bread of bitterness affords too little nourishment to sustain his efforts to build a worthy character, and discredits each attempt he makes to fill the sacred obligations of duty.

Preoccupied in his biography as always with environment, Wright does not concern himself to trace the growth of his own personality. Nothing seems to have shaken the fundamental tenets of his character; frequent visits to drinking dives while still at a tender age did not leave him a drunkard, nor did inadvertent spying on partners at lascivious play turn him into a lecherous youth. Through it all his integrity was left unimpaired, complete, preserved. Little understood at home, more at ease with a book than with any boy of his own age, he had an unhappy and lonely lot.

The results of his many lonely hours can be felt in everything he has written. More concerned with ideas than with people as individuals, perturbed by a social environment that refused to recognize—if it did not deny—his humanity, he came early to place much of the blame for his woes on that environment. So sensitive did he become that he was constantly on the alert for evil to befall him from he knew not where. So resentful had he become while a boy working in Memphis, the attempt of a white man to treat him decently only increased his perplexity, only added to his distrust.

As he grew more and more aware of and became more and more deeply interested in the great world of ideas, he found it impossible to reconcile the conflict between the ideals upon which American society rests and the status to which the South reduced and confines its Negro population. Angered by the arrogance with which white Southerners took as granted their superior status, seething with disappointment and frustration, he determined to leave the South to seek a wider freedom in order to learn who he was and what he might be.

Southern mores and the great wave of materialism that swept the country soon after emancipation account for the environment from which Richard Wright fled. Southern mores alone would have made the lot of the Negro intolerable enough, the all consuming cupidity that kept the country's best brains engaged in a mad scramble for wealth, left little time or energy for concern for the welfare of the newly emancipated freedmen. The machine became a god, material success a sedative. Little thought was given to man as man. Men sought wealth for its own sake. The disappearance of the frontier served to accentuate further the trend. Land was becoming comparatively scarce, hence its value was appreciating. Immigrants were sought no longer with the accustomed avidity. Men were of no great concern—not even white men.

Thus from the Civil War to the beginning of the period of the great world conflicts, the greatest moral question with which the nation must deal has been given little serious, constructive thought. World War II, especially, has served to re-awaken an interest in man himself, and to focus our attention again on the workings of the institutions through which the realization of our ideals may be achieved. *Black Boy,* as an earnest of this trend, indicates a new serious effort to understand and analyze the state of mind responsible for the South of today. For Wright, as for some others, fear is at the bottom of the Southern problem. Fear that grows into hate, and hate that burns itself out with fear again. Fear breeds fear again; the salvation of the South, and the Negro with it, demands the complete eradication of its fear complex.

In language sometimes beautiful in its poetic intensity, reminiscent of DuBois at his best, Wright has in *Black Boy* shown again his gift for original analysis. Eschewing strategic theories and plans—saved possibly for a book dealing with his adult, creative life—he has done much to lead us beyond the ancient, vapid, and painfully threadbare arguments usually presented to condone practices whose reasons for existence are no longer, if they ever were, valid. The acclaim with which the book has been received, together with that extended to *Strange Fruit* and *Fredom Road,* indicates that the time is ripe to extend the bounds of freedom, to build a heaven upon a new earth and end man's inhumanity to man "here beneath the stars." The need for more such provocative books is urgent. Failure to meet it may lose us our last best hope for democracy in our own country and in a world community.

DAVID H. BRADFORD

The Encyclopedia of the Negro. Preparatory volume with reference lists and reports. Edited by W. E. B. DuBois and Guy B. Johnson and prepared with the cooperation of E. Irene Diggs, Agnes C. I. Donohugh, Guion Johnson, Rayford W. Logan and L. D. Reddick. Introduction by Anson Phelps-Stokes. (New York: The Phelps-Stokes Fund, 1945.)

The publication of an *Encyclopedia of the Negro* has long been a matter of concern to the Negroes themselves and to those who have desired more information about the race than is usually found in newspapers and current magazines. Books on the Negro, as a rule, merely treat the race as a problem. Movements affecting the Negro are passed by unnoticed unless they concern other elements of the population or other forces in the social order. Negroes who live useful lives and close their careers with distinction and honor, according to the opinions of the liberal people of the day, receive no mention in the capitalistic controlled and race-hating press. Most assuredly if the Negro does not do more than he has been doing to record his story his race will become a negligible factor in the thought of the world.

It has been highly commendable on the part of persons who in their feeble way have recorded from time to time facts concerning the Negro which have been published in useful form. Unfortunately most of the compilers thus concerned have not approached their task in the light of broad scholarship and scientific research. Many of such works bearing the title of *Encyclopedia of the Negro,* moreover, have not been worthy of the name. The nearest approach of a fair presentation of such data is *The Negro Year Book* which until 1938 was published biennially by the late Monroe Nathan Work. This production satisfied the demand of the average interest in the Negro but served mainly as a stimulus among scholars toward the preparation of a much more comprehensive work.

During the last thirty years the talk about publishing this desired *Encyclopedia of the Negro,* however, has been merely talk. A generation ago one man collected an abundance of reliable and unreliable data but never succeeded in finding the means to finance the publication. He went so far as to publish dummies of the volumes he proposed to bring out. The editors of the proposed *Encyclopedia of the Negro* have advanced a step further to inform the public as to what they intend to publish and how they plan to do it.

If the volume under review must be taken as the best presentation of the appeal for the support of their effort the editors have not done themselves much credit. In the first place, the number of important articles listed is far short of what an informing work on the Negro should contain. Items of importance are not listed— topics which almost anyone acquainted with the background of the present status of the Negro would say cannot be left out. The articles listed leave the impression that they are not compiled by persons familiar with the history of the Negro but are taken mainly from titles of books found in bibliographies of Negro literature. It would be a most unfortunate procedure to develop the work in this way, for most of the works supplying valuable data bearing on the Negro are not so designated. Such facts may be obtained only by scholars well informed by scientific research.

It seems strange, moreover, that the editors would publish such a list to show what they intend to do. They should proceed to the task at once and finish it. They have a large staff of prominent persons who claim to know much about the Negro and at the head of the organization they have Anson Phelps-Stokes, a man who is a millionaire, in the position to finance the work itself. If these intterracial workers of the other race are sincere in the plans set forth they should find the means by which to finance the effort. They should not expect the Negro race to subsidize what has been brought them from so-called friends of the other race. If the Negro is to finance the publication he should write it himself rather than await dictation from without and thus keep the race going around in a circle and getting nowhere.

The editorial board announced is very impressive on paper, but it is clear that, if the work is to be done with scientific objectivity, the staff should be strengthened with scholars who know something about the Negro. The reputation as a race leader or as an interracial cooperationist does not justify the expectation that the work can be done right by those engaged. Dr. Du Bois is now an old man and will hardly do more than pen a prologue and an epilogue for what others may write. Guy B. Johnson has not yet produced anything to warrant the conclusion that he has an encyclopedic knowledge of the Negro. The books which he has produced, so far as they concern the Negro, set forth mainly what the race has not rather than what it has done. In his study of Negro music he discovered that this art is the contribution of the white man; and a few years ago he said in an address at Virginia State College that the Negroes did not proceed properly in trying to force their way into the white universities of the South through the Gaines decision. They should have approached the matter, he insisted, by taking a Gallup Poll to find out where they are wanted and in order not to press the matter where they are not wanted. In other words, the Negro must appeal for his rights, not to the Constitution of the United States which guarantees them, but to the Southern States which denies the race the enjoyment of these rights. With a man of this attitude as co-editor of the *Encyclopedia of the Negro,* we may well wonder what sort of work will be produced. Why the crew took this biased mariner on board is not clear unless the captain of the ship believed that he can cooperate with Anson Phelps-Stokes in finding an angel to pay the freight.

In one respect the staff should be congratulated on its frankness.

According to their list of important topics and the works to be used in developing them, the editors intend to lean very heavily—in fact, unduly heavily—on the works published by the Associated Publishers and the Association for the Study of Negro Life and History. It is difficult to find a page of these listings in their volume without one or more references to the works of these two houses. Unfortunately, moreover, some of the elementary works of these two sources are cited as the sole dependence for developing certain topics—for example Ramos' *The Negro in Brazil* and Delafosse's *Negroes of Africa,* both of which are purely elementary. No man qualified to write on the Negro in Brazil or in Africa would depend solely on books intended to give general information for high school students and undergraduates in college. The intelligent readers of Negro literature will hardly be satisfied with such an inadequate and undocumented publication.

C. G. WOODSON

Color and Democracy: Colonies and Peace. By W. E. B. Du Bois. (New York: Harcourt, Brace and Company, 1945.)

In the proposed reconstruction of the modern world recommendations have been presented to the conferences supposedly engaged in working out the plans by which this new order may be realized. Naturally the races and nations which have been denied consideration in the adjustments and readjustments recently made in the international sphere have become sanguinely expectant of some plan of reconstruction which will assure them their hearts' desires. The assemblies of representatives of nations, as a rule, do not concern themselves with internal problems of nations, but the leaders of the nations combatting the Axis Powers have said so much about security for democracy and brotherhood that elements of the population within these domains have begun embodying their grievances and have tried to air them in these peace conferences. Their chief argument is that the nations through their representatives in these international conferences assembled cannot afford to turn a deaf ear to such complaints inasmuch as the present conflict which they are now trying to bring to a close started from the well known internal problem of the persecution of the Jews in Germany.

In order to bring their grievances before these representatives the Negroes have followed several plans. The spokesmen for the race have urged the consideration of the issue upon officials in their respective countries. The Negro press in Africa, America and the West Indies has agitated the matter through the publication of current developments and the expression of their opinions as editors presenting the demands of the people. The same thought and action have found expression also through the publication of books and pamphlets presenting in permanent form what the Negro wants and the justification of his demands. In *Color and Democracy*, by Dr. W. E. B. Du Bois, the well known leader in shaping the thought of the Negro in this and other matters of public importance, is an outstanding example of this forceful appeal.

In presenting the case the author places his appeal on the broad plane of democracy for all peoples without regard to race or color. He is demanding, then, no special favor for the race to which he belongs but the recognition of all men as justly entitled to liberty and the pursuit of happiness. The author discusses therefore "Dumbarton Oaks," "Disfranchised Colonies," "Unfree Peoples," "Democracy and Color," "Peace and Colonies," "The Riddle of Russia" and "Missions and Mandates." He is mindful of the fact that the British Empire is determined to sustain at the peace table its right to conduct the British Empire as it has heretofore and he does not find much opposition thereto among the authorities of the United States. He prophesies, however, that the failure to deal wisely with these international questions will simply mean another war in the near future, one which will be more self-exterminating than the conflict now apparently coming to a close. What the author is demanding is the destruction of the European empires; for exploitation, trade and subordination of weaker peoples constitute the foundations upon which the European empires are built. There is no evidence that this end can be easily attained. The author finds some hope, however, in the liberal groups now increasing throughout the modern world—friends of freedom who fought the slave trade, slavery, and the exploitation of labor and advocated freedom and liberty for the under man.

C. G. WOODSON

Experiments in Democracy: By USO Divisions of the National
   Board Y.W.C.A. (New York: National Board of the Y.W.C.A.,
   1945. Pp. 80.)

This is a well illustrated booklet showing, according to the publishers, the experiments made in democracy and how they have been
carried out.   These are rather the reports of the activities of the
USO Division of the Young Women's Christian Association in certain areas where the social relations of the races are not exactly a
state of war, as is the case almost throughout the Southern States.
These contacts were such as eating, smoking and drinking at these
places of recreation, planning for such activities and testing how
they work out.   There is nothing exceptional in such contacts.   The
reviewer has been entertained at interracial repasts of Southern
Whites and Negroes in Nashville, New Orleans, and Tampa.

In the Negro-White relationship, however, there are no illustrations showing social contacts of the different sexes of the two races
beyond that of eating at the same table or working on the same
job.   Evidently the book is an effort to show that the races may
associate freely for matters essential to the life and being of both
without bordering the least upon what is known as miscegenation.
This was Booker T. Washington's five-fingers philosophy.   This democracy thus illustrated, therefore, is a qualified democracy like
most of that which we hear about nowadays almost everywhere—
democracy and still not democracy.

This step evidently is about as far as the USO desires to go in
the direction of real democracy, and it is an advance beyond what
is usually practiced by the Young Women's Christian Association.
This body has never permitted the principles taught by Jesus of
Nazareth to interfere with the segregation of the races—the real
religion of the so-called Christians.   As many Negroes are now saying to the Christian Church, so do they say to the Young Women's
Christian Association and the Young Men's Christian Association,
"If they really mean to have democracy in this world, the Church
and agencies working supposedly toward the same end as the
Church should disestablish themselves as Jim Crowing agencies and
reorganize on the principles taught by the Great Nazarene."

At present these Christian organizations are founded upon the
iniquitous principles of segregation in the name of God.   They are
hiding behind the old theory which was the stock-in-trade argument

of the slaveholders. They taught the slaves to be satisfied with their lot because their owners did not enslave them. They were enslaved according to the will of God who had cursed Ham and his descendants. Now, since God had enslaved them there was nothing the Negro or anybody else except an infidel could do about it. The Christian Church of today teaches that its god has ordained the segregation of the races in all matters social, and upon this foundation the Christian Church and its agencies have gone forth to conquer the world for this god which a few liberal minded people of the world now brand as the devil incarnate.

C. G. Woodson

Negro Catholic Writers: By Sister Mary Anthony Scally, R. S. M. (Detroit: Walter Romig & Company, 1945. Pp. 152.)

This is a work intended to invite attention to the number of outstanding Negro scholars and authors who are members of the Catholic Church. The effort of the author is to show not only that the Negro membership in the Catholic Church is increasing but that these persons are a fair sample of the best in the Negro race. The evidence presented consists of the list of these persons, brief sketches of their careers and a bibliography giving their literary contributions.

The book, therefore, works both ways. It will naturally stimulate the interest of the Negro in the Catholic Church and among those not thus impressed it will serve as a manual giving helpful information. The listing as Catholic authors those persons in countries where this religion is the only established faith throws the book out of balance, in a sense, for some of those persons who lived and died as Catholics would have joined some of the Protestant organizations if they had lived in a country like the United States.

The book, therefore, is more effective in conveying the impression of the increasing influence of the Catholic Church among Negroes when we consider solely these Negro Catholics in the United States of America. The competition of the various faiths is shown to better advantage in this country of many widely differing religions, and in this case it does appear that the Catholics have made a remarkable advancement among persons of African blood.

The author speaks of the various efforts made by certain Catholics for the evangelization and education of Negroes in the United

States and does not conceal the fact that there are certain circles in the Catholic Church which close their doors to Negroes seeking admission thereto and students desiring to have their minds enlightened. For example, Georgetown University, a Jesuit institution in Washington, D. C., which was founded by Father Healy, a man known to have African blood, closes its doors to Negroes. These varying attitudes have been ever prominent among Catholics as among Protestants, both having been at one time slaveholding defenders of the institution, while others of the faith attacked the system as an evil. This book shows that the thinking element in the Catholic Church is anxious to remove these evils, and they have been working more rapidly toward this end than the Protestants, who are now losing some of their membership to the Catholic Church.

R. L. WAYMAN

For a New Africa. Proceedings of the Conference on Africa held in New York City on April 14, 1945, together with Addresses by Max Yergan and Paul Robeson. (New York: Council on African Affairs, 1945. Pp. 52. Price 10 cents.)

This booklet comes from an organization which is now in its seventh year. The purpose of this undertaking is to disseminate accurate information concerning Africa, and to ''direct public opinion toward furthering such policies and interests as are consistent with the needs and aspirations of Africans and with international security.'' Who are the persons promoting this movement and why should they be thus engaged? The answer would be a long story.

Max Yergan began life as a worker in the Negro division of the Young Men's Christian Association. He served in the United States and next in India. He was ordered to take up the work of a new field opening in Africa, and his friends in the United States raised a special fund to finance his efforts there. The economic imperialists, fearing that an American Negro might interfere with their depriving the Natives of their land, their labor and their liberty, requested the advice of Thomas Jesse Jones, the protégé of the Phelps-Stokes Fund by which he had been sent to Africa to get control of the mission work undertaken there by Americans. Jones registered a protest against Yergan's coming. Later when Jones's hamstringing was discovered and noised abroad in the United

States, he had to back out of an ugly situation for "a friend of the Negro."

Max Yergan was finally permitted to enter South Africa and did creditable work there for several years; but the unfavorable beginning and the daily observance of the crimes committed against the unoffending Africans caused his soul to rebel against the imperial regime and the lukewarm religious program permitted under the exploiters of the land. He came back to the United States, therefore, and organized seven years ago the Council on African Affairs to work for the elevation of Africans along the line of conflict rather than as the religious element along the line of agreement. His efforts have been successful. The work has rendered the important service of directing to Africa the attention of thousands of persons who heretofore have seldom given the welfare of Africans a thought. The work is receiving increasing support from year to year, and the staff is growing in proportion to the possibilities of carrying out the full program of keeping before the modern world the urgent need for the redemption of Africa from the economic imperialists and the Christians cooperating with them.

Who is Paul Robeson? Why should he be the chairman of an organization of this type and deliver an address on African affairs with respect to the Negro? We know of Paul Robeson as a singer and actor with an international fame justified by his beautiful voice and histrionic ability. His standing is such that he does not have to take up any time with Negroes. He has more contacts with whites than he might well wish for. Paul Robeson, however, appreciates the rock from which he was hewn. Unlike so many other actors and singers who stay as far away as possible from the Negro after they have attained a measure of success, Robeson keeps in close touch with his people, sharing their aspirations to achieve efficiency and recognition; and he has advanced much farther among the members of the other race than those successful Negroes who abandon their fellows altogether. Robeson's wife must have had the same spirit when she talked with the reviewer about the time that her boy was just about beginning to read. She said that she was delighted to find him a real Negro, and she wanted him brought up in the traditions of his people. Although living abroad, she purchased about seventy-five dollars' worth of books on the Negro to direct the development of the mind of the boy in the right way.

He must learn to love his people and to work for their welfare and happiness. This is the invincible spirit of the Council of African Affairs.

The two addresses of these men, therefore, may be easily understood. They want to see the "end of imperialism, imperialist exploitation, and imperialist rivalries." The Africans' share in the victory in this war must be the removal of the evils inflicted upon them by European conquerors, for there can be no assurance of peace if Africa is to continue in the status quo and serve as the jack-pot of World War II. To Africa must be brought a new program of mass education with systematic planning to transform a primitive economy into a modern agricultural and industrial economy. The people of the United States have no direct control of Africa, but they have influence which should be greater than ever in the history of the Americas since we have financed the present war and have taken under our protection both France and England which otherwise would still be under the heel of the Nazis. In the position of the leading nation of the world we can do much to abolish forced labor and unfair trade practices in Africa and to guarantee self-government to modernized Natives. Like others planning along the same line the Conference wants to see established an international authority for colonial affairs, the industrial development of Africa, and its early liberation. These speakers justify their expectations on the declarations made by the leaders of the victorious nations in the Atlantic Charter, at Moscow and Teheran. The friends of Africa emphasize especially the words of the late President Roosevelt who said, "We are determined that we shall gain total victory over our enemies, and we recognize the fact that our enemies are not only in Germany, Italy and Japan: they are all the forces of oppression, intolerance, insecurity and injustice which have impeded the forward march of civilization."

C. G. WOODSON

This Is Our War. By Carl Murphy, Editor. (Baltimore: Afro-American Company, 1945. Pp. 216. Price, $1.00.)

This Is Our War is a selected collection of the reports sent to the Baltimore *Afro-American* by its six war correspondents from Europe, Africa, Alaska and the Southwest Pacific. Carl Murphy, the editor and president of a national newspaper chain, has made an important contribution and addition to the books on the Negro in World War II by collecting in one volume these intimate, day by day stories of the part the colored troops are playing in the winning of the peace.

In the introduction the editor tells us, ''In reprinting these wartime dispatches no effort is made to tell a connected story. This book represents a series of pictures of what war correspondents met in their travels and their interpretations of the reactions of 'GI Joe' to new environments.'' Yet, these stories as selected bring together graphic and personal glimpses of World War II and, on the whole, give the reader a well filled picture and cause for pride in these men.

Included are eye-witness and battle reports by Ollie Stewart of the Invasion of France and the Liberation of Paris; an enlightening and timely report by Max Johnson of his interview with Brazilian troops in Italy, entitled, ''Brazilian Troops Have No Color Line''; also cleverly written articles by Vincent Tubbs on what he saw and heard in the two years he spent in Australia, New Guinea, and many other points in the Southwest Pacific; Art Carter's accounts of Colonel Davis's flyers in Italy; Herbert Frisby's narrative of his experiences while visiting army posts in the Aleutian Islands and Alaska, where he made a study of the contributions and work of the 93rd, 95th, and 97th Negro Engineer Regiments.

Elizabeth Phillips, the first colored woman accredited as a war correspondent, is represented by an article, ''3,000 Miles to a Hospital.'' Francis Yancey, commissioned as a correspondent to cover the Southwest Pacific after Vincent Tubbs' return, has contributed gay and humorous drawings depicting the text of the reports which add greatly to the volume.

This Is Our War is recommended to the home folks generally who are concerned to know how their boys are faring and have fared in the war areas.

ETHEL L. WILLIAMS

NOTES

Books of general use and throwing some light on the Negro in the United States include the following: *A History of American Life*, by twelve authors under the editorship of Professor A. M. Schlesinger and Dr. Dixon Ryan Fox (New York: The Macmillan Company); *Lincoln Bibliography*, in two volumes, by Jay Monaghan (Springfield, Illinois: Illinois State Historical Library, 1945); *To the Counsellors of Peace, Recommendations of the American Jewish Committee* (New York: American Jewish Committee, 1945); *Principio to Wheeling, 1715-1945*, by Earl Chapin May (New York: Harper and Brothers, 1945).

Of social and economic bearing upon the Negro are the following: *Democracy in America*, by Alexander de Tocqueville, a reprint edited by Philips Bradley (New York: A. A. Knopf Company, 1945); *The Children of the Light and the Children of Darkness*, a vindication of democracy and a critique of its traditional defence, by Reinhold Niebuhr (New York: Charles Scribner's Sons, 1945); *An Uncommon Man: Henry A. Wallace*, by Frank Kingdom (New York: Readers' Press, 1945); *Freedom Is More Than a Word*, by Marshall Field (Chicago: University of Chicago Press, 1945); Here may be added also a work of fiction entitled *Winds Blow Gently*, a Quaker story concentrating on the Negro and the South. (New York: Frederick Fell, 1945.)

Books dealing primarily with the Negro include these: *The Land Possessions of Howard University: A Study of the Original Ownership and Extent of the Holdings of Howard University in the District of Columbia*, thoroughly documented, by Beulah H. Melchoir, Washington, D. C. (privately printed); *Experiments in Democracy*, a well illustrated booklet (USO Division of the National Board of the Young Women's Christian Association, 600 Lexington Avenue, New York 22, N. Y.); *Divide and Conquer*, by Allan Sloane and Bob Russell with a foreword by Howard Fast, a play published by the Green Publishing Company, Box 823, Amityville, N. Y.; *An Account of the Physicians of Color in the United States*, a reprint

350

from the BULLETIN OF THE HISTORY OF MEDICINE, January, 1945, being an address delivered before the New York Society for Medical History at the New York Academy of Medicine in New York City, February 3, 1945; *The Armory of God*, by Oscar Sherwin, being a reprint from THE NEW ENGLAND QUARTERLY, January, 1945. Here may be added also *A Traipsin Heart*, a book of poems, mainly racial, by Mildred Martin Hill (New York: Wendell Malliet and Company, 1945).

ARTICLES OF UNITED STATES HISTORY

Articles illuminating the history of the country as it has been influenced by the Negro along with other important factors include: "Dr. Thomas Bray's Trip to Maryland: A Study in Militant Anglican Humanitarianism," by Samuel Clyde McCullough (*William and Mary Quarterly*, January, 1945); "Jonathan Boucher: Champion of the Minority," by Robert G. Walker (*ibid.*); "Vignettes of Maryland History: Part II," by Raphael Semmes (*Maryland Historical Magazine*, March, 1945); "The Vicissitudes of the Chesapeake and Ohio Canal during the Civil War," by Walter Sanderlin (*Journal of Southern History*, February, 1945); "A Confederate Colony in Mexico," by Carl Coke Rister (*ibid.*); "An Analysis of Lincoln's Funeral Sermons," by Jay Monaghan (*Indiana Magazine of History*, March, 1945); "Southern Common Folk after the Civil War," by Thomas D. Clark (*The South Atlantic Quarterly*, April 1945); "A Yankee Professor in the South," by Howard O. Brogan (*ibid.*); "The Background of Reform on the Missouri Frontier," by Marie George Windell (*Missouri Historical Quarterly*, January, 1945).

Articles bearing mainly upon the Negro include these: "Jefferson's Thirteenth Amendment," by Charles Hall Davis (*Tyler's Quarterly Magazine*, April, 1945); "Civil Liberties and Anti-Slavery Literature," by Russell B. Nye (*Science and Society*, Spring, 1945); "The Negro Looks Abroad," by Martin Ebon (*Free World*, May, 1945); "Racial Theory," by E. B. Reuter (*The American Journal of Sociology*, May, 1945); "Douglass' Mind in the Making," by Benjamin Quarles (*Phylon*, First Quarter, 1945); "The Muted South," by Sterling Brown (*ibid.*); "The Negro on Broadway—1944," by Miles M. Jefferson (*ibid.*); "Apostles of Newness," by Oscar Sherwin (*ibid.*); "Southern Students' Dilemma," by Edgar A. Schuler (*ibid.*); "The Mulatto in American Fiction," by Penelope Bullock (*ibid.*).

BOOKS ON THE WEST INDIES AND LATIN AMERICA

Among the most important publications treating matters in this sphere are the following: *Ruy Barbosa: Brazilian Crusader for the Essential Freedoms* (Nashville, Tennessee: Abingdon-Cokesbury Press, 1945); *San Martin: Knight of the Andes,* by Ricardo Rojas (New York: Doubleday, Doran Company, 1945); *La Esclavitud Prehispanica entre Los Aztectas,* by C. Bosch Garcia (Mexico: College of Mexico, 1944); *The Land Divided: A History of the Panama Canal and Other Isthmian Projects,* by G. Mack (New York: Alfred A. Knopf, 1944); *Reliquias Historicas de la Española,* new edition, by B. Ricardo (Santiago: Republica Dominica, 1944); *Cocks and Bulls in Caracás,* by Olga Briceno (Boston: Houghton Mifflin Company, 1945).

ARTICLES ON THE WEST INDIES AND LATIN AMERICA

The most interesting and valuable of these recorded in this restricted field are the following: "Colonization of the Bahamas," by W. Hubert Miller (*The William and Mary Quarterly,* January, 1945); "Is the Twentieth Century South America's?" by C. Langdon White (*Economic Geography,* April, 1945); "Expedición de Francisco Estrampes y Conspiración de Ramón Pintó (1854-55)," by M. Guiral Moreno (*Revista Bimestre Cubana,* 1944, LIII, No. 1, 26-50); "Caribbean Communism," by C. M. Catterns (*Commonwealth and Empire Review,* March-May, 1945); "Bustamente Comes to Power" (*ibid.*); "The Colour Problem" (*ibid.*).

BOOKS ON AFRICA

Recent works bearing on Africa of today include the following: *For a New Africa,* by Paul Robeson and Max Yergan (New York: Council on African Affairs, Inc., 1945); *Through Chaos to Community,* a pamphlet of 20 pages advocating the right sort of peace as seen by the author, John McMurray (London: National Peace

Council, 1944) ; *Makers of South Africa,* by B. L. W. Bret (London : Thomas Nelson and Sons, 1944) ; *Christian and Adult Education in Rural Asia and Africa,* by R. H. P. Sailer (New York : Friendship Press, 1945) ; *The Future of Colonies,* by Sir Bernard Bourdillon (London : Christian Student Movement, 1945) ; *British Military Administration of Occupied Territories in Africa during the Years 1941-1943"* (London : H. M. Stationery Office, 1945) ; *"Thoughts on African Citizenship,* by T. R. Batten (London : Oxford University Press, 1944).

Books mainly scientific include the following : *Elements de Droit Coutumier Nègre,* by Emile Possoz (Elizabethville, Congo Belge : The Author) ; *Prevention and Treatment of Disease in Warm Climates,* by T. Gerald Garry (London : Medical Publications, Ltd., 1944) ; *African Music,* by A. M. Jones, (Northern Rhodesia : Rhodes-Livingstone Institute, 1943) ; *The African as Suckling and as Adult,* J. F. Ritchie *(ibid.).*

ARTICLES ON AFRICA AND THE FAR EAST

The most interesting of such articles recently appearing include the following : "Desert Menace in South Africa" *(Commonwealth and Empire Review,* March-May, 1945) ; "South African Indian Question," by H. S. L. Polak *(Indian Review,* March, 1945) ; "The Colonial Era Ends," by Maurice J. Goldbloom *(Asia and the Americas,* May, 1945) ; "New Guinea," by Effie May Ross *(The Dalhousie Review,* January, 1945) ; "Psychological Background of White Color Contacts in Britain," by K. L. Little *(The Sociological Review,* January-April, 1945) ; "Report, 1944" *(Books for Africa,* January, 1945) ; "Literature Developments in Sierra Leone," by R. A. Johnson *(ibid.)* ; "Report on Adult Literacy among Meru Women," by Mary Holding *(ibid.,* April, 1945) ; "The Place and Content of Translation," by T. Price *(ibid.)* ; "Findings of the Council : Social Security, Non-European Industry, Housing, and Racial Attitudes" *(Race Relations News,* February, 1945).

PERSONAL

MONROE NATHAN WORK

In the passing of Monroe Nathan Work at Tuskegee Institute on Wednesday, May 9, 1945, the nation suffered an irreparable loss. He was born August 15, 1866, in Iredell County, North Carolina, and thus lived to be almost seventy-nine years old. He left a widow, Mrs. Florence Hendrickson Work, whom he married in 1904. They had no children. He was laid to rest at Tuskegee where he had spent his most useful years, and many friends and co-workers joined to pay him the last tribute of respect.

Dr. Work was educated at the Chicago Theological Seminary and at the University of Chicago from which he received the degrees of Bachelor of Philosophy and Master of Arts. His first important service was as professor of Pedagogy and History at the Georgia State Industrial College where he served from 1903 to 1908. Major R. R. Wright was then president of the school. From this post he went to Tuskegee Institute where he functioned most successfully and efficiently as Director of the Department of Records and Research until he retired in 1938. During these years he was not concerned altogether with his tasks at Tuskegee. He took time to participate in all group efforts of social scientists studying the Negro, and he served on numerous boards and committees thus concerned.

Dr. Work's first important achievement in this position was the collection of data from which he published biennially *The Negro Yearbook* which supplied a long-felt need for factual material on the Negro. Almost every Negro high school or college student made some use of this manual and through the libraries of the country it served well the purpose of thousands of both races in this country and abroad.

Dr. Work's next significant achievement was to compile from the results of his researches in this country and Europe data for his *Bibliography of the Negro* which came from the press of the H. W. Wilson Company in 1928. This was the first and, so far, the only effort of the kind to present in one volume the materials bearing on the past and present of the Negro in all parts of the world from the most ancient time to the present. In a work covering such a wide field numerous omissions are inevitable when restricted to the efforts

354

of one individual, but the work is a highly valuable production which has not and will not be soon superseded by something better. At the time of his death he was engaged in revising this work with a view to enlarging it to the extent of two volumes. This remains as a task which he unfortunately could not complete.

Dr. Work was not a publicity seeker, and he never received credit for many things which he accomplished. Only in the many learned circles to which he belonged was he given the recognition which he deserved. In 1928 he was presented the Harmon Award in Education for "scholarly research and educational publicity through periodic publication of *The Negro Yearbook* and the compilation of a *Bibliography of the Negro.*" In 1942 he received the Chicago Alumni Citation in recognition of his forty years of public service. He was undoubtedly one of the most useful and unselfish men of his time.

THE JOURNAL
OF
NEGRO HISTORY

Vol. XXX—October, 1945—No. 4

THE HISTORICAL BACKGROUND OF BRITISH GUIANA'S PROBLEMS

The problems of the British West Indies, in fact of the entire Caribbean area, are basically economic. The root of these problems lies in one fact that can be simply stated: the staple of Caribbean economy, sugar, has for a hundred years been fighting desperately for survival in the world market. Competition has come from two quarters—the extension of cane cultivation in other tropical regions of the globe, and the development of beet sugar in the temperate regions. Cane cultivation, by 1939, was the mainstay of the economy of Louisiana, Hawaii, Java, Fiji, Mauritius, the Philippines, Natal and Queensland, while India and Brazil supplied their own requirements. Beet sugar was encouraged in all the European countries and in the mid-west of the United States. Where beet sugar constituted 14 per cent of total world production in 1852, it represented 51 per cent in 1914 and 38 per cent in 1939.[1] The British Caribbean area produced 3 per cent of the world's output in 1895-1896, 2 per cent in 1941-1942. The British West Indies produced 9 per cent of the world's cane supply in the former year, 3 per cent in the latter. Of the total Caribbean sugar production 17.8 per cent came from British sources in 1895-1896,

[1] H. C. Prinsen Geerligs: *The World's Cane Sugar Industry—Past and Present* (Manchester, 1912), p. 21; *Manual of Sugar Companies, 1943* (New York, 1943), pp. 198-199.

10.6 per cent in 1941-1942.[2] Sugar cultivation is today a political not an economic question. More than any other crop, sugar has been the victim of "tarifs de combat."

The situation of British Guiana is much worse than even the overall picture. With an area of 90,000 square miles, this colony has today a population of less than 400,000. It is true that this population is concentrated on the narrow strip of territory along the coast. Nevertheless, British Guiana, as an economic unit, is underpopulated. Barbados, with 166 square miles, has half the population of British Guiana. Puerto Rico, with 3,400 square miles, has five times as many people as British Guiana. Cuba, less than half the size of British Guiana, has ten times as many inhabitants. It is true that British Guiana's sugar production increased from 54,423 tons in 1860 to 196,502 tons in 1938. But during the same period Cuba's production increased from 447,000 to 2,758,552 tons though it exceeded five million tons in 1925; Puerto Rico's from 51,792 to760,678, though it passed the million mark in 1934; world cane production from 1,340,980 tons to 18,457,284; world beet production from 451,584 to 10,227,486 tons.[3] That is, while British Guiana's

[2]
Year	Caribbean Production	B.W.I. Production	World Cane Production	World Sugar Production
1895-6	1,449,568	258,503	2,839,500	7,160,000
1941-2	5,676,220	603,788	19,147,885	28,552,599

The figures for 1895-6 come from the following sources: Prinsen Geerligs, *op. cit.*, p. 21 (world production), p. 242 (French Islands), p. 244 (St. Croix), p. 266 (Dutch Guiana); *Royal Commission on Trade Relations between Canada and the West Indies*, Part III, Cd. 5370 (His Majesty's Stationery Office, 1910), pp. 282-284 (British West Indies); *Anuario Azucarero de Cuba* (Havana, 1940), p. 59 (Cuba); *Annual Book on Statistics* (Department of Agriculture and Commerce, Puerto Rico, Fiscal Year 1939-40), p. 130 (Puerto Rico); Willett and Gray sheet, dated March 1922 (Dominican Republic). The figures for 1941-2 are from *Manual of Sugar Companies, 1943*, p. 198; for Dutch Guiana from P. H. Hiss: *Netherlands America* (New York, 1943), p. 201; *Annual Report of the Department of Agriculture, British Guiana, for the year 1942*, p. 3.

[3] Prinsen Geerligs, *op. cit.*, 262; *Agriculture in the West Indies*, Colonial No. 182 (His Majesty's Stationery Office, 1942) p. 98; *Anuario Azucarero de Cuba*, p. 59; *Annual Book on Statistics*, p. 116.

production increased three and a half times, Cuba's increased six times (nearly twelve times if we take the year 1925), Puerto Rico's nearly fifteen times (over twenty-one times if we use the year 1934), world cane production fourteen times, world beet production more than twenty-two times.

Despite the difficulties of sugar production, however, sugar has always dominated Caribbean economy. In 1939 sugar and by-products represented three-fifths of the total exports of British Guiana. For the Caribbean has been able to find no substitute for sugar. Trinidad turned to cocoa; West Africa forced it back to sugar. Dominica adopted limes; the industry succumbed to the competition of the Sicilian lemon industry and withertip disease. One hundred years ago West Indian cotton was liquidated by the competition of the Southern United States; its resurrection today, on any large scale, is, under present conditions, highly unlikely. Coffee vanished in the face of the product of Brazil and the East; there is no room today for West Indian coffee in the world market, except for the limited, specialized variety of Jamaica. The five-cent cigar and the cigarette have reduced the once-famed Cuban tobacco industry to negligible proportions. West Indian citrus fruits feel the full blast of competition from Florida, California, and Palestine. West Indian rum has to compete with whisky, scotch or rye. Jamaica's bananas still maintain a precarious existence, with Panama disease and the extension of cultivation in Central America as the question marks of the future.

The West Indies have had to face another serious economic obstacle—competition with other areas and other raw materials for the surplus capital of Europe and America. It is true that North American capital has poured into the sugar industry of Puerto Rico, Cuba, and the Dominican Republic. But oil, iron, coal, steel, tin, rubber, railroads—these and a host of other avenues offer more tempting fields of investment to the capitalists of the older countries.

Finally, one of the crucial problems of the Caribbean is the organization of the local economy. The plantation system has survived as the legacy of slavery. Where it has been abolished, as in Haiti, it is reappearing; where it was largely non-existent, as in Puerto Rico, it has emerged full-fledged in our time. But the plantation system is being increasingly challenged all over the Caribbean today, in Jamaica and Puerto Rico, in Trinidad and Cuba. The great increase of Caribbean population has resulted in terrific pressure on the basic means of subsistence, the land. Land settlement is one of the burning issues of the day.

*   *   *   *   *

British Guiana belongs, economically if not geographically, to the Caribbean area; politically it is a part of the British West Indies. The problems of the Caribbean are thus the problems of British Guiana. In studying British Guiana we have a view of the entire West Indian scene. This is not only valuable in theory. Today it is the road to the solution of the difficulties of the Caribbean. The separated insular units have not been able to and cannot solve their problems in isolation.

The general problems of the Caribbean, however, are aggravated by the special local problems of British Guiana. British Guiana suffers not from the population pressure of the West Indian islands, but from a serious shortage of labor. The land is below sea level and the economy of the colony is dependent upon an elaborate system of sea defenses, irrigation canals and trenches, extensive drainage operations and embankments against flood waters. British Guiana is indeed "made-land,"[4] with each plantation "a complete island within itself; and *dammed* on all sides."[5] This has involved not only large capital investments but

[4] Dr. G. Pinckard: *Letters from Guiana 1796-1797* (Georgetown, 1942), p. 323.

[5] H. Bolingbroke: *A Voyage to the Demerary. An Account of the Settlements there and on the Essequebo and Berbice, 1799-1806* (Georgetown, 1941), p. 18.

heavy recurrent charges for repairs and maintenance, which constitute a serious drain on the colonial exchequer, make the production of a remunerative staple for export mandatory, and render it difficult to envisage a subdivision of the land. British Guiana is as dependent on capital as it is on labor. Without both of these factors, its hinterland will remain undeveloped and its potentialities the subject of the most extravagant schemes.

It remains now for us to trace the historical roots of these problems, general as well as local. British Guiana's present can be understood only by reference to its past.

* * * * *

British Guiana passed too late into the possession of the British Crown. Had it been annexed in the middle of the eighteenth century, before the secession of the North American colonies, when the sugar colonies of the Caribbean were the apple of their mother country's eye, the whole history of the colony and the British West Indian islands would have been different. The problem of labor would have been solved by the slave trade. British Guiana's fertile alluvial coast lands would have attracted British capital in enormous quantities. Barbados and Antigua, cultivating their exhausted soil by the expensive labor of slaves, could never have competed with the profits that would have been extracted from the fresh lands of British Guiana. The British West Indian colonies would have been outdistanced by British Guiana within the Empire, as outside the Empire they were outdistanced by Saint Domingue in 1789 and Cuba in 1840. The virgin and the hag do not compete on equal terms for the favors of the wealthy suitor.

But British Guiana became British only in the early years of the nineteenth century, when the West Indian colonies were falling from grace and sugar's throne was toppling. Wilberforce's motions for the abolition of the slave trade were an annual item on the agenda of the House of Commons. Sugar cultivation was spreading in different

parts of the world—Brazil, India, Mauritius, and Cuba—
and was soon to be extended to others, while beet sugar was
making its first appearance in the world market. The long
war with Bonaparte was undermining the prosperity of
West Indian sugar cultivation, and in 1805 the planters as a
group were bankrupt. Where, fifty years before, West Indian colonies would have been annexed with glee and rejoic-
ing, in 1814 the Earl of Lansdowne protested that it would
be worth paying money to get rid of colonies—British Guiana and Trinidad—which would produce sugar that Britain
could not consume and would withdraw capital which Britain could not afford.[6] The independence of America had put
the West Indian food basket outside the area of empire free
trade, and the sugar colonies after 1783 were forced to grow
more of their own food. The Industrial Revolution had
enormously increased British production and enabled it to
think in terms of production for the entire world, while it
correspondingly called for a greater supply of raw materials, cotton in particular. The sole hope for British Guiana
lay in its reading the writing on the wall. In cotton, not in
sugar, lay its salvation. Cotton was usurping the throne,
sugar was being relegated to the ranks of the footmen. British Guiana in the nineteenth century made the choice it
would have made in the eighteenth. It chose sugar.

* * * * *

British Guiana, under Dutch rule, was a Dutch colony in
little more than name. The Dutch were more interested in
the East Indies and spice than in the West Indies and sugar.
In 1762 Englishmen owned nearly one-eighth of the sugar
plantations of Essequebo, over one-third of those in Demerara.[7] "British enterprise," wrote Dr. Pinckard, "taught
the plodding Hollander that he had overlooked his best in-

[6] *Report of the British Guiana Commission*, Cmd. 2841 (His Majesty's
Stationery Office, 1927), p. 6.

[7] Sir Cecil Clementi: *A Constitutional History of British Guiana* (London, 1937), p. 32.

terests . . .''[8] Where the Dutch colonist developed a garden,
the English colonist established a plantation. The Dutchman emphasized quality, the Englishman quantity. The
Dutchman was out to make his home in British Guiana, the
Englishman was set on making his fortune, whereafter he
would return home. With the same number of slaves, the
Englishman brought more land under cultivation than the
Dutchman; ''the system which the English have introduced,'' wrote Bolingbroke with pride after his visit to the
colony, ''ensures as much cultivation in one year as a Hollander would accomplish in four.''[9]

With the acquisition of the colony by Britain, British
capital poured into the country, to quicken ''the national
slowness of the Dutch.''[10] Plantations were founded at
enormous expense, varying from thirty to fifty thousand
pounds.[11] The planters of British Guiana were inevitably
big capitalists. They ''are usually,'' wrote Bolingbroke,
''persons who possess a capital from 2 to 20,000 pounds.
With less than the former sum they cannot easily commence
their career; nor do they care to forsake it with less than
the latter.''[12] It was a rich man's country, a potential El
Dorado. If only there were no factors which frightened
capital away!

The expansion of the sugar industry was phenomenal.
For every sugar plantation under the Dutch there were
five under the English.[13] In 1745 the colony exported 200
tons of sugar, which increased to 1,120 in 1770, requiring
nine vessels. The export in 1801 was 4,750 tons. In 1805
the steam engine for crushing canes was introduced. Production increased to 14,000 tons in 1814 and 42,000 tons in
1824, while the shipping cleared at the Custom House

[8] Pinckard, op. cit., p. 329.
[9] Bolingbroke, op. cit., pp. 23, 207.
[10] Ibid., p. 207.
[11] Ibid., p. 140.
[12] Ibid., p. 224.
[13] Ibid., p. 19.

amounted to 74,317 tons. In 1830 the vacuum pan arrived, and the world began to hear of the Demerara Crystals. In 1833, the year of emancipation, the colony produced 54,588 tons of sugar.[14]

This expansion of sugar coincided with a contraction of the other two outstanding exports, coffee and cotton. As far as cotton was concerned, Schomburgk, writing in the early forties, attributed the decline to emancipation. "The material obtained by free men cannot compete with that won by slave labour. Were the conditions of Guiana to stand on the same footing with those of the Slave-States of America as regards amount and cheapness of labour, an area of cultivation would then present itself right here along a stretch of some 280 miles of coast-line . . . where all kinds of cotton shrub could be grown with the most magnificent results."[15]

On the general principle, Schomburgk is repudiated by Adam Smith. Smith, representing the industrial bourgeoisie with its new ideas of industrial freedom, claimed that free labor was superior to slave.[16] Both Schomburgk and Adam Smith are wrong. For the competition of free labor and slave is not an abstract question. In given conditions, such as prevailed in both British Guiana and the Southern States, where there was a scanty population and much available land, slave labor is cheaper than free labor. But slave labor in British Guiana in 1830 was vastly more expensive than slave labor in South Carolina.

Schomburgk is equally at fault on the immediate issues involved. British Guiana had followed the general West Indian pattern—sugar first, cotton second. The competition of cotton with sugar for growing space, which was ulti-

[14] A. R. F. Webber: *Centenary History and Handbook of British Guiana* (Georgetown, 1931), pp. 46, 77, 123, 128, 152, 158; Prinsen Geerligs, op. cit., p. 262.

[15] R. Schomburgk: *Travels in British Guiana, 1840-1844* (Georgetown, 1922), Vol. 1, p. 35.

[16] Adam Smith: *The Wealth of Nations* (New York, 1937, Cannan edition), p. 365.

mately determined by the price and protection accorded both in the British market, rendered British Guiana unable to compete with the Southern States where cotton's supremacy was unchallenged. British Guiana's cotton production did not decline, it was annihilated. It was not the Negro who was to blame, but the world market. In 1812 British imports of Guiana cotton amounted to 9,437,473 pounds; in 1833 they were only 1,109,979. In 1842 they were a bare 3,000 pounds.[17]

This was no accident. Sugar was a far more profitable crop than either cotton or coffee. "It is unfortunately but too true," wrote the governor in 1829, "that cotton has lately so fallen in value as not to repay the expenses of its cultivation, which is therefore about to be universally abandoned. Coffee although better than cotton for the planters, is still but little profitable. Sugar is the only produce of export which now affords a reasonable return upon the capital invested."[18] A sugar plantation required one Negro for every acre of land; the average return was estimated at £50 per acre. A cotton plantation required one Negro for every two acres, each acre producing on an average 600 bushels of half a pound of cotton each. At fifteen stivers (15 pence) per pound, the average return for two acres of cotton was £37.10.0. A coffee plantation required two Negroes for every three acres of land. Allowing 450 bushels per acre, and one and a half pounds of coffee per bushel, the average return per Negro on a coffee plantation, valuing the product at 8 pence per pound, was £33.15.0.[19] On the basis of these statistics for the year 1796-1797, the average return from sugar, cotton, and coffee was in the ratio of 40:30:27.

In 1813 the governor of the colony wrote to the Secre-

[17] L. J. Ragatz: *Statistics for the Study of British Caribbean Economic History, 1763-1833* (London, n.d.), p. 16; Schomburgk, *op. cit.*, Vol. I, p. 26.

[18] C.O. 111/67 (Public Record Office). D'Urban to Hay, July 7, 1829.

[19] Pinckard, *op. cit.*, p. 330-331.

tary of State for the Colonies that British Guiana was
"most highly qualified by nature to remedy the principal
inconveniences" of the suspension of the food trade with the
United States. Corn and rice could be cultivated with certain success and in any quantities, whilst Berbice could
raise cattle to any extent with great facility and little expense. "But unfortunately these humble paths to certain
profit are overlooked by people whose whole attention is
absorbed in the expectation of obtaining rapid fortunes by
the growth of sugar, coffee or cotton."[20] Three months later
his successor reiterated that Demerara could supply any
quantity of cassava flour and maize "if sufficient induce-
ments could be offered on the payment to direct capital and
industry to that channel." The obstacle was the mercantile creditor in England, to whom the crops were remitted
to give him a commission in addition to his interest. "The
sale of timber, rice and corn, finding a market at the door,
or near at hand, would be of no advantage to him, beyond
the mere interest of the capital he has at stake."[21] Bolingbroke wrote lugubriously that if the cultivation of rice was
encouraged by the government, British Guiana could rival
South Carolina.[22] Thus it was that Pinckard found "a well-
cultivated garden so extremely rare as to appear quite a
novelty"; those who "court the smiles of fortune, by planting the tropical fields, attend only to the cultivation of sugar, coffee, and cotton, which are often seen growing up to
the very doorway, or almost creeping in at the windows of
the dwelling, not the smallest spot being reserved for garden, pleasure ground or orchard."[23]

But British Guiana had decided advantages over the
British West Indies with respect to sugar cultivation. In
1813 the relative fertility of British Guiana and Barbados

[20] C.O. 111/16. Murray to Bathurst, June 22, 1813.

[21] *Ibid.*, Codd to Bathurst, Sept. 6, 1813.

[22] Bolingbroke, *op. cit.*, p. 17.

[23] Pinckard, *op. cit.*, p. 319.

was estimated at four to one in terms of slave output per capita.[24] In Demerara it took 200 days' labor to produce 5,000 pounds of sugar, in Barbados 400. In the former no outlay of capital for manure was necessary, in the latter it required one-fourth of the labor of the plantation.[25] A Guiana plantation of 600 slaves produced 800 to 900 hogsheads of sugar in a year; Montserrat, with between 3,000 and 4,000 slaves, exported only 1,500 hogsheads.[26] The British West Indies faced the prospect of being denuded of both planters and slaves. The governor of Barbados hastened to acquire a plantation in British Guiana,[27] which became virtually a Barbadian colony. After 1807 the migration of slaves within the British West Indian area was prohibited, unless the slaves were domestics in attendance on their master. A large scale trade in "domestics" thereby resulted; between 1808 and 1825, a total of 9,250 slaves was imported into British Guiana from the older colonies.[28] Bolingbroke viewed the matter with studied nonchalance. It was a natural consequence to expect "the total abandonment of the barren islands for the more fertile soil of the continent." The barren islands were Curacao, St. Eustatius, Saba, St. Martin, Tortola, Tobago, Grenada, and St. Vincent.[29] "Whilst many of the British Islands are nearly exhausted and worn out," so runs one memorandum, the improvement of British Guiana "is in an early and progressive state, and may be extended to a degree hitherto uncalculated."[30]

[24] C.O. 111/16. Codd to Bathurst, Nov. 18, 1813.

[25] *Select Committee appointed to inquire into the Commercial State of the West India Colonies* (H. of C. Sess. Pap., Reports, Committees, 1831-1832, Vol. 20, No. 381), p. 180. Evidence of John P. Mayers, Agent for Barbados.

[26] W. L. Burn: *Emancipation and Apprenticeship in the British West Indies* (London, 1937), p. 70.

[27] Webber, *op. cit.*, p. 123.

[28] See Eric Williams: *"The Intercolonial Slave Trade after its Abolition in 1807"* (Journal of Negro History, April 1942).

[29] Bolingbroke, *op. cit.*, pp. 117-118.

[30] C.O. 111/18. Memorandum respecting the colonies of Demerary and Essequibo, Dec. 1813.

The decision, however, did not rest with the British Guiana planters. Both externally and internally, there were powerful groups intent on restraining this expansion of sugar cultivation.

British capitalism in the nineteenth century had reached the age of maturity. The adolescent suit of monopoly which it had worn throughout the eighteenth century had now become too small. Where formerly it had emphasized protection, it was now advocating free trade. Production had increased enormously. The great textile industry exported in 1830 goods to the value of 31 million pounds, where it had exported one million in 1785.[31] Total British exports rose from 43 millions to 65 millions between 1821 and 1832.[32] Whilst the production of raw cotton in British Guiana had declined catastrophically, British Guiana was negligible as an export market. British exports to the colony amounted to £323,126 in 1814, £414,483 in 1833.[33] It was even worse in the islands, where export figures showed a decline during the same years.[34] The British capitalist, therefore, found himself in the position of giving a very valuable monopoly to the British West Indian planters of his home market in return for an unimportant monopoly of the colonial market, which was unnecessary in any case, as British goods were, then, cheapest and best. The British Guiana planter had no alternative but to buy British manufactures. The British capitalist had many attractive alternatives to British Guiana sugar. It was an intolerable situation.

The British capitalist was therefore determined to make sugar cultivation in Guiana as difficult as possible. Under

[31] P. Mantoux: *The Industrial Revolution of the Eighteenth Century* (London, 1928), p. 258; N. S. Buck: *The Development of the Organization of Anglo-American Trade, 1800-1850* (New Haven, 1925), p. 166.

[32] Customs 8, Vols. 14 and 35 (Public Record Office).

[33] *Ibid.*, Vols. 2 and 38.

[34]*Ibid.* Exports to the British West Indies declined from £4,704,610 in 1821 to £3,813,821 in 1832.

pressure, the government prohibited the grant of new lands except for the raising of ground provisions. In 1817 a grant was made, on these terms only, to one of the most powerful West Indian planters resident in England. This was John Bolton of Liverpool, whose petition had the support of no less a person than George Canning, the future Prime Minister.[35] In 1829 the Colonial Office received a petition from one Mr. Bond, praying that the prohibition on the cultivation of sugar be removed. One official recorded his impression that "sugar cultivation should still be resisted." Another commented that sugar cultivation was "notoriously the most grievous species of occupation" to the slaves. "At all events the general principle will I think be best adhered to of not sanctioning the establishment of new sugar plantations where it can be helped."[36]

The sugar planters of the British West Indian islands, in their turn, saw in unrestricted sugar cultivation in British Guiana a threat to their existence. They therefore brought all their influence—and they had much, though it was on the wane—to bear against this dreaded rival. British Guiana's problem was fundamentally a problem of labor. Reduce the labor supply and the colony was ruined. Thus, with remarkable casuistry, the planters of the older islands condemned the slave trade to British Guiana and Trinidad while condoning it to Barbados and Jamaica, on the curious ground that in the latter case the property had been acquired before any idea of abolition had been entertained.[37] It was not only inconsistent, it was also a breach of faith. It had been stipulated in 1796, for example, when British Guiana was temporarily occupied by British forces, that, in the event of its cession to England at the peace conference, the colonists should enjoy the same commercial

[35] C.O. 111/24. Canning to Bathurst, Sept. 12, 1817.
[36] C.O. 111/68. No date.
[37] *Hansard*, II, 652. Charles Ellis, June 30, 1804.

rights and privileges as the British West Indian Islands.[38] To deny them, therefore, the right and privilege of the slave trade was in reality to deny them everything. In 1806, a bill was passed, with the cordial support of the planters of the older islands, prohibiting the slave trade to British Guiana and Trinidad. The next year, however, found the older planters in increasing difficulties. The war with France had disrupted shipping, and Bonaparte's Continental Blockade had abolished the European market. British West Indian sugar was piled up in England, with no market for the excess over British consumption. The only solution for this overproduction was abolition of the slave trade.[39] The older colonies combined needed only 7,000 slaves a year.[40] Clearly they would not be ruined by abolition. But British Guiana was seriously affected. More than in any other West Indian colony (Trinidad excepted), were Merivale's words literally true: "Slavery without the slave trade . . . was rather a loss than a gain."[41] Abolition of the slave trade was the reply of the planters of Jamaica and Barbados to the competition of British Guiana.

This was the situation in 1823 when the British Government, under pressure from a public opinion infuriated by the death of the missionary, John Smith, formulated a new policy for the West Indies. This was the policy of amelioration, whereby certain basic reforms calculated to improve the conditions of the slaves were to be enforced in the crown colonies of Trinidad and British Guiana. Success in these colonies, it was hoped, would encourage the self-governing islands to initiate similar reforms themselves. The main provisions of the policy were as follows: abolition of the whip, a nine-hour day and six-day week for the

[38] Clementi, op. cit., p. 52.

[39] *Hansard*, VIII, 238-239. Prime Minister Grenville, Dec. 30, 1806.

[40] *Ibid.*, 985, George Hibbert, Agent for Jamaica, Feb. 23, 1807.

[41] H. Merivale: *Lectures on Colonization and Colonies* (Oxford, 1928), p. 303. The lectures were delivered at Oxford, 1839-1841.

slaves, abolition of the Negro Sunday market, regulation of corporal punishment, facilities for manumissions, prohibition of the flogging of women, appointment of a protector of slaves.

The planters of British Guiana were bitterly hostile to this interference "from the other side of the water." They felt "their humanity insulted, their authority enfeebled and their properties and lives consequently endangered."[42] The Council of the colony decided that "if the principle of manumission *invito domino* is to be adopted, it is more for their consistency and for the interests of their constituents that it should be done *for* them than *by* them";[43] and they refused to co-operate. The Court of Policy claimed that certain operations on sugar, coffee, and cotton estates could not be suspended on Sundays without much inconvenience to the proprietors; the British Government had to emphasize that "it is necessary to maintain entire and unbroken the maxim that the owner of a slave has no title to his labour, except during six days of the week."[44] The governor could find no fit person in British Guiana for the office of Protector of Slaves, and had to ask that someone be sent out from England.[45] Even that did not help. "As to my office," wrote the Protector of Slaves, Captain Elliott. in 1832, "it is a delusion. There is no protection for the Slave Population; and they will very shortly take the matter into their own hands, and destroy the Property. The only way of saving these Countries is to give the Slaves a reasonable share in the produce of their labour. I am desperately unpopular. ... The Order in Council is a dead letter, and a dead letter condemned and decried in the most insulting terms. But if it were respected, would the slave have benefited to such an

42 C.O. 111/25. Murray to Goulbourn, Jan. 1, 1818.
43 C.O. 111/55. D'Urban to Bathurst, July 4, 1826.
44 C.O. 111/49. To D'Urban, July 9, 1825.
45 C.O. 111/54. D'Urban to Horton, April 23, 1826.

extent as he ought to be benefited, *and as he looks to be benefited?*"[46]

The success of the policy of amelioration can best be estimated by a consideration of the vital statistics of the slave population. In 1811 the number of slaves was 71,180; in 1817, 79,197; in 1828, 68,326.[47] Compensation was eventually paid on 69,579 slaves.[48] The slave population thus declined over 12 per cent between 1817 and 1833. This decline cannot be attributed to manumissions. Between 1808 and 1821 the number manumitted was 384, between 1821 and May 21, 1826, a further 243 were freed; from Nov. 1, 1826, to May 1, 1827, 177 more.[49] Buxton, with some exaggeration, claimed that the British Guiana slave population was declining at a rate which would depopulate the earth in fifty years.[50]

The legislation of 1823 prescribed the recording of punishments. There were no less than 10,054 punishments inflicted in the course of six months in 1828 upon a population of 62,352 slaves. This represented more than 20,000 punishments a year, or one punishment for every third slave once a year. If the laboring classes in the United Kingdom, wrote the abolitionist Stephen, had been punished in the same proportion, this would have amounted to between six and seven million punishments. "This," observed Stephen, ". . . is the improved condition of society. What it must have been before the necessity of making these matters known was established by laws, it would be difficult to imagine. . . . If contentment be really diffused through a population which are punished at a rate of one punishment

[46] K. N. Bell and W. P. Morrell (eds.): *Select Documents on British Colonial Policy, 1830-1860* (Oxford, 1928), p. 382.

[47] C.O. 111/11; C.O. 111/36; C.O. 111/67.

[48] H. of C. Sess. Pap., Vol. 48, 1837-8. No. 215, p. 360.

[49] C.O. 111/37; C.O. 111/55; C.O. 111/60.

[50] *Hansard*, New Series, XVIII, 1042. March 6, 1828.

for every third person per annum, it at least shows that they are easily satisfied."[51]

The slaves most emphatically were not satisfied, though there were not wanting men who could not understand why they should not be. According to Bolingbroke, they were not slaves at all—they were vassals. "From the moment a Negro is for the first time sold by auction, it is preposterous to call him a *slave*. He is become in the strict legal sense of the word a *vassal*. He is ascribed to the soil, and can invoke its nutritious aid, by law, during sickness, famine, or decreptiude. He has climbed a step in human society." If, in the course of his ascent, the proprietor took "nine or ten hours of labour every day" from him. it left the "vassal" with nearly fifteen hours, in addition to board, lodging, clothes, and luxuries like rum and tobacco. "What British labourer pays for his shelter, his food, his raiment, and his ale-house bill, with the sacrifice of a smaller proportion of his time"?[52] Why, with these patent advantages, Bolingbroke did not suggest that his countrymen exchange places with the slave is not clear. He contented himself, rather with endorsing the slave trade. "The slave trade, properly so called, the trade which redeems slaves to exalt them into vassals, is a benefit to be encouraged by public premiums. Its continuance is of value to the whole Negro race, and is essential to the further progress of agriculture, in the fertile but unpeopled tropical portions of America."[53]

The slave trade was certainly essential to the further progress of British Guiana, but the Negro had his own opinion about its value to his race. The Bush Negroes were a standing example to him of one road to freedom, and he was constantly looking for opportunities of escape and rebellion. In 1808 a Negro revolt was betrayed. The ringleaders were arrested. They consisted of "the drivers, tradesmen, and

[51] C.O. 111/68. Stephen to Hay, Feb. 18, 1829.
[52] Bolingbroke, *op. cit.*, p. 83.
[53] *Ibid.*, p. 86.

other most sensible slaves on the estates.''[54] The planters paid no heed. In 1823 another and more serious slave revolt broke out on the East Coast—''not an unnatural result,'' in the governor's words, ''of misconception as to the discussions and numerous publications that have lately occurred with respect to their state.''[55] The revolt had been so carefully and secretly planned that it took the planters unawares. The slaves demanded ''unconditional emancipation.'' They listened coldly to the governor's expostulations. ''These things they said were no comfort to them, God had made them of the same flesh and blood as the whites, and they were tired of being slaves to them, that they should be free and they would not work any more.''[56] The usual severities followed, the revolt was quelled and the planters went their way, unheeding, concerned solely with the continuance of martial law.[57]

But the Negroes continued restless. ''The spirit of discontent is anything but extinct,'' wrote the governor in the next year, ''it is alive as it were under its ashes, and the Negro mind although giving forth no marked indications of mischief to those not accustomed to observe it, is still agitated, jealous and suspicious.''[58] The home government recalled the governor in the year of the revolt; the Negroes interpreted this as involving ''something interesting to their prospects.''[59] The new governor cautioned against further delay, ''not only for the sake of the intrinsic humanity and policy of the measure, but that expectation and conjecture may cease, and the Negroes be released from that feverish anxiety which must and will continue to agitate them, until the question be definitely set at rest.''[60] The

[54] C.O. 111/8. Nicholson to Castlereagh, June 6, 1808.
[55] C.O. 111/39. Murray to Bathurst, Aug. 24, 1823.
[56] Ibid.
[57] Ibid. Murray to Bathurst, Sept. 27, 1823.
[58] C.O. 111/44. D'Urban to Bathurst, May 5, 1824.
[59] Ibid.
[60] Ibid., D'Urban to Bathurst, May 5, 1824 (Second letter).

governor toured the eastern division of the colony, and notified the home government that 50 plantations had been in revolt, embracing a population of 12,000. "Of one thing I am at any rate certain, that no state of the Negro mind could have been so dangerous as one of undefined and vague expectation."[61]

Thus, in 1833, the British Guiana planter stood with his back to the wall. A formidable combination of adversaries was arrayed against him—the British Government, the capitalists, the humanitarians, and the slaves. Escape was impossible. He was doomed. He could not fight his adversaries in England and his adversaries in Guiana at one and the same time. Whilst Britain was haggling over the price of his sugar, his slaves were refusing to produce that sugar. Emancipation was not only a moral necessity, as the humanitarians emphasized; not only an economic necessity, as the capitalists insisted; it was a political necessity as the slaves demanded. If the government had not stepped in to emancipate the slaves, the slaves would have emancipated themselves.

The first consequence of emancipation was its effect on the labor supply. The compensation per slave paid in British Guiana was nearly £52, in Barbados nearly £21, in Jamaica less than £20.[62] Labor, in other words, was at a premium in British Guiana, and could demand its price. This had nothing to do with race. It was an economic question. It was not the Negro who was responsible but the economic law of supply and demand. The former slaves found themselves in a position similar to that of the feudal villeins in Europe after the Black Death, which wiped out about one-half of the population. When two workers run after one employer wages fall, when two employers run after one worker wages rise.

This came into effect not in 1833 but in 1838. The Eman-

61 *Ibid.* D'Urban to Bathurst, May 15, 1824.
62 H. of C. Sess. Pap., Vol. 48, 1837-8, No. 64, Dec. 11, 1837.

cipation Act of 1833 retained the part-time services of the slaves, under the guise of apprenticeship, for seven years, later reduced to five. Schomburgk complains that the compensation paid to the planters was less than half of the purchase price of slaves from 1822 to 1830.[63] But the planters had had the services of these slaves prior to 1833, they were given the part-time services of the survivors up to 1838, and still received four million pounds. Yet they squawked.

According to Schomburgk, emancipation "was one of the most powerful means of promoting the in-born and hereditary indolence of the Negro." As indications of this he goes on to say: "every former labourer tried to purchase at the lowest rates his own piece of land: he could get his living from out of its produce with the minimum of trouble because his ordinary wants and the inexhaustible productiveness of the Tropics forced him to no great efforts. The scarcity of labour arising from this cause increased the daily pay to such an extent that the free Negro who worked for one or two days could earn enough to live as he liked, comfortably, for the remainder of the week."[64] Governor Barkly in 1849 echoed this sentiment. "The acquisition of a plot of ground," he wrote, "has not been so much the sign of superior intelligence or manly independence, as of unfounded suspicions or a love of uncivilized ease; the freeholders being, I am inclined to think, as a body far less industrious than the older and steadier Negroes, who from confidence in their employers and a desire to work continuously have remained on the plantations."[65]

The myth of the "laziness" of the Negro is one of the most mischievous legacies of the slavery period. Its origin lies in "the hypothesis," as the governor of Jamaica put it, "expressed or understood, that the system of husbandry pursued during slavery was alone suited to tropical cultiva-

[63] Schomburgk, op. cit., Vol. I, p. 23.
[64] Ibid., Vol. I, pp. 23-24.
[65] Clementi, op. cit., p. 174.

tion.''[66] The idea that subsistence farming was equivalent
to indolence was promptly repudiated in England. ''It is
impossible to suppose,'' wrote Lord Howick in the year before emancipation, ''that the slaves (who, though as I believe not more given to idleness than other men are certainly not less so) would if freed from control be induced
even by high wages to continue to submit to a drudgery
which they detest, while without doing so they could obtain land sufficient for their support.''[67] In this, as Lord
Russell pointed out, there was nothing singular or culpable.
No Englishman, who had sufficient capital to keep a shop or
rent a farm, would follow the plough as a day laborer or
work from morning till night as a hand-loom weaver. ''None
of the most inveterate opponents of our recent measures of
emancipation,'' continued Russell, ''allege that the Negroes
have turned robbers, or plunderers, or bloodthirsty insur-
gents. What appears from their statement is that they
have become shopkeepers, and petty traders, and hucksters,
and small freeholders; a blessed change. . . .'' And, in a
noble phrase, he ended by reminding the governor of British Guiana that ''the happiness of the inhabitants of the
colony you are appointed to govern is the chief object.''[68]

The emancipated slaves were willing to work after 1838,
but positively not as wage earners. This aspiration to
peasant proprietorship was clearly more easy of attainment
in British Guiana, with its open spaces, than in Barbados,
where all the land was appropriated. In 1839 six emancipated slaves bought ''Northbrook,'' an abandoned sugar
plantation on the east coast of Demerara, for which they
paid upwards of £2,000, two-thirds in hard cash. ''Orange
Nassau,'' a cotton plantation on the east coast, was bought
by 140 laborers for £11,000. Plantation ''Friendship'' was
purchased for £16,000, nearly half of this in cash. This plan-

[66] Bell and Morrell, op. cit., p. 427.
[67] Ibid., p. 385.
[68] Ibid., pp. 412, 415.

tation was originally purchased for £6,000, and was sold in 1839 for £10,000 before it was disposed of, at the higher rate, to former slaves.[69] As Governor Light wrote in 1839, this evidence "speaks volumes against the determined idleness of the Negro, which a party here would assert."[70]

But for those who, like Schomburgk, equated sugar production and the plantation economy with the prosperity and well-being of Guiana, emancipation was a blunder. The Negro "would be able to live just as much without food and drink, as without whacking."[71] This explains the suggestion made in Barbados that all the provision grounds of the former slaves should be destroyed, to compel the Negroes to work. The British Guiana planters themselves deliberately destroyed all the fruit trees, to deprive the emancipated slaves of a source of sustenance which competed with employment on the sugar plantation, and seriously considered, as late as 1917, a repetition of the procedure when indentured immigration came to an end.[72]

Thus emancipation, in the second place, forced the planter to develop alternative sources of labor. Catholic in his tastes, indifferent to racial questions, he tried Portuguese from Madeira, Maltese, Germans, West Indians from the British islands, and ultimately East Indians. By 1843, 30,000 had been brought in from different sources, but still the need continued.[73] The Europeans were totally unsatisfactory, but it was not the climate to blame. The Portuguese died like flies on the plantations, they multiplied when they took to retail trade. In 1838 two ships arrived with a total of 406 East Indian immigrants.[74] It was the first trickle of the future torrent. The sugar industry of British Guiana, built up by the Negro, was saved by the East Indian. Be-

[69] *Hansard*, Third Series, LXI, 1097-1098. Stanley, March 22, 1842.
[70] *Ibid.*
[71] Schomburgk, *op. cit.*, Vol. I, p. 51.
[72] Webber, *op. cit.*, pp. 168-169.
[73] Schomburgk, *op. cit.*, Vol. I, p. 27.
[74] Webber, *op. cit.*, p. 192.

tween 1835 and 1917, British Guiana imported a net total of 238,000 East Indians.[75]

Thirdly, British capital fled the colony after emancipation. As early as 1825 no one would advance a shilling on West Indian plantations, while British capital was pouring into the far corners of the earth.[76] A very large part of this compensation money never reached British Guiana at all, and was paid to absentee owners and creditors in England. The small slave owner in British Guiana not infrequently was forced to sell out his claim to speculators, and ultimately received sometimes no more than £12 instead of £50 per head.[77] In addition the British capitalists read correctly the signs of the times in England. Realizing that the West Indian sugar monopoly was on its last legs, they hastened to sell out their holdings while there was still time. The Gladstone family, for instance, which received the largest single sum—£85,000—paid out in compensation,[78] sponsored the first immigration of East Indians to British Guiana. When this failed, Gladstone sold out his interests and severed all connection with the colony.[79]

Inevitably, therefore, with the migration of labor from the plantation and the flight of capital from the colony, production declined. In British Guiana sugar exports fell 62 per cent between 1839 and 1842 as compared with the period 1831-1834.[80] "Windsor Castle" Plantation in the forties, appraised at $199,520, was unable to fetch $40,000.[81]

It was all very sad. The sugar planter in Cuba was a millionaire, in British Guiana he was a bankrupt. The West

[75] I. Ferenczi: *International Migrations* (New York, 1929), Vol. I, p. 506-509, 516-518.

[76] *Hansard*, New Series, XV, 385. Lord Redesdale, April 19, 1826.

[77] Webber, *op. cit.*, p. 167.

[78] H. of C. Sess. Pap., Vol. 48, 1837-8, No. 215. The exact sum was £85,606.0.2. for 2,183 slaves in British Guiana and Jamaica.

[79] Webber, *op. cit.*, p. 193.

[80] Burn, *op. cit.*, p. 367.

[81] Schomburgk, *op. cit.*, Vol. I, pp. 64-65.

Indians, now full of the milk of human kindness, began to
excoriate the slave trade to Cuba. A Parliamentary committee in 1831 rejected this explanation, and reminded the
West Indians that depression had "existed in former times,
and at periods anterior to the abolition of the Slave Trade."
Furthermore, the Committee advanced the possibility that
the superiority of the Cuban planter was due far more to
natural causes than the British West Indians were prepared to admit.[82] Natural causes, however, were far less
applicable to British Guiana than to Barbados. British
Guiana had an abundance of fertile land, like Cuba. But
while Cuba was carrying on the slave trade, British Guiana
had been forced to give it up and was denied even East Indian immigrants except on most onerous terms. For this
there were political reasons, connected with the development
of British economy and the trend of British party politics.[83]
Free trade was becoming a religion in England. The blow
which knocked out British Guiana and the British West Indies came not in 1838, with the abolition of apprenticeship,
but in 1846, with the equalization of the sugar duties. In
1846 West Indian production, as compared with the year
1831, had declined in the following proportions: sugar by
one-half, rum by nearly three-quarters, coffee by nearly
three-quarters.[84] As the West Indian sugar planter had been
warned fourteen years before, Britain had renounced
"those provisions of an exploded mercantile system, whereby failing trades have been supported, and uncongenial productions forced."[85] It was the abolition of monopoly and
not of slavery, it was free trade and not free labor, that
"ruined" British Guiana and the British West Indies. The

[82] *Select Committee to inquire into the Commercial State of the West India
Colonies*, pp. 17, 21.

[83] See Eric Williams: *Capitalism and Slavery.* Chapel Hill, N. C., 1944.

[84] *Hansard, Third Series*, XCIV, 692. Bentinck, July 23, 1847.

[85] *Select Committee to inquire into the Commercial State of the West India
Colonies*, p. 17.

architect of "ruin" was not the African free laborer but the British free trader.

* * * * *

Economically, British Guiana today is what it was a century ago, its difficulties aggravated. It is still sparsely populated, its hinterland still unknown. Capital still steers clear of the colony, at least in quantities commensurate with the size of the area. The upkeep of the sea defenses and the drainage and irrigation system still constitutes a severe drain on slender financial resources. The defenders of the plantation economy are still challenged by the protagonists of the subsistence farm. British Guiana's sugar, like the sugar of the British West Indian islands, is still seeking a remunerative market, the prospect of which recedes further and further into the background. The colony is as much a victim of world economy today as it was yesterday—of the religion of free trade in 1844, of the passion for autarchy in 1944.

ERIC WILLIAMS

Washington, D. C.

THE ENGLISH CAMPAIGN FOR ABOLITION OF THE SLAVE TRADE

I

For two centuries after Sir John Hawkins took his first wretched shipload of slaves to America in 1562 and chose to decorate his escutcheon, when knighted, with the representation of a Negro in chains, English opinion was little troubled by conscientious qualms about the injustice of forcing black folk into bondage. Positive official and legal sanctions and even religious apologetics bolstered and sustained the growing slavery system and the profitable trade that developed to supply the labor needs of the sugar islands and the English mainland colonies in America in the seventeeenth and eighteenth centuries.

But in the middle of the eighteenth century the system began to be challenged by scattered objectors. By 1780 their voices had risen to a chorus of protest that could not be ignored. Adam Smith opposed the trade as early as 1760 and in 1776 condemned it as unprofitable in his great work that was to become the textbook of economic statesmanship for the next generation.[1] Hannah More and Cowper penned plaintive poems on the plight of the Negroes, while the pontiff of eighteenth century letters, Dr. Samuel Johnson, dictated to his faithful Boswell an argument in favor of a slave claiming his liberty in the courts of Scotland and surprised grave associates at Oxford on one occasion with the toast, "Here's to the next insurrection of the Negroes in the West Indies!"[2] On academic rostra and in periodicals and pamphlets the abolitionist vanguard began chipping away at the stolid complacency of British opinion.

From pulpits and the conclaves of religious societies came the strongest protests. In the Established Church,

[1] Adam Smith, *An Inquiry into the Nature and Causes of the Wealth of Nations* (London, 1812), pp. 308, 542.

[2] James Boswell, *The Life of Samuel Johnson*, 3 vols. (London, 1924), Vol. II, p. 431.

William Wharton, bishop of Gloucester, and Beilby Porteus, bishop of Chester (later bishop of London) spoke out strongly against the traffic in human beings; and previous residence in the West Indies gave the Rev. James Ramsay, vicar of Teston, in Kent, a fund of first-hand observations to supply his preaching and pamphleteering utterances in the cause.[3] John Wesley, the father of Methodism, who also had been in America and seen the condition of the slaves, sharply attacked the system as inconsistent "with any degree of natural justice." He denounced slave owners and the "butchers" and "wolves" in the trade alike as partners in "fraud, robbery and murder," with hands and homes stained with African blood.[4] Better, wrote Wesley, that the sugar islands be sunk in the depths of the sea than that their prosperity should continue to be dependent upon the murder of "myriads of innocent men" and the enslaving of myriads more.

The most noteworthy early remonstrances were made by the Quakers. George Fox, founder of the sect, carried his denunciations into the heart of the slave area, with sermons in Barbados as early as 1671. There his fellow traveler, William Edmundson, was haled before the governor charged with the offense of trying to Christianize some of the slaves on the island.[5] In 1727 the annual meeting of the Quaker Society in London passed a resolution of censure against Quakers engaging in the slave trade. Successive resolutions (1758, 1761, 1783) threatened and provided for expulsion of members of the sect who persisted in the traffic or abetted it even to the extent of selling or providing

[3] Thomas Clarkson, *The History of the Rise, Progress and Accomplishment of the Abolition of the African Slave-Trade by the British Parliament* (Wilmington, 1816), p. 47.

[4] John Wesley, *Thoughts Upon Slavery*, in Works, Vol. VI, p. 292; see also John Dixon Long, *Pictures of Slavery in Church and State* (Philadelphia, 1867), p. 398.

[5] Clarkson, *op. cit.*, pp. 50-51.

any supplies for slave ships.[6] In 1783 the English Quakers petitioned parliament for prohibition of the trade as "an oppression which, in the injustice of its origin, and the inhumanity of its progress, has not . . . been exceeded, or even equalled, in the most barbarous ages."[7] In the same year they formed a propaganda committee to reach public opinion with articles contributed to the press, particularly provincial newspapers.[8]

In 1772 anti-slavery crusaders were given new vantage-ground by the important judicial decision of Lord Mansfield emancipating all slaves in England—a smashing blow at the established legal sanctions of long standing. Most directly it reversed the ruling opinion rendered in 1729 by Attorney General Philip York and Solicitor General Charles Talbot that "a slave by coming from the West Indies into Great Britain or Ireland, either with or without his master, does not become free."[9] Since 1729 advertisements in the English press for runaways and the slave-chasing practices of owners had helped stir humanitarian opposition. They evoked especially the active efforts of Granville Sharp, who deserves place among the half dozen greatest agitators of the cause. He interested himself decisively in the plight of James Somersett, a slave brought into England and there brutally abused and, when he became sick, turned off by his master, who, however, sought to kidnap and recover him after Sharp and others had restored the man's health. Somersett's claims to freedom, pushed by Sharp as the clearest of a series of cases upon which he had been seeking to establish the emancipation principle in the courts, led to Lord Mansfield's epoch-making decision holding that so soon as a slave set foot

---

[6] *Ibid.*, p. 52.

[7] *The Case of Our Fellow-Creatures, the Oppressed Africans, Respectfully Recommended to the Serious Consideration of the Legislature of Great Britain by the People Called Quakers* (London, 1784), p. 1.

[8] Clarkson, op. cit., pp. 56-57.

[9] *Ibid.*, p. 38.

upon English soil he became free.[10] Though not touching the slave trade or slave-holding in the colonies, the decision heartened humanitarians and spurred abolitionist efforts.

II.

A definite new starting point in the campaign was marked with the formation on May 22, 1787, of the Committee for Abolition of the Slave Trade.[11] It was an outgrowth of the agitation by Quakers, nine of the twelve on the original committee being members of that sect. Sharp, one of the three non-Quaker members, was made its chairman.

Another non-Quaker member, Thomas Clarkson, was destined soon to be the most active and energetic mover of public opinion in the cause. This young man had all the zealotry of the earnestly convinced reformer. His interest in the plight of the slaves, kindled by a Latin essay contest which he won in 1785, burned unflaggingly, with a consuming passion, through years of struggle and discouragement till the final triumph.

His incentive to write the essay which, translated, with additions and changes, became an important piece of antislavery propaganda, came from the Rev. Dr. Peckard, vicechancellor of Cambridge University, who in 1784 had preached to the university body against the slave trade and the next year proposed as subject for a student essay contest: "Is It Right To Make Slaves of Others Against Their Will?" The prize essayist's conclusion was an emphatic negative, with the declaration that the slave trade ought to be continued only "if murder is strictly honorable, and Christianity is a lie."[12] Clarkson's search for materials

[10] Edward Charles Ponsonby Lascelles, *Granville Sharp and the Freedom of Slaves in England* (London, 1928), pp. 32-33.

[11] Clarkson, *op. cit.*, p. 93.

[12] Thomas Clarkson, *An Essay on the Slavery and Commerce of the Human Species, Particularly the African* (Georgetown, 1816), p. 175.

confronted him impressively with the enormities of the traffic, especially as revealed in the book of Anthony Benezet, the American Quaker school-master.[13] The stark and harrowing facts had a profound and gripping effect on his mind and emotions.

"It was but one gloomy subject from morning to night. In the day-time I was uneasy. In the night, I had little rest. I sometimes never closed my eyelids for grief. It became now not so much a trial for academical reputation, as for the production of a work, which might be useful to injured Africa. And keeping this end in mind . . . I always slept with a candle in my room, that I might rise out of bed and put down such thoughts as might occur to me in the night, if I judged them valuable, conceiving that no arguments of any moment should be lost in so great a cause. . . . On returning . . . to London, the subject . . . almost wholly engrossed my thoughts. I became at times very seriously affected while on the road. I tried to persuade myself in these intervals that the contents of my Essay could not be true. . . . A thought then came into my mind that if the contents of the Essay were true, it was time some person should see these calamities to their end."[14]

Clarkson, led to complete self-dedication to the cause, became a timely and forceful instrument as chief investigator and propagandist for the newly formed abolition committee, in whose interest for years he journeyed, wrote and agitated indefatigably to the limit of overtaxed physical powers.

The committee early established contact with the other most outstanding leader of the abolition campaign, William Wilberforce, a man of no less impassioned and persistent zeal than Clarkson, moved by the force of a striking religious conversion to a thorough devotion to humanitarian causes. Wilberforce's precocious interest in abolition was reflected when at the age of fourteen he wrote a letter to a York newspaper "in condemnation of the odious traffic in

[13] Anthony Benezet, *Some Historical Account of Guinea, Its Situation, Produce, and the General Disposition of Its Inhabitants; With an Inquiry Into the Rise and Progress of the Slave-Trade, Its Nature and Lamentable Effects* (London, 1772).

[14] Clarkson, *History*, p. 77.

human flesh.''[15] But the tendencies of his early youth were redirected. His mother, fearful of the effects of a morbid piety on his physically frail constitution, successfully turned his interests into channels of social gaiety. Elected to parliament from York at the age of twenty, as soon as he had completed his university studies at Cambridge, where he was a fellow-student and friend of William Pitt, he plunged into a London life of dissipation.

Then the course of his career was suddenly, sharply changed again. During a tour on the continent in 1785 with a young clergyman, Isaac Milner, their discussions led to an experience of religious conversion that filled Wilberforce's journal with entries of self-castigating introspection and sent him back to England with a purpose to devote his career to the advancement of reform causes.[16] Thenceforward, spending himself in what he conceived to be his divinely ordained mission, he was the principal parliamentary exponent of abolition.

III.

Suppression of the slave trade rather than total emancipation was conceived by the abolition committee to be the immediate objective toward which parliamentary effort could be most practicably directed.[17] A preliminary campaign of public education having been determined upon, Clarkson was dispatched to Liverpool and Bristol, the chief slave ports, on the first of his notable tours of investigation, in search of information and witnesses whose testimony would strengthen the parliamentary attack. Also within a year £2,700 was received by the committee in subscriptions

[15] Robert I. and Samuel Wilberforce, *The Life of William Wilberforce,* 2 vols. (Philadelphia, 1841), Vol. I, p. 17.

[16] *Ibid.*, Vol. I, p. 77.

[17] To other considerations of practical expediency were added constitutional doubts, in line with the philosophy of the American Revolution, as to the power of parliament to interfere in internal colonial affairs, though a regulation of commerce would be more readily conceded. See Robert Livingston Schuyler, *Parliament and the British Empire* (New York, 1929), pp. 118-119.

to be used in broadcasting thousands of copies of anti-slavery tracts. These, together with the stimulation of public meetings, had the effect of flooding parliament with abolition petitions.

In response to this popular demonstration, Pitt, on May 9, 1788, in the absence of Wilberforce, then ill and believed to be near death, moved in the house of commons, without stating his opinion of the subject, that early in the next session parliament take up the "circumstances of the slave trade, complained of in the said petitions, and what may be fit to be done thereupon."[18] This was the opening of a parliamentary siege that was to be continued for twenty years before the trade could be legislatively battered to pieces.

The first debate brought into play both Burke and Fox, whose voices were to be repeatedly heard in the cause—Fox in this session arguing for immediate abolition rather than postponement. Also in this first debate the long and stubborn opposition of the slave trade interests asserted itself in speeches of the Liverpool members, Lord Penrhyn and Mr. Gascoyne.[19] But the resolution, as introduced, was agreed to unanimously. Pending consideration at the next session, a privy council investigation of the trade was authorized by the crown.

Not content to let the whole question drift another year, Sir William Dolben gained permission to introduce a bill to mitigate the miseries of the middle passage by slightly reducing the number of slaves a ship could carry in proportion to tonnage.[20] Even this was strenuously resisted as ruinous by the Liverpool interests. They sent witnesses to testify that the voyage from Africa to the West Indies

[18] Clarkson, *History*, p. 154.

[19] W. O. Blake, *The History of Slavery and the Slave Trade* (Columbus, 1860), p. 190.

[20] *An Act to Regulate the Carrying of Slaves*, in *Documents Illustrative of the History of the Slave Trade to America*, edited by Elizabeth Donnan, 3 vols. (Washington, 1931), Vol. II, pp. 582-589.

"was one of the happiest periods of a Negro's life," during which the slaves made merry and danced upon the deck—though under cross-examination by Pitt and others the dancing, it was discovered, consisted in the slaves, under persuasion of the lash, being forced to jump up and down in their chains for exercise, and the horrors of the middle passage were proved out of the mouths of the slavers' own witnesses.[21] The regulatory measure finally passed, but only by a close vote in the House of Lords, where Thurlow, the lord chancellor, reprehended "this sudden fit of philanthropy," unjustly allowed to "disturb the public mind, and to become the occasion of bringing men to the metropolis with tears in their eyes and horror in their countenance, to deprecate the ruin of their property, which they had embarked on the faith of parliament."[22]

In the taking of evidence before the privy council committee, a process that consumed four months, the anti-slavery elements felt themselves at a severe disadvantage. For while the commercial and planter interests could readily mobilize phalanxes of witnesses directly or formerly connected with the trade and eager, out of self-interest, to paint gloomy pictures of commercial ruin through its suppression and blandly to minimize its cruelties, Clarkson as the abolitionist emissary had to scour the kingdom for competent witnesses who knew the facts about the traffic from direct experience and were willing to face the possible consequences of making their knowledge a matter of official record. Journeying 1,600 miles in two months, a considerable undertaking in the days of stage-coach transportation, he could find only nine persons willing to testify out of forty-seven interviewed — and was discomfited when one Norris, formerly engaged in the trade, who had promised

[21] Clarkson, *History*, p. 168; see also Alexander Falconbridge, *An Account of the Slave Trade on the Coast of Africa* (London, 1788), pp. 23 ff.

[22] Clarkson, *History*, p. 168.

to testify against it, turned up as a spokesman for the Liverpool merchants.[23]

Finally the council after having given nearly all its attention to taking the pro-slavery evidence, pleaded the shortness of time remaining and would admit testimony of but three abolition witnesses, "while our opponents, on the other hand," as Clarkson asserts, "on account of their superior advantages, had mustered all their forces, not having omitted a single man.[24] But the Liverpool witnesses had been subjected to searching cross-examination. The report that emerged was more favorable to the abolitionist cause than anticipated. It had the important effect of leading Pitt to conclude that suppression of the trade would not be commercially ruinous.[25]

IV.

Moving to take up the anti-slavery petitions, the privy council report and other evidence previously taken, Wilberforce on May 13, 1789, launched into his first great parliamentary speech on the slave trade, dwelling eloquently on its evils and seeking to blast the argument that its suppression would be economically disastrous.[26] With telling effect he cited testimony of the Liverpool slavers' own witnesses, to depict the horrors of the middle passage — the fetid squalor of the slave ships, their breathless, crowded misery between decks, and the ravages of disease and death in their human cargoes.[27] The planters, he contended, if the trade were abolished would still have an adequate labor supply, through natural increase if the slaves were well treated, a

[23] Norris for his change of front received the formal thanks of the Liverpool Corporation, which further expressed its gratitude after his death by granting his widow a life annuity of £100. Gomer Williams, *History of the Liverpool Privateers and Letters of Marque With an Account of the Liverpool Slave Trade* (London, 1897), p. 576.

[24] Clarkson, *History*, p. 186.

[25] *Ibid.*, p. 191.

[26] *Ibid.*

[27] William Wilberforce, *Speech on Wednesday, the 13th of May, 1789, on the Abolition of the Slave Trade* (London, 1789), pp. 12-18.

contention supported by statistical computations.[28] He refuted the claim that Liverpool commerce would be ruined by showing that the African trade amounted to only one-fifteenth of the total shipping of that port.[29] As to the argument that ending the trade would menace the supply of seamen for the British navy, he showed that, on the contrary, because of hard usage and disease more sailors died every year in the slave trade than in all the rest of the British ocean marine in two years, with an annual mortality on the slavers of close to a quarter of the total personnel of their crews. Of the 3,170 seamen who sailed out of Liverpool in slave ships in 1787, he declared, only 1,428 returned, 642 dying or being lost, and 1,110 being discharged or deserting because of ill treatment[30]—conclusions which had been worked out painstakingly by Clarkson through careful comparative study of the muster rolls of slavers and other merchant ships.[31]

Burke, Pitt, Fox, William Smith and Grenville ably supported and supplemented Wilberforce's arguments, but Penrhyn and Gascoyne, the Liverpool members, angrily declared facts about the trade were being garbled and distorted, while the London members, Newnham, Sawbridge and Watson, asserted that abolition would menace the commercial interests of the metropolis.[32] The debate, in its arguments and alignments, was typical of those that were to follow from year to year as action was put off with dilatory and obstructive maneuvers by representatives of the vested interests threatened.

The slave trade proponents were put in the strange position in this first debate of having to try to discredit the evidence of their own witnesses who had testified be-

[28] William Wilberforce, *Speech* etc., 28, 34.

[29] *Ibid.*, p. 36.

[30] *Ibid.*, p. 37.

[31] Thomas Clarkson, *Essay on the Impolicy of the African Slave Trade* (London, 1788), pp. 44-67.

[32] Clarkson, *History*, pp. 214-218.

fore the privy council. They secured delay by demanding that more evidence be adduced, which meant putting the matter over till the next session.[33] Delay played into the hands of slavery interests, for as Clarkson declares :[34]

"Though we had foiled our opponents at their own weapons, and had experienced the uninterrupted good wishes and support of the public, we had the great mortification to see the enthusiasm of members of parliament beginning to cool; to see a question of humanity and justice . . . verging toward that of commercial calculation."

When, after the hearing of further evidence, Wilberforce presented his next abolition motion in 1791, it was lost by a vote of 163 to 88.[35] The next year supporters of the trade scored a further victory by pledging the house to the principle of gradual rather than immediate abolition, then taking no further action to carry out even that principle.[36]

V.

Regularly thereafter in each session till 1800 Wilberforce continued to introduce his abolition motions, and as regularly they were beaten. Added to the economic arguments with which the slave trade forces overbore humanitarian considerations were the new tactics, as the French Revolution progressed, of tarring the abolitionists with the odium of "Jacobinism" and attempting to associate them

[33] However, a select summary of the testimony made a tract of forceful appeal for the abolition cause: *Abstract of the Evidence Delivered Before a Select Committee of the House of Commons in the Years 1790, and 1791; on the Part of the Petitioners for the Abolition of the Slave Trade* (London, 1791). In refutation, the pro-slavery interests put out an opposing summary concluding that their "kind treatment and happy situation" being proved by the evidence, there was "absurdity in calling by the name of slaves people who are no more so than Parish Apprentices in England, except as to Duration." *A Summary of the Evidence Produced Before the Committee of the Privy Council and Before a Committee of the House of Commons Relating to the Slave Trade* (London, 1792).

[34] Clarkson, *History*, p. 230.

[35] *Ibid.*, p. 289.

[36] *Ibid.*, p. 317.

in the public mind with the bloody sansculottes of France, with such a ''leveler'' as Tom Paine and with farfetched blame for the sanguinary insurrection in San Domingo.[37] The facts that Clarkson had gone to France in 1789 to attempt to have Mirabeau and other French statesmen move for French co-operation in a policy of English abolition and that the Convention had made Wilberforce an honorary citizen of the French republic were used to support these arguments.

Summarizing the fluctuation of parliamentary opinion, Clarkson records :[38]

''In the year 1787, the members of the House of Commons, as well as the people, were enthusiastic in behalf of the abolition of the trade. In the year 1788, the fair enthusiasm of the former began to fade. In 1789, it died. In 1790, prejudice started up as a noxious weed in its place. In 1791 this prejudice arrived at its growth. But to what were these changes owing? To delay; during which the mind, having been gradually led to the question, as a commercial, had been gradually taken from it, as a moral object. Add to which, that the nation had never deserted the cause during this whole period.''

But poor Clarkson himself was *hors de combat* before the nadir of abolition prospects was reached in the mid-nineties. With his nervous system shattered, memory and hearing impaired, a constant ''confused singing in his ears'' while the floor ''seemed to dance up and down'' under him, he was utterly unable to continue the fight. ''For seven years I had a correspondence to maintain with four hundred persons, with my own hand,'' he records. ''I had some book or other annually to write in behalf of the cause. In this time I had traveled more than thirty-five thousand miles, in search of evidence, and a great part of these journeys in the night. All this time my mind had been on the stretch. The various instances of barbarity, which had come successively to my knowledge within this period, had

[37] Clarkson, *History*, p. 254.
[38] *Ibid.*, pp. 291-292.

vexed, harassed and afflicted it."[39] Disappointment as well as fatigue preyed upon him, and also the importunities of witnesses whom he had induced to testify and who when harassed by the slavery interest in reprisal "came to me, when thus persecuted, as the author of their miseries and their ruin."

Yet even in these years of apparent hopelessness, the effects of propaganda were not all one-sided. So powerfully had the abolition agitation wrought upon the minds of the masses, creating a sense of the deep moral iniquity of slavery, that when parliament in 1791 and 1792 failed to give any apparent heed to more than 300 popular petitions that poured in during those years, a far-reaching movement to boycott the products of slave labor began and was actively encouraged by more propaganda. One pamphleteer went so far as to assert: "Every person who habitually consumes one article of West Indian produce, raised by Slaves, is guilty of the crime of murder."[40] Other appeals passed beyond pleas based on moral obligation by attempting to arouse disgust and nausea, with revolting versons of how West Indian sugar and rum were produced. Naked, perspiring slaves were employed to tramp down the sugar in the casks, it was recited, while "the whole body of a roasted Negro" lately had been discovered in a cask of rum ordered from Jamaica.[41]

So widespread did the boycott become that West Indian interests were alarmed and launched defensive counterblasts. Old ladies gave up sugar in their tea. Even children abjured candy. Clarkson in his journeyings in 1791

[39] *Ibid.*, p. 325.

[40] Thomas Cooper, *Considerations on the Slave Trade; and the Consumption of West Indian Produce* (London, 1791), quoted in Lowell Joseph Ragatz, *The Fall of the Planter Class in the British Caribbean, 1763-1833* (New York, 1928), p. 261.

[41] William Fox, *On the Propriety of Abstaining from West-India Sugar and Rum* (London, 1791) and *A Second Address to the People of Great Brtain: Containing a New, and Most Powerful Argument to Abstain from the Use of West India Sugar* (Rochester, 1792), quoted in Ragatz, *op. cit.*, pp. 262-263.

found no community in which people had not begun to abstain from sweets, as many as 500 persons being involved in the boycott in certain of the larger towns, while in some places grocers ceased dealing in West Indian products. "By the best computation I was able to make, from notes taken down in my journey," he writes, "no fewer than three hundred thousand persons had abandoned the use of sugar."[42] However extravagant that estimate may be, the demand for free labor products induced a ten-fold increase in English consumption of East Indian sugar from 1791 to 1793, at the expense of that of the West Indies.[43]

VI.

After a lapse of five years, Wilberforce and the abolition committee in 1804 felt encouraged to renew a trial of strength in parliament. A principal heartening factor was accession, with the Act of Union, of the new strength of the Irish members, favorable to abolition. The phobic fears of Jacobinism likewise had moderated. Moreover, West Indian opposition was slightly relaxed, with sugar production currently exceeding demand, lessening the need for an increased labor supply.[44]

Hopes were at first fulfilled when Wilberforce's motion won in the Commons by a vote of 124 to 49; but frustration came in the House of Lords, which laid the measure over till the next session. Overconfidence next year meant a setback in the Commons and defeat 77 to 70—a blow that Wilberforce regarded as the most painful of his parliamentary experience.[45] The abolition committee, however, considering the carelessness which had caused absences the night of the adverse vote, felt assured of success at the next session if proper preparation were made.

Clarkson, his health now restored, plunged back into the

---

[42] Clarkson, *History*, p. 295.
[43] Ragatz, *op. cit.*, p. 264.
[44] Wilberforce, *Life of William Wilberforce*, Vol. I, p. 306.
[45] *Ibid.*, p. 314.

fray and was dispatched on another journey to gather new evidence and witnesses in case they should be called for. Old friends of the cause he found steadfast, but with the interruption of propaganda efforts for a number of years, the rising generation, he discovered, was not well informed about slavery evils, though receptive to his exhortations.[46]

In January, 1806, Pitt's death removed a statesman who had grown somewhat lukewarm in support of the cause during the days of its waning strength. Into his place as prime minister came Fox, an unflaggingly consistent advocate, who avowed the ending of the slave trade to be the primary object of his ministry, and who even from his death bed a few months later eagerly followed the final phases of the parliamentary struggle.[47]

A test of strength early in 1806 on a measure to prohibit British ships and merchants from engaging in the supply of slaves to foreigners brought success in both houses. Thereupon Fox flung his full force behind a resolution for suppression of the whole trade "with all practicable expedition," opening the debate with the assertion that if he could carry it, and if he had done nothing else but this in a parliamentary career of forty years, he would "think my life well spent . . . and . . . retire quite satisfied that I had not lived in vain."[48] The measure scored a one-sided triumph by a vote of 114 to 15.[49] This time, guided by Lord Grenville, it also passed the upper house. While declaratory of the sentiment of parliament that the slave trade was inhumane, unjust and subject to suppression as soon as "practicable," this resolution did not actually provide statutory abolition, which awaited the final crucial test (though the conclusion was nearly a foregone one) at the next session. Meanwhile Fox was removed from the head of affairs by death, as Pitt

[46] Clarkson, *History*, p. 332.

[47] *Ibid.*, p. 343.

[48] *Substance of the Debates on a Resolution for Abolishing the Slave Trade* (London, 1806), p. 1.

[49] Clarkson, *History*, p. 337.

had been a few months previously, depriving the cause of his powerful leadership.

In the session of 1807, new tactics were determined upon, reversing previous procedure by launching the first attack in the House of Lords. There the opposition was led by the future king, William IV, then Duke of Clarence, whose attachment to the planter interest had begun during his tours of naval duty in the West Indies.[50] But ably marshalled by Grenville, the abolitionists mustered 100 votes to 35 when the division came at 4 o'clock in the morning of January 6. Thence the bill proceeded on a triumphant progress through the popular chamber, with even one of the members for Liverpool now joining in its support. With success assured, the house burst into enthusiastic cheers for Wilberforce as Sir Samuel Romilly acclaimed him as more to be envied in this impending victory of his long-fought cause than Napoleon at the summit of his imperial glory. The triumph scored on February 24, with a vote of 283 to 16, was decisive and irrevocable. ''Well, what shall we abolish next?'' was Wilberforce's smiling comment to friends.[51] Under terms of the abolition statute, no slavers were to clear from ports in the United Kingdom after May 1, 1807, and no slaves were to be landed in the colonies after March 1 of the following year.

Consternation greeted the event in the West Indies, where rumblings of an abortive independence movement began. In England a costly attempt to wreak vengeance on Wilberforce was made when he had to stand for re-election upon dissolution of parliament on the very day that royal assent was given the abolition measure. Faced by two opposing candidates, for the first time since the beginning of his parliamentary career he was given serious opposition in his Yorkshire district. One of his adversaries, Henry Lascelles, holder of extensive estates in Barbados,

---

50 Ragatz, *op. cit.*, Note, p. 276.

51 John Stoughton, *William Wilberforce* (London, 1880), p. 76.

avowed himself willing to part with all his West Indian property, if necessary, to triumph over Wilberforce. The latter's friends raised an election fund of £65,000 in his behalf,[52] while his opponents together spent more than £200,-000. After a hectic struggle, with the polls kept open for a fortnight, the great humanitarian finally squeaked through to victory by a narrow plurality of 629 in a total vote of 33,972.[53]

VII.

Beyond suppression of the slave trade loomed the more distant goal of emancipation throughout the empire. Beginning actively in 1823, the campaign to that end was pushed for a decade in much the fashion of the fight on the African trade. Just a month before his death in 1833, the venerable Wilberforce, his mantle of parliamentary leadership transferred to his younger disciple, Thomas Buxton, saw the reformed parliament decree general emancipation.

Whatever feeling of elation others had in 1808 upon the successful issue of their long struggle to suppress the slave trade, to the minds of the two devoutly religious chief leaders of the campaign, Wilberforce and Clarkson, it came as a climactic manifestation of the interposition of the guiding hand of Providence in the affairs of men. "For himself, all selfish triumph was lost in unfeigned gratitude to God," say Wilberforce's sons in their life of him, reproducing the entries of thanksgiving and pious invocation that he poured into his diary at this time, as indeed at most other stages of what he conceived to be his divinely ordained work.[54] "Rejoice in the manner of its termination," Clarkson adjures readers of his history of the long contest, "and, if thou feelest grateful for the event, retire within thy closet, and pour out thy thanksgiving to the Almighty for this his

[52] Only £28,000 of this sum was spent, the remainder being returned. Wilberforce, *Life*, Vol. II, p. 34.

[53] *Ibid.*, Vol. II, p. 33.

[54] *Ibid.*, Vol. II, p. 26.

unspeakable act of mercy, to thy oppressed fellow creatures.''[55]

Slave trade suppression came as the earliest great achievement of the new humanitarianism, which brought the impulses of new reforming zeal, (produced largely by the Wesleyan and Evangelical movements) to bear upon the tremendous tasks of amelioration and social sanitation that, for their accomplishment, like the Augean task of Hercules, had long awaited the forceful flow of such a fresh and cleansing current.

LOUIS TAYLOR MERRILL

Beloit College

[55] Clarkson, *History,* p. 348.

THOMAS POWNALL AND HIS NEGRO COMMONWEALTH

Among the eighteenth century Englishmen who were outspoken in advocating Negro emancipation was Governor Thomas Pownall (1722-1805). Although almost forgotten by modern historians who remember him only as the author of *The Administration of the Colonies,* his influence was considerable and his versatility remarkable. He left his mark as colonial governor of Massachusetts during three critical years of the French and Indian War (1757-1760), as an author of two dozen tracts and books on nearly every aspect of British and American life, as a member of the House of Commons during the American Revolution, and as a political philosopher and antiquarian. His wide experience and familiarity with American life made him an accepted spokesman on colonial institutions.[1]

His knowledge of American life made him sympathetic with the colonists and, after the capture of Burgoyne in 1777, a parliamentary advocate of American independence. He believed early independence would salvage American trade for Great Britain and would preserve the many intangibles of friendship. A fight to a finish would give the trade to France and make Britain and America forever hostile. These ideas were most fully expressed in his *A Memorial Addressed to the Sovereigns of America* (1783), which treatise sets forth his views on Negro slavery and his plans for emancipation.

Pownall strangely anticipated the terms of British emancipation in 1833, and his plans of 1783 were as illogical as those of the Act half a century later. He favored (1) gradual emancipation in which the Negro during a period of apprenticeship would work out the price of his freedom

[1] This article is a side light on a larger, unpublished study of Thomas Pownall's life. The most authoritive, lengthy account on Pownall in print is William Otis Sawtelle, "Thomas Pownall Colonial Governor," *Proceedings* of the Massachusetts Historical Society, LXIII (1930), 233-284.

and gain the character to be worthy of his liberty; or (2) something approaching immediate emancipation in which the master would be compensated by the state and the Negro given his immediate freedom. The Negro, in either event, was to remain a valuable, if not indeed an indispensable, part of American society. As a result of his liberation the Negro "emerging to liberty . . . will become what the American community most wants, a beneficial Supply of Laborers, Farmers upon rent, Mechanics and Manufacturers."[2] His plan, he was certain, would appeal to the Americans, for they, in winning their independence, would look favorably upon other oppressed people with kindred feelings.

Pownall did not actively associate with the anti-slavery reformers who gained strength rapidly after the formation of the Abolition Society in 1787.[3] Like many of these men, he was influenced by his study of Locke, Montesquieu, and Adam Smith. By nature a scholar he arrived at many of his conclusions through his philosophical investigations. He held the theory that the equality of every person was ordained by nature, and he denied that distinctions between human beings could be made on the basis of color.[4]

About two decades after his address to America, when he was in his eightieth year, Pownall presented his ideas on equality of Negro capacity with that of the white man and his rights to equality of treatment in economic life and political action. In his *A Memorial Addressed to the Sovereigns of Europe and the Atlantic* (1803) he called for emancipation on the ground that the Negro has the "capacity, powers, and rights of a human being."[5] He did not

[2] Thomas Pownall, *A Memorial Addressed to the Sovereigns of America* (London, 1783), 108-109.

[3] Frank J. Klingberg, *The Anti-Slavery Movement in England* (New Haven, 1926), 73-74.

[4] Thomas Pownall, *Principles of Polity* (London, 1752), 108,109, 140.

[5] Gov. Pownall, *Memorial Addressed to the Sovereigns of Europe and the Atlantic* (London, 1803), 92.

believe that the Negro was a colored white man, but he felt that the Negroes were capable of the same intellectual development if they had an opportunity. In brief, he held that, while the capacities of the Negro were the equal of those of the white man, they were not necessarily identical. In fact, he asserted that there were then in the West Indies some Negroes ready to form an independent government because of their "watching experience" in observing the European rule of their country. To this small number of Negroes "The intercourse, movements, and acts of organized civil government are, by watching experience, known to a sufficient number of particulars amongst them, so as to give that class, *whenever occasion calls forth act,* the means of taking a lead and forming a command which may carry them to every degree of civil organization in government. They feel and know the power as it exists in capacity, so as to give unity and activity to a number of their own class, out of all proportion superior to the European class of inhabitants."[6]

In short, Pownall envisioned a broadening of political control in the West Indies very similar to that championed in Britain in the closing decades of the eighteenth century and actually carried out during the nineteenth and twentieth centuries. It is obvious that, in this *Memorial* just as in his earlier tracts on the American Revolution, he advocated compromise and mutual agreement between white and black before mass Negro rebellion would destroy the white man in the British islands as it had done in Santo Domingo in the 1790's. With these ideas in mind, in his *Memorial* he predicted a great destiny for the Negroes in the West Indies and demanded the establishment of a British Negro Commonwealth as their brothers had done in Santo Domingo. In the American republic the Negro was to be accepted as part of the social order and not colonized back to Africa. In the British American tropics, the white man

[6] *Ibid.,* 93-94.

was to be accepted as part of that social order and not colonized back to Europe. The then unsettled, "revolutionary state of things" of 1803 would grow worse, he asserted, until rebellion would forcibly drive the Europeans from the West Indies.[7] Any repression on the part of England and France to stop this rise of the Negro commonwealth would be futile and lead to unnecessary bloodshed. Instead, the European powers should be prepared to guarantee the West Indians peace and commercial prosperity and recognize the Negroes of the area when they apparently became united, as another independent nation. Their brilliant future as members of an independent West Indian nation, he said, was no secret to the Negroes. Already they had laid the foundation for a nation by the bloody display of force at Santo Domingo. This same kind of rebellion might also be expected in other West Indian islands if a farsighted policy were not formulated by the Europeans. The "only mischief and danger is, the supposing that it can be made a secret of, instead of preparing to meet the event, and providing, as far as human means will admit, to meet this revolution, with such arrangements and measures as may secure a co-existence with it."[8]

The new Negro commonwealth would lay down certain rules for the holding of land in the islands, Pownall predicted, which would bring to an end the exclusive monopoly of the European in the region. There would still be European planters and European controlled estates, but some limitation in the "acquisition of wealth" must be expected. Nevertheless, "it would become the Negro's interest, in every line of interest, to promote, secure, and maintain such settlements of Enuropeans or Americans as would create to them a market of export, but more especially of supply."[9] These rules too would extend to the employment

[7] Governor Pownall, *Memorial*, 94.
[8] *Ibid.*, 96.
[9] *Ibid.*, 98.

of the Negro, who would be hired to the foreigners on contract. The guiding principles apparently would be the protection of the Negro so that he would not fall back into servitude and the encouragement of European interests by insuring them a constant labor supply.

Anti-slavery men in Britain generally met the economic problems of the freedman by picturing him in the possession of a home and a small farm. But just how he was to be transmuted from being a piece of property himself to being a land owner remained a problem unsolved. How to escape slavery and not land in grinding tenancy baffled reformers. Pownall saw this question clearly enough and had as a major solution the creating of a Negro commonwealth which would promote the rights to the land of the freedman without, however, liquidating the lands of the whites. This problem largely defied solution then and still awaits a satisfactory answer for black and white alike.

Pownall's denunciations of the slave of the slave regime, slave trade, and slavery, were much the same as those of James Ramsey, William Wilberforce and Thomas Clarkson, "a wretched policy," and the making of human beings into "the most humiliated beasts of labour."[10] But distinctly new was his idea of a Negro commonwealth, which has a certain imaginative freshness about it that makes it very modern especially when considered in the light of schemes for Negro states in Africa. The African immigrant, who had built tropical America, was like the European immigrant to have a chance to erect his commonwealths on the soil of his productive triumphs. Within the last half of Pownall's life the Negro came to be regarded not as a "beast of labour," but as a man to be charged with the management of his own destiny. This revolution Pownall not only witnessed but promoted.

JOHN A. SCHUTZ

University of California, Los Angeles

[10] *Ibid.*, 91-92.

NEGRO EDUCATION IN ANTE BELLUM MISSOURI

The history of Missouri, containing as it does the Indian, French, Spanish, as well as the American background, rivals that of any state in the Union, if we were to consider antiquity or variety. Marquette and Joliet discovered the mouth of the Missouri as early as 1673, and sixty-two years later the French had established the first permanent settlement at Ste. Genevieve. The more advantageously situated St. Louis was first settled by Laclede and the Louisiana Fur Company in 1764. In 1770 the Spanish took over the Louisiana Territory, but only briefly, for the Treaty of Ildefonso in 1800 gave the whole region back to France, and France promptly sold it to the United States, which took it over on March 26, 1804.

It must be added that, though 1735 was the date of the first settlement in what is now Missouri, it was not until 1769 that the first permanent settlement west of St. Louis was made, at St. Charles. The Boones made their famous trek further into Missouri in 1807. In 1810 Franklin, in what is now Howard County, was settled. When the Missouri Territory was organized in 1812, there were only five counties clustered on the Mississippi. Howard (1816), Cooper (1818), and Boone (1820) were the next to be organized, showing the development along the other principal waterway, the Missouri.

Administratively, the rule of Missouri was varied, even under American sovereignty. An Act of Congress in 1803 put the whole Louisiana Territory under the direction of the President. He made Amos Stoddard commandant of the Upper Louisiana district. An act of Congress in the following year divided the Louisiana Territory into two halves, the Territory of Orleans and the District of Louisiana. The northern half, the District of Louisiana, included present Missouri and was to come under the jurisdiction of the Territory of Indiana, General W. H. Harrison governing.   The Missourians, largely St. Louisans, protested this subordination to Indiana Territory on two counts, lack of self government and failure to protect slavery in Missouri.   Accordingly, in 1804 Congress gave separate territorial status to the area and territorial judges and officials were appointed by the president.

From 1810 to 1812 fifteen petitions went from the newly established territory asking for a higher status. When Louisiana was admitted as a state in 1812, the Territory of Louisiana further north was changed to the Territory of Missouri to the temporary satisfaction on the inhabitants. The new territory was of a higher order and was allowed to have a two-house legislature for local governing. By an act of 1816 Missouri was raised to the highest rank of territories and was allowed to have a legislative set-up with members from each county.

In 1817 Missouri started asking for statehood. An 1818 bill permitted her to form a constitution and a state government was under way. The first attempt of Missouri to gain admittance to the Union was stopped by the Tallmage amendment asking that no more slaves be introduced and that the children of slaves be freed at the age of 25. A third bill, introduced into Congress in 1819, attempted to open the way for Missouri's admission and was more successful. Maine wanted to come in as a "free" state. The Thomas amendment, stating that the Louisiana Territory north of latitude 36° 30′ except Missouri be free from slavery, temporarily stilled the Congressional storm on the question of slavery long enough for Congress to grant permission for the Missouri Constitutional Convention of 1820. Her constitution framed, Missouri was admitted to the Union in 1821, forty years before the outbreak of the Civil War. During that forty years Missouri tried, under ten different governors, to build herself into full statehood.

The antagonisms of the pre-Civil War period did much to discourage unified and constructive action. The State as a whole, indicated by the temper of the governors chosen, was pro-Southern in sympathy. Only St. Louis with the power it wielded was sufficient finally to swing the state from "going Confederate."

The Negro then, free and slave, has played a large part in the history of Missouri. He came early on to the scene and is with us yet. "The first Negro slaves brought into upper Louisiana or the Illinois country came with Sieur Philip Renault, director of the Company of the West, in 1719. On his way from France, Sieur Renault stopped at the Island of San Domingo, and there purchased 500 Negro slaves to work in the mines which were to be opened."[1]

By 1799, Houck tells us, there were 988 slaves in and around St. Louis, as against 6,028 whites, or an average of one slave per white family.[2]

Slavery thus early established was strengthened as an institution in Missouri with the passage of the Ordinance of 1787, prohibiting slavery in the Northwest Territory and thus sending many slave owners to Missouri, shaping in part the future tide of emigration from such states as the Carolinas and Kentucky and Tennessee. Large numbers of Missourians boast of antecedents in these southern states, and their families came here well fortified with the sentiments of the home states.

The desire of the majority of Missouri's inhabitants for slavery for the Negro can be seen in the apprehension, mentioned above, that coming under Indian Territory's jurisdiction might affect Missouri's slavery. The choice of early governors, as already cited, showed pro-slavery sympathy. Though a few men, like Thomas Hart Benton, may have thought of a free Missouri, they were easily frightened from their dreams.[3] The more common attitude of early Mis-

[1] Houck, Louis, *A History of Missouri*, Chicago, R. R. Donnelley and Sons, 1908, V, 2, p. 240.

[2] *Ibid.*, p. 241.

[3] Switzler, William F., *Illustrated History of Missouri*, St. Louis, C. R. Barns, 1879, pp. 221-2.

sourians is best indicated by Violette's statement, "Acceptance of Missouri's Constitution was delayed in Congress over the fact that the legislature was empowered by it to pass any laws necessary 'to prevent free Negroes and Mulattoes from coming to and settling in the State under any pretext whatsoever.' "[4]

As for the education of Negroes in the pre-Civil War period, that must certainly have been a rarity in Missouri, when such education was far from common in northern, supposedly free states. As a matter of record, the schools for whites did not fare very well in Missouri until after the Civil War.

Although the Constitution of 1820 said that education should "forever be encouraged" in the state and further specified that "one school or more shall be established in each township, as soon as practicable and necessary, where the poor shall be taught,"[5] there was much public sentiment against such schools. As had been the case in other new states, the United States government set aside the sixteenth section in every township to help support the schools. But it was five years before the Missouri legislature passed a law having to do with education. This provided that Congressional townships form a district to be controlled by the County Court. In this district schools should be maintained and supported by leases of school lands, penalties, fines, and forfeitures.[6]

Lucien Carr summarizes the condition of the schools in pre-War Missouri as follows:[7]

". . . perhaps owing, also, in some degree to the sparseness of population and to a feeling of prejudice which still lingered in certain

[4] Violette, Eugene M., *A History of Missouri*, Boston, New York, D. C. Heath and Co., 1918, p. 125.

[5] Constitution of the State of Missouri, 1820, Article VI.

[6] Laws of Missouri, 1825, pp. 711-720.

[7] Carr, Lucien, *Missouri; A Bone of Contention*, Boston and New York, Houghton, Mifflin and Co., 1888, pp. 237-8. The quotes, though not acknowledged by Carr, are from Switzer's *History of Missouri*, p. 293.

quarters against the use of schools that were wrongly called 'free,' the cause of public education was in anything but a flourishing condition. In some portions of the State, especially in the remote and thinly populated districts, schoolhouses were necessarily few and far apart; and in those regions where they were more common, they were often 'nothing more than log huts, unplastered and unceiled, with chimneys constructed of sticks, mud, and straw, and without school furniture, unless long, backless benches, made of inverted puncheons, and wide planks fastened to the wall for a writing desk, can be called furniture.' Rude and unsuitable as these buildings would now be considered, they were all that could then be afforded, and not unfrequently, it is to be feared, they were in keeping with the qualifications of the teachers and the elementary character of the instruction given. Webster's Speller and Pike's Arithmetic were the textbooks in general use, and when a boy had 'been through' these, and was able to write 'fine hand,' his education ,so far as these primitive institutions were concerned, may be said to have been completed.

"Such, in brief, seems to have been the condition of public instruction throughout the State of Missouri during the earlier years of its existence. . . . Indeed, when regarded from this point of view, it must be confessed that Missouri, despite the positive injunctions of her constitution to the contrary, had done but a little to forward the cause of popular education."

Switzler says, more succinctly, that despite constitutional provisions, "More than thirty years elapsed after the organization of the State government . . . before a law was passed appropriating any portion of the taxes paid by the people to educational purposes."[8]

That Missouri was not alone to blame for this condition must be admitted. As a Territory, from 1812 on, she had been under the jurisdiction of the Federal government, and this larger organization had set the pattern of legislating idealistically in behalf of public schools, then doing nothing practical to see to it that they came into being.[9] Between 1833 and 1861 Missouri did struggle repeatedly to establish

[8] Switzler, *op. cit.*, p. 292.

[9] Phillips, C. A., *Education in Missouri*, Jefferson City, Missouri, Stephens Printing Co., 1911, pp. 5 and 6.

schools and was laying the groundwork for the establishment of the schools in the post-War period.[10]

When the average salary of the teacher is $117 per year and when the Superintendent calls the school "virtual pigpens," it can hardly be expected that much attention is being paid to the formal education of the slave class. In Missouri, as elsewhere, Arrowood's observations held true: "Down to 1860, the farm house, the rural neighborhood, and the rural church were by all means the most important educational forces in the lives of the most Americans. They were almost the only educational forces in the lives of black Americans."[11]

Prior to the Civil War the attitude of Americans toward the education of Negroes tended to be dictated by economic conditions, as well as by fear of Negro revolts. After 1800, when the Negro became an economic asset, his education was neglected more and more, especially in those areas where his services were valuable and where, accordingly, it was more profitable, even if only in peace of mind, to keep him ignorant.

Such a story as Woodson's *The Education of the Negro Prior to 1861* must be, then, the recital of early attempts, many of them abortive, and the listing of laws enacted to further restrict the possibilities of education for the Negro as the days of the Civil War grew closer. The educated Negro was a rarity. The more usual sight was the entirely untutored and ignorant Negro or the Negro who had used his native ability to take advantage of the only learning available to him, the learning of the plantation, the completely extra-curricular, omnipresent education that is within arm's length of any man awake to life around him.

[10] Some ideas of the gropings of Missouri toward schools can be found in the following sources: Laws of Mo., 1835, p. 137; Laws of Mo., 1837, p. 137; Laws of Mo., 1839, p. 113; Laws of Mo., 1841, p. 142; Laws of Mo., 1853, pp. 148-160.

[11] Arrowood, C. A., "The Education of American Plantation Slaves," *School and Society*, 5: 377-8, March 31, 1941, p. 175.

This was the education of the slave in the South and, to a large degree of the free Negro, even in the North. The Northern Negro and the Southern free Negro were educated by their environment, farm, town, or city. The slave was educated by the plantation system which was his habitat.

In Missouri the plantation system did not flourish. The rice of South Carolina, the cane of Louisiana, and the cotton of the Black Belt did not thrive here, though the latter was to become the leading concern of the southeastern tip in subsequent years. Tobacco was successfully grown in Missouri; but Virginians had discovered earlier that, unlike cotton, rice, and sugar cane, tobacco did not require a large, seasonal, and concentrated labor supply. If Missouri could be said to have grown any staple for export, that would certainly have been hemp.[12] But hemp did not necessitate the plantation system.

Trexler tells us that "As a slave state it (Missouri) was a region of small farms, small slave holdings and relatively few slaves."[13] In his first chapter, "Missouri Slavery as an Economic System," he goes on to say that "Slavery in Missouri was more a domestic than an economic institution."[14] The slaves were more often general farm workers than producers of staple crops. The slaves were used as domestics, especially in the cities; they helped clear the land; they worked as deck and cabin boys on the river boats; they labored in the lead mines; and they worked about the towns and cities much as Negroes do today.

The border state atmosphere which characterized Missouri slavery was further accentuated by the great amount of hiring out of slaves which was carried on.[15] This not only

12 Wetmore, Alphonso, Gazeteer of the State of Missouri, C. Keemle, St. Louis (Harper and Brothers, N. Y.), 1837, p. 28.

13 Trexler, Harrison A., Slavery in Missouri 1804-1865, Baltimore, the Johns Hopkins Press, 1914 (Ph.D. Dissertation), p. 53. Proof for the statement cited is to be found on pages 13-18.

14 Trexler, p. 19.

15 Ibid., pp. 29-37.

made it easier for the slave to buy his freedom eventually, but it also made his acquisition of a trade more nearly possible. In a system which values the handy man above the laborer, the slave had many more advantages when it came to being allowed the opportunity to pick up a practical education.

The nearness of free territory in Illinois, Iowa, and Kansas, the lack of any staple crop requiring strenuous slave labor, and the small farm, small holding situation in Missouri all combined to make life easier for the Missouri Negro than for his brothers to the South, though it is to be doubted that everything was as rosy as Trexler would often like you to imagine.[16]

Trexler may also be brought to task for his treatment of the education of Negroes, which, like his treatment of the free Negro, is virtually lacking. The latter may be excused because of the nature of the title of the book, though Trexler does include an abortive discussion of this classification in his last chapter. Concerning the education of the slave, however, Trexler's errors of omission are more truly sins. In Chapter III, "Social Status of the Slaves," Trexler tells us that elsewhere in the United States fear of servile insurrections had led to laws forbidding the teaching of reading to slaves. "Missouri, however," he goes on to say, "was less subject to social than to political or financial hysteria."[17]

Now although it was not until 1847 that Missouri passed laws to provide specifically that no person should keep or

---

[16] *Ibid.*, especially pp. 37, 49, and 51.

A few instances to disprove Trexler's insinuations could be garnered from any edition of a Missouri paper. The *Liberty Weekly Tribune* gives the following, among others: May 3, 1850, 2-2, slave attempted to poison family; May 7, 1852, 2-3, slave ran away disguised as Indian; August 27, 1852, 1-6, slave drowns herself after being whipped; July 13, 1855, 2-4, slave killed by overseer; January 28, 1859, 1-7, master murdered by slave; and December 5, 1862, 1-4, slave ran away with some of master's property and his neighbor's wife.

[17] *Ibid.*, p. 82.

teach any school for the education of Negroes,[18] Missouri
did pass an act as early as 1817 regulating the travelling
and assembly of slaves,[19] apparently with the intention of
making it more difficult for slaves to plan or to carry out
open insurrection against their white masters. This law
certainly could have been used most effecetively to put a
stop to any attempts at educating slaves. Whether the law
was rigidly enforced or not we cannot say for a certainty,
but it is interesting to note that, in 1833, the law of 1813 was
amended so as to regulate slave travel and assembly even
more strictly.[20] Yet Trexler mentions neither the law of
1817 nor the 1833 amendment.

In Missouri, as elsewhere, in spite of the law of 1847 and
the fine of $500 and the imprisonment of not more than six
months which were threatened as punishments for offend-
ers, some masters did allow their slaves to learn to read,
and many slaves learned to read in spite of masters who
would have whipped them had they known.

That there were ignorant and uneducated Negroes
throughout Missouri, as elsewhere, we know. Featherstonaugh tells us that some of the Negroes were worse than
animals. ''A pack of ragged young negroes performed the
service of chambermaids and waiters, and did it about as
well as a pack of grown monkeys, caught in Brazil, would
do in three months' teaching.''[21]

But despite the failure of Trexler to include mention of
the education of the Negro or of the educated Negro, there
were examples to counteract Featherstonaugh. Although
Shoemaker states that ''Complete citizenship was never
given a Negro (before the Civil War), however, for he could
not be educated, he had no standing in court unless on trial,

---

[18] *Laws of the State of Missouri*, 1847, pp. 103 and 104.

[19] *Laws of Missouri Territory*, p. 498.

[20] *Laws of the State of Missouri*, 1833.

[21] Featherstonehaugh, George W., *Excursion Through the Slave States*,
N. Y., Harper and Brothers, 1844, pp. 34-5. He speaks of St. Louis.

and he was usually treated with contempt and indignity,''[22] the same author gives us two of the infrequent references to schools for Negroes in the same period. He says later, ''The Sisters of the Sacred Heart in St. Charles and Florissant maintained free day schools, and church groups showed an interest in giving instruction to negro and half breed Indian children.''[23] Again he tells us ''The first Sunday School in St. Louis was opened in April, 1818, as a result of the work of the Reverends Peck (John Mason) and Welch (James E.). These missionaries also organized a Sunday School in St. Louis for colored people in 1818. This latter Sunday School began with 14 people, but the enrollment rapidly increased to about 100 and the school proved to be the nucleus of the colored Baptist church in St. Louis, organized about 1827.''[24]

Peck himself said, in 1825, ''I am happy to find among the slaveholders in Missouri a growing disposition to have the blacks educated, and to patronize Sunday Schools for the purpose.''[25]

But it must be remembered that attempts on the part of the white master class to educate the Negro, free or slave, were the exceptions rather than the rule. Another fighting St. Louis minister of the pre-Civil War period, Galusha Anderson laments, ''Although the negroes in St. Louis owned taxable property, assessed year by year at a valuation of hundreds of thousands of dollars, and had long paid annually no inconsiderable school tax, it had been used for the education of white people.''[26]

[22] Shoemaker, Floyd, Missouri and Missourians, Vol. I, The Lewis Publishing Company, Chicago, 1943, p. 574.

[23] Ibid., p. 257.

[24] Ibid., p. 523.

[25] Peck, J. M., Forty Years of Pioneer Life (ed. Rufus Babcock), Philadelphia, American Baptist Publishing Society, 1864, p. 210.

[26] Anderson, Galusha, Story of a Border City, Boston, Little, Brown, and Co., 1908, p. 338.

The Negro's education, if he got one, was more apt to be along the lines indicated by Arrowood, an education gained from the environment. In this struggle for education, he was aided by the nature of Missouri slavery, especially the tendency to let the Negro "work out." Slave or free, Negroes who could work out found much more chance to learn than did the Southern plantation slave. "There was a negro pastor in the city by the name of Richard Anderson. When a boy he was a slave, and had been brought from Virginia to Missouri. When he was twelve years old his master, Mr. Bates, had given him his freedom. He now began to do odd jobs about the city. He became a newspaper carrier, and thus aided in distributing among its subscribers the *Missouri Republican*. While doing this work he learned to read. The newspaper that he carried from door to door was his spelling book and school reader."[27]

Such a story as the above makes us wonder about the beginnings of Negro education. Unfortunately, the Negro himself was not very vocal during this period and could leave us little record. Nor were the white people, aside from a few Northern ministers, interested in observing the colored folk and leaving us records of their life and habits. For this reason there is but scant material to inform us of the social and intellectual life of the Negro.

The only recourse we have is that adopted by Arrowood in his study of the education of the plantation slave; that is, the inference concerning education that may be drawn from what we do actually know about the life of the Negro in that time.

The conditions in Missouri, for our purposes, can be studied most pertinently by following a former slave's recital of his autobiography. Henry Clay Bruce's story may not represent a typical picture of the education of a Missouri slave, but it is a rare record of the conditions in his

[27] *Ibid.*, p. 12.

time.[28] Though Bruce may well have been one of the more intelligent slaves, his life and experiences present much of what could have happened to any other Missouri slave.

Significantly, Bruce was not born in Missouri, but in Virginia.[29] His family was moved to Chariton County, Missouri, in 1844, when he was approximately eight years old. Here he continued the early childhood education he had been undergoing in Virginia. Like any youngster of any color, he had benefited by days out of doors, by the asking of countless questions, by experimenting, and by observing.[30]

Unlike most white boys, he was put to work at the age of nine, hired out to a brick maker in Randolph County. But here he worked with the owner's son, feeding stock and hauling trees. The next year he was hired out again, this time to the owner of a tobacco factory. This was characteristic of Missouri for two reasons: (1) slaves were hired out much more often than in the deeper South and (2) the small ''factories'' of the state were manned with slave labor for the most part.

By the time he was thirteen, Bruce was back in Virginia again. Significantly he tells us, ''I had been taught the alphabet while in Missouri and could spell 'bake,' 'lady,' 'shady,' and such words of two syllables, and Willie took great pride in teaching me his lessons each day from his books.''[31] This ability to spell was discovered by his Virginia owner who made a great to-do about it. Like many a master, he thought that reading was permissible, since it

[28] Bruce, Henry Clay, The New Man: Twenty-nine Years a Slave, P. Anstadt and Sons, York, Pennsylvania, 1895.

[29] Newspaper items such as the following, indicating the importation of Negroes, were common: ''Description of twenty-five Negro boys and girls, late from Virginia, to be sold by G. P. Dorris'' in Liberty Weekly Tribune, Feb. 9, 1849, page 3, column 1.

''Dr. Perry en route to Missouri (from Virginia) with nearly 100 slaves to be sold'' also in Liberty Weekly Tribune, May 18, 1849, p, 2, column 2.

[30] Bruce, op. cit., pp. 17-20.

[31] Ibid., p. 25.

opened the Bible to the slave; but writing was forbidden, for much evil might come of it, in the master's opinion.

In 1850 Bruce was brought back to Missouri and hired out to a tobacconist; in 1854 he was splitting rails for a farmer; in 1855 he was back in a tobacco factory again; in 1856 he went to work as a farm hand, working his way up to the post of foreman or supervisor. Certainly the nature and variety of these tasks illustrate conditions in Missouri. If we were to add that his two brothers meanwhile were trained as bricklayers and his mother was hired out as a cook, the versatility demanded of Negro slaves is apparent.

Of the general level of intelligence among Missouri slaves Bruce says, "In order to show that education and intelligence are the great powers which have been the means of dispelling the gloom of superstition and voodooism among the Colored people, especially, I will state that the Colored people of Missouri, particularly those of Chariton, Howard, Carroll, and Randolph Counties, were above the ordinary slaves in the more extreme Southern states in intelligence and education."[32]

Yet, though the level of slave intelligence in Missouri was higher than in the more Southern states, "A colored man who could read was a very important fellow, for they (the slaves) would come miles and bring stolen papers for him to read to them at night or on Sunday."[33] We should remember at this point, however, that the white people were often hardly more literate than this at the time. Bruce tells incidents of slaves fooling the white patrols by presenting them with any piece of writing and calling it a pass.[34] Certainly the slaves often showed more intelligence than their opponents when they outwitted the patrols time after time.[35]

Learning must have been sweeter to the slave, since it

[32] Bruce, op. cit., p. 58.

[33] Ibid., p. 86. This reading was mainly in connection with Fremont's bid for the Presidency and the hopes it brought the Negroes.

[34] Ibid., pp. 96 and 97.

[35] Ibid., pp. 97-100.

was a forbidden fruit, to a certain extent at any rate. Negroes could and did learn despite state laws to the contrary. "Slavery in some portions of Missouri was not what it was in Virginia, or in the extreme South, because we could buy any book we wanted if we had the money to pay for it, and masters seemed not to care about it, especially ours, but of course there were exceptions to the rule."[36]

Certainly the laxity of control that accompanied Missouri's policy of hiring out Negroes differed greatly from the policy found in the deep South. Bruce says, "When the factory closed at sunset, we were free to go where we pleased until sunrise next day. I remember that the M. E. Church, South, allowed the Colored people to meet in the basement of their church, and their minister preached to them every Sunday, commencing at three o'clock, p.m., and his text was not always from Luke xii 47 or Titus ii 9."[37]

That the slave had money with which to buy books, should he want them, is indicated by Bruce's assertion that the slaves gave a $45 suit to one of the white ministers whose sermons they particularly appreciated.[38]

As in the South, when a colored preacher held forth for a slave congregation, there was supervision and often censorship by the master class.[39] But the Negroes did meet in spite of any laws to the contrary. Bruce even mentions a school for slaves established by a Southerner who had immigrated to a 700-acre farm near Brunswick, Missouri. Since he intended to free his slaves and give them his lands and property, he and his wife started a school on the plantation to teach the slaves those things they would have to know in order to cope with life as free men.[40]

Though the Germans who had settled in Missouri would appreciate such humanitarian sentiments,[41] many Mis-

[36] Ibid., p. 67.
[37] Ibid., p. 71.
[38] Ibid., p. 72.
[39] Loc. cit. and p. 73.
[40] Ibid., p. 76-77.
[41] Ibid., p. 90 states that Germans never hired slaves.

sourians objected strenuously. The master of Bruce's sweetheart was a case in point, "I was engaged to marry a girl belonging to a man named Allen Farmer, who was opposed to it on the ground, as I was afterwards informed, that he did not want a Negro to visit his farm who could read, because he would spoil his slaves."[42]

As the Civil War approached, conditions for the Negroes in Missouri, as in the South, got worse.[43] Owners were filled with a fear of losing their investments and/or their lives. They guarded their slaves more strictly, punished them more severely. The whole situation became more and more critical.

For the free Negro in Missouri conditions were never so rosy as they were for the slave.[44] The free Negro had even less of a chance to be granted privileges, because he lacked the patronage and protection of a master. He was cared for less, because he didn't mean $500 to $1,000 to some white man. As the War came on, these free Negroes, suspected of intrigue with slaves, were harried from pillar to post. No wonder newspapers often carried stories of Negroes returning gladly to slavery.[45]

To conclude the story of Bruce, it should be remarked that, before the War started, he borrowed a horse from his master and escaped over to Kansas, taking with him his bride-to-be.

There is a more didactic lesson in this, for our purposes, than is suggested by this romantic conclusion. The whole book illustrates many of the truths concerning the nature of slavery in Missouri: the Missouri Negro was often born out of the state and transported in; he was a jack-of-all-trades, used most often as a general farmer's hand, but found also as a bricklayer, cook, miner, domestic, carpenter, or factory

[42] Bruce, *op. cit.*, p. 108.
[43] *Ibid.*, p. 76.
[44] *Ibid.*, p. 77.
[45] *Liberty Weekly Tribune*, April 30, 1858, 4-1; April 29, 1859, 2-4; November 2, 1860, 1-7.

worker; more often than not the slave would be hired out, living under less strict supervision, able to make a little money of his own; if he wanted to, then, it was possible for him to get a rudimentary knowledge of reading and writing, as well as vocational and religious education.

What goes for the rest of the slave territory goes for Missouri, too, modified only by the revealing details of Bruce's story. Slavery, like the university, turned out all sorts of men. The great majority of the slaves never learned to read; their masters didn't encourage it, perhaps because it was an accomplishment theirs only recently if at all, but more likely because it would not improve the economic value of the slave and because they, the masters, feared the element of insurrection that might come with learning. Yet, in spite of the opposition of the masters, many slaves did learn to read, taught by children, by mistresses, by religious masters, by the men who were teaching them trades.

The real training of slaves, their real education, came not so much from the book, secular or religious, as from the work they did. They were compelled to learn the household arts, the crafts, the trades. In Missouri more than elsewhere, since there was more reward for individual initiative and accomplishment here, slaves could develop good work habits along with their knowledge of a skill. In a system where they were hired out, their social education came through their learning to get along with those with whom they worked. Their moral and religious education came from better masters and mistresses and from such ministers as Bruce describes.

Undoubtedly this "university" graduated many fine slaves. But some one else controlled the slave too much. His opportunities for development were far too limited. He still had to cross over the river to a freer land before he could really develop and grow to his full height.

R. I. Brigham

Yankton College

NOTES ON THE BAKONGO

The people known as the Bakongo, referred to erroneously as the tribes of the Congo, vary much in their appearance and cannot be treated as one nation. It is well known from the traditions of the people of this area that the so-called Bakongo were not originally what the Europeans discovered them to be when the adventurers first spied Africa in the fifteenth century. The people had been attacked by various hordes moving into that region and had warred among themselves so often and so long as to result in numerous migrations. The admixture of the various tribes consequently so confused matters that even had these tribes fairly well preserved history it would be difficult to tell when the story applies to the one and when not to the other. The Bakongo according to their traditions never reached a state of permanent organization on a large scale. Small groups, or tribes, tended to hold together, but these were not strong enough to withstand the combined force of two or three others or of some warring king with a large following. Such a conqueror might build and maintain for some years a large state, but the preference of the people for the rule of smaller circles would not permit such sovereignty to endure.

In the region of the Congo proper are found people of unusual height and well developed bodies and in the Ituri forest, Aruwimi, and elsewhere appear the dwarfs known as Pygmies who seem to be unrelated to the majority of people classified as of Bantu stock. As a rule these Bantu are characterized by a long head, broad nose, prognathic jaw, thick lips, thin legs, chocolate-brown color, and not very hairy body. Yet among them appear members characterized by a slightly round head, somewhat thinner lips, an all but prominent nose, a more hairy face, and a lighter color than the large majority. Seligman shows this variation in his record of the cephalic index and stature of those

421

of the Fiote of Fjort of the Lower Congo with a dolicephalic head and stature of 66 inches; the Bakongo to the South of the Congo near the cataracts to the Stanley Pool, with a cephalic index of 65 and stature of 74 inches; the Bangalla about the bend of the Niger, a little more dolicephalic and a little taller; the Basoko of the Congo-Aruwimi area, with a cephalic index of 80 and stature of 63¾; in the tributaries of the Congo the people like the Baluba almost brachyce-phalic; the Batela of Lubefu, with a cephalic index of 78.

The people of the area are fetishists except so far as Christianity has had some influence to the contrary. Mo-hammedanism has not invaded this area to the extent it has in the case of West Africa and the Sudan. Cannibalism has survived here and there. The people speak an agglutinant dialect of the Bantu language, but those in the tribes on the borders of the Ouelle-Oubangui-Chari speak monosyllabic dialects of the Sudanese order. Their main source for a living is agriculture. They have such industries as working in iron, brass, ceramics, and wood. They are great metal workers and are noted for their beautiful carving in wood and ivory and for the decoration of their productions in metal. For beautifying the body they make collars, brace-lets, anklets and the like from brass. Yet the dress of the majority is the apron string made from leaves and grass while a few of the well-to-do don cotton garments.

The Bakongo entered history by the discovery of the Congo in 1484 by Diogo Cam. A chief was spoken of as having a residence at Mbanea-Kongo, now San Salvador, far in the interior from the Kwanza in the South, as far as Kwilu-Nyari to the North, as far as Kwango from the sea. The king had various and magnificent titles. It seems that the Bakongo came from some place and conquered the Ambundu.

From the Mbrizi to the Kwanza the population must have been dense. The Bakongo drove out or assimilated the clans north of the Loje. Those situated to the South had to pay tribute. The greater part of these were grouped later under a chief-blacksmith named Musuri, who was proclaimed Ngolo de Ndongo, of the name of his "residence" and constituted a sort of kingdom of Angola. He freed himself from the suzerainty of Kongo, but one of his successors was again subdued by the king of San Salvador, in 1559. It was not until six years later, during the invasion of the Yagas, or Jagas, who devastated the Kongo that the Ngola Dambo made himself independent.

This freedom from one yoke was merely to come under a harder one, the Portuguese. The two ambassadors who had been sent to the king of Portugal to attract European commerce to the banks of the Cuanza were escorted back by Paul Diaz de Novaes in 1560. The astute Ngolo took possession of the goods and persons sent from Portugal, but he finally turned Diaz loose. As a result Diaz came later with a small army and in 1589 founded the colony of Angola. The kings could keep their title of "Ndongo a Nogola Kiluanji-Kia Sambo," but the real government remained with the Portuguese who were hard masters. The Ngola did not willingly submit. The last of these kings, Joas Arii, rebelled. He was defeated in 1671 and committed suicide by hurling himself from a precipice.

This conquest displeased the king of San Salvador. As soon as he got rid of the terrible Yagas he undertook to reestablish his suzerainty over the Ambundu. Already in 1752 Alvare I had sent against the Ngola the chief of Sogno. As a result of the battle of Musulu, the king of Kongo had to accept as frontier the southern bank of the Dande. He did not discontinue the use of the title of the king of Angola and kept the island situated in front of St. Paul de Loanda. This island was taken from Alvare III, in 1621, by Correa de Souza, governor of Loando, who, aided by the Yagas or Jagas, defeated the Bakongo at Nambu a Ngongo and permitted his savage allies to ravage the country. The title of King of Angola was definitely lost at the battle of

Ulanga, at Pedra di Nkosi, in 1666. Antonio I was defeated there by an army composed of 400 Portuguese and 6,000 Negroes who had two cannon. Tristan de Cunha, Capitão Geral d'Angola, notified the conquered that, from the days of Paul Diaz, the chief of San Salvador had lost the right to the titles of king of Angola and of Matamba and that henceforth he must abstain from using them.

The result of the Portuguese colonization was to nullify the relations between the Bakongo and the Ambundu; but to the great disadvantage of the Bakongo. For although the arrival of the Europeans developed the commerce it was based upon the slave trade. This trade led to the destruction of the prestige and authority of the king, the cohesion of the tribes, the peace. Everything was slowly ruined by St. Paul de Loanda. This city began to replace Pinda as a commercial port. The caravan route of Pinda, by Mfuma—Ngongo and Mokutu to San Salvador was more and more abandoned, while coffles of slaves loaded down with ivory, raffia stuff, or articles from Europe ran without ceasing the long route which connects Saint Paul with San Salvador. In this locality the road forks to go by the Mbata to Kundi on the Kwango, or by Nsundi or Mpumbo (Stanley Pool). The trip from Saint Paul to San Salvador and return required three months. Along the way were found lodging places for the caravan, and slave markets. The slaves, of whom Saint Paul exported more than 10,000 in favorable years, were principally the Ambundu, people of Mbamba and Mbata, and the rest Negroes of the Upper Congo, purchased by the Banfumgumu of Kundi and the Bateke du Pool. They were exchanged for European stuffs—glassware, knives, sabres, porcelain or brass cooking utensils. The traffic stirred or added fuel to the covetousness of the chiefs, driving them to the point of selling their own subjects and then those of their neighbors. The European contact then, instead of being helpful to Africa as it has been to Asia and America, was a drawback. Africa was already retarded and Europe came upon the scene to make it worse. This was the principal cause of African wars prior to the European occupation. The African himself, left to himself, prefers peace.

The people along the river bank continued to maintain a small slave market of Pinda. This place recovered only in the second half of the seventeenth century when the Sogno became independent of San Salvador. In the nineteenth century Ambrisette replaced Saint Paul and Pinda and attracted many slavetraders from the interior of the country, even from Kwango. This trade continued until the establishment of the independent state and ceased only during the last few years. It introduced flint muskets which took the place of the bows and arrows.

The Matamba country, of which the kings of Kongo were suzerains, was inhabited mainly by the Ambundu, and in the Southeastern part by the Holo and the Bangala. This situation was changed by the invasions. A warlike race had come down from the Southeast, probably from Lunda. About 1558, in a formidable rush they crossed the middle Kwango. Then they invaded Kongo dia Mulaza, Mbata, Mpanguu Mpemba, and as far as the Sogno. In passing they burnt the villages, massacred and devoured a large number of inhabitants. The King Alvare had only time enough to escape into the Island of the Hippopatami situated in the lower stream. In 1574, Captain François de Govea sent by King Sebastian of Portugal, arrived with a detachment of 400 Portuguese and with the aid of a Native army defeated the Yagas and drove them from the Kongo. A part of the invaders crossed the stream and settled upon the bank of the Kwilu-Nyari in the country called Bokkemeale. They continued there their depredations but finally adopted more human customs. A part of the Yagas were driven back toward the Kwango. To the north of the Kongo dia Mulazza, to the east of Mbata, they dislodged some Bakongo clans, mixed with others while dominating them.

It was thus that were established the independent tribes of
the two Lula, one on the Nsele, the other upon the Lumene,
the lordship of which the kings of San Salvador often ar-
rogated to themselves. More to the south they ruled over
the people whom writers call Hokango or Bacango, and who
dwelt on the two banks of the Kwango. In the beginning of
the seventeenth century a nephew of Ilunga, the founder of
the kingdom of Lunda, named Kasongo came and fought on
the right bank of the Kwango. He annexed diverse groups
of Yagas and became in that way the Muata-Kiamvu de
Kasongo-Lunda. His domain covered the two banks of the
east Kwango and was extended as far as the right bank of
the Kwilu as far up as Mitschakilia. Van Wing says that the
last Muata established himself in Portuguese territory, and
his depredations and his cruelties had ruined his authority.

More to the south the Yaga chief Imbe Kalandola cut
out a kingdom between the Cuanza and the Kwango. Several of the Yaga tribes were won over by the famous Anna
Nzinga Mbandi Ngola, queen of Angola and of Dongo, when
she warred against the Portuguese (1625-1655). When she
adopted the code and customs of the Yagas she lost her
kingdom but conquered the Matamba. She dominated the
whole of the upper Kwango and inflicted even a defeat on
the Muata-Kiamvu of Kasongo. She was converted to
Christianity after an expedition against the chief of Wandu.
For some years the Capuchin had a flourishing mission in
Matamba, the center of which was Nzinga Kabaza, or Sainte
Marie de Matamba. At the death of Anna Nzinga, her sister Barbara Nzinga, converted also, succeeded her, but she
returned very soon to her ancient customs. Her husband,
Antonio Nzinga Mona, destroyed even the seat of Sainte
Marie and uprooted Christianity in all his country. The
Capuchin Mission (1654-1670) had established frequent re-
lations between the Congolese kingdom and Matamba. After
the departure of the missionaries the country returned to
its former state and was no longer influenced except from

Cuanza. The short-lived mission of the Capuchins had nevertheless sufficed to make penetrate some Christian ideas among the Bayaka of the Middle Kwango, of which one still finds vestiges.

To the northeast, the Kongo kingdom was limited by the Anziga, or Ancica, that is, the country of the Bateke, or the kingdom of Makoko. The principal town is called by authors, Monsoles, where was held a large slave market and ivory market. The Portuguese of Loango and of San Salvador sent there their Pomberos, that is, slaves instructed and exercised by the Portuguese, in order to direct the caravans which they were sending to Pombo (Mpumbu, country of the Bawumbu in Kikongo). Already before the arrival of the Portuguese the Bawumbu were the intermediaries for the trade between the Upper and Lower Congo. They constituted a sub-tribe of the Bateke. A part of them live to the south and east of Pool, within a radius of forty kilometers. Others are settled upon the Kwango near Kundi. The Pombéros have crossed Africa from west to east. One finds them mentioned by Portuguese authors and others. Dapper relates that a Kaffir had probably come from Mozambique to Angola. It is certain also, according to native traditions, that the Pombéros went sometimes as far as Lake Leopold II, to Masa Mandombe. The Kikongo words which are found even among the tribes of the Great Lakes are probably due to these bold Pombéros.

To the east and north of Pombo is situated the Fungeno area, that is the region of the Bamfungunu or Bamfunuka or Bamfumu. It extends between the Nsele and the Kwango from the 5° of south latitude. To the north of the 4° the population is rather composed of real Bateke, to the south of 5° there is a mixture of Bakongo and Bayaka. Ancient writers describe these people with their characteristic traits. These people are dependent on the Grand Makoko. They are really a sub-tribe of the Bateke. They had a trade in beautiful mats and still have that specialty.

To the north of the Makoko country was the kingdom called Giribuma which is really the Babuma country. Authors report also on Kwilu-Nyari and in the parts north of the Makoko kingdom, the Mbaka-Mbaka, or Pygmies. Authors have confused the kingdom of Makoko and the Anziga country but almost all the authors put Anziga under the domination of Makoko. This is an error due to placing the "residence" of Makoko far beyond Pombo, says Van Wing (Stanley Pool). "They exaggerate the distance from Pombo to the coast. Anziga, on the contrary, was for them adjacent to Nsundi, neighboring province of San Salvador."

The other regions of the Upper Kwilu-Nyari were little known in the 16th and 17th centuries. The copper mines were nevertheless known because of the commerce between Loango and Bateke. The writers were unacquainted with Mayombé. They were not so well informed about the kingdoms Ngoy, Kakongo, and Loango, of which the kings of San Salvador for a long time claimed suzerainty. These kingdoms extended from the mouth of the Congo to the Kwilu-Nyari. They were established by Bakongo who emigrated from the left bank of the Congo. In Ngoy the Bakongo customs have been kept pure. At Kakongo and especially at Loango the digression is more considerable.

As to the origin of the first kings of the Congo we have some information from ancient historians. Païva speaks of Meshicongo as a foreign nation. These people came down from the interior and it is thought that they came originally from lord of Kongo di Amulaca, who conquered the powerful kingdom of Kongo, the natives of which were Ambundu of another race.[1] Cavazzi is more precise. He says: "In Corimba in the region of Kwango, one named E. Mima Nzima, married to Lukeni lua Nzanza, daughter of Nsaku Lau and of Sirokia de Mpuku a Nsuku had by her a child named Lukeni. This Lukeni became a strong and bold warrior who ransomed the people, especially those at the fords

[1] Païva Manso, Vicomte de, *Historia da Congo*, Lisbon, 1877.

of the Kwango. He had assembled about him a band of his stamp. One day he murdered his pregnant aunt. As a result of this high crime he was proclaimed chief Mutinu. He invaded the province of Mpemba Kasi, and established there his capital Mbasa a Nkanu. He established laws and organized his kingdom. His maternal uncle, descendant of Nsaku Lau, was able to keep the province of Mbata, but it had to recognize the sovereignty of Lukeni and received the title of Neakon dianene Kongo, which, according to Cavazzi, signifies grandfather, ancestor of the Kongo. Lukeni had a competitor, Mabambala Ma Mpangalafi whose successors protest annually by the mouth of a woman against the usurpation of Lukeni.'' It is not clear, however, whether the two countries mentioned by these two authors are two different countries or the same country mentioned under different names.[2]

In the Archives of the Congo, published in the *Revue Congolaise,* January, 1914, page 207, one finds that ''the kings of the Congo descended from a very wise and skilful artisan who was called in by diverse peoples as an arbitrator of their disputes, and who thereby succeeded in marrying his daughters to the neighboring chiefs.'' Thus it is said, were formed two families, one called the Chimolaza and the other the Chimpanzu. This document bearing date of the end of the 17th century, is confused with a tradition concerning the origin of the royalty and the rivalries which broke out in the second half of the 17th century between the ancient royal clan, whose Mpangu branch often occupied the throne, and the clan of the Ne Nlaza, which contrived to have one of its members Antonio I ($+$ 1666) elected king.

With respect to the question as to the Congo kings' deriving their origin from a very able artisan, it is again stated precisely by Cavazzi who makes of this ancestor the

[2] Ade M. Cavazzi,*Istorica descrizzione degli tré regni Congo, Angola e Matamba,* Bologna, 1687.

inventor of the art of forging iron.[3] A similar tradition ascribes this to the kings of Angola. It is probable that these are variants of a general theme, for other Bantu people have similar origins.

The local traditions indicate that the ancestors of people of the Inkisi region came from the Kwango and that it was from the Kwango that they departed to found Kongo di Ntotila or San Salvador. These traditions for the most part do not go farther back than San Salvador as the original home of the people, but several chiefs informed R. P. Van Wing that the first chiefs of the tribe came from the Kwango. There is besides the tradition of the Bankanu, a very mixed Bakongo people who inhabit the region of Kwilu an affluent of the Congo and the affluents of the Kwilu, the Gubizi, the Tawa, and the Benga. Their principal town was Bbansa Kongo, situated in the angle formed by the Kwilu and its affluent the Tawa. They say that their Congo kingdom was founded by the great chief Na Kongo when he had passed the Kwango. This Kongo of Kwilu is the Kongo dia Amulaka, which is the same as Kongo di Yaka. Yaka is for the Bakongo the country of the Bayaka, descendants of the "terrible Yagas or Jagas," who in the 16th and 17th centuries invaded the kingdom of Kongo, commencing with the frontier region of Kwango, that is, by the way of the country of the real Bankanu and that of their neighbors, the Bambata.

The Bakongo of the Inkisi region, namely, the Bampangu, the Bankanu, and the Bambata have a keen recollection of the ferocious contests in which their ancestors, the Bayaka of Kwango engaged. Yaka or Yaga still means in Kikongo miseries and troubles. The Bambata call the Bayaka *Gayaga*. Their neighbors, the Bankanu call them *Mayaka*. It should be added that Van Wing considers as imaginary Cavazzi's Corimba and Agherima reported as

[3] Ade M. Cavazzi, *Istorica descrizzione degli tré regni Congo, Angola e Matamba*, Bologna, 1687, p. 136.

the kingdom and capital of the Kongo. Van Wing thinks that Cavazzi is merely carrying forward thereby an error of Ptolemy with respect to the map of Africa.[4]

As to the names of the kings of the Congo there are various discussions by Païva, Cavazzi and others; but they confuse rather than clarify. Van Wing says they were: First, Nimi a Lukeni (in the 14th century); then Nanga kia Nlinu Kongo, after whom we are not sure as to names and periods. Then came Nkuwu a Ntinu. Next came the second period of the Congo history when the Christianized kings had control from 1491 to 1656. During the next period, one of competion, we have one king ruling at San Salvador from 1666 to 1710, another at Kibangu from 1669 to 1680; and still another at Mbula from 1697 to 1710. During the nineteenth century one king ruled apparently all of the ancient realm.

The insignia of the king were grand. Three iron bracelets, sack of pineapple fibre, and an ivory chair on a platform. He wore a mitre of palms, a brass bracelet, a horse tail, the emblem of royalty, a lance, bow and arrow, and a baton. At first the people were organized as clans on the African order. Later they were made "Europeans" by the Portuguese. The Church began to show the influence there with the first mission which came as early as 1482.[5] From this nucleus have developed in the usual imperialistic fashion most of what is now the Belgian Congo and Portuguese Southwest Africa.

C. G. Woodson

---

[4] R. P. Van Wing, *Etudes Bakongo*, pp. 17-27.

[5] O. Dapper's *Nanwkeurige beschryving der Afrikoansche Gewesten* (Amsterdam, 1676); Ravenstein's *The Strange Adventures of Andrew Battel of Leigh in Angola and Adjoining Regions* (London, 1901); Th. Simar's "Le Congo au XVI siecle" in the *Revue Congolaise*, 1911, pages 226 *et seq.*; H. Bentley's *Pioneering on the Congo* (London, 1900).

BELIZE: A STORY OF PRACTICAL AMALGAMATION[1]

In 1839, President Van Buren sent John L. Stephens on a special mission to Central America. The following excerpts, quoted from the latter's book, *Incidents of travel in Central America, Chiapas and Yucatan,* were selected solely to record the author's observations on the Negro at one point in the travels, Belize (British Settlement, Central America), and do not purport to be a condensation nor a critique of the book which is not, essentially, about Negroes.

Being instructed by the President with a Special Confidential mission to Central America, on Wednesday, the third of October 1839, I embarked on board the British brig Mary Ann, Hampton, master, for the bay of Honduras. My only fellow-passenger was Mr. Catherwood, an experienced traveller and personal friend.

On the eleventh we were moving gently between Cuba and St. Domingo, with both in full sight. On the twenty-ninth we were driven inside the Lighthouse reef, and, avoiding the regular pilot-ground, at midnight reached St. George's Bay, about twenty miles from Balize. A large brig was lying at anchor, with a pilot on board, waiting for favorable weather to put to sea. The pilot had with him his son, a lad about sixteen, whom Captain Hampton knew, and determined to take on board.

It was full moon when the boy mounted the deck and gave us the pilot's welcome. I could not distinguish his features, but he was not white; and his voice was as soft as a woman's. He took his place at the wheel, and, loading the brig with canvas, told us of the severe gales on the coast.

At seven o'clock the next morning we saw Balize, appearing like Venice and Alexandria, to rise out of the water. We landed in front of the warehouse of Mr. Coffin, the consignee of the vessel. There was no hotel in the place, but Mr. Coffin undertook to conduct us to a lady, who, he thought, could accommodate us. At the extreme end of the principal street we met the "lady,"[1] Miss

---

[1] This use of quotation marks is the author's. Judging by the text, one may say that Mr. Stephens was ignorant of Miss ———'s character and had not known her long enough nor well enough to say whether she was a lady or a "lady."

————, a mulatto woman, who could only give us board. Mr. Coffin kindly offered the use of an unoccupied house on the other side of the river to sleep in, and we returned.

By this time I had twice passed the whole length of the principal street, and the town seemed in the entire possession of blacks. The bridge, the market-place, the streets and stores were thronged with them, and I might have fancied myself in the capital of a Negro Republic. They were a fine-looking race, tall, straight and athletic, with skins black, smooth and glossy as velvet, and well dressed, the men in white cotton shirts and trousers, with straw hats; and the women in white frocks with short sleeves and broad red borders, and adorned with large red earrings and necklaces; and I could not help remarking that the frock was their only article of dress, and that it was the fashion of these sable ladies to drop this considerably from off the right shoulder, and to carry the skirt in the left hand, and to raise it to any height necessary for crossing puddles.

On my way back I stopped at the house of a merchant, whom I found at what is called a second breakfast. At the head was a British officer, and opposite him was a mulatto; on his left was another officer, and opposite him was also a mulatto. By chance a place was made for me between the two Colored gentlemen. Some of my countrymen, perhaps, would have hesitated about taking it, but I did not; both were well dressed, well educated, and polite. They talked of their mahogany works, of England, hunting, horses, ladies, and wine; and before I had been an hour in Balize I learned that the great work of practical amalgamation, the subject of so much angry controversy at home, had been going on quietly for generations; that colour was considered mere matter of taste; and that some of the most respectable inhabitants had black wives and mongrel[2] children, whom they educated with as much care, and made money for with as much zeal, as if their skins were perfectly white.

I hardly knew whether to be shocked or amused at this condition of society; and in the meantime, joined Mr. Catherwood, to visit the house offered by Mr. Coffin. It was situated on the opposite side of the river and the road to it was ankle deep in mud. The upper story was tenanted by a family of Negroes; in the yard was a house swarming with Negroes; and all over, in the yard and in front, were picturesque groups of little Negroes of both sexes, and naked as they were born. We remember Captain Hampton's remark, that Balize was the last place made.

---

2 The author used the word *mongrel*, by which he doubtless meant *mulatto*. The word *mongrel* does not refer to the human race

At this day Balize contains a population of six thousand, of which four thousand are blacks, who are employed by the merchants in gangs as mahogany cutters. Their condition was always better than that of plantation slaves; even before the act for the general abolition of slavery throughout the British Dominions they were actually free; and on the thirty-first of August 1839, a year before the time appointed by the act, by a general meeting and agreement of proprietors, even the nominal yoke of bondage was removed.

The Negro schools stand in the rear of the Government House and the boys' department consisted of about two hundred, from three to fifteen years of age and of every degree of tinge, from nearly white to two little native Africans bearing on their cheeks the scars of cuts made by their parents at home. These last were taken from on board a slave-ship captured by an English cruiser, brought into Balize, and, as provided for by the laws, on a drawing by lot, fell to the share of a citizen, who, entering into certain covenants for good treatment, is entitled to their services until they are twenty-one years old.

From the Negro school we went to the Grand Court. The court consists of seven judges, five of whom were in their places; one of them was a mulatto. The jury was empannelled, and two of the jurors were mulattoes; one of them, as the judge who sat next me said, was a Sambo[3] or of the descending line, being the son of a mulatto and a black man. I was at a loss to determine the caste of a third, and inquired of the judge, who answered he was his, the judge's brother, and that his mother was a mulatto woman. The judge was aware of the feeling existing in the United States with regard to colour, and said that in Balize there was, in political life no distinction whatever, except on the ground of qualifications and character; and hardly any in social life, even in contracting marriages.

I had noticed the judges and jurors, but I missed an important part of an English court. Where were the gentlemen of the bar? Some of my readers will perhaps concur with Captain Hampton, that Balize was the last place made, when I tell them that there was not a single lawyer in the place, and never has been; but lest some of my enterprising professional brethern should forthwith be tempted to pack their trunks for a descent upon the exempt city, I consider it my duty to add that I do not believe there is the least chance for one.

As there is no bar to prepare men for the bench, the judges,

[3] Some Spanish dictionaries define ''sambo'' as the offspring of a Negro and an Indian.

of course, are not lawyers. Of the five then sitting, two were merchants, one a mahogany cutter and the mulatto, second to none of the others in character or qualifications, a doctor. This court is the highest tribunal for the trial of civil causes. Balize is a place of large commercial transactions and there was no absence of litigation; the calendar was large, and the courtroom crowded.

There was no case of particular interest. In one the parties became excited, and the defendant interrupted the plaintiff repeatedly, on which the latter, putting his hand upon the shoulder of his antagonist, said, in a coaxing way, "Now don't George; wait a little, you shall have your turn. Don't interrupt me, and I won't you."

I remarked that regularly the merits of the case were so clearly brought out, that, when it was committed to the jury, there was no question about the verdict; and so satisfactory has this system proved, that, though an appeal lies to the Queen in Council, but one cause has been carried up in twenty-two years. Still it stands as an anomaly in the history of English jurisprudence; for, I believe, in every other place where the principles of the common law govern, the learning of the bench and the ingenuity of the bar are considered necessary to elicit the truth.

At daylight the next morning I was roused by Mr. Walker for a ride to the barracks. In half an hour we reached the barracks. The soldiers were all black, and are part of an old Jamaica regiment, most of them having been enlisted at the English recruiting stations in Africa. Tall and athletic, with red coats, and, on a line, bristling with steel, their ebony faces gave them a peculiarly warlike appearance. They carry themselves proudly and call themselves the "Queen's Gentlemen."

We returned to breakfast, and immediately made an excursion in the government pit-pan. This is the same fashion of boat in which the Indians navigated the rivers of America before the Spaniards discovered it. European ingenuity has not contrived a better, though it has, perhaps, beautified the Indian model. Ours was forty feet long and six wide, and made of the trunk of a mahogany-tree. It had large cushioned seats. It was manned by eight Negro soldiers, who sat two on a seat, with paddles six feet long, and two stood up behind with paddles as steersmen. It was an unusual thing for his excellency's pitpan to be upon the water; citizens stopped to gaze at us, and all the idle Negroes hurried to the bridge to cheer us. This excited our African boatmen, who, with a wild chant that reminded us of the songs of the Nubian boatmen on the Nile, swept under the bridge, and hurried us into the still expanse of the majestic [Balize] river. Before the cheering of the Negroes had died away we were in as perfect a solitude as if removed thousands of miles from human habitations.

We had an eager desire to penetrate to the famous Lake of Petén, but the toil of our boatmen reminded us that they were paddling against a rapid current. We turned the pit-pan, and with the full power of the stream, a pull stronger, and a chant louder than before, amid the increased cheering of the Negroes, swept under the bridge, and in a few minutes were landed at the Government House.

In order that we might embark for Yzabal [port of Guatemala] at the hour appointed, his excellency, Colonel M'Donald, had ordered dinner at two. Before rising, Colonel M'Donald, like a loyal subject, proposed the health of the Queen; after which he ordered the glasses to be filled to the brim, and, standing up, he gave, "The health of Mr. Van Buren, President of the United States."

The steamboat lay in front of the Government House, and the black smoke, rising in columns from her pipe, gave notice that it was time to embark.

CORINNE DEAN

A NOTE ON "DIVIDE AND CONQUER"

A state's political policy is determined by what it deems its own interests. When the state becomes an empire these interests more often than not entail the subjugation of other peoples, for few, if any, people, with a clear understanding of its implications, have voluntarily accepted a state of vassalage.

The problem is not very difficult for the conqueror when the invaded territory is inhabited by one homogeneous people. But when it is inhabited by different peoples the leaders of empire have made the problem equally easy for themselves by the simple rule of "Divide and Conquer." This, of course, imperialists vehemently deny. And direct evidence for and against this point of view is not often obtainable, for man has never tended to proclaim proof of his departure from the laws of justice and fair play. But here we have direct evidence that the aim of this imperialism was unequivocally to divide and rule.

It comes in the following letter from Valentine Morris, Governor of St. Vincent, to Lord George Germain, dated March 25, 1777.[1]

In further detail of mine of fifth and nineteenth inst[s]. I have the satisfaction, and honor, to inform your Lordship that by dint of address, by properly working on their different passions, and by some treats, I have happily effected a breach of that Alliance between the runaway negroes, and very many, I might add therefore greater part if not all of the Charibs, which altho denied at first by many of them, was at last avowed by others, and was daily growing stronger and stronger, threatening with infinite danger this Colony—having first by the several excursions I constantly had caused to be made into the woods, in that part of the Island which belongs to us, dislodged the runaways from their several detached Settlements therein, the consequence was that the great Band (which is deep in the Charib country and who we had so lately failed cutting entirely off, merely from the intelligence those received of our motions from the Charibs) received them with open Arms, destroying the provisions of their Settlements I had forced the lesser band to desert, confined these, when blended with the greater, to consume what had been calculated only for the old Band

[1] Colonial Office 260 vol. 4 ff. 86.89ᵛ—Public Record Office—London.

437

at Rabacaw; and had the effect I foresaw, of occasioning some plunder on the nearest Charib settlements, which lay open to them; this on the one part, added to my calling together, and treating both at the outposts, and here, many of the Charib Chiefs, laid the grounds of that Jealousie, and distrust, which I wanted to avail myself of—the consequence was some overt Attempts of acts of violence on the part of the negroes, in the night, against the women of the nearest Charib settlement, and at attempt to cut off the Chief of the same for having been with me and received presents as they said.

I snatched the occasion, offered the Chief protection for his wives and children, within the precincts of our posts near there, which is very strong, against such Enemys; and offered himself also a guard of Soldiers, whenever he should want to call for them; this, and many other similar manoeuvres, too tedious to minutely trouble your Lordship with, but which I have been playing even prior to my last letter of the nineteenth instant, widen'd the just forming breach. I pointed out to all the Chiefs, the apparent facility with which I had dislodged from our part of the Island, most, or all of those settlements which had been in it; & how surely I could always do it; shewed them how the ones in their country encreased to a formidable degree, far out of their power now as they saw, to be controuled by them, detached in interests, and in so many different Tribes. I comvinced them that these must still greatly encrease by being an Asylum to all of our runaway Negroes, which must end soon in the falling on them, & taking from them their Lands, which it must as I said be perfectly indifferent to us who possessed, as we laid no claim to it. The reasoning was plausible, the thing before their Eyes gave a growing proof of what I said, their own fears, which some alleged of the negroes being too strong for them to dare to join in attacking or endeavouring to dislodge them, still furnished me with fresh Arguments, and at last the far greater number of the Chiefs have been in with me, and by my Command with the Officers of the outposts nearest to them, and have all in their way solemnly swore *by eating a little dirt* that they will go out, and assist the Troops and Colony in any Attacks whenever I order them.

RUTH ANNA FISHER

BOOK REVIEWS

They Seek a City. By Arna Bontemps and Jack Conroy. (New
York: Doubleday, Doran Company, 1945. Pp. 266. Price, $3.00.)

The saga of the American Negro is not confined, as many believe, to the Atlantic Seaboard. Coronado, Cortez, De Soto and
Balboa found use for colored explorers in their search of new lands
and gold during the period of Spanish influence in the Americas.
Reports confirm the belief that the French also utilized the services
of black adventurers. The engrossing story of Jean Baptiste Point
Du Sable, the founder of the great mid-western city of Chicago, is
the initial chapter of a moving and thrilling account of the nomadic
wanderings of a mix-blooded explorer whose name, today, is rather
closely associated with this progressive mid-western municipality.

The western expansion movement is inextricably interwoven
with many pioneers of colored blood. The arresting tale of black
people who tramped the prairie lands, crossed the uncharted rivers
and scaled the lofty highlands is recalled most vividly in the highly
interesting story of Arna Bontemps and Jack Conroy, entitled,
They Seek a City, a tale based upon authenticated documents and
depicting the hardships encountered in a quest for greater freedom
and economic security. On the heels of these fearless black explorers followed a host of fellow Americans seeking relief from the
harshness of slave economy. The authors bring into bold relief the
daring adventures of hitherto unknown characters who have left
a deep imprint upon western life. Few people recognize the names
of James P. Beckwourth, who antedated John Jacob Astor in fur-
trading. Little is known of William Still of "Underground Railroad" fame. John Jones, cultured Chicago business man is a forgotten entity. "Pap" Singleton, self-styled "Moses of the colored
exodus," who led thousands from the south into Kansas following
the Civil War because of intolerable conditions in that section, has
never appeared in the chronicles relating the development of that
State.

In their adventuresome tale, the authors describe the migratory
movements of Negroes seeking a better land in which to live, grow
and rear their children. Into four periods are divided these whole-

439

sale removals from southern states. "Mudtowns" characterize the first settlements in northern and western communities and the poisonous fangs of racial prejudice extend throughout the areas occupied, but such a feeling did not deter the black citizen in his quest for a haven safe from the bigotry and hatred found in his former abode. Out of "mudtowns" above the Mason and Dixon line has come more hope for the future. Out of these early, unkempt communities have originated a galaxy of outstanding American citizens who have made their contribution to the progress of our nation. In Chicago, the hub of the western migratory movement, Cincinnati, a laboratory of racial achievement, St. Louis, the center of gravity which aided the new comer to gain his equilibrium, Detroit, the bristling heart of industrial life and a score of other cities stretching across to the Pacific, the colored migrant brought his wares and his troubles.

The Columbian Exposition held in Chicago in 1893 offered an excellent opportunity for colored America to pool its resources and gifts. Here, Douglass, Dunbar, Ida B. Wells, W. P. Dabney, Harry Burleigh, Will Marion Cook, Robert S. Abbott and many others gathered to say to the world that black men demanded recognition for their achievements. From the deep South, W. C. Handy had come. In the wake of the author and composer of the "St. Louis Blues" came Scott Joplin, rag-time king from Texas, Adah Mencken, famed and beautiful actress from New Orleans, and the beginning of the New Pekin Theatre in Chicago, which opened new doors to colored performers in the world of music and song.

In seeking a city, the authors do not omit the barriers placed by labor unions and self-styled protectors of white supremacy. They discuss the plans devised by believers in the colonization movement to deport citizens of color to foreign climes. Characters like Marcus Garvey, Drew Ali, Mrs. Gordon and W. D. Fard come into the picture for an interpretation of their motives as they are concerned with the welfare of Negroes in these United States.

Historical in background, sociological in content and rich in character material, this volume merits the careful consideration of the American public. In these days of "restrictive covenants," economic proscriptions and social regimentation, a rear glance at the spirit and faith of Black America should serve to quicken our senses towards our duty to a group that has come with the explorers, remained through every change in our national life and now faces the future undauntedly with sanguine hopes and dogged determination.

JAMES EGERT ALLEN

The Land Possessions of Howard University. A Study of the Original Ownership and Extent of the Holdings of Howard University in the District of Columbia. By Beulah H. Melchor (Washington, D. C., 1945. Pp. 85.)

Many phases of the history of Howard University are yet to be written; so that it may be assumed that in time monographs and histories will appear to enlighten those persons interested in the growth and influence of this institution.

Miss Melchor in a very able manner has surveyed the various land holdings of Howard University. She has divided her study into two parts. Part one "treats the original ownership of the campus and the history of the land transactions pertaining to various portions thereof from 1651 until 1943." Part two "treats the numerous landholdings of Howard University in many parts of the city, their original ownership and disposition made by the University of some of these tracts."

It is of interest to know that the present site of the campus of Howard University was in 1651 a part of the great Manor of Calverton, a vast tract of land of about ten thousand acres set aside by Lord Baltimore as an Indian reservation.

According to the author the larger part of the original land which formed the Howard University campus was at one time a part of "Plain Dealing, a subdivision of the old area known as Mt. Pleasant," a large one thousand acre tract originally patented to Robert Peter in 1791.

On May 25, 1867, the trustees of Howard University agreed to purchase about 150 acres of this land at a thousand dollars an acre. John A. Smith, however, from whom the land was finally purchased could not give a clear title to the 150 acres so he let the trustees have 149 acres for $147,000. From this time on Miss Melchor enumerates many land transactions, most of which decreased the size of the campus. These transactions she divided into three groups. First, the purchase of various campus tracts made by General Oliver Otis Howard; second, the land transactions of Howard University with the Federal and District governments; and third, the sale by Howard University of building lots to many private individuals.

In addition to frequent sales of its property, Howard University constantly reclaimed portions of the original tract and purchased other lands not a part of the original tract. Miss Melchor has compiled a list of deeds, relating to the sales and purchases made by Howard University in the campus subdivision, arranged according to the specific blocks to which they relate.

The second part of this study is concerned with the land owned by Howard University in the various sections of Washington, D. C. "Of great extent were the land possessions," states Miss Melchor, who lists all these possessions among which were "Jamaica," "The Miller Tract" or "Le Droit Park," holdings in the subdivision of "Mt. Pleasant," tracts in Meridian Hill and land in what was known as Ingleside.

Within the city limits, Howard University owned at one time land in all four sections of Washington. "In the northeast practically three whole city squares were at one time owned by the University. About five acres of land in southeast Washington and slightly less than a half of a city square in southwest Washington were once listed among the land possessions of Howard University. A number of small lots located in various sections of northwest Washington were also owned by the University.

Miss Melchor goes into a detailed study of the processes by which Howard University obtained this land. Her conclusions are that Howard University increased its holdings by purchasing tracts of land sold at auction. In some instances where deeds contained restrictive covenants and it was impractical to hold them the University sold the lots soon after the purchase of them.

The difference in the land policies of General Oliver O. Howard and Dr. Mordecai W. Johnson, the two presidents of the University who contributed most to the expansion of the land holdings of the University, is that General Howard was interested in the land tracts in various remote sections of the city and Dr. Johnson has been interested in the extension of the holdings near the school.

The author of this study has examined many original documents, most of which were located in the Division of Surveys, Interior Department, Washington, D. C.; the Land Commissioner's Office in Maryland; the Office of the U. S. Engineer; the Supreme Court of the District of Columbia; the Library of Congress; the Auditor's Office, in the District Building and the Office of the Recorder of Deeds. In addition, Miss Melchor used printed books, periodicals and newspapers for her study. Twenty-six appendices enhance the historical value of the monograph.

DOROTHY B. PORTER

Inching Along: An Autobiographical Story. By Henry Damon Davidson. (Nashville: National Publication Company, 1944.)

Inching Alang is not an interesting book for the general public. It is not brought out in the style which will please the average reader. The author undertakes to give an account of his life and the work that he did in founding the Centerville Industrial Institute, which is now the Bibb County Training School, Centerville, Alabama. He goes into the details of his numerous experiences and sometimes violates the law of proportion in saying too much about one thing and not enough about other things of greater importance. At times the book borders upon self-adulation when the same story might be presented more effectively in other words.

This story, however, is of incalculable value to the historian who desires to portray the past of the Negro and will be of still more value to the investigator of the distant future when he will find it necessary to reproduce the best he can the scenes of present-day life in the midst of which he may be able to see the Negro as a factor. Books of this type are eagerly welcomed by the serious student of history as it has been influenced by the Negro in America, because most of the records of the past have been made by biased minds—commentators, editors, lecturers and authors, who have not considered the Negro worthy of thought and consciously or unconsciously have said very little about this race. Every time a Negro of a long and useful career like that of Henry Damon Davidson leaves an account of his experiences with his own people and others about him, he renders historical research a great service. Here we are not only able to understand his contacts with the people of Alabama, including the local judges and the governor of the state, but with others like Dr. James Hardy Dillard of the Slater and Jeanes Funds, with Booker T. Washington, and finally with H.

Council Trenholm who wrote the introduction to the book. All these connections and experiences combine to make *Inching Along* a valuable work for documenting the history of the Negro.

C. G. WOODSON

The Virgin Islands and Their People. By J. Antonio Jarvis. (Philadelphia, Pa.: Dorrance & Company, 1945. Pp. 178. Price $1.50.)

This book is a brief statement within 178 pages. It is not, therefore, a definitive history of the Virgin Islands. It is, however, a commendable undertaking in the much needed work of acquainting the world in general, and the people of the United States in particular, with the natives of this group of islands, their problems and their possibilities. The author has written before in this field and this volume is a second reprinting of an earlier work. He is a native of the Virgin Islands and is occupied mainly today as a teacher in the school system of his home at Charlotte Amalie, St. Thomas. As such he has been engaged for the last twenty years. In his preparation for this work he studied at De Witt Clinton High School and at Columbia University in New York City. He is the author of several other books, two of which are *Brief History of the Virgin Islands* and *Bamboula Dance,* a book of poems. For ten years he was the editor of *The Daily News,* a paper which he established in St. Thomas. He is, moreover, an artist whose paintings have been accepted on such occasions as the San Francisco Golden Gate Exposition, exhibits of the Harmon Foundation, and shows in various colleges. He was once awarded an *Opportunity* prize as a winner in fine arts.

As a writer with some appreciation of what the public wants and what it will absorb, he does well to attract attention by referring to the ancient landmarks of the Virgin Islands established under the control of the Danes. He writes in clear language about the salubrious climate and useful plants, worthwhile animals and valuable fisheries. After presenting the picture of the country he projects it upon the screen as a part of the general view of the Caribbean area with respect to other settlements and colonists that influence the Virgin Islands and by which the group is itself influenced. Describing the natives of the Virgin Islands, who form 65 per cent of the population, he penetrates the background of these people and especially the mulatto class developed from the race admixture of German, French, Spanish, Russian and Dutch as well as Danish. He devotes a whole chapter to showing that the white French Americans and Puerto Ricans changed the Virgin Islands, thus causing the Negroes to lose ground. These people, as a whole, he shows conclusively deserve a higher rating than being referred to as neglected, poor and unpromising. Another chapter he devotes to the essentials of the history of the Island from 1493 to 1847 when, without many dangerous disturbances, the Danes held the land. In 1848, however, came a real uprising which resulted in the emancipation of the slaves. Under American rule the Islanders have both suffered and prospered, but the author does not despair; he sees some evidence of the growth of democracy; he has faith that when these people and their problems are properly known the world will learn to love, respect and honor them with all the rights and privileges of citizens.

C. G. WOODSON

African Journey. By Eslanda Goode Robeson. (New York: The John Day Company, 1945.)

This work has an all but misleading title for the reason that it does not show a deep penetration of the interior of the African continent. It is really a diary interspersed with observations. It seems that most of the experiences of the author were restricted mainly to the coast. This, however, does not mean that the work is not of value as a book of travel. One touching even the ports along the coast of Africa can easily see sufficient of the life of that continent to evoke prolonged comment on the situation there in contradistinction to conditions obtaining elsewhere. For the account which the author has given the public must be grateful because we are very much in need of additional comment on what has transpired and is still transpiring in Africa.

It is hardly likely that the author was permitted to look into many of the conditions which she desired to examine. Most of the travelers in Africa, unless they are known to sympathize with the economic imperialists, are not allowed to study conditions there. The Africans themselves of most of these possessions, moreover, are not permitted to leave for education elsewhere with the expectation of returning. They are not wanted in the country after being thus spoiled by contact with the equalitarians and race-problem-solving agencies of Europe and the United States. In this way the authorities in control in Africa hope to safeguard the system of forced labor and other devices for exploiting the Natives just as the ruling class in the South endeavored to safeguard slavery before the Civil War and thus brought it to pass that the only way the institution could be attacked was from without.

As a rule Negroes are not permitted to conduct investigations in Africa. A few who have gone there as missionaries have reported on the inequalities, injustices and atrocities in some areas. Most of the Negro missionaries to Africa, however, have not been sufficiently trained to present their thoughts in literary form. Some of them, moreover, assume the attitude of treating the Native as an undesirable who can be saved only through such psalm-singing as they bring. Such observers are blinded thereby to what is actually going on and what it portends for the future. The public should welcome, therefore, the production of Mrs. Robeson as a step in the right direction; and in the projected reconstruction schedule to follow this war, other Negroes with the same purpose may have an opportunity to delve more deeply into African affairs.

C. G. Woodson

The Congo. By John Latouche and Andre Cauvin. (New York: Willow White and Company, 1945.)

This is a book which gives in readable style the facts of the history of the conquest and the administration of the Congo by its rulers. The book is evidently intended to invite the attention of the world to this large possession of Belgium, in order to inculcate some appreciation of what has been done to develop the country and to make its resources available to other parts of the world. The book deals with the history of the Congo, both as a possession of the Belgian Crown under the title of the Congo Free State and as administered later under the Government as the Belgian Congo. As to the importance of additional information concerning European imperialism, especially at the present time, there can be no doubt.

The book, however, is *ex parte.* The author gives the bright side of the story and omits the unfavorable aspects which, if presented, would show mistakes that the economic imperialists of our day should try to avoid. He says practically nothing about Stanley who used his knowledge gained from the exploration of the Congo as a pawn which he would give to any government in Europe in a position to pay for such data in order to establish a claim to that land. He does not go into the details of how Leopold II outwitted the other European imperialists who failed to grab this large area of the African domain. The author is silent also on the diplomatic ineptitude of the United States of America in recognizing Leopold's Congo Free State and thus giving the possession standing in the international sphere. We thus made it possible for Leopold to commit some of the worst atrocities ever inflicted upon natives in exploiting the rubber industry of the Congo, and the world, standing aghast, could not legally interfere.

On the other hand, the author tries to make excuses for Leopold II by saying that his employers in the rubber industry who committed these atrocities were not necessarily Belgians themselves. Leopold II employed French, Swiss and English adventurers to conduct his enterprise in the Congo. The author writes also of the improvements which have taken place since the reorganization of the Congo under the control of the Belgian Government. He mentions better schools, technical training activities, medical service and avenues for employment opened up by the mining interests, the commercial agencies and the great trusts operating in the country. He fails to show, however, that the Natives are still being worked at starvation wages. While the standard of living has been raised, wages have been kept low and to meet the requirements of the new order and pay the taxes exacted by the Government, the Natives are not much better off than they were before except that they are not being killed when they reach their extremity and cannot carry their burdens any further.

C. G. WOODSON

Build Together Americans. By Rachel Davis DuBois. (New York, Philadelphia: Hinds, Hayden & Eldridge, Inc., 1945. Pp. 270. Price $2.00.)

Rachel Davis DuBois deserves much credit for her patience and for her faith in humanity. This mad world does not please a sympathetic soul like hers, and she has ever worked to effect changes to brighten the way of the handicapped elements of the population of the United States. She has tried first one experiment and then another, in all of which she may have achieved some positive good. She has left no stone unturned in embracing every opportunity for new experiments in the world-wide human laboratory.

In this book entitled *Build Together Americans* she has given an account of adventures in intercultural education. She first tries to show what our American culture is. Here her statement is very direct with the exception that she runs into the difficulties of trying to present in a few words the many contributions which have entered into the making of the so-called American culture and reasons why those thus functioning should not be ashamed of the rôles they play in the drama. She discusses such difficult problems as prejudice, personality, the rôle of the school in advancing new ideas, the play of social psychology, the treatment of wounded personalities, and other aspects of the situation which must be understood by those attempting intercultural education. In other words, she has not only given a clear statement of what ought now to be done, but she has also presented a number of things which should not be done; or, if they have been done, should be abandoned. The book is filled with actual facts for guidance and specific directions for inculcating in each group an appreciation for the culture of the others.

One difficulty, however, the author does not overcome, namely, that of the arguments by the race-hating class to the effect that these very differences in culture are good grounds for the justification of race-hate in that each element resists the encroachment of any other of a marked difference because each race desires to remain what it is. It requires much more vision than the race-hating class has to understand how these differences enable the differing elements in cooperation to enrich our culture with significant contributions which, when properly understood and assimilated, would make the United States outstanding among the nations of the world. In this work the author deserves the commendation of all citizens who take seriously the building of a new democracy for tomorrow.

One suggestion as to bibliographical treatment may be offered here, but not as a criticism, because a bibliography is always out of date as soon as it is printed. Since the preparation of this valuable work have appeared a number of productions which are being widely circulated in the interracial and intercultural circles; and in a new edition of this work these titles should appear. For example, the author mentions among "Children's Books" Jane Dabney Shackelford's *Child's Story of the Negro,* but says nothing about her more recent work, *My Happy Days,* which is being widely used in the schools for intercultural purposes. Likewise she failed to add *Tobe,* by Mary Gentry Sharpe, a production which has been extensively used in inculcating an appreciation of the rural Negro boy.

C. G. WOODSON

The Story of the Springfield Plan. By Clarence I. Chatto, Alice L. Halligan, and John Granrud. (New York: Barnes and Noble, Inc., 1945. Pp. 201. Price $2.75.)

As a result of intercultural education which is now moving the whole country we have heard much about the Springfield Plan. We can better understand what has been undertaken in that industrial center in Massachusetts when we realize the fact that, although it was established as most New England cities were, with the native element and for a long time retained this aspect, Springfield has in recent decades changed into a community of varied industries attracting persons of all nationalities and from all levels of human society. For a long time Springfield proceeded as most cities have done in trying to leave these foreign elements in isolation while the true Americans proceeded in their accustomed way. Now that many of these centers having a preponderance of so-called foreigners who in our democratic government exercise sufficient political power to control such centers themselves, it has become necessary to come to terms with these conflicting social forces and organize the whole community for the good of all. The Springfield Plan, then, undertakes to integrate with the life of the community such formerly discordant elements as the Roman Catholic, Jew, and even such dissimilar racial elements as the Negro, Indian and Chinaman. This is in substance the Springfield Plan.

In the book giving the story of the working of this plan appear chapters on the background of the story with the Mayor of Springfield playing the leading rôle, the schools as aiding both in teaching and living according to this new way of life, and the cooperation of citizens with the school system in the important task of democratizing the entire community. They face their work as an unfinished task of democracy and show a determination that our profession of belief in the free principles enunciated in the Declaration of Independence and the Constitution of the United States shall no longer continue as hypocritical outbursts for the Fourth of July and George Washington's Birthday.

It is encouraging to workers thus concerned that other cities likewise interested in attaining the objective of real democracy are studying this plan and gradually incorporating it into their school systems and the administration of their towns and cities. These centers in other parts of course, have not all taken the plan so seriously as Springfield itself has done, but the data given indicate clearly that it is a movement with very great vitality and will eventually move the thinking element in all parts of the country except the backward areas where the unenlightened are organized against democracy. These books and others will help to disseminate these new ideas of democracy and will thus record at least another noble effort to advance toward liberty and freedom with equality and justice for all.

J. L. MOORE

An Uncommon Man: Henry Wallace and 60 Million Jobs. By Frank Kingdon. The Readers' Press (New York, 1944), Pp. 94. $1.00.

This book about one of the most controversial figures in public life today does not propose to be a definitive biography of Henry Wallace up to the present time. From the point of view of the historian, such would be impossible without the perspective that only time can furnish. It is rather an extensive discussion of his social and economic philosophy and the manner in which it has evolved during his public career. It seeks to trace the growth of Wallace's ideas concerning the solution of America's economic and social problems and the manner in which these ideas have come to represent the views of a considerable portion of the American public.

Mr. Kingdon places the emphasis in his book on the practical idealism of Henry Wallace and the timeliness of the philosophy which he has expounded during the years which have elapsed since he became the Secretary of Agriculture in Roosevelt's first administration. Much attention is devoted to a discussion of the conflicts which Wallace has experienced since becoming Vice-President of the United States in 1941. In vivid fashion the author has pointed up the character of Henry Wallace by contrasting him with Jesse Jones with whom Wallace, as chairman of the Board of Economic Warfare, had a bitter quarrel during the early months of the war. Both in that conflict and in the more recent controversy over the appointment of Wallace to Jones' job as Secretary of Commerce, Jones was depicted as "The Past" and Wallace was portrayed as "The Future." Kingdon viewed it as a conflict between "Business as usual," on the one hand, and a broad socioeconomic philosophy on the other; and in his discussion the author never leaves the reader in doubt that he favors the Wallace brand of humanitarianism.

The author then discusses the views of Wallace on almost every important social and economic problem: agriculture, industry, science, religion, race relations, full employment, housing, politics, international relations, and social security. In all these areas Wallace has a point of view which Kingdon regards as liberal. Wallace views the myth of racial superiority as absurd. He thinks that full employment is fair employment. He strongly advocates an Economic Bill of Rights that will not only constitute a "toughening fiber for free enterprise," but will also give strength and meaning to our earlier Bill of Rights. The function of government in realizing a full life for everyone is to stimulate and encourage private enterprise, and, when necessary, to step in and maintain full employment at public expense.

Mr. Kingdon is an avowed supporter of the ideals of Henry Wallace. He does not attempt any criticism of Wallace unless his admission of Wallace's political ineptitude be regarded as a criticism. For example, in the discussion of the conflict between Jones and Wallace over the use of public funds to raise the living standard of workers the author said, "Wallace had a concern for the workers. Jones had none. He would frankly say that they were none of his business. Wallace would say that everybody engaged in the work into which he was putting the money of the United

States was his business. If this seems like sentimentalism or nonsense to you, gentle reader, give this book right now to the salvage drive, for you will never understand Hanry Wallace'' (p. 19). In another place (p. 94), the author shows his unreserved enthusiasm for Wallace when he said, ''Which comes first, property values or human values? That is the issue. If we put property first, we get one kind of world. If we put human beings first, we get another. These are the Two Worlds that are struggling for the mastery of tomorrow. Henry Wallace has made himself the advocate of the world of human values. He is the uncommon man become spokesman for the common man. The story of his political battles is an enlightening comment on the nature and meaning of the profoundest social developments of our times.''

Mr. Kingdon's enthusiasm for Henry Wallace does not prevent him from presenting a full discussion and comprehensive analysis of the program which his ''prophet'' has evolved to attain sixty million jobs for peace-time America. The implications of such a program are clearly set forth on page after page of the book, such as when he says that Wallace ''believes that private industry, agriculture, labor and government working together under a Constitution assuring liberty can organize our resources and wealth in such a way as to provide permanent employment for sixty million workers'' (p. 88). The author, moreover, has undertaken to explain and interpret the program of Wallace to an American public that has become increasingly curious about this man who occupies such a unique position in American life today. If the book suffers at all, it is from the intolerance which the author has of the critics of Wallace and the impatience which he manifests with those who do not understand the Secretary of Commerce. In its approach and treatment, it comes close to being one of those partisan documents which appear near or during an election. But it is certainly more than the ''run of the mill'' campaign documents, for it is an able and inspiring presentation of the case for a philosophy of life which, if realized, will launch America into an era of prosperity and plenty the like of which it has not heretofore experienced.

JOHN HOPE FRANKLIN

North Carolina College for Negroes

NOTES

Books which bear indirectly upon the Negro in treating other matters of national importance include the following: *Diplomat in Carpet Slippers,* a new view of Lincoln, by Jay Monaghan (Indianapolis: Bobbs-Merrill Company, 1945); *Lincoln as President-Elect,* by William Barringer (Springfield, Illinois: The Abraham Lincoln Association, 1945) *Intimate Memories of Lincoln,* edited by Rufus Rockwall Wilson (Elmira, New York: The Primavera Press, 1945); *Seaman A. Knapp, Schoolmaster of American Agriculture,* by Joseph Cannon Bailey (New York: Columbia University Press, 1945); *In Memoriam, the Tribute of a Sorrowing Group on the Passing of the Late Franklin Delano Roosevelt,* edited by George W. Westerman (The Isthmian Negro Youth Congress, 1945).

Books approaching the present situation with programs of reconstruction and taking the Negro into consideration include: *Primer for White Folks,* a symposium, edited by Bucklin Moon (New York: Doubleday, Doran Company, 1945); *The Springfield Plan,* by James Waterman, illustrations by Alexander Alland (New York: Viking Press, 1945); *The Story of the Springfield Plan,* by Clarence L. Chatto and Alice L. Halligan (New York: Barnes and Noble, 1945); *Design for America,* an educational exploration of the future of democracy, by Theodore Brameld (New York: Hinds, Hayden and Eldridge, Inc., 1945); *Build Together Americans,* adventures in intercultural education, by Rachel Davis DuBois (New York: Hinds, Hayden and Eldridge, 1945.)

Of special importance to students of Negro History are the following: *All Brave Sailors,* the story of the Steamship Booker T. Washington, by John Beecher (New York: L. B. Fisher Company, 1945); *Race Riots Aren't Necessary,* by Alfred McClung Lee (New York: Public Affairs Committee, Inc., 1945); *Early Negro Church Life in New York,* George W. Hodges (published privately by the author, 312 Manhattan Avenue, New York 26, N. Y.); *War-Time Changes in the Occupational Status of Negro Workers,* a reprint, by Julius A. Thomas (New York: National Vocational Guidance Association, 525 West 120th Street, New York City); *Vocational and Educational Survey for the Kanawha County Negro Schools,*

453

by Andrew H. Calloway, assistant superintendent of schools and director of the survey (Kanawha County Schools, Charleston 1, West Virginia); *Religion in Higher Education among Negroes*, by Richard I. McKinney (New Haven: Yale University Press, 1945).

ARTICLES OF UNITED STATES HISTORY

Articles of United States History dealing incidentally with the Negro include: "Civil and Military Relationships under Lincoln," by J. G. Randall (*The Pennsylvania Magazine of History and Biography*, July, 1945); "A Frenchman Visits Norfolk, Fredericksburg and Orange County, 1816," by L. G. Moffat and J. M. Carrière (*The Virginia Magazine of History and Biography*, July, 1945); "Origin of Seward's Plan to Purchase the Danish West Indies," by Halvdan Koht (*American Historical Review*, July, 1945); "Evolution of Emerson as an Abolitionist," by Marjory M. Moody (*American Literature*, March, 1945); "What Rutherford B. Hayes Liked in Emerson," by Lyon N. Richardson (*ibid.*); "The Pattern of Migration and Settlement on the Southern Frontier," by Frank L. Owsley (*The Journal of Southern History*, May, 1945); "Ante-Bellum Attempts of Northern Business Interests to 'Redeem' the Upper South," by George Winston Smith (*ibid.*); "Incidents of the Confederate Blockade," by Kathryn Abbey Hanna (*ibid.*); "Puerto Rico—The Forty-Ninth State?" by Belle Boone Beard (*Phylon*, second quarter, 1945); "Light for Men in Darkness," by Samuel Adams Lynde (*ibid.*); "Discipline for Today," by Marc Moreland (*ibid.*); "Racial Prejudice," by Helen V. McLean (*ibid.*); "A French Reactionary Visits the South," by Edward A. Jones (*ibid.*).

Of special importance to the study of the Negro are the following: "Should Congress Pass a Law Prohibiting Employment Discrimination?" (*Congressional Digest*, July, 1945); "The Negro Looks Ahead," by Martin Ebon (*Free World*, May 1945); "Some Methodological Considerations for a Comparative Study of Slavery," by Bernard J. Siegel (*American Anthropologist*, July-September, 1945).

Articles dealing with civil rights include the following: "Summary of Civil Liberties Cases in the 1944 Term of the United States Supreme Court," by John R. Stockham (*National Bar Journal*, September, 1945); "The Role of Lawyers in the Negotiations for

Permanent World Peace,'' by José Coll-Cuchi (*ibid.*) ; ''Adminis-
trative Law: A Threat to Our Constitutional Guarantees,'' by
Raymond Pace Alexander (*ibid.*) ; ''Report of the United Nations
Conference,'' by Perry W. Howard (*ibid.*).

Books on Latin America and the West Indies

Brazil, an interpretation, by Gilberto Freyre (New York: A. A.
Knopf, 1945) ; *Our American Neighbors,* prepared by the Coordina-
tor of Intra-American Affairs (Washington, D. C.: Public Affairs,
1945) ; *Le Racisme et le métissage devant la science,* second edition, Achile Aristide (Port-au-Prince, Haiti: Compagnie Litho-
graphique, 1945) ; *Apuntes de un Cooresponsal: Guerra de Inde-
pendencia,* by Modesto A. Tirado (La Habana: Molina y Compania,
1942) ; *1895 y 1898, dos Guerras Cubanos,* by Emilio Roig de Leuch-
senring (Habana, 1945) ; *Bibliotecas de Autores Cubanos* (Habana:
Editorial de la Universidad de la Habana, 1945).

Articles on Latin America and the West Indies

''Bolívar and Spanish-American Cooperation,'' by Harold A.
Bierck, Jr. (*Pacific Historical Review,* June 1945) ; ''Historia de
historiadores dentro de la democracia norteamericana,'' by Samuel
Flagg Bemis (*Revista Bimiestre Cubana,* January-February, 1945) ;
''Esclavitud y anexionisno en Cuba,'' by Adrian del Valle (*ibid*) ;
''Historia local de la Habana,'' by Jenario Artiles (*ibid.*).

Books on Africa

Books mainly scientific in this field include the following: *Europeans in West Africa,* by John William Blake for the Hakluyt Society (London: Robert Morehouse) ; *The Succession of Bemba
Chiefs,* by W. V. Brelsford (Lusaka, North Rhodesia: Government
Printer) ; *The Akan Doctrine of God,* a fragment of Gold Coast
ethics and religion, by J. B. Danquah (London: Lutterworth
Press) ; *The Fulani of Northern Nigeria,* F. W. de St. Croix (La-
gos: Government Printer).

Books devoted mainly to government, politics or economics include: *The Price of Peace,* by William Beveridge (New York: W.
W. Norton and Company, 1945) ; *Makers of South Africa,* by B. L.
W. Brett (London: Nelson and Sons) ; *The Economic Development
of Africa,* by Sir Alan Pim (London: The Anti-Slavery and Abo-

rigines Protection Society) ; *Ourselves and Empire,* by H. W. Foster (London: Macmillan Company) ; *African Politics in High Commission Territories,* by Lord Harlech (Lovedale: Lovedale Press) ; *The Colonies: The Labour Party's Post-War Policy of the African and Pacific Colonies,* by the Labour Party (London: The Transport House) ; *Tanganyika Territory: A Study of Economic Policy under Mandate,* by Charlotte Leubuscher (London: Oxford University Press) ; *The Colonies and Their Future,* by the Liberal National Council (London: Liberal National Council).

Less serious works on Africa by travelers and observers include the following: *African Journey,* by Eslanda Goode Robeson (New York: The John Day Company, 1945) ; *What do the People of Africa Want?* by the same author (New York: Council on African Affairs) ; *First Americans in North Africa,* by Louis B. Wright and Julia McLeod (Princeton, 1945) ; *Congo,* by John Latouche and André Cauvin (New York: Willow White and Company, 1945) ; *Native Peoples of the Pacific World,* by Felix M. Kessing (New York: Macmillan Company) ; and a novel entitled *Rooster Crows for Day,* a trip up the Congo, by Lucien Burman, with sketches by Alice Caddy (New York: E. P. Dutton, 1945).

ARTICLES ON AFRICA

The most important scientific articles recently appearing are: "Pangani: the Trade Centre of History," by H. C. Baxter (*Tanganyika Notes and Records,* June, 1944) ; "Sukuma Twin Ceremonies—Mabasa," by H. Cory (*ibid.*) ; "An Annotated List of Ancient and Modern Indigenous Stone Structures in Eastern Africa," by C. Gillman (*ibid.*) ; "Honden-oorlog," by E. Boelaert (*Aequatoria,* VII, 2, 1944) ; "Godsgebeden bij de Baluba" (*ibid.*) ; "Over de Mukanda en Zemba bij de Tshokwe" (*ibid.*) ; La grossesse et l'enfantemente chez les Nkundo," by P. Nogoi (*ibid.*) ; "Pages d'histoire africaine: Essai de reconstition des lines de famille paternelle, qui relient entre les populations soudanaises du Nord du Congo Belge," by Basil Octave Tanghe (*ibid.*) ; "The Marriage of a Swazi Princess," by Hilda Kuper (*Africa,* July, 1945) ; "La paleolithique au Congo Belge d'apres les recherches du Docteur Cabu," by Henri Breuil (*Transactions of the Royal Society of South Africa,* xxx, 2, 1944) ; "African Suicides in the Bamenda Division, British Cameroons," by M. D. W. Jeffreys (*ibid.*) ; "Les industries paleolithiques de la terrasse de 15 metres et d'un chenal secondaire comble, plaine de Piemont de Leopoldville, d'apres les fouilles et protographies du Docteur Cabu" (*ibid.*); "A Journey among the Primitive Tribes in Madagascar," by Olive Murray Chapman (*Scottish Geographical Magazine*, lix, 3, January, 1944); "Notes on the Bassa-Koma Tribe in the Igala Division," by Mile Clifford (*Man*, xliv, 95, September-October, 1944); "The Installation of the Shilluk King," by P. P. Howell (*ibid.*).

To these should be added: "Ibeji Statuettes from Yoruba, Nigeria," by L. R. Meyerowitz (*ibid.*); "La cérémonie funeraire dans le Kissi," by Coundono Djoumé (*Education Africaine*, xxxii, 108, 21-7); "Notes sur les Holes," by Boubu Hama (*ibid.*); "Autobiographie d'une femme banen," by Mme. R. Dugast (*Bulletin de la Société d'Etudes Camerounaises*, June, 1944); "Inter-tribal History through Tribal Stories," by Miss M. E. Head (*Bulletin of the Uganda Society*, June 1944); "Jurisprudence; Formalitié solonelle du marriage" (*Bulletin des Jurisdictions Indigènes et du Droit Coutumier Congolais*, xii, 10, July-August, 1944); "Coutumes et institutions des Barundi," by Eugene Simmons (*ibid.*); "Le pays et la population Matakam," by G. Lavergne (*Bulletin de la Société d'Etudes Camerounaises*, September, 1944); "Duyangar: Rites agraire et classe d'age," by J. Mouchet (*ibid*); "Stone Age in East Africa," by Julius Lewin (*ibid.*, September, 1944); "Prospectus for Field Research in the Position and Treatment of the Aged in Primitive and Other Societies," by Leo W. Simons (*American Anthropologist*, July-September, 1945); "The Rule of the Kings of Baganda," by Hamu Hukasa (*Bulletin of the Uganda Society*, June, 1944); "Ugabire: a Feudal Custom among the Waha," by J. J. Tawney (*Tanganyika Notes and Records*, June 1944); "African Art," by H. Clarence Whaite (*Journal of the Royal Society of Arts*, November, 1944).

Articles dealing mainly with matters of government and politics include the following: "The Future of Native Authorities," by Bernard Bourdillon (*Africa*, July, 1945); "Colonial Development and Welfare," by the same author (*International Affairs*, July, 1944); "Les Problèmes des Mulâtres," by G. Hulstaert (*Africa*, July 1945); "Le Marbat: Marche au Betail de Louga," by J. Robin (*ibid.*, April, 1945); "The Sanusi of Cyrenaica," by E. E. Evans Pritchard (*ibid.*); "Final Obsequies of the Late Nana Sir

Ofori Atta, K. B. E.," by Kwamie Frimpong (*ibid.*); "Integration of Native Life in a Reserve," by J. H. Farquhar (*Native Affairs Department Annual*, 1944); "Native Tribunals in the Gold Coast," by H. B. Thomas (*Journal of Comparative Legislation*, November, 1944); "Lord Lugard," a general appreciation (*Africa*, July, 1945); "Lord Lugard, Great Colonial Administrator," (*The Anti-Slavery Reporter and Aborigines Friend*, July, 1945); "Impressions of Ethiopia Today," by J. G. Grimwade (*ibid.*); "The Machinery for Colonial Development" (*ibid.*); "South African Native Policy," by G. Heaton Nichols (*The United Empire*, May-June, 1945); "African Colonial Administration," by Rennell Rodd (*ibid.*); "Development in Colonial Administration," by Rennell Rodd (*Fortnightly*, July, 1945).

PERSONAL

WALTER HENDERSON BROOKS

On July 6, 1945, Walter Henderson Brooks, a prominent member of the Association for the Study of Negro Life and History, died. He was born a slave in Richmond, Virginia, August 30, 1851. His parents were Albert R. and Lucy (Goode) Brooks, ranking among the most enterprising Negroes of the city. Their children were born under Christian influence in a home where the family altar was maintained and Christian precept and example took precedence in their daily life. Emancipated in 1865, this son had this training to build upon. He attended schools on the elementary level in Richmond and then studied at Wilberforce Institute at Carolina Mills, Rhode Island. He was thereby sufficiently grounded to enter Lincoln University in Pennsylvania in 1866. At Lincoln he studied from 1866 to 1873. He completed by 1872 the course leading to the degree of Bachelor of Arts and spent one year in the theological course.

While a student he joined the Presbyterian Church at Lincoln University and along with Archibald H. Grimké served there as an elder. But Walter Henderson Brooks' beginnings were in the atmosphere of the Baptist Church, and on returning to his home in Richmond, Virginia, he joined the First African Baptist Church. He was ordained a minister in this denomination December 24, 1876. For two years, from 1874 to 1876, he served as Sunday School Missionary in the employ of the American Baptist Publication Society. As a missionary the young minister had to supply homes, churches and schools with such suitable literature and hold Sunday School institutes for the edification of Christian workers. To direct this work wisely and successfully was a most important duty which in our time cannot be easily evaluated.

Dr. Brooks next accepted the pastorate of the Second African Baptist Church in Richmond and served there four years. In 1880 he resigned this pastorate and went to Louisiana to serve as Sunday School Missionary for the American Baptist Publication Society. There his efforts for the uplift of his people morally and spiritually were crowned with success, but in 1882 came to him a call to the

459

pastorate of the Nineteenth Street Baptist Church, of Washington, D. C. Believing that this post offered him a field for greater usefulness in the ministry, he accepted and served this congregation from that time until his death.

During his pastorate the Nineteenth Street Baptist Church grew steadily toward the ideal of a model congregation with the pastor and his followers working toward a common goal of saving humanity. It is the mother church among the Negro Baptists, and out of it developed most of the large Baptist Churches of the city. The Nineteenth Street Baptist Church was so organized and conducted as to reach the community through its numerous clubs and societies. The young people were trained in a thoroughly graded Bible School which was supplied with teachers employing the latest methods of religious education. The cause of missions was well maintained at this center. Schools engaged in the enlightenment of the Negro found support there. The pastor himself gave one thousand dollars to Lincoln University, his alma mater, when it was raising an endowment fund of $400,000. No worthy cause serving humanity was ever turned away empty-handed. In fact, this congregation was a striking example of how the Negro church has had to function as a substitute for meeting needs which among people otherwise circumstanced would be supplied by various agencies.

This Christian leader, from the very beginning of his ministry in Virginia was an ardent temperance worker. In his zeal in this work he sometimes pressed his views so far that he made enemies among the lukewarm and indifferent members of the church. On the other hand, he made great friends. By 1875 his efforts in this sphere had brought him into international prominence. He served as chaplain in the Anti-Saloon League of the District of Columbia as long as it functioned in this city. He was a delegate to the convention which organized the American National Anti-Saloon League with Hiram Price as its first president. In recognition of his national standing as a religious leader several schools including Howard University conferred upon this tireless worker the degree of Doctor of Divinity and Lincoln University, his alma mater, the degree of Doctor of Laws.

Some years later Dr. Brooks became one of the three Negro ministers who figured in the storm that made the separation of the Negro Baptists from their white coworkers inevitable. Answering the petition of Negro Baptists for participation in the production of religious literature, the American Baptist Publication Society requested Dr. Walter H. Brooks, Dr. E. K. Love and Dr. William J. Simmons to make such literary contributions; but on protest from Southern white Baptists, withdrew the request. The Negro Baptists regarded this as adding insult to injury and declared their independence of these religionists still devoted to the pro-slavery principles of their former oppressors.

This independent effort shocked the Northern white Baptists and did not please those of the Southern jurisdiction who in a way had given some cooperation in keeping Negro missionaries in Africa. They had never realized that the Negro would resent an insult. Ministers conspicuous in this country had to take a stand on this question. The development was still further in the direction of the independence of the Negro Baptists, however, for in 1885 Dr. William J. Simmons, hoping to effect a merger of all Negro Baptist Bodies, launched the American National Baptist Convention at St. Louis. Ten years later Dr. E. C. Morris effected an organization taking over all these predecessors under the name of the Baptist Foreign Mission Convention which later became the Foreign Mission Board of the National Baptist Convention, was organized in 1886. In 1915, however, after fighting for years the white Baptists who had influential workers among Negroes to show the wisdom of cooperation with them, the Negro Baptists themselves divided. Dr. Brooks stood like a pillar of cloud and fire in leading his people through all these changes.

Dr. Brooks believed in domestic happiness. He was thrice married. In 1874 he married Eva Holmes, the daughter of the Rev. James Holmes, the pastor of the First African Baptist Church in Richmond. She bore him ten children before she passed away in 1912. These children were: Warren Randolph (deceased); Ottie Maria (deceased); James Gordan (deceased); Alberta Gertrude (Mrs. William H. Terrell); Eva Celestine (deceased); Julia Evangeline; Perzelia Goode (deceased); Walter H. Brooks, Jr. (deceased); Antoinette Allison (Mrs. Louis A. Mitchell, of Paris, France); and Albert Neal Dow. In his second marriage in 1915, he took for his companion Mrs. Florence H. Swann (deceased). In his third venture in 1933, he married Mrs. Viola Washington who survives him.

Lafayette McKeene Hershaw

On September 2, 1945 passed from this life Lafayette McKeene Hershaw, one of the colorful figures in Negro-American History. He was born May 10, 1863 in Clay County, North Carolina, the son of Abraham and Anne (McKeene) Hershaw. He was of both French and African descent. In his education therefore he emphasized the language of his Gallic forbears, and he read French and spoke the language fluently. In 1888 he married Charlotte Monroe who died some years ago, leaving three daughters, Rosa Cecile, Alice May, and Fay M. Hershaw.

The very beginning of Hershaw's career was colorful. At the age of thirteen he was hired to some "gentlemen" who later turned out to be moonshiners. They took the boy with them into the Southern mountains where they were attacked and fought a desperate battle with federal officers who during the seventies were trying to round up these outlaws. In the midst of battle Hershaw saw some of these culprits shot down and others overpowered and put under arrest. Hershaw himself, being under age, had no share in the enterprise and was merely held as a witness.

Hershaw entered Atlanta University where he studied from 1879 to 1886, when he was awarded the degree of Bachelor of Arts. He later studied law at Howard University and obtained there in 1892 the degree of Bachelor of Laws. Hershaw's first important service, however, was that of a teacher and principal in the Atlanta Public Schools from 1886 to 1890. That year he came to Washington to serve as an executive in the United States Civil Service in which he attained the position of land examiner in the Department of the Interior. From this position he was recently retired after having served the United States Government forty-two years.

As a citizen of Washington and of the nation he made himself felt far and wide. As a lawyer he never practiced extensively although he was a member of the local bar. He became a teacher of law in the Robert H. Terrell Law School of which he was once president. As such he was most successful in developing this institution into an accredited law school turning out graduates who have made themselves felt in their practice in the courts. He belonged to the Oldest Inhabitants Association of the District of Columbia and made some contribution to local history. For twenty-eight years he was a trustee of Atlanta University.

Above all Hershaw was a fighter for the rights of his people. He was once president of the Bethel Historical and Literary Association, once the outstanding national forum for the discussion of such questions. He functioned also as the president of the Pen and Pencil Club which in another way advanced the same interests. He was one of the thirteen organizers of the Niagara Movement out of which developed the National Association for the Advancement of Colored People. In fact, there was no commendable movement projected for the welfare of his race that he did not aid in some way. To a very great extent his life was one of sacrifice for the good of humanity.

In the advancement of the interest of his race, Hershaw, nevertheless retained the friendship of many of the distinguished whites with whom he became acquainted in Atlanta. One of these was Hoke Smith who served as Secretary of the Interior under Grover Cleveland, and later became United States Senator. After his elimination from politics, Smith remained in Washington to practice law, and Hershaw frequently called on Smith. One morning when Hershaw came in and greeted his friend, Smith, pointing to a copy of *The Negro in Our History* lying open before him at the page of a Negro slave tied to the ground and the overseer laying it on heavily with his cowhide, said abruptly, ''Do you know this man Woodson up here on Ninth Street?''—''Yes, I do,'' replied Hershaw. ''He is a good friend of mine.'' ''I am very sorry if he is your friend. You have a damned poor friend. Why in hell would a man who calls himself an historian put a thing like that in a book? That picture would cause bloodshed.'' What Hoke Smith really disliked about the book, however, was that elsewhere he is referred to as an unprincipled politician in a class with Ben Tillman, Cole Blease and James K. Vardaman. It does not appear that Hershaw's association with Hoke Smith softened his attitude toward the Negro.

Hershaw had close contact also with Woodrow Wilson. Their friendship began in a most vital way. When Wilson failed as a lawyer in Atlanta and finally decided to try his luck at post graduate work at Johns Hopkins, Hershaw befriended him by standing for a suit of clothes for Wilson at Eismans's, and the late world leader never forgot Hershaw. When the members of Wilson's cabinet began to segregate Negroes in the Civil Service the President sent word to the office where Hershaw was, saying, ''I understand that you are segregating Negroes in the various departments, but there is one man, L. M. Hershaw, whom you must not segregate. He is a white man.'' When Wilson came into the presidency Hershaw was receiving only $1,800 a year. Before Wilson went out of office Hershaw was receiving twice that amount. Hershaw, however, was not trying to advance himself in these contacts. Frequently he talked to Wilson about the injustice of the segregation of the members of his race in the Civil Service, and Wilson expressed his desire to see the Negro enjoy every right guaranteed other citizens, but he would not force his personal views upon the entire country.

Hershaw told of another experience of great interest. He called on Woodrow Wilson a few days after he had been visited by the committee appointed by Congress to call on the President to see whether he was physically fit to discharge the functions of the office after having the stroke which resulted in his death. The gentlemen, after talking as some length with the President, arose to leave and said that they were glad to find him mentally fit and would so report to Congress. They said, moreover, that they hoped that he would improve. Albert B. Fall, a member of this delegation, lingered behind to say, ''And Mr. President, we will pray for you.'' Thereupon Wilson said, ''Don't you pray for me. If you do, I am sure that I'll go to hell,''—''A scoundrel,'' said Wilson to Hershaw, ''he will die in the penitentiary.'' That prophecy came true in Fall's conviction in the Teapot Dome Scandal. This raises the question as to what Wilson knew at that early date about Fall's questionable transactions.

INDEX OF VOLUME XXX